HISTORY OF KERALA

History of Kerala

Prehistoric to the Present

Rajan Gurukkal
Raghava Varier

Orient BlackSwan

HISTORY OF KERALA: PREHISTORIC TO THE PRESENT

ORIENT BLACKSWAN PRIVATE LIMITED

Registered Office
3-6-752 Himayatnagar, Hyderabad 500 029, Telangana, India
e-mail: centraloffice@orientblackswan.com

Other Offices
Bengaluru, Chennai, Guwahati, Hyderabad,
Kolkata, Mumbai, New Delhi, Noida, Patna

First published 2018
Reprinted 2020, 2022, 2026

041687

ISBN 978-93-5287-380-7

Typeset in
Gentium Basic 11/13
by Shine Graphics, Delhi 110 094

Maps cartographed by
Sangam Books
(An imprint of The Agricultural Development Commercial Credit And Industrial Investment Company Private Limited)

Printed in India at
Yash Printographics, Noida

Published by
Orient Blackswan Private Limited
3-6-752 Himayatnagar, Hyderabad 500 029, Telangana, India
e-mail: info@orientblackswan.com

Contents

Maps

Glossary of non-English Terms

agniparīkṣa	ordeal by fire
ainkammāḷar	five castes of artisans and craftsmen
ainnūṟṟuvar	the five hundred
āḷ	bonded labourer/slave
āḷaṭiyār	subjected tillers under the kārāḷar
ancuvaṇṇam	an organisation of overseas traders, probably headed by Jewish leaders
angāṭi/ankāṭi	fair/markets
ankam	mandatory tax for resolving disputes by duel
aṟunūṟṟuvar	the six hundred
aṭiyāḷar	servile group, subjected tillers
aṭiyāymai	servile state
āṭṭaikkoḷ	annual rent due
āyiravar	the thousand
brahmadēya	royal land grant to brāhmaṇas
brahmasvam	land held by brāhmaṇas
campū	a combination of poetry and prose
cērikkal	the ruler's land; i.e., land traditionally held by the ruling lineages
cēris	settlements of hereditary artisans/ craftspeople
cunkam	kind of octroi
devasvam	land held by the temple
eḻa	payments received from confiscated property
eḻunūṟṟuvar	the seven hundred
granthavari	palace records written on palm-leaf manuscripts
irumpuvaḷa	iron bangle
janmi	landlord

jāti	'that which one is born in'; a trans-familial identity of relative status recognised by one's own families
jīvitam	(or virutti) landed property received on lease as service tenure by temple functionaries for the services rendered by them
kaccam	regulatory code
kallumāla	stone bead-chain
kārāḷar	tenants/lease-holders
kari (land)	black land; i.e., water-saturated land made of alluvial soil
kaṭama	hierarchical obligations
kiḻān	the elder in the sense of the headman
koḻa	bribe
kuṭi	domestic segments
kuṭimākkal	descent group
maṇigrāmam	an organisation of overseas traders, probably headed by Syrian Christian leaders
maṇipravāḷam	literary works that employ an admixture of Tamil and Sanskrit
maṛavar	mercenaries/warriors
māṭampis	landed aristocrats
mūkkutti	nose stud
munnūṛṛuvar	the three hundred
nagaram	town/marketing centre
nānādēśikaḷ	an organisation of long-distance overland traders from various regions
nāṭu	agrarian settlement; production unit of land larger than *taṛa*, which was in turn larger than *dēśam*, the production unit of ūr
nāṭuṭayavar	owner of the nāṭu
nāṭuvāḻi	local ruler (of the nāṭu)
paṇam	unit of currency
pāṇar	bards
paṛampu	garden land
pāṭṭam	land rent

Perumāḷ	the biggest of all nāṭuvāḻis
piḻa	fine
Pulavar	scholarly bards
purayiṭam	household
sandeśakāvya	messenger poem
sthānam	positions of power in the order of seniority under the *kūṛu* system of inheritance
swarūpam	principality or local ruling house; Neṭiyirippu swarūpam (Sāmūtiri or Zamorin of Kozhikode), Perumpaṭappu swarūpam (kingdom of Cochin)
Tamiḻakam	the Tamil macro region
tiṇai	ecotype
tiṛai	tributes in kind
ūr	clan settlement
vaḷanciyar	an organisation of long-distance overland traders
vaḻi	fee for permissions
veḷḷāḷar	farmers under irrigated agriculture
vēntar	(along with vēḷir) chieftains during the Tamil Heroic Age—the Cēras, Cōḻas and Pāṇḍyas

Transliteration Key to Diacritics used in the Text

ā = pronounce as in 'aap'
ī = pronounce as in 'Egypt'
ū = pronounce as in 'usual'
ē = pronounce as in 'acre'
ō = pronounce as in 'opium'
ca = pronounce as in 'chat'
ṭ = pronounce as in 'top'
ṇ = pronounce as in 'money'
ta = pronounce as in 'thunder'
ḻ = pronounce as in the French name 'Jean'
ṛ = pronounce as in 'wrap'
ḷ = pronounce as in 'stolen'
ś = pronounce as in 'Siva'
ṣ = pronounce as in 'fashion'

Preface

Doing a comprehensive history of Kerala in English has been a project in our minds ever since the publication of our two-volume *Kerala Charithram* ('History of Kerala') in Malayalam, which have run into several reprints. There has been sustained pressure on us from students, teachers and the general readership for such a concise history of Kerala. This book is in a way materialisation of that long-standing project. We owe the drive to execute it in the present form to Orient BlackSwan, whose assiduous persuasion and support has been the prime mover. Our volumes in Malayalam could cover the history from the earliest to 1800 CE only. In this volume, we have covered the history almost up to the modern times to cater to the needs of students graduating in history.

The book starts with the prehistory of Kerala that includes the Early Iron Age, and goes on to the early historical and historical times that subsume the region as part of the Tamiḻakam (Tamil macro region). Subsequent history covering the history of agrarian settlements; formation of the state, initially as overarching provincial chieftaincies and later as independent states in correspondence to agrarian expansion; overland and overseas long-distance trade run by the Arabs, Persians, Jews, Nestorians and Syrian Christians; the arrival of the foreign trading companies; the Mysorean inroads; the British dominance; peasant movements; impact of the national freedom movement; the making of the linguistic state; the Aikya Kerala Movement; the Communist Movement leading to the Communist Ministry; and the making of the modern Kerala are discussed. The book ends up with the summing up of the salient features of contemporary life.

We retain the perspective and methodology that we have followed in our volumes in Malayalam, which insist upon analysing the material processes first and explaining the relations, institutions, structures and processes against their background. Our narrative is, therefore, inherently explanatory with an explicit precedence of the economic and social over the political and cultural aspects of history. Naturally, there is subordination of the dynastic history to the holistic history of the land and people. Due to this perspective and methodological preoccupation, the narrative abstains from describing aspects such as the social, economic, political, cultural, etc. as independent facets.

History is an unmanageably vast domain of knowledge even when we confine it to that of a small landscape like Kerala. It is a bewilderingly complex assortment of facts unless they are sorted out into an order of events. Chronology is the primary device with which we can order events of the past, but that gives us only a catalogue. History is not a catalogue of events. It is not their narration either. Events narrated as stories do not constitute history. Even a descriptive narrative on specialised aspects cannot serve the purpose because history is to enable theoretical comprehension of the whole rather than give an empirical account of a part. History unveils the principles that link parts to the whole. As a field of specialised knowledge, history is an explanation of events in terms of causation and generalisation of intellectual depth. You cannot explain events without a theory that helps identify their causality and sequence. Further, the past is inevitably in fragments and it constrains historians to piece them together. Theory helps historians see whether the fragment turns up as a signifier, so that the signified is known, and enables them to fill the gap between fragments. Sources show the outer manifestations of the process. It is not the description of these surface manifestations which constitutes history, but the historian's interpretation of the process at the bottom. Therefore, there is no history without theory and the only theory of history to comprehend history is historical materialism enunciated by Karl Marx. Accordingly, history is the history of material processes of change in means, forces and relations of production. Several anthropological and sociological theories help you explain the niceties and nuances of the process. Historicising indispensably involves conceptualisation. Similarly, theme selection in historiography depends almost entirely on ideological presupposition. All this makes perspective quite crucial in understanding as well as writing history.

As in the case of the other social sciences, objects of history too are invariably subjective. Historians deal with these subjective objects and generate knowledge that is inevitably subjective. Naturally, the knowledge of history is made up of subjective interpretations by historians. Historians attempt at hypothetico-deductive analyses to make sure that their inferences are compatible to the premises. Nevertheless, objectivity is a mere rhetoric, not only in historiography and the other social sciences, but also in the physical sciences. In historiography, objectivity cannot signify anything more than methodological transparency about the source basis of inferences. What historians logically construct on the basis of theory is their proof and quite often not the empirically given. Such proofs are not out there for anybody to go and pick. Only the theoretically knowledgeable make sense of these proofs.

What we have attempted in this volume is an outline of the history of Kerala from the earliest to the recent, percolating the outcome of even latest researches. At the same time, the constraint to be brief precluded the scope for including the various debates in the historiography of the region. We have tried to point out the major differences of opinion among renowned historians in certain serious matters. Conceived as a textbook at the undergraduate level, we have not bothered to make the volume supported by citations and footnotes. Nevertheless, a detailed bibliography is given at the end in order to show the works we have depended on.

We are indebted to several scholars who have helped us in various ways for doing this volume in its present form. It would not have been possible for us to complete the work without their support and encouragement. We express our sincere gratitude to all of them. They are too many to be acknowledged individually and personally, but some of them have to be specifically mentioned here. At the outset, it is our privilege to acknowledge M. G. S Narayanan's critical comments that have been of great help. We acknowledge the encouragement given by K. N. Panikkar, Kesavan Veluthat, K. N. Ganesh and Michael Tharakan. We have been immensely benefitted by academic discussions with them in their respective areas of specialisation. Our thanks are due to P. T. Thomas and Prabha Chatterjee who translated certain portions from our Malayalam publications. We are grateful to Krishnaraj for the maps. Last but not the least, we express our indebtedness to Orient BlackSwan for producing the volume so well.

Bengaluru
20 June 2018

RAJAN GURUKKAL
RAGHAVA VARIER

I

Landscape, Sources and Historiography

Features of the landscape ecosystem of Kerala, sources of the history of human adaptation to it and the gradual development of historiography constitute the content of this chapter.

Landscape

Kerala is a 38,855 sq km land strip situated between 8°18' N and 12°48' N latitudes and 74°55' E and 77°24' E longitudes on the south-western coast of peninsular India. It is a landscape distinct for the sandy, loamy plains with undulating tracts of red soil sandwiched by the forested Western Ghats on the east and over 780-km-long coast of the Arabian Sea on the west. The red soil terrace droops towards marshes and waterlogged plains that at certain places fall even below the sea level. Geologically, Kerala is a relatively young landmass that was made through a series of transgressions and regressions by the sea over a few million years.

Delimiting physical features, such as the largely unbroken Western Ghats of altitudes ranging from 3000 to 8000 feet above sea level and the continuous sea line, have encouraged a few historians to see Kerala as a geographical isolation within the subcontinent, while many others see it as a landscape amenable to external contact, thanks to the Palakkad Gap of the Ghats and strategic seaboards. Anamuti of the Western Ghats is the highest peak in peninsular India and Kuṭṭanāṭu is the lowest land. There are other passes like the Periya Gap that connects to Coorg and Thamarassery Pass that links to Mysore. Similarly, Bodinaikkanur Pass, Kampam Pass, Ariyankavu Pass and Aruvamozhi Pass connect Kerala to the neighbouring state of Tamil Nadu. Māḍāyi, Kannur, Kozhikode, Kadalundy, Ponnani, Koṭunkōḷūr, Paṭṭaṇam, Kochi, Kollam and Vizhinjam are examples of Kerala's strategic seaboards. Other notable physiographic points of Kerala are Ezhimala in the north and the Varkkala Cliff, that juts out into the Arabian Sea, in the south.

There are 44 rivers that drain the Kerala landscape. Barring three east-flowing tributaries of the river Kaveri, all rivers of Kerala flow to the west and into the Arabian Sea. The major rivers of the state are Valapattanam, Chaliyar, Perar (Bharatapuzha), Periyar and Pampa, which are all over two hundred kilometres long. Several other water bodies, such as lakes and backwaters, also characterise the landscape. Among them the largest is the Vembanadu Kayal, spread over an area of 160 sq km between Alappuzha and Kochi. Kayamakulam and Ashtamuti are the other big lakes in the state. Sastamkotta Kayal is the only sweet water lake in Kerala. Kumbala, Kalnad, Bakel and Kavvay are the main lakes of north Malabar.

Kerala is an agro-climatic zone with relatively heavy rainfall due to the South West and North East monsoon winds. In the state the high ranges of Idukki district get the highest rainfall. Human habitation began in the high ranges first (c. 25000 years BP) and descended to the red soil hillocks (c. 5000 years BP) as well as the undulating tracts that recline into the water-saturated and waterlogged landscape. For a very long period (till about 6th–7th centuries CE), people lived as unevenly-evolved descent groups—uneven in terms of techno-economic and socio-cultural development, and expansion of population—and remained confined to the red soil terrain. It was probably around the seventh and eighth centuries CE that human adaptation to the water-saturated and waterlogged landscape occurred, through the making of paddy fields by draining the water and reclaiming the productive soil. We do not know the exact historical process of this reclamation. While it is certain that it must have involved enormous labour, who mobilised the labour force, how, when and under what organisational or institutional means are all matters of sheer conjecture.

Sources

Kerala's historical sources are varied as in the case of any other region. They consist of conventional categories such as archaeology—i.e., architectural remains, epigraphic and numismatic records—and archives and literature, and non-conventional categories like folklore and place names.

Archaeological Remains

Archaeological remains, the most archaic among which belong to prehistoric times, constitute the primary source of Kerala's history. The earliest major collection of Stone Age tools is of Michael Todd's, which seems to have contained several microliths belonging to the late Stone Age (5000 years BP). Some stone tools of the middle Palaeolithic Age (38000–30000 BP) have been discovered at a few places on Kanjirapuḻa in Palakkad district and Shendurney (Thenmala) in Kollam district. There are a few prehistoric rock-art sites like those in the Marayur forest, which are assigned to the Mesolithic Age (30000–25000 BP), and those at Eaṭakal and Tovari in the Wayanad forest, which are assigned to the Microlithic Age (25000–7000 BP). The rock art of Tovari is important in that it depicts the terraced field of cultivation, thereby pointing to the beginning of agriculture, most probably in the Neolithic phase (7000–3000 BP).

The most widespread archaeological remains in Kerala and south India belong to the Iron Age (c. 1000 BCE–c. 200 CE) and they are in the form of burial systems like dolmens, cists, rock-cut chambers, stone circles, cairns and urns. As some of the burials are huge stone alignments, they are known as 'megaliths' and that gives the age its name. Spanning across many centuries, Iron Age burials overlap the prehistorical and early historical phases. These remains are rich in data, for the grave goods include not only iron artefacts but also a variety of pottery and beads of semi-precious stones like carnelian. They indicate the technology of iron smelting, artefacts production, ceramics and lapidary, besides whatever they symbolise in association with the type of the monument they are found in. Although there are many megaliths all over the state, as elsewhere in peninsular India, very few have been systematically excavated and studied. Excavations have been carried out at sites in Umichipoyil near Kanhangad, Punnol near Mahe, Kuppakkolli in Wayanad, Ānakkara in the Malappuram district, Machād, Pa<u>l</u>ayanur, Porkaḷam near Kunnamkulam, Paṭṭaṇam and Koṭunkōḷūr in Thrissur district, and Māngād in Kollam district. These monuments provide clues to the architectural knowledge and practice of their times.

The site at Paṭṭaṇam, a village in Ernakulam district, is one of the few sites that have been systematically excavated over several seasons. The site is situated on an ancient channel of the Periyar river. Paṭṭaṇam has yielded a wealth of relics of Iron Age habitat—the earliest assemblage of Black and Red Ware, superimposed by the ceramic assemblage of western Asia consisting of shards of Phoenician Torpedo Jars and Turquoise Glazed Ware along with Indian Rouletted Ware and an unidentified ware presumably local, besides a variety of organic and inorganic categories of archaeological objects such as wood, plant fibre, spices, vegetables and nuts as well as beads and bead materials, uncut gemstones, copper, bronze and iron objects, several copper coins, backed bricks, triple grooved roof tiles and potsherds of different types including the early Roman such as Amphorae and Terra Sigillata. Shards of Torpedo Jars and Turquoise Glazed Wares (jars and bowls) are indicative of the maritime contacts of the pre-Roman Egyptian phase (664–332 BCE). Beads of semiprecious stones such as beryl, carnelian, quartz, agate, amethyst, garnet, chalcedony and onyx, and glass constitute the most voluminous quantity among the craft-goods excavated. There are remains of a platform made of lateritic rubble and lime with brick lining, presumed to be part of a wharf, and a partly withered canoe.

Architectural Remains: Kavu shrines, brāhmaṇical temples, Jain basadis, Buddhist relics, mosques, synagogues and churches from the tenth century CE onwards and palaces from the eighteenth century CE onwards exhibit distinct types of construction and artistic styles. They represent contemporary modes of worship and religious ideologies. Therefore, analysis of architecture is essential for understanding the composition of the cultural history of Kerala. Compared to other areas in south India, huge temple architecture and rich sculptures are absent in Kerala. Unlike elsewhere in the country, the early temples of Kerala are not constructions by kings and hence they are not huge architectural and sculptural accomplishments. Any impressive royal monument is an architectural statement of power. Those like Trikkulasekharapuram and Tiruvanchikkulam temples (built c. 9th century CE) are monuments with royal connections, but are still small monuments. Even among later temples huge structures are absent and the only exception is the renovated structure of Padmanabhaswamy Temple in Thiruvananthapuram, the *gōpuram* (gatehouse tower) of which is relatively big and strikingly different from those of the rest in the state. It is the political stature of the famous Tiruvitāmkūr king Anizham Tirunal Marthandavarma (1705–1785 CE), the founder of absolute monarchy in the kingdom, which the architecture symbolises.

Coins: The numismatic sources of Kerala history are of two types: (*a*) direct evidence, consisting of ancient Roman coins and north Indian punch-marked coins; and (*b*) indirect evidence, in the form of references to coins in inscriptions and medieval poetry. Roman and punch-marked coins have been discovered from several sites in Kerala, mostly as accidental discovery of treasure trove from north Kottayam, Eyyal, Valluvalli, Panangad, Kanhirapally and Paṭṭaṇam. While in some places only a handful were found, in other places big hoards of coins were discovered. For instance, the north Kottayam hoard contained rare silver punch-marked coins of 53 varieties issued by the kings of Gangetic northern India, belonging to disparate periods between the sixth and fourth centuries BCE. These coins are distinct for their attributes of fineness. Numismatic studies show that most of the Roman coins belong to the period between the first and third centuries CE. The coins vouch for the transactional relations between Graeco-Roman mariners and inland merchants on the Kerala coast. However, the presence of coins alone is not enough to believe that there was trade between Rome and the coast of Kerala. Various other factors of contemporary exchange practices have to be examined to determine the nature of the involvement of Roman coins in them.

Inscriptions: There are about half a dozen Brāhmi inscriptions in Kerala as the earliest inscribed relics found in different parts, including Ulladukkam east of Kasargod, Eaṭakal cave in Wayanad, Netunkayam near Karulayi, Nilambur, and on a potsherd at Paṭṭaṇam, dating back to the early centuries of the Common Era. Ceran Iḷamkaṭunko, son of Perumkatunko, son of Atan Cellirumporai, figures in the Brāhmi labels of Mangulam and Pugalur in Tamil Nadu respectively. A potsherd of the Indian Rouletted Ware found among the excavated finds at Paṭṭaṇam, and probably dating to the second century CE, has the Brāhmi label *amaṇa* (*sramaṇa*, a term used for non-brāhmaṇā sects like the Jains and Buddhists) inscribed on it. This find indicates the presence of inland merchants from northern India, probably *upasaka*s (devotees of Buddhist monks) of some heterodox religious groups.

Most of the inscriptions of Kerala are in old Malayalam language engraved on stone in the Vaṭṭeḻuttu script and belong to the period between the ninth and twelfth centuries CE. These are inscriptions starting with an auspicious expression, quite commonly '*swasti śree*', mentioning the name and year of the Perumāḷ's (the king's) reign as a time marker. The mention of the king's name has created the misconception that these inscriptions are *śāsana*s (royal proclamations), though very few royal statements have also been found. These inscriptions are primarily the decisions made by the assembly (*sabha, ūr*) of brāhmaṇā landlords or the temple committees (*paraṭai*). Few instances of such decisions have been recorded in copper plates as the Vāḻappaḷḷy Plates, the Tiruvalla Plates, the Māmpaḷḷi Plates and the Kilimanoor Plates exemplify. Recently, a *prasasti* (eulogy) has been discovered from Kurumathur near Arekode in Malappuram district. The record eulogises the Perumāḷ Rajasekhara and is important because it provides a reliable date concerning the reign of the king. This is the only one of its kind to be obtained from Kerala. Two other well-known copper plates are the Tarisāppaḷḷi plates and the Jewish plates, which have registered the ruler's grant of rights and privileges—including those over land and the service persons—to the Christian and Jewish merchant leaders, respectively.

Although these inscriptions contain matters relating to the temple, they also indicate a wide variety of economic, social, political and cultural affairs. Initially, when political history used to be the main concern of historiography, the political content of inscriptions—especially the name and date of the king—mattered. Subsequently, when socio-economic history became important in historiography, the use of inscriptions as a source material acquired a new dimension. Socio-economic history demanded the search for indications of social and economic institutions, ideas, groups, relations, functions, structures, systems and processes. This heralded a new dimension to understanding inscriptions that were originally used just for reconstructing the genealogy and chronology of kings. Inscriptions have been transcribed, translated, edited and published in the different volumes of the *Travancore Archaeological Series*, *South Indian Inscriptions* and *Ramavarma Research Institute Bulletin Series*, besides a few journals. There are several stone inscriptions dating to the thirteenth to fifteenth centuries CE, without any significant content other than indications of the period.

Archival Material

It seems that by that time the usual practice was to record details of transactions and deeds in *ōlakkaraṇam* (palm-leaf records). Many prominent households had started maintaining their own archives as *nāḷvaḻi* (daily accounts) that often contained mention of events and occasions. Vanneri *granthavari* (palm-leaf manuscript), Kūṭāḷi granthavari, the Guruvayur temple records and Kavaḷappāṟa records are examples of inscriptions belonging to this period.

There is a commendable body of archival material in the form of records of the Portuguese, the Dutch, the French and the English East India Companies, and the royal government records of the Tiruvitāmkūr palace and the Sāmūtiri's (Zamorin) court. These records are an important part of the primary category of source material that enables a rich historiography of Kerala since the seventeenth century CE. Even the local chiefly families of the time were document-based and in the habit of keeping records, as in the case of the Kūṭāḷi records. Ruling houses and big temples maintained their archive of daily affairs in the form of granthavari, of which the Matilakam granthavaris of the Padmanabha Swami temple in Thiruvananthapuram and Kozhikkotan granthavaris of the Sāmūtiri's palace are rich in terms of historical data.

Palace archives acquired a new mode of documentation with the penetration of the printing press and British power even into regions of royal governance. The pattern of documentation in Madras Presidency entered Tiruvitāmkūr as well, with the publication of the government records and assessment reports. The publication of *Selections from the Records of Travancore* (1860) is an example. Documentation not only meant mere everyday accounting and book-keeping, but also the preparation of a comprehensive account of the land, people, resources, social composition, customs, practices, culture, history and so on. As the record of everyday transactions, granthavari was supplemented by the preparation of a comprehensive manual. This was the historical context of the making of the *Travancore State Manual* (1906), which was written and published under royal order. The *Manual* was written by V. Nagam Aiya, and covered the physical features, boundary, geology, climate, rainfall, meteorology, flora, fauna, population statistics, social composition, history and archaeology of the princely state of Tiruvitāmkūr (Travancore). This was followed by the seven volumes of *Castes and Tribes of Southern India* (1909) written by Edgar Thurston as part of the British colonial project of knowing the land and people thoroughly for managing them effectively.

Literary Sources

The descriptions and notes of Graeco-Roman navigators constitute an important category of source that should be treated as a primary source of Kerala's history. *Periplus of the Erythraean Sea* by an unknown mariner (first century CE), *The Natural History* by Pliny (first century CE), *Geography* by Ptolemy (second century CE) and an illustrated Christian topography called *Cosmas Indicopleustes* (sixth century CE) are prominent examples of literary sources. They give brief accounts on the ports, marts and merchandise of the south-western and south-eastern coasts of India and contain references to the people and rulers of the regions. We can gather a lot of information about the ancient ports, their location, accessibility, products and so on from these writings. As the writings are contemporaneous to what they describe and on the basis of firsthand experience, they constitute a very import category of primary source material.

There are several other works from the subcontinent, contemporaneous to what they contain, which come under the category of literary source material for the historiography of Kerala. Unlike the Graeco-Roman works, these are imaginary writings of the truly literary type but with allusions to certain matters of their times. Tamil heroic poems, forming the oldest codified compositions of oral tradition in Tamiḻakam, rank foremost among them. They are popularly called Sangam literature, after the tradition about the Maturai *cankam* under the Pāṇḍyas, which talks about three cankams and the destruction of numerous poems of the first two cankams by a flood. Traditional scholars of Tamil have interpreted 'cankam' as a royal academy of poets under the Pāṇḍyas. However, recent research has shown that the cankam was an assembly of heterodox monks, which collected, redacted and classified the poems into different anthologies. It is well-known today that there is a time lag of at least three or four centuries between the composition of the poems and their classification into anthologies, and that therefore, the expressions 'Sangam literature', 'Sangam Age', 'Sangam polity', 'Sangam society' and so on are misnomers. These expressions are misnomers because they give the feeling that it is the literature by the Sangam and of the period of the Sangam. Similarly, they give the false impression that the Age of the Sangam and the period of the polity and society reflected in the poems are the same. These are poems that directly or indirectly glorify the values and passions of heroism. The popular usage apart, 'Tamil heroic poems', as K. Kailasapathy calls it in his work *Tamil Heroic Poetry*, is the appropriate way of addressing this corpus of literature.

The Tamil heroic poems are grouped under three categories: *Eṭṭuttokai, Pattuppāṭṭu* and *Patineṇkīḻkkaṇakku. Eṭṭuttokai* consists of eight anthologies, viz., *Naṭṭiṇai, Kuṟuntokai, Ainkuṟunūṟu, Patiṟṟuppattu, Paripāṭal, Kalittokai, Akanānūṟu* and *Puṟanānūṟu. Pattuppāṭṭu* consists of ten songs, viz., *Porunarāṟṟuppaṭai, Ciṟupāṇāṟṟuppaṭai, Perumpāṇāṟṟuppaṭai, Tirumurukāṟṟuppaṭai, Mullaippāṭṭu, Maturaikkānci, Kuṟinjippāṭṭu, Paṭṭiṇappālai, Malaippaṭukāṭām* and *Neṭunalvāṭai.* The category of *Patineṇkīḻkkaṇakku* consists of *Nālaṭiyār, Nānmaṇikkaṭikai, Innanāṟppatu, Iniyavainārpatu, Kāṟnāṟppatu, Kaḷavaḻināṟppatu, Aintiṇai ayimpatu, Aintiṇai eḻupatu, Tiṇaimoḻi eḻupatu, Tiṇaimālai nūṟṟaipatu, Kainnilai, Ainilai Kuṟal, Tirikaṭukam, Ācārakkōvai, Paḻamoḻi, Ciṟupancamūlam* and *Mutumoḻikkānci.* There are the twin epics of *Cilappatikāram* and *Maṇimēkalai*, and two other texts, *Takaṭūryāttirai* and *Peruntēvanār Pāratam*, as part of the old Tamil literature. They are not part of the Sangam works but are considered along with them. There is the famous grammatical text of Tamil called *Tolkāppiyam* and its various commentaries, all of which are not directly useful as source material for the historiography of Kerala.

The chronology of Tamil heroic poems is problematic and there is only a tentative knowledge about the date of the various collections. Among the *Eṭṭuttokai* collection, the poems are mostly of the turn of the Common Era, except *Kalittokai* and *Paripāṭal* that were written later. Similarly, most poems of *Pattuppāṭṭu* are of the early centuries of the Common Era. The other texts are largely of the sixth to tenth centuries of the Common Era. Since mortuary practices like urn burial, cremation and erecting of heroic monuments, and artefacts like ornaments and tools figuring in the poems have archaeological attestation in megaliths and related grave goods, an overlap of the early historical period with the period of the heroic poems is evident. However, the Megalithic Age spans several centuries, perhaps over a millennium. It is believed that the poems are contemporaneous to the last phase (c. third century BCE–second century CE) of the Megalithic culture. In short, archaeological attestation hardly helps us determine the dates of the poems in the collection.

There are certain poetic notions such as *akam* (internal) and *puṟam* (external) as well as *tiṇai* (the landscape ecosystem) and *tuṟai* (the opening site) that are helpful in classifying the poems in the anthologies. Generally, these poems deal with the life and culture of the heroic society. Many of them extol the heroic exploits of the ruling chieftains of the period, as poems in *Puṟanāṉūṟu* and *Patiṟṟuppattu* illustrate. *Patiṟṟuppattu*, which is specifically about the exploits of the Cēra chieftains, is an important source of the historiography of Kerala. Although poems of *Akanāṉūṟu* deal with love, even there the context is invariably that of the heroic society.

Another type of literature consists of the devotional texts by the Alvars and Nayanars (Śaivite and Vaiṣṇavite hymnists) of the hagiological tradition in southern India. They belong to the period between the eighth and the first quarter of the twelfth centuries CE. The Perumāḷs who ruled from Mahodayapuram (Koṭunkōḷūr) belonged to both Śaivaite and Vaiṣṇavite sects. Cēramān Perumāl Nāyanār and Kulaśēkhara Āḷvar were esteemed personages of the Śaivite and Vaiṣṇavite sects. The famous Śaivite devotee Sundaramūrti Nāyanār was a friend and contemporary of Cēramān Perumāḷ. *Ponvaṇṇattantāti, Mummaṇikkōvai* and *Ātiyula* are works by Cēramān Perumāḷ. They reflect many facets of contemporary Kerala society. Sundaramūrti's songs, which contain a panegyric on the deity of the Thiruvancikkuḷam temple, throw light on Kerala's contemporary social and political life. Likewise, the Vaiṣṇavite devotional songs of Kulaśēkhara Āḷvār are included in the *Nālāyiraprabadham* under the title of *Perumāl-Tirumoḻi*. He is usually identified with Sthāṇu Ravi Perumāḷ who ruled Kerala during the second half of the ninth century CE. *Mukundamāla*, a Sanskrit devotional work, was also written by Kulaśēkhara Āḷvār. Their works provide much valuable information about Kerala's devotional cult well known as the Tamil *bhakti* movement. *Periyapurāṇam* of Cekkiḻār and *Divyasūricaritam* are the main hagiological texts that have some relevance to Kerala historiography.

The plays *Āścharyacūḍāmaṇi* by Śakthibhadran (considered to be a contemporary of Sankaracārya), *Tapatisamvaraṇam* and *Subhadrādhananjayam* of Kulaśēkhara Varma also have to be mentioned among literary sources as they were written during the Perumāḷ rule. Though they deal with the epic and purāṇic stories, they contain certain allusions to the socio-cultural life in the Age of the Perumāḷs (c. 800–1124 CE). Further, they shed light on the development of Sanskrit theatre and certain other performing arts in association with the temple of Kerala. *Laghubhāskarīya-vyākhya*, a work of astronomy by Sankara Narayanan, interpreting Bhaskara's *Lakhubhāskarīyam*, is considered a source material for the period of Sthāṇu Ravi Perumāḷ (844–c. 883 CE) as the period of writing the work has been reliably fixed on the basis of certain accurate information contained in it. Apart from astronomy, the work contains references to major sites like the observatory situated near the capital at Mahōdayapuram. It is a work of great relevance to the history of Kerala's science and technology. Orrakkūttan's *Takkayyāgapparaṇi* (twelfth century CE) is another significant literary source of its period. The book refers to the olden Vanci (*mūtūr-vanci*) as the first capital of the Cēra rulers and talks about the eventual shift to Mahōdayapuram.

A class of literature that relates to courtesans and dancing girls has a lot of importance as a source material shedding light on the urban growth and aristocratic material culture in Kerala.

Poems like *Uṇṇiyaccīcaritam*, *Uṇṇiccirutēvīcaritam*, *Uṇṇiyāṭīcaritam*, *Uṇṇunīlīsandeśam* and *Kōkasandeśam* are well-known examples of this kind. Sanskrit works like *Sukasandeśam* and *Kōkilasandeśam* are also important literary source materials. These works belong to two different poetic traditions, namely the *campū*s (a combination of poetry and prose) and the *sandeśakāvya*s (messenger poems), and are of importance to the socio-cultural and economic history of Kerala. For example, the *maṇipravāḷam* (an admixture of Tamil and Sanskrit) works like *Uṇṇunīlīsandeśam* provide a long list of exchange goods available in the markets, bazaars and places of seasonal fairs. These lists are pointers to the development of different technological skills involved in various arts and crafts of hereditary nature, such as the alloy metallurgy involved in making bronze objects. Piecing together the facts available in these literary texts, one can have a good idea of the development of technology and craft production in contemporary Kerala. From these texts we can understand that craftsmen obtained raw materials like copper, tin, zinc and mercury through traders from distant places within the Indian subcontinent and beyond. The literary works also provide the structure of dispersed villages of Kerala and the functions of the constituent elements of artisan and service groups thereof.

The anonymous sixteenth century CE work *Candrōlsavam* reflects the contemporary social and cultural life of the leisurely upper-caste people. Another sixteenth-century poet called Mahiṣamangalam Nārāyanan extols the virtues of his patron Keśava Rama Varma in *Rājaratnāvalīyam*. Similarly, *Kaṇṭiyūr-marram Paṭappāṭṭu* (battle-lore) by Nīlakaṇṭhan from Cēppād is an important source that provides some information about the political situation of the local ruling lineages of late-sixteenth century Kerala. It mentions the trading corporation of Maṇigrāmam. Another *Paṭappāṭṭu*, whose author is not known, shows the political situation of Perumpaṭappu Swarūpam between 1646 CE and 1670 CE. *Māmānkam Kiḷippāṭṭu* by Kāṭancerri Nampūtiri, a court poet of Bharani Tirunāḷ Mānavikṛaman (1684–1705 CE) is a very important source for the late-seventeenth century history of the Sāmūtiris in general and the study of the political ritual of Māmānkam in particular. It provides a detailed description of the Taippūyyam festival of 1693 CE and two Māmānkams of 1694 CE and 1695 CE. There are a few *cāvēr pāṭṭukaḷ* (suicide mercenary lore), such as *Kanṭarmēnōn Pāṭṭu* and *Rāmaccappaṇikkar Pāṭṭu* of the late-seventeenth century CE, that celebrate the heroism of fighters who died in Māmānkam encounters. An anonymous work called *Mārttāṇḍa Māhātmyam* and Rāmapurattu Varier's *Kucēlavṛttam* and *Bhāṣāṣṭapati* are significant literary works relevant to the history of Mārttāṇḍa Varma (1729–1758 CE). Kunjan Nambiar's *Tuḷḷal Pāṭṭukaḷ* is another composition which provides a lot of clues about the various social and political practices of the eighteenth century CE.

Book of Duarte Barbosa, the first Portuguese travelogue (1516 CE) by Duarte Barbosa, a co-navigator of Magellan, is an important source for understanding the socio-economic and politico-cultural conditions of Kochi and Malabar. Barbosa had stayed in these regions for almost fifteen years, initially with his uncle who was in the Portuguese navy and later independently as a servant under Francisco de Albuquerque. Having learnt Malayalam, Barbosa served as Albuquerque's interpreter, and soon developed direct contacts with the rulers of Kannur and Kozhikode where he spent most of his days.

Hortus Malabaricus, a Latin compilation of medicinal plants in Kerala, the earliest such comprehensive account ever made, is a rare source material for acquiring contemporary knowledge about the medicinal plants and their uses. The work was conceived by the Governor of Dutch Malabar, Hendrik van Rheede (1636–1691 CE). In fact, the description of medicinal plants and their uses was first written in Malayalam and then translated into Portuguese before being turned into this Latin compilation. In twelve volumes, this compendium provides detailed descriptions of over 742 plants with sketches true to the original. These volumes help us know about the system of herbal classification that traditional physicians in Kerala followed during the period.

Folklore: Folk songs constitute a very significant set of literary source that provide insights into the history of community life beyond mainstream society. We possess a rich body of folk literature in heroic poems such as the northern and the southern ballads (*vaṭakkan pāṭṭukaḷ*), and the ritual songs of North Malabar (*tōrram pāṭṭukaḷ*), most of which have been published. *Iravikkuṭṭippiḷḷai Pāṭṭukaḷ*, which extols the exploits of Iravikkuṭṭi who confronted the Nāyaks of Tirumalai and met a heroic death at Kaṇiyākuḷam in 1634 CE, is the most important among the southern ballads. There are ritual folk songs (tōrram pāṭṭukaḷ) that accompany divinised performances of different types, such as Teyyam performances in North Malabar and the Muṭiyērru performance in southern Kerala. *Valiyatampi Kunjutampi Katai* about the conflict between Mārttāṇḍa Varma and his cousins, *Divānveṭṭi Katai* about Rāja Kēśavadās, *Putuvāṭa Pāṭṭu* about Kottayam Kerala Varma of eighteenth century CE are other southern ballads. Northern ballads (vaṭakkan pāṭṭukaḷ) are mainly *Taccōḷippāṭṭukaḷ* and *Puttūrampāṭṭukaḷ* that praise the heroic encounters of the Nair fighter Taccōḷi Otēnan of sixteenth century CE and the heroic exploits of the Tiyya fighter Ārōmal Cēkavar of seventeenth century CE, respectively. They provide interesting accounts that shed light on the social and political customs of the times. Other folk songs like *mārggamkaḷippāttukaḷ*, *kalyāṇappāṭṭukaḷ* and *paḷḷippāṭṭukaḷ* of the Christian community and *māppiḷappāṭṭukaḷ* of the Muslim community of the region are of great importance as an indirect source of Kerala's socio-cultural history of the seventeenth and eighteenth centuries CE.

Folklore, consisting of oral traditions by way of songs and story narratives that generations 'continue to hug to their bosom,' contain the hopes, despair, fears, anxieties, dissents and revolts of a people. It is a compendium of the knowledge of folk life, its culture and its cosmos, providing explanations to the problems and suggesting resolutions. They are not intended to be historical records that historians seek, but there is history embedded in them and more significantly, the way the folk understood their past. Therefore, folklore form a part of the indirect and non-conventional sources of history, the value of which has been increasing in historiography in recent times due to the need to understand the history of the social, political, economic and cultural affairs of the subalterns. In the absence of other sources, folk traditions are the only means with which the life and culture of the common people can be studied. We can discover the historical outlook of the folk on past events rather than their historicity, as Romila Thapar points out in her study of historical traditions of early India, *The Past Before Us*.

Place Names

The study of place names (toponymy) as a source of historical understanding is still in its infancy in our country because of the excessive importance given to linguistic facts like historical grammar, phonology and etymology. To a great extent place names are linked to such related subjects as geography, history, sociology and anthropology. If they are analysed using appropriate methodology, place names can provide a lot of insight into a number of issues of geographical, sociological and anthropological importance. To illustrate, several place names such as Chanthakkunnu, Kanjikuzhi and Kozhikode are suggestive of geographical positions like elevation, depression and protrusion. Similarly, several place names like Palakkad (dry land), Maruthōnkara (wetland), etc. indicate geographical features. Through place-name studies it is possible to locate historical landscape ecosystems, zones of agro-biodiversity, fields of different crops like millets and pulses, salt pans, places of endemic plants and animals, etc. Old trade centres, ferries, ports, urban centres, royal sites and other politically- and culturally-important institutions can be ascertained from place-names. Toponymic evidence can shed light on the means of subsistence, mode of human habitation and property relations. Sometimes place names help the historian identify the social composition of each habitation unit. A number of place names indicate sociological and anthropological traits. For instance, certain place names like Nāykkanūr, Kuṛavankōṇam, Paṛayarukaṇṭi, Nāyarampalam, Jōnakamēḍu, etc. signify social constituents like ethnic groups, caste groups and religious groups. Place names like Panamkāṭu, Chamakkāla and Mutirakkaṇṭi indicate specific vegetation or agricultural practices.

HISTORIOGRAPHY

Where does Kerala's tradition of writing history begin? This inquiry takes us back to Atula's *Mūṣakavamśa kāvya*, a historical poem dating to the tenth century CE, a period anterior to Kalhaṇa's *Rājatarangiṇi* by a century. Its theme is eulogy of the Mūṣaka kings of Kōḷattunāṭu in the extreme north of Kerala, from the founder of the dynasty Rāmaghaṭa to the poet's contemporary Srikanṭha. The poet narrates in the first six *sargas* (cantos) the origins of Rāmaghaṭa Mūṣaka, a line of kings anointed by the sage Paraśurāma, the legendary exterminator of kshatriya kings. By linking the Mūṣaka ruling lineage with the *Yadus* (the Yādava lineage), this Kāvya incorporates the lineage into the purāṇic genealogy and thereby helps acquire high legitimacy. The next four sargas recount the exploits of Nandana, a descendant of Rāmaghaṭa, and the ninth sarga narrates the stories of all the ninety-five Mūṣaka kings. In the following three sargas the history of nineteen of ninety-five kings is given. The kāvya ends with a detailed account of the *abhiṣeka* ritual of the king Srikanṭha.

There are two other historical traditions, Keraḷōlpatti and the Keraḷamāhātmyam, closely connected to the Paraśurāma legend of the creation of Kerala. The view of Gundert that these texts were written down in the eighteenth century by the Nampūtiri brāhmaṇas cannot be accepted because of the existence of Keraḷōlpatti manuscripts belonging to the sixteenth century CE. It makes little sense to ask when exactly historical texts like these were put to writing for they become written texts only after long use as oral traditions. What we see as historical traditions embedded in the folklore, like Vaṭakkan pāṭṭukal and invocatory songs like tōṛṛam pāṭṭukal, are allomorphs of Keraḷōlpatti. In fact, Keraḷōlpatti is not just one unified text. It represents diverse versions in one and the same diction.

There are many Keraḷōlpattis eulogising and legitimising different *swarūpams* (local ruling houses), and institutionalising their customs, rituals and social practices.

Keraḷōlpatti text has three parts of which the first draws upon the legendary creation of the land and settling of the brāhmaṇas into thirty-two *grāmas*, while the second enumerates the Perumāḷs who were invited to be the reigning kings. In the concluding part, obviously an extrapolation, the respective *nāṭuvāḻi* (local ruler) is shown as a blessed recipient of sanction from the last of the Perumāḷs. It is this part that seeks textual legitimacy for the local ruling lineage that makes each Keraḷōlpatti text to be apparently different from the other. Places, persons, rituals and customs mentioned in the non-legendary portions of Keraḷōlpattis are historical and verifiable in the light of epigraphic evidence. A text of temporal one-dimensionality and characteristic disregard for the sequence of time and events, Keraḷōlpatti precludes historical veracity. A striking example is the mention of Udayavarman Kōlattiri, Madhavācārya, Sankarācārya and Mayūraśarman of disparate periods transacting with Paraśurāmā. The order in which they are mentioned upset their chronological sequence.

While *Mūṣakavamśakāvya* poetises the origins and continuity of the Mūṣaka dynasty, Keraḷōlpatti narrates the legendary creation of a land mass and institutionalisation of its ownership. The *vamśakāvya* embodies the past consciousness of a society, which emphasises the primacy of *vamśa* and *varṇa*, whereas Keraḷōlpatti does the same of a society which emphasised rights over land. Both of them represent the forms of history and modes of appropriation of the past that could cater to the needs of their societies and time. However, as it encompasses the origin stories of a large land, its people, and their rituals, customs and practices, the Keraḷōlpatti is able to function as valid history for a longer period compared to that of the kāvyas whose scope was too limited in time and space. Factors like the persistence of the social formation without much change, the political continuity of the nāṭuvāḻi swarūpams, and the elasticity of the textual structure to adjust itself with new developments account for the long survival of Keraḷōlpatti. Its influence lasted even to recent times, as evidenced by the event of a member of the Kōlattiri family, namely Karippattu Unittiri, accepting the title of Udayavarman Kōlattiri Vaṭakkan Perumāḷ (sixteenth century CE) in pursuance to the Keraḷōlpatti tradition.

The coastal trading community of Kerala had to encounter certain new challenges with the arrival of the Portuguese, which adversely affected the economic interests of the Marakkars, the prominent Mohammedan trading families on the Malabar coast. Portuguese merchants imposed control over traders in the Indian Ocean with the patronage of the Sāmūtiri, the ruling family of Calicut, and obstructed these families from engaging in coastal trade. This predicament prompted the aggrieved to invoke the communal fraternity of other Mohammedans to strengthen resistance against the Portuguese. A community history of the Mohammedans capable of exciting communal sentiments became a need of the hour and that accounts for the birth of the book by the Arab writer Shaik Zainuddin called *Tuhfat-ul-Mujāhiddīn* (1583), which with its Arab sense of realistic past made a breakthrough from the indigenous tradition established by Keraḷōlpatti. Distinct from the genre of storytelling, Zainuddin's work for the first time provides the Mohammedans of Malabar with a reliable community history, rendered plausible through a narrative of events in chronological sequence. This triggered corresponding attempts at building community consciousness and religious identity by the Portuguese Jesuits through Latinisation, which was a move to compel the Christians to conform to the customs, traditions, beliefs, etc. of the Latin Church. This required the use of history and religion as binding factors to develop communitarian fellowship. The drafting of the Synod of Diamper (1599) and the writing of a Church history by Michel Geid (1694) may be viewed as examples.

A more realistic past consciousness became necessary in Tiruvitāmkūr in the wake of serious changes that took place in the power structure of the nāṭuvāḻis as a result of economic growth at the instance of agrarian expansion and foreign trade. An assertive state power emerged stretching its long arms even to the innermost recesses of the domain by quelling the *māṭampis* (landed aristocrats) and monopolising commercial resources. The infrastructure for the working of the state power improved and the royal circuit became extensive through land and water with a corresponding rise in the number of activities. These necessitated systematic bookkeeping and maintenance of archives at the palace and demanded the adoption of Western perspectives of writing dynastic histories. This is the historiographical context of *Tiruvitāmkūr Caritram* (1867) by Vaikkattu Pāchchu Mūttatu, a distinct work not structured in the mould of Keraḷōlpatti and Keraḷamāhātmyam. The author declares that it was written after consulting several sources of information such as Koṭṭāram granthavaris, personal accounts by palace bookkeepers, official correspondences, contemporary folk songs and traditions maintained by the aged. He was aware of the need to confirm the reliability of the sources through their mutual corroboration. History was a true statement of the character, benevolence, fortunes and other virtues of a great personage. That the narration of the past should be a truthful statement was something new in contemporary historical practice. It is this awareness of Pāchchu Mūttatu that underlines his importance in the historiography of Kerala. He knew that history was a rational description of the events of the past in the chronological order, though by events he would mean only the life events of great men. The problems and limitations of such a perspective are explicit. What is notable about Mūttatu is not his methodological success, but the recognition of the fact that there should be a method to do history and that it should be declared at the outset. His declaration of the sources and the method followed in their analysis, however brief and inadequate as it is, helps us understand the potentials and drawbacks of the book.

The presence of the British power and the spread of the English language in Tiruvitāmkūr necessitated writing the region's history in English, more as a part of contemporary political expediency to apprise the British of the greatness of the ruling house. In fact, it became possible to mentally escape the ignominious plight under colonial subjugation by describing the region's past glory in the language of the subjugators. Shangoonny Menon's *A History of Travancore* (1878) was written under such circumstances. Government records, old *curuṇas* (palm leaves) and copper plates were the primary sources of Shangoonny Menon's book. He has acknowledged using stone inscriptions of Coimbatore, Tanjore, Trichinopoly and Malabar for writing his book. In addition to engaging himself in taking notes, he had officially employed several assistants for the collection of data from distant places as well as out of various original documents. Nevertheless, these researches seldom helped him to substitute the legendary origins of the land and people with history. Though he begins the history of Tiruvitāmkūr in the fourteenth century, hardly does he succeed in driving it beyond the immediate past with reliable spatio-temporal specificity. The factually well-founded discussions in his book are more or less confined to the palace history of nineteenth-century Tiruvitāmkūr. As in the case of Pāchchu Mūttatu, history meant royal history to Menon too, and the central purpose of the book seems to have been recounting the fortunes and exploits of the kings of Tiruvitāmkūr. But, his predecessor's concern for criticism and authentication of documents is not present in Shangoonny Menon, probably with the same degree of rigour. However, his high dignitary status and royal patronage brought the book greater recognition and official authenticity. The genealogy prepared by him was repeated as the authentic one every year in the Tiruvitāmkūr royal calendar.

It was under the peculiar circumstances of Malabar that the historiography of Kerala took a step forward both factually and methodologically. Malabar had come under the British rule by the close of the eighteenth century. To rule the ruler should know closely the people to be ruled. Traditions and conventions were not enough for the British to govern the civil society as they resorted to the rule of law based on statutory sanction rather than hereditary rights and customary practices. The traditional forms of history, such as Keraḷōlpatti and Keraḷamāhātmyam, had no relevance to colonial bureaucrats who rejected such compositions as fictitious. They required factual accounts with spatio-temporal clarity. The first response to this requirement is seen in Samuel Mateer's *Native Life in Travancore* (1883). A realistic topography, rational history and detailed statistics became essential for the colonial government that was emerging in contemporary British Malabar. Being a need of the administration, often the administrators themselves took to the task of writing history very much as a part of their official activities, thereby giving rise to Mannuals and official chronicles. *The Malabar Mannual* by William Logan (1886) is an outstanding product of the context. As one who had imbibed the contemporary European historical and social knowledge, Logan in his *Malabar Manual* presented a new subject and analytical method in Kerala historiography. His historical outlook encompassed fresh insights from geology, anthropology and folklore, palaeontology and economics. But most of the reference materials for the preparation of a comprehensive Kerala history had not yet surfaced. Moreover, his ambition did not go beyond what was necessary for administrative purposes. Except for the statistics and details of archaeological findings, there was no appreciable search for authoritative sources or production and discovery of evidence. However, Logan's *Manual* had profound influence on the composition and form of similar manuals and historical writing in general in Tiruvitāmkūr and Kochi.

New methodological advances can be witnessed almost during the same period, though not under similar circumstances, in the historiography of the kings of Tiruvitāmkūr, made possible with the spread of new Western sciences. Even a history of the lineage of the kings had to be written scientifically. In short, scientific analysis and utilisation of sources gained unprecedented importance, mainly due to the appearance of a class of readers equipped with new knowledge. Teaching of history in universities added momentum. Similarly, the publication of official journals brought to light new materials. Under these circumstances the study of ancient descriptions grew as a part of contemporary epigraphy. *Some Early Sovereigns of Travancore* by P. Sundaram Pillai (1894), based on a scientific analysis of inscriptions, represents this new trend in historiography. He calls the inscriptions 'dying declarations of antiquity'. He gave lectures to make the common people aware of protecting these monuments. He conversed with a still larger audience by writing in official journals like *Indian Antiquary*. In his studies, Sundaram Pillai ascertained the name and period of some hitherto unknown kings of Tiruvitāmkūr. Incidentally, he discusses the variety of facts appearing in these inscriptions. Unlike the accepted practice, his method was to mention the sources as and when they appeared and to reserve definitive opinions for want of proof. Though he was acquainted with several branches of knowledge, such as Philosophy, Tamil, Sanskrit and English, he did not try and formulate a holistic historical perspective, probably due to the Western positivist approach. As a result, his studies focused mostly on the inscriptions, a category of primary source material, and the chronology and genealogy of kings. This was his concern also because the royal history of Tiruvitāmkūr abounded in chronological ambiguity and geological gaps.

In the initial decades of the twentieth century, there appeared a new social perspective in the historiography of Kerala due to the rise of an educated middle class. Westernised passions and values provided by modern education equipped them with a new civic sense, social culture and respect for the rule of law. Moreover, it was a time when a new political consciousness and patriotism were growing throughout the country in the wake of the Indian national movement. This in turn stirred regional self-consciousness that manifested in the form of provincial patriotism and love of the vernacular. A social structure engendering the political leadership of the educated middle class necessitated regional historical awareness complimenting national consciousness. K. P. Padmanabha Menon represented such a regional historical awareness and national consciousness. As a member of a noble family, a barrister and a radical modern thinker, he furiously reacted to the existing conservative customs and social institutions. The sum total of his intellectual activity being the responsive politics of social criticism, it was essential for him to know the roots of conservative institutions, practices and ideas. Menon got opportunities for this in his official capacity as well. An example is his *Matriarchal Committee Report and Memorandum of 1908*. He was not satisfied with a report on the prevailing custom of matriliny and hence sought to study the history of this social institution by analysing the observations of well-known anthropologists.

Padmanabha Menon would then go on to write *Kochi Rājya Caritram* (1912–14) in two volumes, motivated by patriotism and love of modernisation. The first volume contains ancient and Portuguese history, and the second contains the history of the Dutch and the British. Historiography, according to Menon, was a means for the people to know their past history. He narrates the social history of the people by describing institutions like kinship, marriage relations, matriarchy, right of inheritance, etc. His historical curiosity was not confined to the history of Kochi alone, but spread all over the Malayalam-speaking region, its pattern of settlement, social customs and manners. Not confident of considering what he wrote as a continuous history of Kerala, he presented the historical facts of the land known to him in the form of descriptive notes attached to the correspondence of Bishop Canter Visscher's letters. However, when these notes were published (1924–37) the editor called it the history of Kerala. Menon discriminated his sources between primary and secondary with respect to their reliability. His main source material consisted of inscriptions, literary works, notes of foreign travellers and government records. He did not ferret out mere descriptions from his source material, but interpretations and explanations as well. Viewed in this light, he can be viewed as the first gifted historian of Kerala in the modern sense. However, he had no theoretical perspective about the social system or political structure for interpreting the institutions or practices he studied.

Around the same time K. V. Krishna Iyer wrote his book on the history of the *Zamorins of Calicut*. For the reconstruction of ancient history he literally relied on the legends of Kerala, and for the history after the coming of the Portuguese, he depended on the accounts of foreign travellers, place chronicles and literary works such as the heroic ballad *māmānkam kiḷipāṭṭu*. There is an appreciable attempt on his part to construct the early history of the Sāmūtiris (known at that time as Ēṛanāṭu chieftains) by piecing together the bits of information from available rock inscriptions and copper plates. Moreover, the history of the Sāmūtiris is not placed in the broader background of Kerala, as has been done in *Kochi Rājya Caritram*.

New ideologies came into play as a result of national reconstruction and social reformist movements in the provinces towards the late nineteenth and early twentieth century. This in turn produced philosophical consciousness of a society free from exploitation and gave birth to movements for social emancipation. It was driven by the realisation of the miserable human condition which had become all the more miserable under the *jāti-janmi-nāṭuvāḻi* system, popularly known as the Kerala feudal system. Organised peasant movements acquired more and more strength. One of the programmes of these organised political movements was the interpretation of history based on Marx's theory. E. M. S. Namboodiripad's *Keralam Malayāḷikaḷuṭe Mātrubhūmi* (Kerala, the Motherland of Malayalis) (1946) and K. Damoderan's *Kerala Caritram* (1966) came out in this political atmosphere. These scholar-politicians aimed at imparting objective knowledge of social relations at the instance of history.

New source material for the reconstruction of early history began to surface through the discovery and publication of inscriptions and archaeological reports. Most of the inscriptions belonging to the Perumāḷ rule were published by T. A. Gopinatha Rao, K. V. Subramanya Iyer and Ramanatha Iyer in the *Travancore Archaeological Series*, and Anujan Achan and A. G Warier in the *Ramavarma Research Institute Bulletin*. Apart from archaeological findings by the British officers, a few planned excavations by experts of the Archaeological Survey of India also improved the source of historical understanding. Old Tamil heroic poems, popularly called Sangam Poems, and the later Tamil Bhakti literature augmented the scope of historical inquiries.

It was Elamkulam Kunjan Pillai who first discussed the various issues in Kerala's history by making use of these new additions to the source of history. Linguistics was his main area of research, and his study of the developmental processes of the language of Kerala in ancient inscriptions enabled him to disentangle a number of historical issues. He identified the Perumāḷs appearing in these documents, fixed their period with the support of credible proof, and thus gave a chronological order to a critical juncture in Kerala History. Faced with teaching Kerala history he had only the works of Shangoonny Menon, Logan and Padmanabha Menon to rely on as textbooks. Naturally his task was not to write a new history of the land, but to throw light on the dark chapters and bring in continuity of the narrative. His method was largely that of source-based rational imagination of the past and explanatory description with ideological presupposition and contemporary consciousness. He was reacting to contemporary social problems like Padmanabha Menon, but with more awareness about the social system and political structure. His major contribution is the differentiation made between the Cēra chieftains eulogised in Tamil heroic poems and the Cēra Perumāḷs invoked in the inscriptions. He called these later Cēras as Kulaśēkharas and was able to provide clarity about their chronology with sequential relationship among various historical events. Sharp observations, provocative comments and sustained debates over identifying the kings and fixing their dates by rigorously examining the inscriptions and candidly interpreting the historical context and implications, make him distinct in the historiography of Kerala.

In addition to the compulsions created by the prevailing social conditions and the intellectual need as stated, there was the formal academic pressure of universities which encouraged the study of Kerala history. University-based academic research in history began with K. Marthanda Varma who obtained the state's first PhD in history in 1948 for his thesis on the Sāmūtiris of Kerala. P. K. S. Raja published his *Medieval Kerala* (1853), focusing on the period between fifteenth century CE and eighteenth century CE and covering the socio-economic and political history of the principalities of Tiruvitāmkūr, Cochin, the Sāmūtiri and Kolattiri with trade relations under the Portuguese and the consequences of the Mysorean invasion. K. M. Panikkar's *A History of Kerala* (1960) was another work. Panikkar's historical inquiries were stimulated by the disturbing claims by the dominant European powers. His historiography was triggered by his annoyance towards the capitalist development of West European nations and their colonial exploitative enterprises in Asia. He was a strong critic of the Eurocentric belief that everything of value, such as religion, philosophy, art and even science, arose in the Aegean coast. According to him, such assertions by the West were meant to destroy the morale of Asians. He felt that it was extremely important to make people aware of the alarming rise of Western Imperialism, and this objective accounts for his writing of the history from 1498–1945 CE. M. G. S. Narayanan inherited the commendable scholarship of Elamkulam and made substantial improvement in it through the discovery of new inscriptions, fresh readings of the old inscriptions, construction of a more reliable chronology, more convincing identification of rulers, rectification of their sequential order, fresh conceptualisation and better characterisation of the polity, society, economy, culture, religion, art, architecture, etc. His *Perumals of Kerala* (1972) is the first accomplished work that presented the history of an era by taking Kerala as a single cultural unit. M. G. S. Narayanan tries to structurally identify the society of Kerala during the period of the Perumāḷ rule with conceptual presuppositions about the social systems in world history. He conceives the history in the broad perspective of socio-economic development, and examines political institutions, community settlements, land relations, culture, literature, religion and other aspects of the past of Kerala. Other early publications of academic research are those of A. P. Ibrahim Kunju who wrote a comprehensive history called the *Rise of Travancore: A Study of the Life and Times of Mārtāṇḍa Varma* (1976) and C. K. Kareem who wrote the *Administration of Kerala under Hyder Ali and Tipu Sultan* (1973). T. I. Poonnen's *Dutch*

Hegemony in Malabar and its Collapse, 1663–1795 (1978) is the first major work on the Dutch in Kerala. K. S. Mathew's *Portuguese Trade with India in the Sixteenth Century* (1983) was the first study of the Portuguese period done after consulting Portuguese records. M. O. Koshy's *The Dutch Power in Kerala, 1729–1758* (1989) is a work that provides some information about the political events that accounted for the rise and decline of the Dutch East India Company during the period.

Brahmin Settlements in Kerala (1981) by Kesavan Veluthat follows the same methodology and narrative style of M. G. S. Narayanan. Veluthat adds fresh historical facts about the traditional brāhmaṇa settlements. There was a growing need for the resurrection of the past with the emergence of social reform movements and organisations based on caste. It was in this background that a few works that enabled castes with an oppressed past as well as present to acquire a sense of identity and caste-based self-respect, were produced. Most of them glorify the ancient days of the respective caste, such as the works of Kanippayur and Chentharassery.

One that denigrates the past as a whole is *Jātivayavasthayum Kerala Caritravuam* (The Caste system and Kerala History) by P. K. Balakrishnan (1992), which tries to prove that the society of Kerala had been in a static and primitive state until the nineteenth century. Balakrishnan does so by exposing the biases of Elamkulam and rejecting his characterisation of Kerala history as a figment of imagination in the absence of reliable source material. In the process, he discredits temple inscriptions, the main category of primary source. Unfamiliarity with the source material and methodological indifference make his work a biased attack on biases. However, the strong negation in the book did excite a critical rethinking of the glorified chapters in the state's early history.

Studying history in the light of the theory of productive systems is an accepted method of scientific research. *Keralathinte Innalekal* (The Yesterdays of Kerala) by K. N. Ganesh (1990) reflects the shift in Kerala historiography and portrays the life of the people of Kerala from ancient times till the present. His focus is the human–nature interface and the various systems and relations of production. Close scrutiny of the source material, production of new evidence and conceptual interpretation are characteristic of his method. His aim is not to provide a chronological history of the state, but to highlight select aspects of social life in the perspective of the history of the present.

II

Prehistory

Earliest evidence of ancient human habitation in Kerala dates to the Upper Palaeolithic Age (25000 to 30000 years BP). For convenience the Stone Age is divided into the Lower Palaeolithic and Upper Palaeolithic Ages. As elsewhere, in India too, the characteristic feature of the Palaeolithic Age is the prevalence of a specific kind of pebble-butted axe made out of large pebbles found in river beds. The stone axe has three of its sides, barring the handle, form rough curved edges by flaking. Such stone axes have been found only on the banks of river beds in North West India and the Deccan. In the Lower Palaeolithic Age, people lived in natural rock shelters at high altitudes and on big game-hunting with the fleet-footed deer in the prairies of the rainforests. Lower Palaeolithic antiquity goes back to five lakh years from the present, dated through Electron Spin Resonance (ESR) test on the stone tools discovered at the archaeological site of Athirappakkam near Chennai. Upper Palaeolithic antiquities of south India are presumed to be 40,000 to 50,000 years old. Mesolithic sites (30000–25000 BP) with paintings are assigned to 25,000 to 38,000 years from the present. A slightly late phase of the Upper Palaeolithic Age is called Mesolithic Age and it falls between the Upper Palaeolithic and late Stone Age (or Microlithic Age).

Palaeolithic people could survive only in high altitude environments. Originally they co-existed with mammoths that lived in high altitude icy mountains and hunted this huge animal using stone-tipped spears on a face-to-face encounter. Sometimes they drove the animal into swamps or other landscape traps. Since all this involved lot of collective physical combat with the animal, archaeologists called it big game hunting. Recent studies have shown that they used to scavenge too. They are said to have scavenged the bone marrow from the animal waste left by big predators. There is no such high altitude environment of ice-capped mountains in the Western Ghats of Kerala and signs of human habitation going back to such a hoary antiquity. However, recent studies have shown the presence of the people of the Upper Palaeolithic Age in the high ranges of Kerala.

Stone Tools

Some Upper Palaeolithic tools like choppers have been reported recently by P. Rajendran in his archaeological studies along the banks of the river Kanjirapuḻa in Palakkad district. Similar studies on tools by Padmanabhan Thampi in the Koodakkad reserve forest of Marayur have shown the presence of habitation during the Mesolithic period. In May 1982 more pieces of evidence surfaced at a few places on the right bank of the river Tīrthakkara and in the caves of the Chenthuruni hills that is surrounded by the tributaries of the river Achenkovil. Upper Palaeolithic implements such as choppers flaked out of pebbles have also been discovered in Kerala. These are relatively small flake-tools with curved edges showing features of local distinction. Normally the core was preserved after use while the choppers were abandoned on river banks where the hunters process the hunt. These people might have lived on hunting the gaur, tahr and deer, probably by using the stone tools hafted to long sticks. Such tools were common during the Mesolithic phase of the Stone Age, which is well-known for rock-paintings.

Upper Palaeolithic and Mesolithic antiquities of Kerala are not scientifically dated as yet. What we have is a relative dating based on comparative archaeology applied to the stone tools and paintings of the sites in Andhra, Karnataka and Tamil Nadu. Accordingly, archaeologists have presumed the Upper Palaeolithic and Mesolithic tools and paintings to be 25,000 to 30,000 years old.

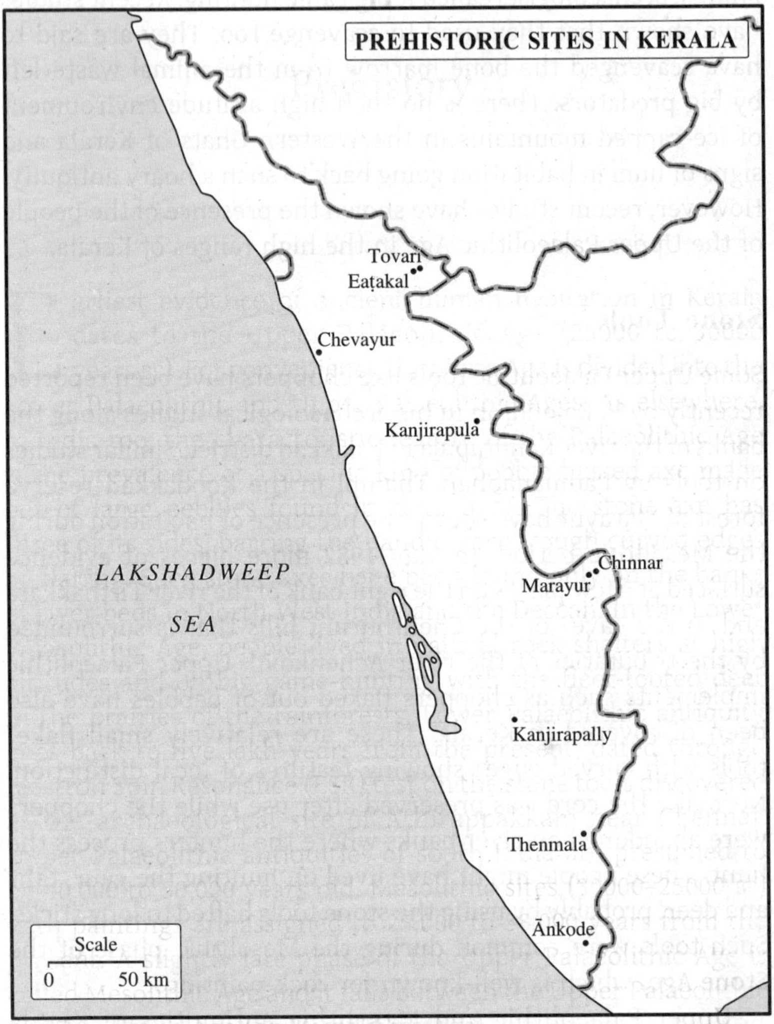

Note: 1. © Government of India, Copyright 2018.

2. The responsibility for the correctness of internal details rests with the publisher.
3. The territorial waters of India extend into the sea to a distance of twelve nautical miles measured from the appropriate base line.
4. The spellings of names in this map have been taken from various sources.

Rock-Paintings

Prehistoric art works constitute a vital source for understanding the overall living environment of their times. They are mainly in the form of etchings, paintings and bruises on the surfaces and walls of the rock shelters. While some are identifiable pictures, many others look like symbols and abstract motifs. Whether the prehistoric people had seen them as art or magic is a matter of debate. Nevertheless, it is evident that these depictions relate to the means of subsistence and survival of the people who made them. Padmanabhan Thampi, an archaeologist and a specialist in prehistory, was the first to draw scholarly attention to the various rock-art sites in Kerala. His studies are mainly on the rock-paintings on the Marayur hills. A few rock caves with paintings have been identified recently at Ālampaṭṭi hamlet in the Chinnar Wildlife Sanctuary near Munnar in Devikulam taluk. Ālampaṭṭi is close to Marayur, a hill station that is already on the map of rock art with sites such as Āṭṭaḷa and Eḻuttaḷa that bear paintings. In one of the Ālampaṭṭi rock caves there is a line drawing of the Sambar deer and in another cave several graffiti marks and handprints, all in red ochre colour. Red ochre, made of silica, clay and iron oxide, is famous for its permanence. The pigment has been used since prehistoric times and paintings in red ochre occur all over the world. It has been mainly used as the colour of primeval emotion and a sign of blood, symbolic of puberty and, hence, fertility rites.

Rock-paintings give some idea about the Stone Age people's ritual practices and beliefs with which their everyday life was probably linked. During the Mesolithic phase people are said to have drawn or painted hunting scenes on their cave walls not as art but as part of magic, i.e., the depicting of hunting could've been a prior ritual enactment under the belief that it could invigorate them with enough strength for real hunting. Several rock-art historians have interpreted this ritual depiction of the hunter, the animal and the hunting act as magico-religious and called it sympathetic magic, meaning symbolic representation of actions with the hope of better results in their real performance.

It is well known that red ochre made of silica, clay and iron oxide, seen in the prehistoric caves all over the world, represents both the colour of primeval emotion and a sign of blood symbolic of puberty and, hence, the cult of fertility.

Microliths

In Kerala what follows the 'chopper' culture is the Late Stone Age period noted for its small stone tools or microliths. It appears that the habitat of people during the Late Stone Age period was the red soil slopes and marshy plains where they subsisted on trapping smaller animals, birds and fish. Naturally, their tools were smaller. Microliths were reported from the quartzite tracts in the plains of Kerala, because these tools are made of small quartz chips flaked from rock dykes with the help of a core and shaped into tiny stone blades and points. These could be hafted to wooden sticks or bones for use as axes, knives and sickles. Sticks fitted with stone tips might have been used to hunt animals, the blades to scrap animal skin and the sickle to reap wild cereals. In Kerala, microliths made of quartzite flints alone have been found, whereas in other places in India and elsewhere microliths made of semiprecious stones such as carnelian, lapis lazuli and jasper have also been found. Kanhirapally in Kottayam district, Marayur in Idukki, Keezhillam in Ernakulam and Kanjirapuḻa in Palakkad are some Microlithic sites in Kerala.

As in the case of the Upper Palaeolithic period, Microlithic tools of Kerala have not been scientifically dated because they have not been discovered in any precisely datable stratified context. Using comparative archaeological method, therefore, archaeologists have tentatively dated the microliths of Kerala as being at least 10,000 years old.

Beginnings of Agriculture

Neolithic or the New Stone Age in human history was far more than a mere Stone Age. Apart from the fact that the people of the age used well-shaped and well-ground tools of smooth surfaces, they invented agriculture, domesticated animals, manufactured earthen pots, fabricated cloths and made use of fire for cooking. In many respects of culture, the Neolithic Age stands out totally distinct and far advanced than the other stone ages. As the age that marked the transition from food gathering to food production, ushering in the first major socio-economic transformation, the Neolithic phase is often conceived as a revolution.

Agriculture and cattle-rearing triggered a fundamental change in the living of the people. The assurance of food promoted a larger population, which in turn boosted production. The Neolithic Age marked the beginning of various handicrafts too. Earthenware of different sizes and shapes have been found among the relics of the Neolithic culture elsewhere. Clothes and ornaments made by people of this age have been found. A certain type of specialisation of arts and crafts might have existed across the scattered settlements and the people might have exchanged their products. As in the case of the Microlithic people, Neolithic people also had beliefs and rituals, but they were predominantly of the fertility cult. Fairs and festivals developed during this age, thereby bringing together these collectives around cult spots and facilitating exchanges.

Neolithic axes were made with gneiss or granite rock that was locally available. Polished celts (hand axes) are the tool types typical of the Neolithic Age across the world, though the raw material differed from place to place. The tool technology evident in stone axes, flakes, blades and beads seems to have spread all over the world during this age. Stone axes were made through flaking, pecking, grinding and polishing. Finished axes were symmetrical in shape and their working edge was well polished. Some of the axes bear marks of use at the convex working edge on the right angle. Antiquities of the world Neolithic culture date back to about 12,000 years before the present and those from the earliest Indian site date to about 5,000 years before present. In south India, the oldest known Neolithic site is dated back to 4,000 years before present. Apart from a host of stray finds of hand axes and a few rock-art depictions, and some stratified indications (indications from roughly datable strata or layers on the walls of an excavated trench) here and there, we have no archaeological evidence of habitation sites of the Neolithic culture in Kerala. There is no reliable dating of these remains either. Comparing them with remains from the neighbouring regions for relative dating seldom helps because their features vary from site to site. However, it may be presumed that Neolithic people might have reached Kerala from Tamil Nadu and Karnataka sooner or later. This presumption of migration is drawing from the absence of habitation sites and the discovery of Neolithic tools at a few places, obviously brought by migrants from the settlements in the neighbouring states.

The archaeologist Philip Lake was the first to discover Neolithic axes in Kerala in 1891. He discovered them at the foot of the Kannyakad hills. Later, William Logan (1887) and Fred Fawcett (1901) had collected a few quartz flakes, a fragment of a Neolithic celt and a couple of beads from the Wayanad area. Polished stone axes and beads that are typical of the Neolithic phase were then reported from Kalpetta and Pulppalli in the Wayanad district and the riverbeds of the Periyar in Alwaye. Hand axes were collected as stray finds from Thamarassery, Puthady, Parambikkulam and Kundurmedu. Though very limited in number, the stray finds of the Neolithic hand axe in Kerala shows distribution across all the three physiographical zones, viz., the lowlands, midlands and highlands. Most of these pieces of evidence come from the surface, seemingly as objects carried away by people from other places, precluding stratified contexts and the possibility of fixing provenance. Also, it is probable that some of the artistic representations on walls of the rock-shelters of Eaṭakal, Ānkode and Marayur are a product of the Neolithic culture.

Neolithic artefacts discovered in Kerala show that the culture had obviously got diffused from the sites of the neighbouring states and evolved here almost parallel to the development in other regions of south India. Despite differences in the raw material, Neolithic hand axes found in Kerala represent the typology typical of the culture elsewhere. In spite of the dominance of hand axe among the tool types discovered, certain features peculiar to the ecosystems—hilly forests, water-saturated swamps, river valleys, water bodies, high altitude grasslands, etc.—had evolved here. Nevertheless, there is no way to reconstruct the culture exactly, as it evolved out of the material processes of human adaptation to the ecological conditions of Kerala.

The principal means of subsistence all over the world during the Neolithic Age was agriculture or stock-rearing as determined by the ecosystems. In south India, there is Neolithic evidence for both pastoral as well as agricultural means of subsistence under appropriate ecosystems. In Kerala, the Neolithic means of subsistence was presumably a combination of gathering and primitive cultivation, supplemented by hunting/fishing. However, stock-rearing was never a major subsistence strategy even in highland Kerala that has no dearth of pastures. Extensive pastures in Kerala are confined to the high-altitude mountain ranges of Idukki district, and this accounts for indications of pastoral base in the Neolithic paintings at Marayur that depict stock-rearing corroborated by the stratified deposits around the time of the paintings.

Total absence of habitation sites and excavated material keeps us ignorant of the ethnic, organisational, institutional, customary and ritual aspects of the Neolithic material culture. However, in the light of existing knowledge about the culture in neighbouring regions, we assume that the earliest kin-based village settlements (*ūr*) in Kerala date back to the Neolithic phase. Probably the earliest Proto-Dravidian-speaking communities of Kerala must have lived in these villages. It is clear that the Neolithic people here as elsewhere had cultivated the slopes of the hills after burning the natural vegetation. This assumption is supported by the wild rice found in mid-forests and generic place names that mean 'rice fields'.

It appears that the Neolithic culture was not widespread in Kerala. The waterlogged and marshy landscape along midland Kerala with a lot of small animals such as gray hare, tortoise, porcupine, monitors and crocodiles, and several aquatic creatures like fishes and turtles, must have kept many Late Stone Age people confined to the Microlithic subsistence culture until the arrival of the iron-smelting people. In various places in Palakkad, Kozhikode, Wayanad, Thrissur and eastern parts of Ernakulam this seems to have been the sequence of cultural transformation. It appears that the Neolithic phase of Kerala was very brief as it soon got exposed to the use of iron.

Overlap in Rock Art

The Mesolithic culture in Kerala seems to have continued till around 3000 BCE from where probably the Microlithic culture begins. As regards the question of successive Stone Age cultures, it is to be borne in mind that as a general rule a technologically superior one succeeds one that is at a lower level. However, this need not necessarily imply the complete disappearance of the inferior type with the inception of the superior one. They often co-existed, as is the case even today. Along with people of the Microlithic phase, the chopper culture existed, but in their own habitats. These sequences as well as the coexistence are attested by the multilayered rock-art.

All the major rock-paintings in Kerala are multilayered and obviously belong to disparate phases from the Mesolithic down to the Iron Age. It is quite possible that there are Microlithic superimpositions on Mesolithic rock-paintings and Neolithic and Iron Age superimpositions on the Microlithic. The Marayur hood rock-painting, for instance, is a typical example. Here, we see a big human figure with wavy lines, a graffiti very frequently met with at many places in south India and Sri Lanka on Iron Age pottery. However, this depiction is superimposed over certain other depictions, probably of three different cultures. There are several dolmens that represent huge rock-cut burial monuments, indicating the possible connection to the Iron Age. There about two hundred depictions of dolmens all along the surface of the Ālampaṭṭi rock. There are red ochre paintings at various dolmen sites of south India. Similarly, the rock-art at sites such as Tovari, Eaṭakal and Ānkode is layered, representing cultures probably from the Microlithic and Neolithic to the Iron Age, through depictions with indications of hunting, domestication and cattle-keeping.

Engravings at Tovari and Eaṭakal rock-shelter, located on the hill called Ampukuttimala in the Wayanad district, are with certain comparisons and contrasts. Tovari engravings are smaller and thinner incisions on a spherical stone with a roof-like structure. They depict implements such as stone arrow-heads and crow bar of triangular shape, set in such geometrical shapes as squares and circles. There is also a drawing seemingly that of a stylised bind. Since these incisions are too thin to be made with a stone axe, it is reasonable to presume that they were made with microliths and, therefore, slightly anterior to the Eaṭakal engravings. At the same time, the crow bar drawn along with a square divided into eight segments seems to depict fields of terraced farming.

Eaṭakal, literally meaning the gap between stone blocks, is a huge natural rock-shelter. Since these are weathered rock, they can easily be carved using a stone axe. Several pictures can be found engraved on the rock-walls on either side, in different styles enabled by deep and shallow incisions, most of which are of 1–2 cms wide and 2 cms deep with shallow edges on both ends. There are human figures in postures of a ritual dance, and animals such as elephants, wild dogs and deer in the forest environment. Moreover, there are wheeled carts with the driver, various images, geometric forms and orthographic symbols. Neolithic hand-axes were reported to have been collected from the site by Fred Fawcett who discovered the rock-engravings in the cave in 1901 CE.

Ānkode, locally known as Pāṇḍavampāṛa, is located at an elevation of 1,000 feet in the village of Perumkadavila of the

Neyyattinkara taluk in Thiruvananthapuram district. It is a weathered rock comparable to the rock of Tovari and Eaṭakal, with the entire surface easily amenable to deep engraving. Neolithic hand-axes were reported to have been recovered from the site. The Āṅkode engravings are 1.9 cm deep and 1.5 cm wide, which could be executed using a sharp stone flake such as the Neolithic hand-axe, as in the case of the Eaṭakal engravings. However, there is no comparison between the figures at Āṅkode, too small in volume and diversity, and those at Eaṭakal. Mesolithic tools were reported to have been discovered at the site in the stratified context, with the signification of chronological sequence.

Early Iron Age

Historians do not agree from where iron was introduced into south India and Kerala. Some argue that the iron technology which came to north India through the Gangetic plains from Asia Minor reached the south through central and western India. Two radio carbon dating tests—one of Atranjikhera in north India showing the date around 1025 BCE and another of Halluz in Karnataka showing the date around 1105 BCE—indicate that iron came to south India slightly earlier. Scholars have pointed out that the technology of iron smelting and casting in south India differed from that of north India. Throughout the south, including Kerala, iron tools are found as part of grave goods in megaliths as well as within burial urns.

The advent of iron must have enabled the ancient people to clear forests and cultivate fresh areas, and protect themselves and the crops. Iron improved weaponry unprecedentedly and democratised combat. It is natural that the practitioners of iron working would exercise power over alien collectives and claim a share of their produce. Those who thus acquired control over reclaimed land, iron weaponry and a share of what others produced could establish hegemony over the people with inferior technology and economy.

Economy

It is widely agreed upon by scholars that Early Iron Age people were of different tribes and clans of uneven capabilities in accessing the technology of iron. Their means of subsistence varied from hunting and gathering to agro-pastoralism and crafts production. Hunting-gathering was the most primitive form of subsistence and agriculture was the most advanced form of subsistence. Animal (cattle and sheep) herding, shifting agriculture and crafts production converged in the life of agro-pastoral people who constituted the dominant society of the phase. We get clues to the Early Iron Age economy from archaeological studies. Iron Age social formation of the Tamil south was by and large a combination of pastoral activities, highland agriculture and crafts production. In the sense that an economy means a given pattern of production, consumption and exchange, Early Iron Age economy was one of kinship-based production, redistributive consumption and reciprocity-based (goods-for-goods) exchange.

Specialised crafts like copper, gold, silver smelting, bronze-alloying, lapidary and ceramics were continuing to develop along with iron smelting over the first millennium BCE. Though the history of Bronze Age civilisations date back to 2500 BCE, it is the persistence of bronze technology and its co-existence during the first millennium BCE, which we mean in the present context. However, copper, gold, silver and bronze objects are relatively very few, while iron objects of a wide variety were aplenty. Swords, daggers, knives, burins, arrowheads, tripods, lamps, hooks and points are among the burial objects made of iron. Instances of sickles and ploughshares, rarely though, have been reported from a few places like Wayanad. Etched carnelian beads of various designs dominate the lapidary artefacts. Bangles, ear ornaments and rings constitute the rare objects of copper, silver and gold. Among fine ceramics Black and Red Ware and Red Slip Ware are predominant.

Iron smelting was a local craft practised by specific tribes or clans. Local presence of raw material for iron production accounts for this. Iron slag and related remains have been found at various sites of the granite rich and lateritic regions like Malappuram and Wayanad districts. A few river basins were sources of gold. Ponnani and Beypore river basins have a long tradition of gold washing. Gold must have reached from the Nilgiri hills as well.

Society

Early Iron Age society can be imagined only in the light of archaeological studies. Archaeological remains of the period predominantly belong to the burial monuments and their contents. They show variations in the nature and quantity of material goods and the size of the burial monuments. This variation suggests that there was some sort of differentiation of status and ranking among the persons interned in burials. Some of the burial monuments are quite huge, very elaborate and multi-chambered. Early scholars like William Logan have taken huge monuments as burials of chieftains or those belonging to the upper strata and the simple monuments as burials of ordinary people or those of the lower strata. Nowadays most scholars do not consider the differentiation in the size of burials and their contents as an indication of social stratification during the period. Instead they take it as a sign of ranked society with chieftains of different ranks.

Recent studies in social formation perspective do not agree with the postulation of the presence of a stratified society during the Early Iron Age since people were by and large semi-tribal in character. We imagine the nature of Early Iron Age society by extrapolating the living conditions reflected in Tamil heroic poems, popularly called Sangam poems. There were small and big agro-pastoral chieftains, who were regularly engaged in cattle-lifting from one another. Naturally, they were big fighters and it led to the making of the heroic society with heroism as the main passion. This accounted for the erection of burial monuments and hero stones. Since they were made of huge stones, these monuments are called megaliths. Huge and elaborate burial monuments are obviously of bigger chieftains who were indeed heroes. Certain individual fighters who had heroic deaths might have been conferred a higher status, accounting for the erection of huge burials as monuments of commemoration.

Archaeological Remains

Some of the earlier archaeological discoveries of Iron Age remains in India by J. Babington in 1823 include the Megalithic burials from Chirakkal taluk of Cannanore district. William Logan (1887), A. H. Longhurst (1911), A. Ayyappan (1933), L. A. Cammiade (1930), M. D. Raghavan (1936) and several others were early investigators into this culture. Systematic investigations of the megaliths in Kerala began only in the late 1940s and early 1950s with V. D. Krishnaswami (1949) undertaking a detailed field survey of burial types and B. K. Thapar (1948) excavating the Megalithic site at Porkaḷam. L. A. Krishna Iyer (1929) was the first anthropologist to study the tribal people's relationship with megalith-building. Several archaeologists have studied various sites during the last few decades. The studies of the Kerala megaliths have focused only on issues like typology, chronology, authorship and distribution as elsewhere in the country, whereas other details too can be studied, such as habitat, habitation, means of subsistence, technology, social formation, relations, institutions, ideas and polity. Many Megalithic sites have been surveyed and recorded in every district of Kerala, although there is as yet no specialised state-wide study of the subject matter, unlike Tamil Nadu or Karnataka.

Megalithic sites known earlier from Thiruvananthapuram district include the cist burials (rock-cut chamber quarried into the surface) at Pirappancōde, urn burial and dolmens at Pulimath, and urn burials at Srīkāriyam and Veḷḷaikkaḍavu. In Kollam district, menhir sites (memorial stone or victory stone) at Anjirānḍil, Chillayam, Paṇayam, Pavitrēśwaram and Perinad have been recorded. The sites in Pathanamthiṭṭa district are Kadukutti, Koduman and Pūtankara. Several megaliths have been reported from Kottayam district and they include the menhir and cairn circle (burial circle) from Atirampuḻa, Dolmens from Kainakari, cist and urn burials at Kallūr, dolmen in Kuṟavilangād and Mannānkaṇḍam, and menhir at Tirunakkara. Among the six southern districts of Kerala, Idukki stands ahead of others in the case of Megalithic sites that are too many. The reported sites include menhirs at Ālappāṟa, Bison valley, Chinnakanāl, Kaccanpāṟa, Karnamuhi, Mūkkanpāṟa, Pōttankōlu, Pūppāṟakkutty, Ambalamēḍu and Sūrianallur. At Veḷḷappāṟa and Mēppāṟa both dolmens and menhir have been reported. Dolmens have been reported from Ariyanad valley, Bōḍimēttu, Chakkimēḍu, Iḍamalayār, Kūrkkuḻi, Maṟayūr, Muthukād, Peirakanāl and Thudathur. Stone circles, dolmens and urns have been reported from Vaṇḍipperiyār, Pāmpāḍumpāṟa, Pannivayakkara and Śānthanpāṟa.

Mulamthuruthi, Thondannur and Tripunithura in Ernakulam district had yielded the Megalithic evidence of dolmens, multi-chambered rock-cut caves and menhir respectively. A large number of Megalithic sites was reported from various parts of Thrissur district and they include mainly dolmens from Karunathara, Mulankunnathukavu, Vadakkethara and Varanadarappalli; urn burials from Edakkulathur, Eland, Eranallur, Kakkad, Kandanasseri, Karalam, Kamimangalam, Kondazi, Nadathara, Nattika, Panjapallipaambu, Pazhayannur and Porathussery; rock-cut caves at Choondal, Chevannur, Eyyel, Mangadu and Mullassery. *Kudakkal* (umbrella- or mushroom-shaped burial monument made of lateritic stone) from Ariyanur, Cheeramangad and Kadanasseri; cairn circle with capstone at Porkaḷam, and cist and urn burial at Machād.

Several Megalithic monuments have been reported from Palakkad district and they comprise hood stone at Alanallur; menhirs from Anakkatty and Kottathara; cist burials at Edappal and Thiruvilluamala; dolmens from Elavanchery, Kangad, Manjalur, Pallassana and Vadakarapatti; rock-cut caves at Elambullassery, Vaniyampara and Vellinezhi; and *toppikal* (resembling a cap, as the name suggests) at Ungallur. A few cist

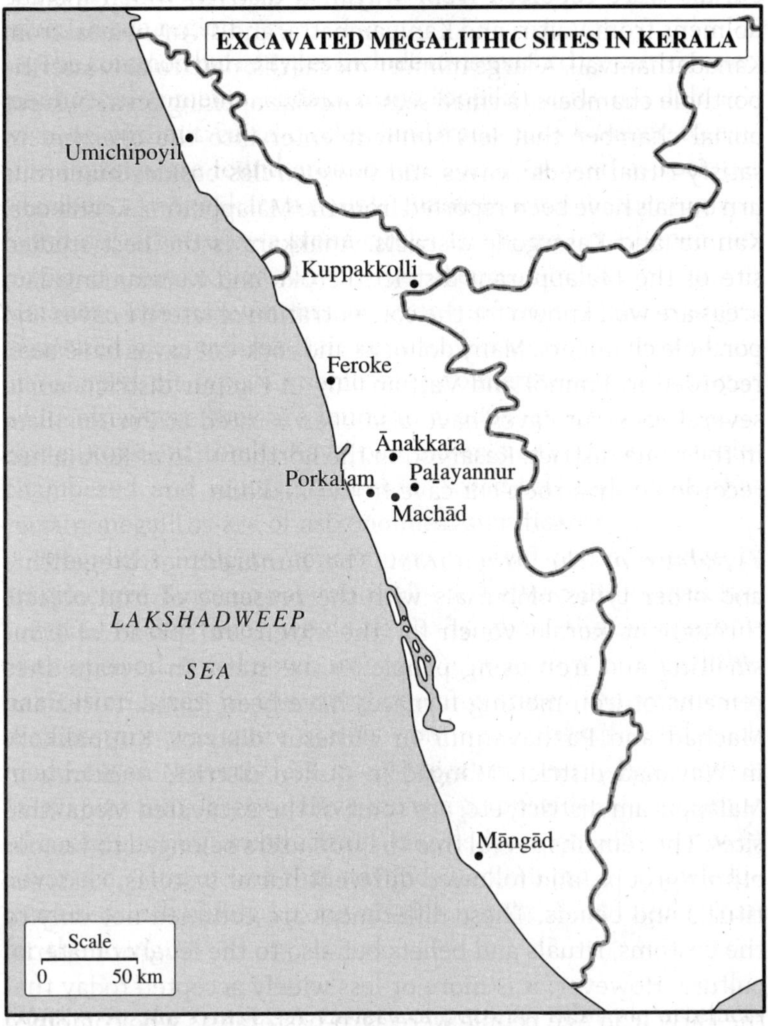

Note: 1. © Government of India, Copyright 2018.
2. The responsibility for the correctness of internal details rests with the publisher.
3. The territorial waters of India extend into the sea to a distance of twelve nautical miles measured from the appropriate base line.
4. The spellings of names in this map have been taken from various sources.

burials were reported from Wayanad district, which include dolmens from Vaitiri and Kaniyambatta, and an urn burial from Kanadathamvail. A large number megaliths, particularly lateritic porthole chambers (a small semi-circular opening on a rock-cut burial chamber that lets sunlight enter into the chamber to satisfy ritual needs), caves and stone circles besides numerous urn burials have been reported from the Malappuram, Kozhikode, Kannur and Kasargode districts. Ānakkara is the best studied site of the Malappuram district. Feroke and Kunnamangalam areas are well known for the concentration of laterite caves and porthole chambers. Many dolmens and rock-cut caves have been recorded in Punnōl and Vaṭṭianallūr in Kannur district, while several rock-cut caves have also been located at Perumkulam in the same district. Kasargod in the northern tip of Kerala had recorded only a rock-cut cave from Pilikkode.

Typology of the Megaliths: The hundreds of Megalithic and other types of burials with the presence of iron objects throughout Kerala vouch for the extensive spread of iron-smelting and iron-using people in the state. In certain sites remains of iron-melting furnaces have been found. Porkaḷam, Machād and Pazhayannur in Thrissur district, Kuppakkolli in Wayanad district, Māngād in Quilon district, Ānakkara in Malappuram district, etc. are some of the excavated Megalithic sites. The remains reveal that the iron users belonged to various ethnic groups, and followed different burial systems, customs, rituals and beliefs. These differences are confined not only to the customs, rituals and beliefs but also to the level of material culture. However, it is more or less widely accepted today that the Early Iron Age people were agro-pastoralists who combined hunting, cattle-keeping and dryland agriculture, especially the cultivation of a variety of millets. Iron Age has a long history of highland cultivation, cattle-keeping and hunting. Ethnographic evidence of iron smelting and artefact exchange among the tribal people are available. For example, the ūrāḷi of Wayanad is said to have been traditionally an iron-smelting tribe that used to supply iron artefacts to the Paṇiayar, Kuṛumar and Kuṛicya tribes in the region.

The common burial types include urns marked by cairn circles, menhirs, alignments, kudakkal and toppikal, cists and dolmens with or without cairn-circles, and rock-cut chamber tombs. Stone circles are found around urn burials as well as rock-cut chambers. At Ānakkara a double chamber with an opening was found demarcated by a stone circle. There are urn-shaped pits reported from excavations in the laterite table-land of north Malabar. The monuments of Umichipoyil near Kanhangad excavated by Jayashree Nair constitute a good example of the urn-shaped pit type. At some sites dolmens are found singly, while elsewhere they are found in groups enclosed by a stone circle. Rock-cut tombs have two major subtypes, viz., single-chambered and multi-chambered. Some scholars think that certain megaliths are of astronomical significance.

Megaliths indicate contemporary level of knowledge in architecture. Since no habitation site of the Megalithic phase has survived to our times, we do not know about the architecture of the period. It is known from the archaeology of Megalithic habitation sites in the neighbouring states that domestic architecture was quite simply confined to wattle and daub mud houses. Nevertheless, many Megalithic burial monuments in granite and laterite have survived, providing a facsimile of contemporary architectural knowledge that was relatively advanced. This means that advanced architectural knowledge was used in building strong abodes for the dead rather than for the living.

Objects in the Grave: A variety of pottery, multiple artefacts made of iron, a few copper, bronze and gold pieces, beads of semiprecious stones like carnelian, and various terracotta items are the main objects in the Iron Age grave. Black and Red Ware is the typical pottery type associated with Iron Age as well as the megaliths. Russet-coated and painted ware with wavy line pattern and other decorations, black ware, red ware and red-slip ware are the commonly found pottery types in the Megalithic sites. Both the wheel thrown as well as hand-made types of pottery are found in the Megalithic sites. Huge urns (1.5 m in height) and large jars with various decorative features have been reported from different parts of Kerala. An urn with hooks inside has been discovered and is kept at the archaeological museum of School of Social Sciences, Kottayam. Bowls, legged jars and cooking pots are commonly found in many sites as part of the grave goods. Various terracotta objects other than pots are also seen in certain graves.

Among the metal artefacts from the burials, an enormous amount of iron objects including weapons of offense, household and agricultural implements are reported. Swords, daggers, hooks, nails, iron spindles, spear-heads, knives, tridents, rods with forked ends, tripod stands, axes, chisels, bill-hooks, unusually shaped cutting tools and lamps are the main artefacts that have been reported. Some copper items like bowls and bangles and a few bronze items like bells and small vases have also been reported. There are a few instances of gold objects like coins, thin sheets and ear ornaments that have been discovered as part of burial goods. Etched carnelian beads of various shapes and dimensions constitute the main lapidary items found in the Megalithic graves. Some of them are distinct for their radial, horizontal and vertical lines of decoration. Beads made of jasper, agate, feldspar, quartz crystal, etc. have also been discovered at certain sites.

Pattern of Distribution of Megaliths: What is generally said about the distribution pattern of megaliths has limitations because of the incomplete and uneven nature of the available survey data. The pattern suggested by various scholars is influenced by the results of regions intensely surveyed. For instance, the well-surveyed Periyar river basin is considered as the area of maximum concentration of megaliths while the least-surveyed Kasargode and Alappuzha districts are considered as areas of poor distribution. Likewise, it makes little sense to speak about the concentration of Iron Age people on the basis of visible monuments like megaliths because the invisible may be much more in number. The only pattern of distribution evident is that of the raw-material based concentration of the burial types. In the granite-rich areas dolmens and cists dominate, while in the laterite table-land rock-cut chamber tombs, stone circles and kudakkal dominate. In river deltas and coastal tracks that have neither rock nor laterite, urns dominate. Thus, the pattern is that along the rocky slopes of the Western Ghats and the rocky red soil tracts the concentration is of dolmens; in the sandy and loamy plains the concentration is of urns; and in the laterite hills the concentration is of the rock-cut chambers. All the types of kudakkal and toppikkal are interspersed in red or loamy soil areas with granite and laterite. Porkaḷam is an example of the convergence of various types. Although it is indeed the availability of the material that seems to have determined the type, in places with material for all types, the preference of the local community seems to have mattered.

Of about thirty major Megalithic sites in the state, fourteen are located in Kollam district. Out of them Abhayagiri, Peruman, Kaḍavūr and Kokkōṭṭumūla are sites of menhirs; Karimpāḷūr, Orukōthupāṛa, Valiyapāḍam and Porēḍam are sites of the urn burial type; Kalluvācca, Kūvakkād, Orukkōthupāṛa, Valiyapādam and Peruman are sites of dolmens; and Ayīram, Anchal and Arippa are sites of cists. Abhayagiri and Kalluvācca that contain remains of slag were sites of iron smelting. Similarly, the remains at Ezhavannikōṇam in Thiruvananthapuram district indicate the presence of an ancient iron-smelting site there. At Chenkalthaḍam in Pathanamthiṭṭa district a huge urn burial was discovered. In Muthiramala near Kallūppāṛa in the same district relics of laterite chamber tombs were explored. Three sites at Kunnōṇni in Kottayam district and Embīram in Alleppey district have yielded several urn and cist burial types. Laterite rock-cut caves and urn burial types have been found at Kuṭṭikkunnu in Kōṭṭūrvayal of Kannur district, and Pullumala and Paḻangād in Kozhikode district.

Although hundreds of Iron Age burial sites have been identified, very few habitation sites have been identified thus far. In fact, there is no clearly-identified Iron Age habitation site in Kerala. Paṭṭaṇam is the only excavated site with an Iron Age stratum of non-burial context. Unlike megaliths and other monuments such as cairn circles, which are prominent on the surface, habitation relics are sub-surface material and escape the attention of the archaeologist. There are a few Carbon-14 dates of organic relics from Paṭṭaṇam but no thermoluminiscence dating of the potsherds. Generally, the Megalithic-Iron Age antiquity in Kerala has been dated to around c. 1000 BCE–c. 500 BCE. Megalithic practices seem to have continued till the turn of the Common Era and urn burial practice must have lasted till the second century CE.

III

Early Historical Period (c. 300 BCE–c. 300 CE)

Historians identify the closing phase of the Megalithic Iron Age (c. 200 CE) as the early historic period. In the history of Kerala this period refers to the interregnum between the late phase of the Iron Age and the emergence of the Perumāḷ rule. This is the period of the Tamil heroic poems. These poems mention Tamiḻakam (or the Tamil macro region) of which Kerala was part. Tamiḻakam, inclusive of Kerala, over a millennium between c. 500 BCE and c. 500 CE, is a typical socio-economic aggregate that becomes intelligible when characterised by using the framework of the social formation theory. According to the theory, social formation refers to a combination of unevenly-evolved economies structured by the dominance of one among them, which need not necessarily be the most superior in terms of technology and productivity. This is perhaps the best paradigm one can think of for representing the human affairs and social processes of this region that are characterised by cultural homogeneity and economic heterogeneity. When we integrate clues from the various sources such as archaeological relics of iron, epigraphs, ancient coins, contemporary Graeco-Roman writings and Tamil heroic poems, we discover that forms of subsistence during this period were hunting/gathering, herding-cum-shifting cultivation, plough agriculture and crafts production. Though they were adapted to different ecosystems, these forms of subsistence were obviously unequal in terms of productive forces and productivity of labour. The social formation was the aggregate of the economic, social, political and cultural transactions of the peoples of these different forms of subsistence.

Their coexistence and interaction were marked by the dominance of the people of agro-pastoral means of subsistence. This seems to have dissolved into a new social formation during the sixth or seventh centuries CE.

The peoples all over Tamiḻakam, irrespective of the form of subsistence, were descent groups split into domestic segments (*kuṭi*) and clustered around the respective clan settlement (*ūr*). Each ūr was a self-sustaining system made up of kuṭis that were independent production units based on the kin labour of the concerned descent group (*kuṭimākkal*). Despite the differing strategies of subsistence from ecotype to ecotype,* kinship was central to the division of labour. In all forms of production, kuṭi functioned as the repository of familial labour, consisting of the young (*iḷaiyar*) and the old (*muṭiyar*) among the agnatic kins and affinal relatives. The primacy of kin labour precluded the possibility of social stratification of any perceptible kind. Interspersed within these kin-based production units of the clan settlements of the various chiefdoms existed brāhmaṇa households with a different system of productive relations that was devoid of kinship.

Although at the level of social formation the land strip that we distinguish as Kerala was not distinct during the period, there existed differences in ecological terms. Kerala's relatively well-inhabited zones of Iron Age were predominantly of the *kuṛinci* ecosystem that corresponded to the red soil ranges and plains. Next in importance was obviously the *neytal* ecosystem, thanks to the lengthy littoral and fairly-extensive backwaters. As regards the other micro ecosystems, the *mullai* (the pastoral landscape ecosystem) was virtually absent, the *pālai* (the dry landscape ecosystem) very rare and *marutam* (the wet landscape ecosystem) was confined exclusively to a few pockets of highland fields and elevated alluvial plains. Major forms of subsistence in the region must have been hunting/gathering, shifting cultivation,

* We use 'ecotype' as a landscape type in this context. To get the same meaning we will also use 'landscape ecosystem'. For instance, a *tiṇai* is an ecotype or a landscape ecosystem.

crafts production and dryland agriculture of the semi-forested red soil midlands. As in Tamiḻakam, the social formation in the red soil plains of Kerala too was a system of multiple forms of subsistence structured by the dominance of dryland agriculture. Here semi-forested red soil tracts, as elsewhere in Tamiḻakam, were peopled by descent groups dispersed as kuṭis clustered into self-sustaining ūrs conducted under their headmen. However, there are a lot of ecological differences between the agro-climatic zones of Kerala and those of the rest of Tamiḻakam in terms of seasons, rainfall, permeability, landscape, soil structure and so on. What comes up as the most striking difference about the wet-rice landscape ecosystem is the excess of water in the case of Kerala and its scarcity in the case of the regions elsewhere in Tamiḻakam. This would suggest a great deal of differences in the nature of cultivation followed and labour processes required in these regions. In the wetlands of the former the management of excess water has been the central problem, whereas in those of the latter irrigation has been central.

Socio-Economic Milieu

Around the turn of the Common Era, the Kerala region was marked by an advanced level of technology in terms of metal-smelting, weaving, glass-making, stone-cutting, pottery and other crafts, as mentioned in indigenous literary sources and foreign notices. Archaeological evidence corroborates this fact in terms of metal-works, glass-making, weaving, pearl fisheries, stone-cutting and pottery. During this period metal-working included the alloy metallurgy of bronze casting. Barring small brick-constructions, elaborate burial cists and rock-cut chambers, no monumental buildings have been testified by the relics, though the excavations vouch for a fairly good knowledge in architecture. Excavation of habitation sites reveals that dwellings were only of the hutment type during this period. Stone-cut benches and cots in the big burial caves shed light on the kind of furniture that was used, and these were obviously not in huts. Big burials must have been accorded to headmen of prominent descent and chiefs who could have commanded the collective labour of the clan. Utensils of a wide variety, implements, lamps and other artefacts suggest the specialisation of crafts among the people. While how the people worked and who controlled each craft under what social conditions constitute the most crucial aspects for us to characterise the social formation, it has to be borne in mind that these details can never be known precisely.

It appears that the headship over clan kin ties, i.e., the chiefly power, largely constituted the source of authority to command collective labour. Chieftains of higher levels could command the labour of his mercenaries (*viṭutolil*) who seem to have included potters and metal-workers. Probably the most subjugated kind of labour they commanded may have been of the captives. Since the chieftains were warriors, they could probably command people who did all kinds of specialised labour. There are references in the Tamil heroic poems to warriors (*maṛavar*) offering paid service of protection to caravan troupes of salt merchants (*umaṇac-cāttu*). The means of payment mentioned in the source is *dravya* (wealth).

As already noted, the principal social mode of labour realisation was familial/co-operative, but at least a few—such as metal-working and pottery—that come under the category of skilled labour must have been full-time trades of specialists and therefore hereditary. As the most extensively used metal, iron had a central place among metals as the base of weapons which are significant for a society of predatory operations, i.e., a situation in which communities were plundering against one another under the leadership of their chieftains. Moreover, the practice of burying iron objects along with the dead had pushed a great deal of iron out of circulation, presupposing continuous iron-working as a full-time occupation of hereditary specialisation. Production of earthen pots, a characteristically brittle artefact, was obviously a continuous full-time activity, for their use was extensive both for the living as well as the dead. Such hereditary full-time artisans/craftspeople may have usually been in the headquarters of *vēḷir* and *vēntar* chieftains, who were the bigger and the biggest types respectively. These chiefly settlements were the major redistributive pools of resources and could therefore support more full-time craftspeople. Another full-time function that was hereditary in nature was that of the maṛavar. Every ūr needed full-time warriors because the main mode of political appropriation of resources was predation. In association with the chiefly households there were three other full-time hereditary functionaries, viz., the *pāṇar* (bards), *paṛaiyar* (who played a kind of raid drum called *paṛa*) and *tuṭiyar* (who played a small drum called *tuṭi*).

In ports like Muciṛi and Toṇḍi there seem to have existed settlements (*cēris*) of hereditary artisan/craftspeople. Probably both the ruling authority and organised merchant groups must have used the labour of this category of servile people under conditions of coercion and relations of labour transcending kinship. The poems refer to captives working in pearl fisheries. The emergence of new hereditary occupations is implied by the vēntar level of political control. The vēntar was the most resourceful and hence the most powerful category of chieftains wielding control over several communities even outside his own ethnic group. This resource-rich position and command transcending kinship ties would have enabled the vēntar to possess permanent workforce of his own. In the process of predatory operations and redistribution (i.e., centralised pooling of resources for distribution), some kind of differential allocation of new position, status, roles and prestige within the complex redistributive relationships was natural. Gradually hereditary occupation groups were emerging in the chiefly settlements, especially in the coastal towns, marketing centres and ruling headquarters. The beginnings of differential allocation of positions and the formation of a simple hierarchy were likely at the instance of the highest chiefly authority represented by the vēntar. However, the poems do not contain pointers to a clearly stratified society. Social differentiation was confined to the binary between *uyaṛntōr* (the high-born) who comprised brāhmaṇas, and *i̱lipiṛappāḷar* (the low-born) who comprised the people. That the second category comprised all people suggests a very flexible kind of social division and lack of indications to the existence of intermediary positions confirms the fluidity. Similarly the people were conceived as two mutually-opposed groups, viz., *puravalar* (people with resources for redistribution) and *iravāḷar* (people with no resources to subsist and hence dependents). Most people had something to subsist and, therefore, they redistributed the left-over to dependents, whose number was relatively lesser because it was largely a semi-tribal community and inherently accommodative.

Exchange

In addition to the early forms of customary exchange practices, formal exchange seems to have become more extensive towards the closing phase of the Iron Age that overlaps with the period of the Tamil heroic poems. Punch-marked coins that reached from the Gangetic region, the names of the specialist merchants seen in the Tamil brāhmi label inscriptions, evidence of organised merchant body (*nikamam*), the Roman coins brought by long-distance traders and the writings by the Graeco-Roman geographers provide evidence of mercantile circulation of resources. There were several tributary channels to the pan-Indian exchange routes diverging from Pratiṣṭhān (or Paithan), the main centre of exchanges in the Deccan, to different parts of Tamiḻakam. Kerala was well connected to the network through her ports like Muciṛi and Toṇḍi, as well as inland markets. It appears that the volume of goods exchanged from the coasts of Tamiḻakam, both the west and the east, across the sea and on land, was amazingly high.

However, the overall nature of contemporary internal exchanges, as depicted in the heroic poems, was largely that of reciprocity based on use-value. It was primarily a system of goods for goods exchange (*nēr-koḷ*) based on haggling (*notuttal*) that involved no notion of exchange-value, price and profit. This does not preclude the existence of route communication and formal points of exchange. Contemporary networks of exchange were fairly large and people of different ecosystems with diverse resources entered into frequent transactions. There were fixed points of exchange such as *āvaṇam* or *angāṭi* (fair) as well as occasional markets like *nāḷangāṭi* (day market) and *antik-kaṭai* (evening shop). Poems refer to a kind of commodity loan (*kuṛittumāretiṛpai* or *kuṛiyetiṛpai*) to be returned in the same kind and quantity which precludes the notion of interest. Even the exchange of specialist goods was primarily based on the notion of use-value.

This necessitates a rethinking about the nature of south India's exchange relations with the Roman world. There is no clear evidence of ancient Tamils organising trade with Rome. The nature of internal exchange shows that the lack of evidence is not altogether accidental. All evidence in this regard points to the coming of the foreign traders, particularly the Greeks and Arabs in their vessels for shipping of goods. It was hardly trade for the Tamil society, the forms of exchange of which were reciprocity, redistribution, gifting, goods for goods and barter. Trade—distinguished as exchange-value or profit-oriented exchange, using money as medium of exchange, means of payment and measure of value—was not the form of exchange in early communities. Mere presence of coins is not enough to confirm that a society was monetised. There should be evidence for the use of money both as a means of payment and measure of value, which sources hardly vouch for in the case of ancient Tamil society. The description of this exchange relation as Indo-Roman maritime trade is a loose generalisation. On the contrary, there are a plenty of indications in the sources to believe that the society was largely non-monetised, and that the Roman coins functioned as a part of social valuables and not as money. The survival of coins as hoards fresh from the mint and with apertures or loops on many suggests that they were preserved as treasure and often used as ornaments. This does not rule out the possibility of the use of coins as a medium in higher transactions and as an item of gift enhancing status and ranking.

Exchanges and incessant interaction among the self-sustaining entities with one another accomplished a common horizon of shared cultural practices facilitated by the Tamil language. Exchange involved circulation of ideas, which meant dissemination of knowledge systems and worldviews. Long-distance exchange relations did carry forces of production and strategies of subsistence from one place to another, modifying and transforming the pre-existing ones as agreeable to the ecosystems and social relations. To a great extent the dissemination of the brāhmaṇical, Jain and Buddhist knowledge systems and worldviews did determine the nature of institutional transformation in Late Iron Age Tamiḻakam. Brāhmaṇ presence in Tamiḻakam is attested by allusions in the Tamil heroic poems around the closing centuries of the first millennium BCE. It is important to note that most of the traditional brāhmaṇa settlements of Keraḷa have megaliths or urn burial complexes close to them, suggesting their rise adjacent to the pre-existing human settlements. There is hardly any direct evidence of an equally ancient Jain or Buddhist presence in the region, though it is reasonable to assume their ideas to have spread at least to those areas that are accessible through exchange routes. Descent groups even of Kerala find mention in the Aśōkan edicts. Scholarly bards, particularly the brāhmaṇ poets (*pulavar*) from the north, accustomed to the administrative tradition of the Maurya-Sātavāhana reigns, carried ideas of state power, periodic exaction and bureaucracy right to the ears of the vēntar-level chieftains. However, as major institutions like the state never come up as a transplant, in spite of being exposed to both brāhmaṇical and heterodox religious ideologies, the chiefdom-level polity remained the same until the dissolution of the social formation. In short, the result of these internal and external influences was presumably further development of the social milieu of clans segmenting into lineages and lineages splitting into domestic groups that subsisted on multiple forms of economies based on kin-based relations of production, redistributive system of social appropriation and predatory political control.

Political Conditions

Each descent group had its headman called *kiḻār* who pooled and redistributed the resources of the ūr. This elementary structure of chiefdom acquired varying degrees of complexity depending upon the numeric strength as well as the nature and extent of redistributive social relationships. The three categories of chieftains in the ascending order were kiḻār, vēḷir and vēntar, and the redistributive social relationships of this order involved a corresponding increase in complexity. This order was naturally the order of the resource strength as well. However, the chiefly levels from kiḻār to vēntar were not structured into a single system of formal hierarchy of power distribution with a running thread of political control. Vēntar-level chieftains were patrons of Vedic rituals and assumed titles of status and legitimacy relating to their patronage. They were theoretically independent from one another, however the more powerful and incessant predatory marches demanded the allegiance of others below.

In this manner the three vēntar lineages of Cēras, Cōḻas and Pāṇdyas began commanding the resources of numerous settlements within a region through predatory control and subjugation, sometimes extending over the domains of the veḷir, and soon emerged as well established ruling powers without clan ties. The resource potential of these vēntar level chieftains was obviously very high. Roman exchange contacts must have enabled them to secure gold, silver, horses and other prestigious objects as the poems would have us believe. Plunder was the principal means of exacting resources and was beyond the control of clan ties for all categories of chieftains. Predatory campaigns and booty redistribution as the central means of resource sharing were fundamental to the maintenance of the chiefly status. Prestations and predatory exactions were the usual modes of chiefly appropriation of resources, and gifts and redistribution their instituted channels of social sharing. Even for the highest chiefly lineages, collective appropriation through the institution of redistribution was the common practice, though they received prestations from their own people and exacted tributes (*tiṟai*) from the enemies.

Poems glorify the *mūvēntar*, the three ruling lineages of Cēra, Pāṇḍya and Cōḻa, as the great rulers of Tamiḻakam and historians mostly resonate this by calling them kings and assuming them symbolic of state power. They seem to have assumed royal titles, as evidenced by those attributed to a Cēra chieftain: *imayavar-ampan* and *vānavar-ampan*, the Tamil forms of *dēvānampriya* (the beloved of god) used by the Mauryan Emperor Aśōka. However, the absence of various factors like periodic exaction, formally-organised militia, bureaucracy and juridico-political institutions show that it was not a state system but only a pre-state chiefdom. These features of early historical agro-pastoral social formation—predatory campaigns, redistribution, prestations, gifts and non-stratified society—show that state formation could have been unlikely at that stage.

Cēras in *Patiṟṟuppattu*

Cēras held sway over the kuṟinci-dominated zones of the Western Ghats towards the sea. They are referred to in the poems as *kānaka-nāṭan* (the chief of the forested *nāṭu*) or *malaiyan* (the chief of *malai* or hill). While praising Cēramān Kōtai Mārpan in the *Puṟanānūṟu*, the poet Poikeyār expresses confusion about how the chief should be addressed. His confusion is as to whether the chief could be called *nāṭan* as he owned marutam lands or *ūran* as he held kuṟinci lands or *cēramārpan* as he possessed coastal tracts. This would suggest that the Cēra region was a mixture of diverse ecological zones with the predominance of hills and forests, though its resource base was primarily derived out of the hills and forests. In a poem of *Puṟanānūṟu*, incidentally, the poet Paraṇar refers to the hill products (*malaittāram*) and sea products (*kaṭarrāram*) of Cēran Cenkuṭṭuvan and the gold that reached ashore by boats.

The Cēras are the only line of chieftains with a collection of eulogising songs solely for them, and this collection is called the *Patiṟṟuppattu* (a collection of hundred poems by ten poets). It is said that originally the *Patiṟṟuppattu* was a collection of ten sets of ten songs, each ten dedicated to ten Cēra chieftains, but the first and the last tens are lost. It is from the surviving eighty songs, dedicated to eight Cēras, that we get the Cēra genealogy, ideas about their exploits, the structure of political power, sources of legitimacy and the nature of authority in contemporary Kerala.

Utiyan Cēralātan of Kuzhumur, well-known as *perumcorrutiyan* (literally, the Utiyan famous for his great rice feasts), is the first known Cēra chieftain. As mentioned earlier, he was praised in the first ten songs (*pattu*) of *Patiṟṟuppattu*, but this set of ten poems dedicated to him is lost. It is from a few poems by Māmulanar in the *Puranānūṟu* that we get some information about Utiyan. He is said to have been defeated in the battle of Veṇṇi against Karikāla Cōḻa. Moreover, the poems also report that Utiyan was wounded at the back, a big shame in contemporary society, and he was therefore compelled to commit suicide by observing the ritual fast unto death (*vaṭakkiruttal*; the ritual sitting in penance facing the north until death) to save himself from disgrace.

Utiyan was succeeded by his son Neṭum Cēralātan, who has been praised by Kaṇṇanār in the second set of ten poems of *Patiṟṟuppattu*. He was referred to as imayavar-ampan. Some historians thought that the phrase meant a king with the sky as the boundary of his kingdom, but as mentioned earlier it is widely held to mean 'the beloved of God' today. Kuṭanādu is mentioned to have come under Cēra control during his period. Poems extol his benevolence, and victories over seven crowned kings and the subsequent achievement of the title of *Adhirāja*. Māmulanar mentions the defeat of the Kadamba chieftain by Neṭum Cēralātan and the exhibition of valuables brought by him as booty. He is said to have defeated not only the Kadambas, his principal enemy, but all the kings of the land between Kanyakumari and the Himalayas. Kaṇṇanār praises him on defeating the Yavanas (Graeco-Romans) who were supporters of the Kadambas. It is mentioned in the *patikam* (colophon)[†] that he had gifted a part of Umbarkkāṭu (Ānamalai) to Kaṇṇanār. According to Kaṇṇanār, Neṭum Cēralātan was killed by a Cōḷa ruler in battle. Māmulanar notes that before the end of his long reign of 58 years, his brother Palyānai Celkezhukuṭṭuvan, the hero celebrated by the brāhmaṇa pulavar Pālai Gautamanār in the third ten of *Patiṟṟuppattu* as *puḻiyār kōn*—i.e., the lord of Puḻināṭu—had died. Kaṇṇanār notes that Antuvan Cēralātan, another brother of Neṭum Cēralātan, was also no more by the time of Neṭum Cēralātan's demise. Antuvan Cēralātan is said to have assisted his brother in all battles, and patronised brāhmaṇas and Vedic sacrifices. Kalankāikkaṇṇi Nārmuṭi, who was eulogised in the fourth ten of the *Patiṟṟuppattu* by Kappiyarru Kappiyanār, had predeceased his father Neṭum Cēralātan. Aṭukoṭṭuppāṭṭu Cēralātan, another son of Neṭum Cēralātan, is eulogised as the hero of the sixth ten of the *Patiṟṟuppattu*. He too predeceased his father. His title seems to indicate that he was famed for his skills in dancing, drumming and singing.

So Neṭum Cēralātan was succeeded by his second son, Vel Kezhukuṭṭuvan, the hero of the fifth ten of *Patiṟṟuppattu* by the brāhmaṇa pulavar Paraṇar. He is celebrated as *kaṭal pirakōṭṭiya kuṭṭuvan*, a phrase that refers to his prowess in the sea; he seems to have routed his enemies, obviously pirates, back into the outer sea. He is said to have extended his control from Kollimalai in the east to the port towns of Toṇḍi and Māntai on the western coast. Also called *cenkuṭṭuvan* (the illustrious ruler), he is famous in history as the elder brother of Ilanko Aṭikaḷ who wrote the *Cilappatikāram* and as the hero who brought the rock for Kaṇṇaki's idol all the way from the Himalayas. Historians have tried to determine Cenkuṭṭuvan's period on the basis of his synchronism with Gajabāhu, the ruler of Sri Lanka during the second century CE. M. G. S. Narayanan has convincingly dated *Cilappatikāram* as a late ninth century CE work. Cenkuṭṭuvan is said

[†] A *patikam* is a colophon added later as a brief introduction by those who had collected, redacted and put the poem as part of an anthology.

to have joined the battle of succession between two claimants to Cōl̲a power, and had supported Kiḷḷi, one of the contestants. He is also said to have helped Kiḷḷi in the Cōl̲a battles of Iṭumpil and Valyur against the Kadambas. Cenkuṭṭuvan is said to have crushed the Kadambas in spite of the Yavanas extending them naval support. He is said to have defeated the Kongus and a warrior chief called Mōkur Mannan. Cenkuṭṭuvan's attack of the Koṭukur fort and the destruction of the Kadamba army camping there has been praised by Paraṇar.

Celvakaṭumko Vazhyatan (also mentioned as Azhi Atan) is hailed by Kapilar as the most illustrious Cēra ruler who was victorious over his Pāṇḍya and Cōl̲a contemporaries. During his time the Cēra rule extended from Kollimalai in the east to Toṇḍi and Māntai on the west coast. He is also called the lord of Pul̲ināṭu and Kollimalai as well as the lord of Puhār, the Cōl̲a capital. He is praised as being an extremely benevolent ruler who distributed among the pāṇas (bards) all the treasures that he acquired through his plunder campaigns. He is said to have generously extended the gift of villages to brāhmaṇas. Tradition holds that he had gifted an extensive area of land to Kapilar. Historians opine that Celvakaṭumko could be Ātan Cēral Irumpoṛai who figures in the Pukaḷur inscription.

Perum Cēral Irumporai, praised as the chieftain of Pul̲ināṭu, Kollimalai and Puhār, and the hero of the eighth ten of *Patirruppattu*, sung by Arisil Kizhar, was Celvakaṭumko's son. He is said to have defeated the combined armies of the Pāṇḍyas, Cōl̲as and Aṭiyamān, the chief of Takaṭur. Having destroyed Aṭiyamān's city of Takaṭur, Perum Cēral Irumporai acquired the title of Takaṭur Erinta Perum Ceral Irumporai. It shows that he had defeated his Cōl̲a contemporary. He is also praised as a great patron of the brāhmaṇas and Vedic sacrifices. Kunrur Kizhar celebrates his son Ilam Cēral Irumporai in the ninth ten of the *Patiṟṟuppattu.*

Yānaikatcai Māntaran Cēral Irumpoṛai was Perum Cēral Irumporai's successor and probably the hero of the last ten of the *Patiṟṟuppattu.* The decline of the Cēras began by the time of Māntaran Cēral's ascendency. It is said that the Pāṇḍya ruler

Neṭumceḻian defeated and captured Māntaran Cēral. However, he is said to have managed to escape and restore his chiefdom. Māntaran Cēral's successor Kanaikkal Irumpoṛai is said to have defeated a local chief called Mūvan. He is alleged to have pulled out the teeth of the vanquished and planted them at the gate of the port town of Toṇḍi. Kanaikkal Irumpoṛai is said to have committed suicide by observing vaṭakkiruttal after his defeat in the hands of the Cōḻa ruler Cenkaṇṇan.

Political Structure

As indicated above, the songs of the *Patiṟṟuppattu* contain invaluable clues to the structure of political power, nature of authority and sources of legitimacy. Many of the features attributed to the Cēras in these poems are applicable to the other vēntar too, but that they are specifically assigned to the Cēra lineage is important. Like the vēntars, the Cēras are praised as performers of *velvi* (Vedic sacrifices), devotees of the war goddess *Korravai*, and worshippers of the protector god *Murukan.* However, unlike the case of the other two of the mūvēntar, these poems equate the Cēras with the Vedic gods Surya, Agni, Marut, the *pancabhūtas*, the constellations and the *navagrahas*. These comparisons remind us of the *lōkapāla* (protector of the world) theory of the *itihāsa-purāṇa* (epic and purāṇic) tradition. The poets eulogise the Cēras as wearing garlands made of seven crowns. A poem says that Koperumcēral Irupoṛai protects his kuṭimākkaḷ the way a mother takes care of her child, and this reminds us of the concept in the second edict of Aśōka (Separate Edict II) that equates the relation between the king and his subjects with that of the parent and his children. However, the simile of the mother is very important in the context of the kinship-basis of contemporary polity.

In a poem by Kārikkaṇṇanār of Kavirippumpaṭṭinam in the *Puṟanānūṟu* there are indications to the expansion of the predatory control beyond their original ūr (*mutūr*), obviously through the process of subjugation. One poem shows Cēramān Kuṭṭuvan Kōta seated as the *uṭaiyōr* (lord) of a mutūr in the place of its original chief. The subjugation process seems to have involved three different methods: subordination with tributary obligations, expulsion and marital alliance. There are many references in the poems to all these methods of enlarging the domain of the vēntar. The chiefs of Nānjilmalai, Pāyarmalai and Veṭṭāṟu are noted as Cēra vēntan's subordinates who had the obligation to fight in times of raid. A few poems praise the chiefs Tirukuṭṭuvan, Tirukkilli and Tirukkannan as the *ēnāti* of the Cēra (i.e., *sēnāpati* or the chief of soldiers). Similarly, Paṇṇan, the kiḻān of Ciṟukuṭi and Aruvantai, and the kiḻān of Ampar were Cēra subordinates with tributary and military obligations.

Sometimes chiefs in the fringes were subordinated by two vēntar chiefs, and they allowed the obligation to shift from one to the other in regular intervals. In addition to such subordinates, there were many village chiefs called *cīṟūr-mannar* (the chief of a *cīṟūr* or small village), mostly maṟavar headmen, who functioned as the warrior headmen of the vēntar. The vēntar sometimes made them village chiefs (*ūr-mannar*) in lieu of the latter's obligatory service (viṭutoḻil) in the predatory campaign. Several poems are in praise of such warrior-chiefs who were ready to rush to their vēntar in times of emergency and die fighting for him. Since limitations of contemporary transport and communication facilities necessitated it, control seems to have been maintained by stationing the kinsmen of the vēntar at different points for collateral management of resources in the expanded area. The poems show that the people in subjugated areas could remain fearless only by parting with the vēntar a share of their resources in the form of *tiṟai* or *koḷ* (tributes in kind). Often the vēntar had to raid the settlements to exact tiṟai, for the bigger chieftains always preferred to resist, rather than volunteer, paying tribute.

The structure of the vēntar-level of political power was relatively complex since its redistributive social relationship was elaborate. It involved some kind of a simple hierarchy from vēntar to the kutimākkal, with kilār or *mannar* as intermediaries, but cutting across kinship and distancing the vēntar from the kuṭimākkal. However, during the pre-raid or post-raid feasting (*untāttu*) the vēntar did drink and dine with the maṛavar at his residence. A complex redistributive political economy based on raids precludes the formation of a structured polity with defined positions and functions: the only institutions of some political character mentioned in the poems are the *avaiyam* (*sabha*) which seems to have functioned as an assisting body of vēntar. The members of this body seem to have been mainly warrior-chiefs and the scholarly pulavar. However, the image of a king was quite well-known to the bards who eulogised the mūvēntar as crowned kings, albeit without any correspondence to reality. However, even the pulavar do not seem to be glorifying the vēntar as accomplished rulers with the *saptānga* attributes mentioned in the *Arthaśāstra*.

The poetic expressions and descriptions in *Patiṛṛuppattu* are clear about one aspect of the nature of the political authority of the Cēras: that they were seeking to legitimise it by drawing heavily from Vedic itihāsa-purāṇic-śāstraic brahmanism. Their authority is characterised in terms of purāṇic–śāstraic notions of leadership and status legitimised by comparing and associating them with epic characters. In fact, a poem claims that Cēramān Perumcōrrutiyon conquered the land of the Pāṇdavas and hosted a feast for both the Pāṇdavas and the Kauravas after the Bhārata war. There are references in the poems to Cēras possessing an army of the classical four-fold division, conquering many rulers and subjecting them to a subordinate position. In several songs, the Cēras are described as the overlord of all monarchs in the lands between the Himalayas and Kanyakumari. It is futile to go by such poetic expressions as these are embellishments applied for praising the vēntar and not statements of reality.

The Edicts of Aśōka referred to the Cēras not as individual rulers but as clans of kindred descendants, as expressions such as *satiyaputo* and *kēraḷaputo* suggest. There seems to have been a lot of difference between the image that the poets attribute to the vēntar and the reality. We know that the whole of Tamiḻakam did not belong to them and there were other tribute-receiving chiefs like Atiyamān, who were almost vēntar in status. A poem in praise of Neṭumān Anci warns all the chiefs of agrarian settlements to rush to him with tiṟai if they wished to retain their ūrs. Many of the hill chiefs were uncompromisingly opposed to the vēntar. For instance, Pāri of Paṟampumalai offered strong resistance to the vēntar, though he was subsequently defeated and killed. Among the vēḷir chieftains, the Āy chieftains (c. seventh century CE) held sway over the region from Kanyakumari to most of the northern part of Kerala up to Tiruvalla. Antiran, Atiyan and Titiyan were prominent among them. Another vēḷir was the Ezhimala chiefdom in the north. Nannan was the main ruler of this chiefdom, and he has been celebrated in Tamil heroic poems as the lord of the region comprising Coimbatore, Wayanad and Gudalur.

There was no notion of precisely-demarcated territory and poems would fix the Himalayas as the northern boundary of each vēntan, whose control beyond the core waned and constantly fluctuated and had to be frequently refreshed through predatory campaigns. The reality was that vēntar were also chiefs, but the crucial difference was their greater resource power, larger redistributive intercommunity relationship and better access to cultural sources of legitimisation in comparison to the vēḷir. They were surrounded by brāhmaṇa pulavar of the Vedic tradition and a few were well informed of the śāstraic-purāṇic notions of kingship. Pāṇas and their heroic compositions were the main strength behind their name, fame and legitimacy. They kept the image of the vēntar alive by roaming around the land with their songs in praise of the vēntar's exploits. Predatory marches, their ravaging of settlements, arbitrary redistribution of the ūr, and the consequent migration and subsequent immigration were characteristic features of the content of the poetry of the period under review. This was a situation of pre-state chiefdoms heading towards the formation of a state system that had relatively evolved juridico-political features, i.e., laws or normative stipulations and ruling power.

Material Contradictions

The material processes of co-existence and interaction of conflicting forms of subsistence continuously generated contradictions at the economic level. Mutually-conflicting economies formed a system that was dominated by pastoral agriculture, and this persistently gave rise to forces that aimed at dissolving the system itself. This was a social formation that was structured around the dominance of dryland agriculture, and herding, predatory politics, redistributive social order and heroic culture were its fundamental institutions. It appears that the complex redistributive system and the instituted practice of gift (*koṭai*) had been generating contradictions that accentuated the process of erosion of kinship and segmentation of clans.

Of all the contradictions, the most striking was the plight of plough agriculture which failed to secure its conditions of expansion. Predatory campaigns of chieftains and the entailing destruction of agriculture and settlements of farming communities strangulated the plough-based wet-rice agriculture, despite its status as the superior technology in terms of productivity. That such a form of subsistence could not dominate was a major contradiction of the social formation. Predatory raids sometimes involved the capture of the ūr and its redistribution among warrior chiefs implied the imposition of a predatory right of the alien chief over descent groups. In the case of gifts of ūr, probably, the grant of the right of exaction to warrior chiefs beyond clan kinship must have given rise to the chiefly lineages branching off from clans.

As pulavar and Vedic priests brāhmaṇas seem to have been given gifts of ūr, not in the form of actual land grants but as a part of the redistributive system. Such gifts must have given rise to individual holdings against communal holdings. However, the gifts of ūr to brāhmaṇas would mean formation of their households, involving far-reaching changes in terms of relations of production, because it was much more than the superimposition of an alien right of exaction. Being a non-cultivating group, brāhmaṇas had to depend on the familial labour of neighbouring clans for the cultivation of their land. This meant making some permanent arrangement for the supply of labour for these brāhmaṇa households, which is a system transcending kinship. In due course, brāhmaṇa households must have emerged as independent units of production with working clan families attached to them. In fact, poems refer to brāhmaṇa households as *pārppanaccēri*, which in the present context signifies an alternative system of production relations counterpoised to what was dominant. As noted earlier, a nexus of new relations representing traits of an alternative ideology based on the Vedic, purāṇic and śāstraic texts, instead of heroism, soon developed. Actually, the development of this alternative system itself was a process that may have generated and aggravated systemic contradictions.

Low labour productivity was a basic drawback of the social formation. Limitations of kin labour added on to it. Economic re-productivity was steadily declining. This caused another serious problem. Thus, it was not possible for the socio-economic aggregate to continue as a system for a longer period with its low labour productivity and ever-falling potential of economic reproduction. Actually, the incompatibility between relations of production based on kin labour and plough-based forces of production demanded a larger set up of productive relations that involved non-kin labour. And, this was yet another contradiction. In short, in due course, the social formation was headed for an inevitable breakdown with the maturing of its built-in contradictions towards the end of the third century CE.

Transformation Scenario

While there is no direct evidence for a total crisis leading to the dissolution of the Tamil heroic society, a disjunction is explicit in both archaeological and literary sources, which in terms of their existing chronology and historical context would have us believe that the principal chiefdoms went into oblivion by the close of the third century CE. None of the heroic poems sing the exploits of a chieftain belonging to the period after the third century CE, nor can the historians clearly identify any chieftain of the well-known chiefdoms reigning during that period. Heroic compositions of the typical bardic diction too seem to have been discontinued by this time. There is a corresponding discontinuity of the institution of raids and booty redistribution. This is synchronised by a marked decline in the post-third century layers of major archaeological sites. While sites with Buddhist association provide some evidence of continued development, largely there is a gap of about two centuries between the heroic chiefdom and the establishment of monarchy in Tamiḻakam.

Historians have associated this period of discontinuity with the inroads by a predatory people known as the Kaḷabhras who belonged to the uplands of Karnataka. They are said to have swept through the domains of the Tamil chieftains and caused their eclipse. This has led to the construction of an interregnum labelled after the Kaḷabhras. Recently, historians of south India have rejected the Kaḷabhra episode as being based on weak evidence. In fact, an invasion thesis might do for explaining the replacement of the chiefdoms rather than their disappearance. There is no clear indication of substitution, though the rulers mentioned in the Pulānkuṛichchi rock inscription of fifth–sixth century CE from the region of the Pāṇḍya chiefdom do not belong to any known lineage. There were various developments of a fundamental nature other than the disappearance of chiefdoms. For instance, an invasion would not be enough for explaining the ushering in of major socio-economic and political changes. Often historians attribute the causes of radical social transformation to one invasion or the other. Actually, an invasion cannot lead to fundamental reconstitution of a socio-economic system, which happens only as a result of basic contradictions in the economy. Invasions do aggravate economic contradictions, but do not cause them and lead to the total disintegration of the socio-economic system. Therefore, historians' construct of invasion is a weaker explanation of the systemic discontinuity that we see in social history.

There are incidental allusions in a few copper plates of the eighth–ninth centuries CE to a traditional memory of the brāhmaṇas about an evil period of hardship that they were doomed to face. It was a period chaotic enough for the brāhmaṇas to have represented as the Kali age. However, there is no reason to believe that brāhmaṇas all over south India were affected by the Kaḷabhra attack. Kerala, for instance, had been affected by no such onslaught from the part of the non-brāhmaṇas. Unlike elsewhere in Tamiḻakam, where brāhmaṇas at times experienced non-brāhmaṇ threats to their gift villages, in the Kerala sub-region there were no rivals to the brāhmaṇas who owed the land enjoyed by them to none other than Paraśurāma. However, the problem of socio-economic and political discontinuity remained as elsewhere, providing ground for a conjuncture of crisis in the whole region.

Several historians believe change is gradual. But the drawback of this perspective is that it naturalises change and precludes the relevance of a causal explanation for transformation. Serious historical analysis which enables explanation involves conceptualisation of the emerging properties and their causal interconnections. There were a series of radical transformations at the fundamental level that caused the discontinuity. Theoretically, the maturing of the contradictory dynamic of the social formation engenders all great transformations in history. In our case, conditions such as the dominance of the agro-pastoral economy, its relation to predatory politics, the limiting influence of plunder raids on wet-rice agriculture, the complex redistribution that generated differentiation and the mismatch between kin labour and plough technology are constructs based on direct clues in sources. Matters such as the contradictory structure of the social formation, the ever-intensifying incompatibilities between productive relations and forces of production, limitations of kin labour and the continuous decline of the reproductive ability of the economy are conceptual abstractions or constructs based on clues in the sources. It is significant that the present state of knowledge about the chronology of the heroic poems and the absence of evidence for the continuation of the chiefdoms go well with the ever-intensifying contradictory dynamic immanent in the heroic society. Predatory marches, migrations and disintegration of kinship were steadily accentuating the process of the dissolution of the social formation. As argued earlier, the social formation persistently gave rise to forces of its own destruction and met with the inevitable collapse. This accounts for the alleged discontinuity of the economic and politico-cultural system of heroic society, and establishes the absence of evidence for the continuity in the poems as not accidental.

Transformations of Kerala

Due to the ecological differences of the landscape of Kerala from the rest of Tamiḻakam, the process of transformation of the social formation involved certain unique features. Extensive forests, large catchments, numerous micro watersheds, many natural aquatic networks of rivers and streams, and well-drenched aquifers constituting wet plains, vast stretches of waterlogged/saturated depressions, thickly-vegetated large marshes and isolated swamps surrounded by undulating lateritic midland terrains merging with hillocks and low-lying fluvio-marine landforms make the landscape of Kerala a major ecological distinction. The most striking difference about this wet-rice landscape ecosystem is the excess of water in the case of Kerala and its scarcity in the case of regions elsewhere. This would suggest a great deal of difference in the nature of cultivation followed and labour processes required at the two sub-regions. As observed already, the management of the excess water was the central problem since the days of the very inception of agrarian settlements in the wetlands of Kerala, whereas in the other regions irrigation was a problem. In order to construe the nature of historical landuse in an agro-climatic region, we need evidence of necessary technology and social relations during the period in question.

Low-lying wet plains were largely inaccessible to cultivation, though people from the Late Stone Age onwards seem to have subsisted on fishing and hunting in the waterlogged/saturated landscape. Lateritic hill slopes and undulating midland terrains besides the small pockets of wetlands in the Western Ghats and the foothills were the main productive zones of Kerala in the age of the Tamil heroic poems. In the wetlands people grew paddy and sugarcane while in other parts they cultivated a wide variety of millets and short-term dry crops. These were supplemented by cattle-keeping. Though the technology of wet-rice agriculture was known, its extension to the inhospitable landscape through reclamation of heavily-vegetated marshes and waterlogged expanses was impossible, for it was far beyond the reach of the familiar labour of clannish households. Needless to say, it was a very hard task that demanded massive labour.

Tamil heroic poems are perhaps the only source for assuming the existence of brāhmaṇa households in ancient Kerala. It is certain that the number of brāhmaṇa households was obviously very small in those times and they must have been within the domains of hunter chieftains, small and big. In the plains they must have concentrated in areas of wet-rice landscape ecotypes adjacent to the red soil terraces and between the forested hill tracts and waterlogged lowlands. The expansion of paddy cultivation beyond these small patches was not easy under the socio-political set up of the heroic age, as we have already seen. It was not possible for the period to expand plough agriculture to lowlands that were marshy and waterlogged, because the task necessitated a variety of factors such as a fairly-evolved technology of water management, knowledge of seasons, specialised social division of labour, effective institutions for the realisation of labour and a competent class for the coercive mobilisation of massive labour.

Material processes and the socio-political structure that evolved in Kerala during the period were more or less the same as those of the rest of Tamiḻakam. However, certain antecedents were remarkably different. The absence of royal land grants to brāhmaṇas and the claim of the brāhmaṇical origin-legend of Kerala—assigning to Paraśurāma's axe the credit of reclaiming 160 *kātam* (an ancient measure) of land that lay between Gōkaṛṇam and Kanyakumari—are perhaps the most striking among them. This is a clear indication of the direct acquisition of arable land by brāhmaṇas without being obligated to anybody. They sprang up on their own as sparsely-distributed individual households along the red soil fringes of the alluvial ecosystem using clan labour in the neighbourhood.

The transformation of individual brāhmaṇa households into corporate village settlements was the result of economic processes. It appears that the culturally contingent brāhmaṇical authority, ritual charisma, legitimacy, social command, structures of control, institutional devices, the various systems of knowledge and technologies of management succeeded in coercing the massive labour of the clans for the conversion of the wetland ecosystem of Kerala into paddy fields. Indeed it must have been a long process of two or three centuries and involving a series of simultaneous transitions.

As the processes that led to the dissolution of the chiefdom-level social formation of the descent groups were the same as those in the places elsewhere in Tamil̲akam, and as the alternative to it was to evolve from the production relations of brāhmaṇa households, the emergent social formation in Kerala was more or less the same. What was crucial about the new formation was its binary basis between landholding and landlessness which eventually got mediated by intermediaries to form a complex structure.

Specialised division of labour, its crystallisation into hereditary occupations and their non-economic coercive modes of social realisation were the main characteristics. In short, the social formation of ancient Tamil̲akam with its contradictory structure, ever-intensifying incompatibilities between productive relations and forces of production, limitations of kin-labour and the continuous decline of the reproductive ability of the economy faced the inevitable dissolution crisis by the mid-first millennium CE. Dissolution process comprised a series of transitions of simultaneity—the transitions of the economy, division of labour, social relations, political structure and religious ideology. They collectively signified the dissolution of the ancient social formation of redistributive economy based on kin labour into another dominated by wet-rice agriculture based on hereditary occupation groups slowly getting institutionalised as castes. While these were common to the whole of the Tamiḻakam, the Kerala sub-region witnessed an additional transformation—a major human-ecological transformation. This was the traumatic and fundamental transformation of the low-lying wetland ecosystem that the landscape owed to the making of paddy fields out of the waterlogged and water-saturated lowlands.

In this historical process of dissolution of agro-pastoral social formation into the paddy dominated in Tamiḻakam, formation of *veḷḷāḷar* (farmers under irrigated agriculture) settlements with their pulaya tillers, the castes of artisans and the castes of craftsmen was crucial. Another crucial phenomenon there was the emergence of *brahmadēya* villages (royal gift-villages to the brāhmaṇas) with tillers, artisans and craftsmen. Veḷḷāḷa households and their settlements might have existed in Kerala, especially in the southern parts. However, the emergence of brāhmaṇa settlements in the river valleys was the most decisive in the social and human ecological transformations specific to the land.

IV

Brāhmaṇa Settlements and Agricultural Expansion (c. 800 CE–1200 CE)

The central agrarian requirement in the landscape ecosystem of Kerala was draining off the water from the marshes. We do not know exactly when and by whom the low-lying wetlands of Kerala were reclaimed by draining the water through canals and distributaries and transformed into rectangular paddy fields. However, it appears that the making of the paddy fields and the rise of brāhmaṇa settlements were synchronous. In the previous chapter the human ecological processes behind the reclamation of the waterlogged and marshy landscape ecosystem into paddy fields have already been discussed.

Largely the tiṇai-based agricultural practices continued but with a shift to paddy as the dominant crop around the eighth century CE, giving its technology or methods of cultivation, labour processes and property relations precedence over everything. Towards the end of the previous chapter we discussed the features of these transformations. Here in this chapter we seek to provide more details. Agricultural production, land relations and institutional means of labour mobilisation decided the socio-economic system. Who owned and controlled the paddy fields was decisive. An equally significant question was what institutional form of labour mobilisation and ideological means of coercion ensured productive services. Institutions like service tenure and caste turned entire occupations hereditary. Subsequently, caste proved to be the most oppressive of fetters. All this determined the nature of laws and structure of the ruling power of the period. Our sources, in order to understand these economic, social, political and cultural processes, are limited. They are mainly in the form of about two hundred temple inscriptions belonging to the period between c. 800 and 1200 CE. Most of them are inscribed on stone and a few on copper plates.

Brāhmaṇa Settlements

Unlike elsewhere in south India, there is no brahmadēya charter in the case of brāhmaṇas of Kerala. Keralōlpatti, the traditional chronicle of the brāhamaṇas, assigns their origins in Kerala to the Paraśurāma legend that speaks about the reclamation of the land of Kerala from the sea for the settling down of the brāhmaṇas. The legend shows that the brāhmaṇas owned their settlements to none other than Paraśurāma himself, precluding the role of kings who had invited and settled brāhmaṇas all over south India. What it means is that the brāhmaṇas had migrated to Kerala on their own without the patronage of the kings of the land. According to tradition, the early brāhmaṇas had come from Ahichchatra, probably Āryāvarta of the Gangetic region. There is a strong presumption that the brāhmaṇas migrated to Kerala through Tamil Nadu. The famous thirteen brāhmaṇical temples of Kerala were part of the 108 *divyadēśams* of Tamil Nadu, and integral to the Tamil bhakti movement, which was as much a temple movement as a brāhamaṇa movement. In short, it is reasonable to think that the brāhmaṇas migrated to Kerala mainly from the neighbouring parts of Tamil Nadu.

Several historians suggest that the brāhamaṇa migration to Kerala was from Karnataka. They connect Ahichchatra to Aihole of Karnataka and argue for the brāhmaṇa migration through the Tulu region. They observe certain comparable features among the brāhmaṇas of Karnataka and Kerala. Further, the presence of certain old Kannada usages in the inscriptional language (old Malayalam) supports this suggestion. An early Keralōlpatti tradition legitimising the status and ranking of Kōlattiri, mentions a royal initiative in settling 237 brāhmaṇa households from Tulu villages such as Vilakkar Gunavanta and Iṭupuncha during the reign of Udayavarman Kōlattiri. This migration might have occurred during the period of

Mādhavācārya in the twelfth century CE and those migrants, known as *emprātiris*, continue to follow the tradition of the Tulu language and culture even to this day. The nampūtiri brāhmaṇas claiming the highest social ranking had considered them inferior.

According to the Kēralōlpatti tradition of the 64 brāhmaṇa villages established by Paraśurāma, 32 were in the Tulu region and 32 in Kerala. The 32 settlements identified in Kerala are Payyanur, Perumchellur, Ālathur, Kārantho!, Chokiram, Panniyur, Karikkāṭu, Iśānamangalam, Trissivaperur and Peruvanam between the Perumpuzha and Karumanpuzha rivers; Chamunda, Iringadikudal (Irungāṭikkuṭal), Āvaṭṭipputhur (Avittathur), Paravur, Arāṇikkaḷam, Mūḻikkaḷam, Kuzhavur, Adavur, Chenganād, Iḷibhyam, Uḷiyannur and Kazhuthanād between the Churṇi river and Kanyakumari; and Ettumanoor, Kumaranellur, Kāṭmaṛuku, Āṛammuḷa, Thiruvalla, Kidanganur, Chenganur, Kaviyūr, Veṇmaṇi and Nīrmaṇṇu. All these have been more or less accurately identified. Of these, 17 settlements have in their temples inscriptions belonging to the period between the ninth and tenth centuries CE. Four of these settlements appear in the temple inscriptions of other settlements and three in contemporary literary works. Seven settlements have not been mentioned anywhere other than in the tradition.

The distribution of the brāhmaṇa villages shows that they are invariably in the agro-climatic areas suitable for paddy which was the chief economic resource of the period. Naturally, paddy fields represented the most significant form of contemporary wealth and a landlord was virtually the lord of the paddy fields. It is important that the region between Peruncellūr (Taliparamba) and Karikkad (Malappuram), which is not ideal for paddy cultivation due to the tidal salination of even the upstream, had not attracted the brāhmaṇas. In the case of the land north of the Korapuzha river (Elathur river), the land strip between the Western Ghats and the Arabian Sea tapers, resulting in the contraction of fertile midlands. Fertile lands remain scattered between the hills and the sea in north Malabar, and vast stretches like the Eṭavaṭakkan field are a very rare feature. Since the rivers are shorter in this region, tidal seawater reaches upstream and makes the low-lying fields saline and unsuitable for rice cultivation. Moreover, survey reports show that the land is not ideal for rice cultivation due to the chemical activity of oxides in the soil. Rapid permeability of water, leaving the soil too hard to be tilled in summer, and the predominance of iron-rich red soil add to its unsuitability. Therefore, those in search of fertile alluvial soil were not attracted to this region. All the traditional brāhmaṇa villages are therefore situated on the fertile riverbanks of the Periyar and Perar rivers.

There were brāhmaṇa villages outside the list of 32 settlements and their village assembly was known as *sabha* in contemporary inscriptions. A document belonging to the twelfth year of the reign of Indeswaran Kōta, i.e., 955 CE, has been found in the Subramanya temple at Chembra near Mahe in Kerala. It contains a reference to the village assembly in Eṭannūr. A tenth-century inscription from Thiruvattur temple near Taliparamba says that 24 brāhmaṇas were brought from the brāhmaṇa settlements at Vaikom. Unfortunately, the first part of this inscription is lost and, therefore, it is not possible to know who founded the settlement and when. In southern Kerala too the expansion of brāhmaṇa settlements was more or less of the same pattern. The Kollur maṭham copper plates mentions the landgrants to 23 brāhmaṇa families and their settlement. In the Kilimanur copper plates of 1169 CE, some 10 brāhmaṇas from eight settlements are said to have been brought to Thiruppālkkaḍal temple. All these sources speak of the establishment of new villages out of old ones. These newly-settled villages are not included in the traditional list. The method followed was to bring brāhmaṇas from their old settlements, established in the tenth century, to found new ones. It was not the Perumāḷ of Mahodayapuram, who founded the settlements, since according to Keralōlpatti the brāhmaṇas were the people who brought Perumāḷs to Kerala. As already noted, the earlier brāhmaṇas themselves were founders of their settlements in Kerala and might have been the result of self-directed and self-supported migration of the community. Perhaps the chieftains in the fringes might have provided some help. However, it is important that brāhmaṇas do not acknowledge indebtedness to any human agency. Keralōlpatti holds fast to the Paraśurāma legend and the description thereof aims at legitimising the history of the brāhmaṇa community in Kerala. The Keralōlpatti legends are also part of the ideology that legitimises the rights and privileges of the chieftains. These legends, as we know them now, must have taken shape probably during the twelfth and thirteenth centuries, in the wake of the consolidation of the jāti-janmi-nāṭuvāḻi system.

A village, irrespective of its identity as brāhmaṇa or non-brāhmaṇa, was called ūr in Kerala, unlike in Tamil Nadu where a brāhmaṇa village was addressed as brahmadēya and a non-brāhmaṇa village as ūr. The brāhmaṇa landlords jointly formed an assembly called *sabha* that enjoyed proprietory control over the persons and property of their ūr. The members of the sabha were called *sabhaiyār* as well as *ūrār.* The ownership of land in the ūr was virtually in the hands of the brāhmaṇas, either in the form of *brahmasvam* (held by brāhmaṇas) or in the form of *devasvam* (held by the temple).

Non-Brāhmaṇa Villages

A non-brāhmaṇa village (ūr) was held traditionally by the ruling lineages including the local chieftains and its land was called *cērikkal* or the ruler's land. Originally, these villages must have been predominantly red soil tracts with small fields that required irrigation. The village created through the land grant of the Tarisāppaḷḷi copper plates of 849 CE is an example. This land grant mentions veḷḷāḷar as a category of tenants (*kārāḷar*) who made the subjected tillers (*āḷaṭiyār*) plough the fields. However, the plates do not call the land granted cērikkal, and the land presumably belonged to the chieftain of Vēṇāṭu. Another example is the Tirunelli copper plates of 1005 CE which registers a landgrant by Kuṟumpoṟai, the local chieftain of the east Kuṟumpoṟaināṭu, giving his Kīḻkāṭṭipuḻa cērikkal as free hold to the Tirunelli temple. It is evident in the copper plates that the veḷḷāḷar along with other functionaries like the *ainkammāḷar* constituted the village. In the case of the non-brāhmaṇa village also the landlords were the heads. Due to the absence of inscriptional evidence it is unclear if the veḷḷāḷar were the landlords. In the inscriptions of Tamil Nadu, an ūr is both the village headed by the veḷḷāḷar landlords (*veḷḷān-vakai*) and their assembly.

A few inscriptions of Kerala sometimes refer to ūr and sabha separately, presupposing the village assembilies of the non-brāhmaṇa and brāhmaṇa landlords respectively. Whether the nāṭuvāḻis or veḷḷāḷar were the landlords in such villages is not clear. The Triprangode inscription of 944 CE speaks about the unanimous decisions taken by *ūrpaṭṭar* (*bhaṭṭa*s of the village), *āḷkōil* (nāṭuvāḻi) and *potuvāḷ* (the mediator of the temple). Ūrpaṭṭar, obviously brāhmaṇas and hence members of the sabha, are mentioned independent of others. A Chembra inscription of 955 CE mentions the ūr and the sabha of Ēṭanūr in the context of a decision. However, in another Chembra inscription (c. tenth century CE), the ūr alone takes decisions. In the Thrikadithanam inscription of 1050 CE, decisions are taken jointly by ūrār, *paraṭaiyār* (the temple's executive) and sabhaiyār. Whether the non-brāhmaṇa village was managed by an assembly of its landlords or by the nāṭuvāḻi is not certain. Some of the villages, owned and controlled by rulers, were called cērikkal settlements. There were a few Jain settlements also in the red soil highlands. Every village had more or less the same pattern of settlement as regards its functionaries who sometimes varied depending upon the nature of the main econocommercial centres.

The stone and copper plate inscriptions of the ninth, tenth and eleventh centuries clearly show that the 32 traditional brāhmaṇa settlements in Kerala from Payyannur and Cellur (modern Taliparambu) in the north to Tiruvalla in the south had already been established by that time. The actual number of brāhmaṇa settlements in Kerala was greater than what is given in the traditional accounts, for some settlements which are not included in the list are met with in some early medieval epigraphic records. The Chōkūr inscription of the seventeenth regnal year of the Cēra King Kota Ravi Perumāḷ (c. 898 CE) mentions the sabha, assemblies of the settlements of Valiceri (modern Balusseri in Kozhikode taluk of Kozhikode district) and Pulikkalpurai which is yet to be identified. The Chembra inscription of the twelfth regnal year of Indu Kota (c. 955 CE) refers to Ēṭanūr near Mayyazhi (French, Mahe) in Kannur district. Expansion of the agrarian society outside the listed brāhmaṇa settlements is attested to in the Wayanad plateau beyond the Western Ghats in the Cēra period itself. The successful efforts for reclaiming the low-lying *kari* lands (literally, 'black land'; water-saturated land made of alluvial soil that gets submerged under tidal flow) in the Kuṭṭanāṭu area are also indicated by inscriptions.

Epigraphs refer to some non-brāhmaṇa settlements in addition to the aforementioned brāhmaṇa settlements. For instance, a non-brāhmaṇa settlement on the seashore of Kurakkenikkollam (modern Kollam) was originally owned by the rulers of Vēṇāṭu. Later, in c. 849 CE, it was granted to a foreign merchant named Maruvan Sapīr Īśo to meet the daily expenses of the Christian Church which was established by him. In addition to these there are several allusions to the cērikkal lands of the local ruling families that were occupied by non-brāhmaṇa groups. Thus we can identify two types of agrarian settlements—the brāhmaṇa and the non-brāhmaṇa settlements. And, there are two sub-types under the non-brāhmaṇa settlements—the cērikkal settlement and the merchant community settlement. Clear felling of the forests and reclaiming land for cultivation was an ongoing practice in the Cēra period and continued in the post-Cēra period also. The Kilimanur inscription of Kollam Era 343 (1168 CE) shows that a new brāhmaṇa settlement was established in southern Kerala. Similarly, a new settlement was created at Tiruvadur near Talipparambu in the north, bringing brāhmaṇas from the traditional settlements of central Kerala.

Irrespective of whether the settlements were of the brāhmaṇa or non-brāhmaṇa type, they were of a dispersed pattern. Accordingly, the spatial organisation and occupational structure of the villages were also unique. With all essential occupation groups attached to it each village settlement was a self-sufficient entity. Since a brāhmaṇa settlement was invariably temple-centred, the occupation groups included the various service personnel of the temple too. When a new settlement was created, the services of artisans and craftsmen were ensured by attaching them to it. All royal charters in the form of copper plates vouch for this. For example, the Tarisāppaḷḷi plates of c. 849 CE contain provision for attaching occupational families like *īḻavar* (toddy tappers), *vaṇṇār* (washermen), *taccar* (carpenters) and *vāṇiyar* (oil mongers) to the donated land. Similarly, the Kollur Maṭham plates of c. 1189 CE vouch for the practice of attaching oil mongers, potters, washermen, etc. to the settlement.

Agrarian Settlements

Generally there were two seasonal harvests of paddy, one in the month of Kanni (August–September) and the other in the month of Makaram (December–January), each leaving four months as the duration of cultivation. An additional harvest was possible in certain areas with enough water, while in dry areas short of water and low-lying wetlands with excess water only one harvest was possible. However, in all areas the labour process was such that labourers had to be available throughout the year for one function or the other, such as ploughing, sowing, transplanting seedlings, weeding, harvesting and threshing. This had given rise to various specialised arts and crafts as well. Each plot of land thus required permanent workers of its own and this led to the institutionalisation of the system of attaching tillers to the land. Among such attached tillers of subjection and immobility, ensured by means of jāti restrictions such as untouchability, the pulayas constituted the main group. Mentions of pulayas as attached tillers and those transacted along with the land are found in the Tarisāppaḷḷi copper plates of Quilon, certain inscriptions at the Trikkākkara temple and the Tiruvalla copper plates. Various other functionaries directly and indirectly required for agriculture became hereditary occupation groups who were accommodated under the caste system. These groups were attached to the settlement or village. In contemporary society, there were no independent workers since they were either attached to the landlord or to the landed institutions like the temple. Tarisāppaḷḷi copper plates mention carpenters, washermen and other workers granted along with land to the church.

Each settlement was formed as part of the village and constituted an intelligible production unit with its proprietors, intermediaries, necessary occupation groups and tillers. Tarisāppaḷḷi copper plates of 849 CE contain references to the formation of a settlement under the sanction of Ayyan Aṭikaḷ Tiruvaṭikaḷ, the ruler of Vēṇāṭu, who donated land to Maruvan Sapīr Īśo, a merchant leader and probably a Bishop. Along with the grant of land, the ruler makes provision in the charter for the artisans and craftsmen essential for the new settlement. A similar instance of granting a few vāṇiyar and veḷḷāḷar along with the land is seen in the Kollur Maṭham copper plates of 1189 CE to ensure the supply of oil and ghee to the temple. In the Vīrarāghava copper plates of 1225 CE, the Perumāḷ makes provision for the transfer of craftsmen like *kollar* (blacksmiths), taccar, etc. All this shows that a contemporary settlement had its own tillers and cultivators attached to the land, and artisans and craftsmen (ainkammāḷar), besides other functionaries like washermen, physicians and astrologers. In short, an agrarian village of those times was a relatively self-sufficient settlement of people with various specialised occupation groups of hereditary character, as their names suggest. In brāhmaṇa and royal settlements there would be some additional service personnel, as seen in the case of the merchant settlement of Kollam, which had service personnel such as *tīyamāḷuvan* (supervisor of toddy tapers) and *matilnāyakan* (the security headman of the boundary wall). These workers were also part of hereditary occupation groups, who became endogamous castes—tiyya and nair respectively—during subsequent times. This pattern of settlement continued for several centuries. Even to this day plot names indicating the occupation groups survive all over the villages of Kerala.

Plot names such as *kollantetoṭika* (blacksmith's field), *taṭṭānkanḍi* (goldsmith's portion), *mūśārikkaṇḍi* (bronzesmith's portion), *pāṇarukaṇṭi* (bards' portion), *kaṇiyānpaṛambu* (astrologer's plot), *pulayakkuṭi* (pulaya huts) and *paṛayankkuḻi* (paṛaya pit) are a few examples.

Agrarian Relations

The system of ownership of land was central to contemporary agrarian relations. In principle all land belonged to the king. Inscriptions mention about various types of ownership, such as brāhmaṇa property (brahmasvam), temple property (devasvam) and cērikkal. The number of households in each brāhmaṇa settlement varied and according to the respective inscriptions they were 10, 16, 18, 27, etc. Each brāhmaṇa household and its land was owned by the eldest among brothers. This system of ownership is called primogeniture. However, the ownership was not absolute proprietorship. It meant only lordship over a system of multiple levels of property rights. The lord had the right of the highest level called *janmam* or *iṭayīṭu.* He leased the land out to tenants (kārāḷar) at a certain measure of paddy as rent (*pāṭṭam*). This level of property right of the kārāḷar was called *kārāṇmai.* The various artisans and craftsmen who were the settlers in the land had the right to occupy their household premises. This level of right of the occupants (kuṭis) was called *kuṭimai.* At the bottom were the subjected tillers called *aṭiyāḷar*, fated to be in the servile state (*aṭiyāymai*).

In the case of devasvam land the temple was the landlord. This landed property was collectively owned by the brāhmaṇā village lords (ūrār or sabhaiyār) who shared the property with the responsibility of certain specific services to the temple for which it was endowed. Each of such groups of landlords (*gaṇam*) with obligatory responsibility was generally known after the service endowment concerned. For example, a Trikadithanam inscription mentions gaṇams such as the uttrāṭagaṇam (responsible for the rituals on the asterism named *uttrāṭam*) of the temple, the Perunna inscription mentions the tirunāḷgaṇam (responsible for the rituals on *tirunāḷ* or *tiruvātira*) of the temple, and the Tiruvalla copper plates mention the existence of tiruvōṇagaṇam (responsible for the rituals on *tiruvōṇam*), tirunāḷgaṇam, tiruvātiragaṇam (responsible for the rituals on *tiruvātira*) and uttragaṇam (responsible for the rituals on *uttram*). The gaṇam rented out the land and managed the affairs with the rent he collected. The temple paid its functionaries with service tenures in land known as *virutti* and *jīvitam* (both terms literally mean, means of life). Those who got land as service tenure further leased it. Agrarian relations of non-brāhmaṇa villages were also more or less of the same tenurial system. Pāṭṭam (land rent) varied from two-fifths and one-third to one-fifth of the crop as decided on the basis of the nature of the crop and the level of the yield. Pāṭṭam is called *mēloṭi* (the higher share) and *kaṭama* (obligatory dues) in the temple inscriptions. In land documents, there are specific directions as to whom the rent was to be paid and when. The pāṭṭam was to be paid by the tenant to the landlord twice a year, after each harvest season. Normally the leaseholds remained hereditary and not used to be transferred at the will of the landlord so long as the kārāḷar paid the pāṭṭam regularly. When the property was sold the tenancy was retained. However, certain inscriptions show that, under certain circumstances, probably under the situation of default in rent, the tenancy could not be transferred at will. Tenants who cultivated the temple lands had the obligation to fulfil their responsibilities attached to their land, for example, the supply of rice or other goods for the temple. Inscriptions stipulate that a defaulter would be penalised by exacting double the due and in case of further irregularity the tenants would forfeit the kārāṇmai.

The kārāḷar in their turn were entitled to obligations from the people below them. As already mentioned, various kuṭis like the ainkammāḷar and other subjected workers like īḻavar, vaṇṇār, etc. linked to agriculture were under them. Actually, the entire households of kuṭis constituted the kārāḷar among whom the occupation groups had only the small household premises as their holdings. Being full-time artisans and craftsmen, their household premises hardly comprised paddy fields, and naturally their dues were in the form of produce from the garden-land (*paṛampu* or *kara*). This was the the case with various other functionaries like the village astrologer, physician and those engaged in the performance of rituals. The Chembra inscription mentions *kuṭittala* as an area where the kuṭis lived. It stipulates that the landlords should not divide the kuṭittala, implying that it is the kuṭimākkal's hereditary right of occupancy in land. At the lowest rung were the āḷaṭiyār, the most subjected group almost like slaves, and addressed as 'pulayar' in several inscriptions.

Social relations are human relations themselves as engendered by the system of production and distribution of resources. Communities involved in the production process enter into different kinds of labour relations that are manifested in the form of rights over means of production and produce. The distribution of resources depends on these rights. Social relations are thus the sum total of these relations. The various social groups were automatically structured in a hierarchy on the basis of the differences in their rights and entitlements in the tenth century CE. They were glued together by mutual obligations of protection from above and obedience from below. These obligations included military and non-military duties.

Circulation of Resources

Paddy was the main agricultural resource of the period. Actual tillers, i.e., the pulayar, harvested the paddy and took it to their immediate lords who were the leaseholders (kārāḷar). At this stage a small share of the harvest, normally the worst remnants, is redistributed among the tillers and other servile dependents linked directly to agriculture. The kārāḷar in their turn gave the due share by way of pāṭṭam to the landlord, who could be the nāṭuvāḻi, or the temple or the brāhmaṇa or the church. At these two levels the paddy gets stocked as surplus out of which the artisans, craftsmen and other functionaries are paid their dues by way of reward for their services. Out of their surplus, the landlords had to pay *āṭṭaikkoḷ* (annual due) to the local ruler as well as the Perumāḷ. We understand this pattern of circulation of paddy from the extant source material, especially temple inscriptions.

The temple was the most important centre of resource mobilisation and redistribution. This does not mean that the paddy was mobilised and stored in the temple. Dues to the temple were collected by the brāhmaṇa landlords as members of the various gaṇams that were entrusted with the responsibility of meeting expenditures of specific functions and services in the temple. What the temple seems to have stored was the rice required for its daily services, for the occasional feast to the brāhmanās and for paying the priests and other servants. The temple's executive committee (*paraṭai*) seems to have kept detailed accounts of all this, and this was overseen by the sabha which made the entire major transactions of the temple's resources. All the traditional brāhmaṇa village temples were landed magnates with enomous resource control. According to the Tiruvalla copper plates (tenth–eleventh centuries CE) the total measure of paddy that reached the temple by way of dues was 27,105 paṛas. Similarly, this temple had owned and controlled paddy fields extensive enough to sow paddy seeds measuring about 30,000 paṛas. Other big temples such as those of Trikkākkara, Irinjālakuda, Mūḻikkaḷam, Chengannur and so on were also comparable in the strength of their resources.

A part of the rice collected at the temple was given as remuneration to the temple servants. For instance, the Neṭumpuṛamtaḷi inscription of c. 900 CE (the seventeenth regnal year of Kōta Ravi Perumāḷ) mentions the amount of paddy to be given to labourers, dancing girls, etc. A detailed account of the amount of paddy given to the temple servants, drummers, musicians, security guards, florists, etc. is given in the Tiruvalla copper plates. Expenditure varied from temple to temple. Some of the temples like the Pāthivapuram, Tiruvalla and Mūḻikkaḷam had *śālas* (Vedic learning centres) attached to them. According to the inscriptional evidence the Parthivapuram śāla in Aynāḍ had to feed 95 brāhmaṇa pupils (*caṭṭas*) and their teachers (bhaṭṭas). According to an account there were 175 pupils in the

Tiruvalla śāla at a time. There were more than hundred pupils in the Mūḻikkaḷam śāla. Certain temples had treatment centres (*āturaśāla*) too.

The pattern of resource mobilisation and redistribution was not different in the non-brāhmaṇa villages with cērikkal land from those in the land of the Christian merchants or Jainas. Since the land held by the merchants was in the centre of commercial transactions, the crops of cultivation and the nature of economic resources certainly differed. The service personnel, functionaries and dependents who shared the resources were also different. Since the Jainas were not agriculturists but traders, like the Christians, their settlements were at points of exchange on the trade routes in the red soil region, and hence the nature of their resources too had a marked difference. Nevertheless, the overall pattern of circulation of the resource in all these settlements must have been more or less the same because the relations of labour and conditions of appropriation could not have been radically different from place to place. The subjected labour, tenurial relations, lordship and hierarchy were integral to the social order of the period. Hence the mode of resource mobilisation and the course of its distribution could not have been different.

The rulers, both at the local as well as supra-local levels, had their own land, the cērikkal. A *nāṭuvāḻi* could be a small chieftain holding a village or a big chieftain of a larger *nāṭu.* A chieftain, small or big, was a landlord with his service personnel, kārāḷar, kuṭis and āḷaṭiyār, besides a certain number of mercinery fighters ready to die for him. A bigger chieftain was an overlord of a few lesser lords with a relationship of obligation and larger number of fighters. A supra-local chieftain had larger nāṭu and more number of lesser lords under him besides a greater number of fighters. In short, the juridico-political power and the number of fighters of the chieftain were greater as the extent of area, people and resources under his control increased. The biggest of all chieftains (Perumāḷ) had the maximum area, people, resources and mercinery fighters at his disposal, which enabled him to offer protection to the landlords under him and exact protection dues (*rakṣābhōga*) from them and annual dues (āṭṭaikkōḷ) from their settlements. The Pantalāyinikollam inscription shows that āṭṭaikkōḷ was one-sixth of the total agricultural produce. However, the system of resource mobilisation and pattern of redistribution remained the same, except the difference in size. Inscriptions mention the nāṭuvāḻis and their nāṭus often with an indication of the total strength of the fighters attached. Mentions of the *munnūṟṟuvar* (the three hundred) of Nanruḻaināṭu, the *aṟunūṟṟuvar* (the six hundred) of Vēṇāṭu, the *eḻunūṟṟuvar* (the seven hundred) of Kiḻumalaināṭu and the *āyiravar* (the thousand) of the Perumāḷ, are examples of the nāṭus and their respective strengths of fighters.

It is explicit in various ways that contemporary Kerala had an agrarian economy of marginal surplus. A society with increased surplus would show off its wealth in the form of monumental buildings such as huge temples, elaborate sculptures and luxurious ceremonies. Such evidence are in plenty in several regions in Tamil Nadu, particularly in the form of huge monuments enabled by the paddy surplus of the Kaveri delta and the wealth acquired through conquest. Kerala never had such a huge surplus in paddy due to ecological reasons. Both the Pāṇdya and the Cōḻa kingdoms had paddy inflation, as evident in the contemporary gold–paddy ratio that was 1:100 in these kingdoms as against 1:20 during the same period in Kerala. The wealth of the Cēra Perumāḷs was not comparable to that of the fabulously rich Pāṇdyas and the Cōḻas. Therefore, it is not accidental that the temples of Kerala are relatively small and largely devoid of architectural or sculptural splendour.

Temple Functionaries

The temple had various servants for discharging its ritual and non-ritual functions. *Tantri* (the chief priest), *potuvāḷ* or *samnjitan* (the secretary or the mediator or the *madhyastha*), *śānti* (priest), *vārier* (the functionary in charge of flowers, oblations and cleanliness of the sanctum) and *uvaccakaḷ* (drummers) were the regular functionaries of the temple. The tantri is the the temple's highest ritual sanction. Under various contingent situations the temple might be deprived of the purity of its premises (*prāsāda*) and the sanctity of the idol (*bimba*). Then it is the tantri, who orders to close down the temple for special rituals such as *aṣṭhabandhakalaśa* and *gōnivāsa* for the restoration of the temple's purity. In a few temples two types of potuvāḷ are mentioned: (*a*) *aka-potuvāḷ*, who takes care of matters internal to the temple, probably the rituals affairs; and (*b*) *puṛa-potuvāḷ* for looking after external affairs. They figure in certain temples as *uḷpāṭan* and *perumutiyan*, customarily together, and are mentioned in certain Trikkākkara inscriptions in connection with the collection and accounting of the temple revenue. In the Chembra inscription of 955 CE, *paṭai uḷpāṭan* is mentioned as responsible for the maintenance of the land set apart for rituals. Vārier literally means a member of a *vāriyam* (committee) and figures in south Indian inscriptions in the context of committees responsible for administering the various resources of the brahmadēya villages. In a tenth century CE inscription from Cheḷannūr there is a reference to *ūr-vārier*, obviously connected to the administration of the temple village. However, in general the term vārier appears in the temple inscriptions in the context of the upkeep of the sanctum premises. These functionaries were paid through service tenure in land called virutti or jīvitam, meaning the land set apart for the service.

Theatre personnel like dancers and dramatists, both men (*cākkaiyār*) and women (*nangaiyār*), were also attached to the temple. An old Tamil poem in the *Puranānūṛu* refers to *kūttacākkyān* of Paṛaiyūr (cākkaiyār of Paṛavūr). All these theatre artists appear in the Chōkūr temple inscription of 898 CE in the fifteenth year of Kōta Ravi Perumāḷ. Cākkaiyār were actors in the Sanskrit dance-dramas of Kerala. Kollur Maṭham inscription gives an interesting reference to Cākkaiyār virutti. There are also references to *kūttu* (dance drama) presented at temple festivals. A Trikadithānam inscription, dated 976 CE, speaks of kūttu staged for 10 days of the *utraviḻā*. Similarly, the Tiruvalla copper plates mention the payment made for staging the *kāḷiyānkam kūttu*, two fourth scenes of the Sanskrit play

Bālacaritam by Bhāsa. Cākkaiyār and nangaiyār were performers with long years of professional training in the Sanskrit theatre (*nāṭyaśāstra*) for performing in the traditional temple theatre called *kūṭiyāṭṭam*. This is perhaps the oldest *dēśī* version of the early Indian Sanskrit theatre, which represents its *mārgī* (great tradition) form. Among the allied theatre artists were *kāndaṛpikar* (musician) and *naṭṭuvanār* (dance instructor).

Nangai, also mentioned as nangaiyār or *nangacci* in inscriptions, were temple dancers. They were performers in kūttu (*kūttacci* meaning woman who performs *kūttu*) and kūṭiyāṭṭam (dance-drama) in the temple theatre (*kūttampalam*). Some of them were of the landlords' families. The Neṭumpuṛamtaḷi inscription of the seventeenth regnal year of Kōta Ravi Perumāḷ (900 CE) mentions nangaiyār of three different categories—the ideal, the middle level and lower (*uttama*, *madhyama* and *adhama*)—and their differentiated remunerations. Some of the women dancers (*kūttu strī*) in the temple were dedicated as slaves at the feet of the deity (*tēvaṭiyāḷ*). A few of these women at the service of god (*tēvaraṭiyāḷ strī*) were of noble or royal birth and of high socio-economic status, as evidenced by the case of Tribhuvana Mahādevi (daughter of Kulaśēkhara Āḷvār) *alias* Ciritara Nangacci, who figures as a donor of land in the Neṭumpuṛamtaḷi inscription of the eleventh regnal year (975 CE) of Bhaskara Ravi. Although it denotes the *dēvadāsi* system, the term was not in use in contemporary records. The aforesaid inscription registers Ciritara Nangacci's land grant to the temple for meeting the rice requirement of the temple. Plots of land called *nangapaṛampu* and *nangacckikunnu* still exist in the vicinity of the Chōkūr temple. Another instance of women of the royal family dedicating themselves as tēvaraṭiyāḷ strī is seen in an inscription of the Kaṇḍiyūr temple. In common parlance, the terms kūttu strī and tēvaraṭiyāḷ strī, became *kūttacci* and *tēvaṭicci* respectively. Over the years some of them were turned into temple courtesans, as in the case of the dēvadāsis elsewhere in India, under the pressure of the lasciviousness of local rulers, landlords, big merchants, etc. Subsequently, the terms kūttacci and tēvaṭicci acquired abusive meanings in alignment with the dissolute life, which the material culture and social structure imposed on them.

There were several menial servants in every temple, as in the case of any other institution, and they are mentioned in a few inscriptions. The Tiruvalla copper plates contain a somewhat lengthy account on temple servants, and provide information about guards, collectors of firewood, servers of food, cleaners of waste-food, dehusking women, sweepers, etc. Inscriptions mention their remuneration by way of daily share of rice. Some of the women attached to the temple as the adhama category (poor) of nangai were engaged in different kinds of menial jobs like cleaning the temple courtyard, dehusking the paddy and pounding the rice.

It is explicit that there were a wide variety of people who had entered into different kinds of transactions with the temple. Inscriptions do not contain any reference to those people. However, the inscriptions of the temples like Tiruvalla, Kiḷimanūr, etc. mention merchandises like salt, jaggery, camphor, cedar, sandal and silk, which were brought from distant lands. They refer to the exchange rates of a number of goods. For instance, the Tiruvalla copper plates give the rate of a given measure of pepper for 16 measures of rice, 360 bananas for 100 measures of rice, a certain quality of camphor for 17 measures of rice, and so on. Who brought them and under what terms or conditions are not available in the inscriptions, but certain merchants (*ceṭṭis*) figure as donors and devotees making offerings to the temple. Cēravanāṭṭu Ceṭṭi of the Chōkūr inscription of 898 CE, and Alankāra Ceṭṭi of Pantalāyinikollam are some examples.

Marumakkattāyam: The discussions under agrarian relations and temple functionaries provide some idea about the pattern of property relations and the entailing social organisation of the period. A crucial component in the context of property relations and social organisation is the system of inheritance. The contemporary system of inheritance in the region was *marumakkattāyam*, which literally means the order of inheritance of the household (*taravād*) property by *marumakkal* (sister's children)—a matrilineal system of inheritance. That is, descent and the inheritance of property were traced through females. Several castes followed the system, but it was predominant among the nair community whose women had liberty and the right to property.

Redistribution

Compared to the temples of Tamil Nadu, the temples of Kerala had very limited and nominal transactions of wealth. Only two kings, a few local chieftains and two brāhmaṇas donated land to temples and that too of an insignificant size. Most of these references are found in the Tiruvalla copper plates. Main transactions of the temple were the redisrtibution of goods collected as offerings. An inscription of the tenth regnal year of Indu Kōta found at the Trikkākkara temple registers a Cēra queen's donation of a small strip of cērikkal land to the temple. Similarly, there are a few inscriptions at the Trikkākkara temple registering certain gifts of the chieftain of Kālkkaraināṭu. Some minor land grants are recorded in the inscriptions of the Chōkūr and Neṭumpuṛamtaḷi temples. The proprietory right over the land granted to the temple was redistributed as shares of the gaṇam among the brāhmaṇa landlords who owned and managed the temple. Subordinate rights were redistributed among the temple servants who in their turn redistributed the rights of occupancy and cultivation to the settlers on the land. Several intermediary rights emerged as a result of this redistribution process.

Apart from land endowments many objects of gold also reached the temple by way of gifts. An inscription in the Tirunadikara temple mentions a gift of 5 *kaḻanju* of gold by Sthanu Ravi Kulaśēkhara's daughter. The Trikkākkara inscription of the sixteenth regnal year of Brāhmaṇas Ravi records Kōta Keraḷa's gift of 40 gold coins to the temple. Another inscription of the same temple mentions Cherumattapuzha Kōta Nārāyaṇan's donation of 10 kaḻanju of gold. In an inscription of the forty-second regnal year of Bhaskara Ravi a certain Kuvalāyini Kovindan's donation of 6 kaḻanju of gold to Trikkākkara temple is mentioned. Moreover, gold reached the temple as fines imposed on its tenants and servants for default of dues and dereliction of duties. There are engravings in the Trikkākkara, Trikkoḍithānam, Kumāranallūr, Neṭumpuṛamtaḷi, Tiruvalla and many other temples that lay down the amount of fine for various offences. Gold thus received by the temple was given out at interest on pledging a proportionate measure of land against the transaction. The Chōkūr inscription of the fifteenth regnal year of Kōta Ravi Perumāḷ (898 CE) registers Cēravanāṭṭu Ceṭṭi's donation of 60 kaḻanju of gold to feed some brāhmaṇas, stipulating that the expenses thereof were to be met with the interest on the gold. The Trikkākkara inscription regarding Cherumattapuzha Kōta Keralan's gift of 20 kaḻanju of gold to the temple, and redistributed to four brothers namely Tēvan Nārāyaṇan, Tēvan Subramaṇyan, Tēvan Cuvākaran and Tēvan Cēntan, stipulates 5 per cent interest to be paid in the form of rice and ghee. The Trikkākkara inscription of 999 CE records that Mākaṇṇapally Kaṇṭan Nārāyaṇan borrowed 10 kaḻanju of gold on the condition of paying the interest as ghee to the temple. Several temple inscriptions mention about investing gold on land. A Trikkākkara inscription clearly stipulates that the gold on repayment must be used for buying up lands and that the gold loan should not be repaid in gold. A few other inscriptions there record instances of buying land with gold. It means that the temple was interested in enlarging its landed property. The Trikkākkara inscription of 959 CE in the sixteenth regnal year of Indu Kōta mentions a certain Karillattu Kaṇṇan Kumaran who bought land from the chieftain of Kālkkarai nāṭu. Another document records a land transaction by ulpāḍan and perumutiyan for the temple with gold. Through these redistributive transactions the temple acquired control over land, gold and people. It was mandatory to pledge land against every gold loan. The Tiruvalla copper plates mention a dancing girl who paid 290 paṛas of paddy to the temple by way of interest against the gold she borrowed.

These transations show that gold was more a means to acquire land, the chief means of production rather than a store of wealth by itself. The practice of gold loans presupposes its use as a medium of exchange in land transactions, although its function in contemporary society was still not as money but as the most precious ornamental metal. It is evident that the main source of gold was the long-distance traders who acquired them mainly in the form of *dīnārs* and *dirhams.* It was the local chieftains and landlords who showed interest in acquring gold, obviously because the precious metal was of immense ornamental value and indicated high status and ranking. Gold was the most important object of gift too, which had a crucial role in the maintenance and enhancement of power relations. There is no clinching evidence to know the land-gold ratio in terms of value. In a Trikkākkara inscription dated to 968 CE and of Bhaskara Ravi stipulates the interest for 20 kaḻanju of gold. It helps us fix the exchange rate of gold and land. This shows the land value in Kerala was much higher than what it was in contemporary Tamil Nadu and that at no point in time was Kerala's productive surplus in paddy comparable to that of Tamil Nadu.

Exchange

In an agrarian economy of the aforementioned pattern of resource circulation, commodity production and market would be unlikely. A possible conjecture is that the ainkammāḷar would have produced artefacts not only to cater to the needs of the landlords but also for exchange at fairs. However, this was a settlement-centered activity of the community concerned, giving rise to social products and not commodities with fixed prices determined under market conditions. Organised commodity production and independent exchange centres had not come into existence. Markets, in the technical sense, did not exist. Only periodic fairs at certain conventional points of exchange were held in the countryside. These exchange centres were seasonal and periodic fairs where merchants from different places converged. Nevertheless, as we have already seen, agriculture and exchange networks were expanding during the period of the consolidation of brāhmaṇa villages. They continued with changes in the agencies, networks, institutions and structures. The influence of the Romans from the Eastern Mediterranean died out completely by the end of sixth century CE, but the Arab influence sustained due to improved networks and contacts. Nestorians, Jews and Chinese coexisted with them, with relatively influential zones of their own.

The main social products were agricultural implements, household utensils, pottery, clothes, ornaments, salt, oil, jaggery, ghee, etc. Of these goods salt was perhaps the only essential non-local item that had to reach the people through merchantile circulation. Jaggery also need not have been available in all villages. However, unlike salt, jaggery was not an essential item without a substitute. Most goods were produced locally by the artisans and craftsmen attached to the settlement. The artisans and craftsmen did not own their raw materials in certain cases. For instance, the potters had to take the clay with the landlord's permission. Similarly, the blacksmiths had to depend on the landlords for extracting iron ore and the goldsmiths could make ornaments only with the gold and silver given by the landlords or merchants. In short, the production of artefacts was also subsumed by the social relations of agrarian economy. Production was demand-driven and exclusively limited to the requirement of the local society. Such a production system hardly necessitated trade relations. However, there were hawkers and peddlers dealing with items like clothes, oil and other goods that were not manufactured in every settlement. As cotton was not cultivated in Kerala, cotton thread had to be brought from outside. Contemporary Pāṇdya and Cōḻa inscriptions abound in references to weavers' guilds, and divisions and sub-divisions among them. The prevalent hierarchy of weavers show production relations transcending family ties. In Kerala, however, the situation was different. The weavers settled in streets of their own, but there is no mention of weavers' streets in the inscriptions of the Perumāḷ period.

The oil mongers and weavers who were there only in major settlements must have reached out to nearby settlements. Tharisapalli copper plates make a provion for the oil mongers to supply oil to the church. As the only fuel for lamps oil was an essential item of all religious institutions, and the regular endowment of oil or ghee for the institution of *tirunontāviḷakku* (permanent lamp) in the temple underscores the importance of oil in contemporary society. Oil was extracted from gingelly which used to be cultivated all over Kerala till recent times. Coconut was another source of oil. The term *vāṇiyan*, though it means 'merchant' in the generic sense, is used to mean a caste of oilmongers even today. A potter is mentioned in certain inscriptions as *kalavāṇiyan.* Sources of the period do not mention weavers.

Long-distance traders like Arabs, Jews, Persians and the Chinese were reaching the seaboards of Kerala during the period mainly in search of spices. This had a long history going back to the days of the Classical Roman Empire (c. first century BCE–second century CE), when merchant mariners of the Eastern Mediterranean reached the ports of Naura, Toṇḍi, Muciṛi and Nelcynda Kerala on the coast to trade spices. And, as mentioned earlier, trade with the Romans dwindled along with the decline of the Roman Empire. However, the exchange seems to have been continued by the Arabs and Jews nominally till c. fourth century CE. As recent excavations at Paṭṭaṇam (identified as Muciṛi) suggests, the Arabs, Jews and Persians seem to have revived the exchange relations after a gap of three to four centuries. Chinese traders also seem to have joined them. During the period of the Perumāḷs the seat of the rulers was Muyirikōde (the highshore of Muciṛi), Koṭunkōḷūr (Mahodayapuram). In the inscriptions of the ninth and tenth centuries CE there is evidence of the presence of long-distance merchant bodies, such as *ancuvaṇṇam* (an organisation of overseas traders, probably headed by Jewish leaders), *maṇigrāmam* (an organisation of overseas traders, probably headed by Syrian Christian leaders), *vaḷanciyar* (the name of an organisation of long-distance overland traders) and *nānādēśikaḷ* (the name of an organisation of long-distance overland traders from various regions). It was during this period that certain new trade centres developed, the oldest among them being Kurakkēṇi Kollam or Pantalāyinikollam, which is distinct from the southern Kollam. The Tarisāppaḷḷi copper plates show that foreign merchants' settlements-cum-market (Kollam *nagaram* founded by Maruvan Sapīr Īśo, presumably a Syrian Christian merchant leader) was bounded by a wall (*matil*) and goods reached the market in carts (*vāyanam*) and boats (*paṭa*). Similarly, the Jewish deed of 1000 CE granted by Bhaskara Ravi Varma Perumāḷ gives us the impression that Muyirikōde was the site of the palace and that there existed a market at Koṭunkōḷūr (Mahodayapuram). Several old songs of the Jews refer to Kōtanagari, another name of Mahodayapuram, as the erstwhile headquarters of their community.

These two title deeds (Tarisāppaḷḷi and the Jewish plates) grant the conventional 72 rights and privileges of a local ruler to the two merchant leaders (Sapīr Īśo and Joseph Rabban). This means the merchant leaders were made rulers of the two markets, viz., Kollam and Koṭunkōḷūr. It is evident that in Kerala during the ninth and the tenth centuries CE, ports and coastal markets were controlled by the merchant bodies called ancuvaṇṇam and maṇigrāmam. Most historians are of the view that leaders of these merchant bodies were Jews and Syrian Christians respectively. It has been traditionally accepted that Sapīr Īśo, the head of the maṇigrāmam of his time, was a Syrian Christian community leader, and that Joseph Rabban, the head of the ancuvaṇṇam of his time, was a Jewish community leader. However, in light of inscriptions from south India in general, it appears that maṇigrāmam was an organisation of long-distance overland merchants who were Christians, Arabs and Jews. Those who have signed as witnesses of the Tarisāppaḷḷi deed are prominent Jewish, Syrian, Palestinian and Arab merchants. Similarly, ancuvaṇṇam seems to have consisted of Persian, Arab, Christian and Jewish merchants. Of these the Arabs had an upper hand in the maritime trade through the Arabian Sea.

Several accounts of Arab travellers throw light on the trade carried out by the Arabs and the Chinese with Kollam. The oldest is perhaps the ninth century CE account by Sulaiman, an Arab trader who had direct contacts with Kollam. Sulaiman's work mentions that the Chinese had trade relations with Malabar, where they had established a firm foothold during the Tang Dynasty (818–907 CE). In Malabar, Kollam was the favoured port of call for Chinese ships. Sulaiman mentions that each Chinese ship anchoring at Kollam had to pay 1000 dirhām as duty. There are a few other works of the ninth century CE that attest to this, such as the accounts of Abu Said and Ibn Khordadbeh. By the eleventh century there are a few more works by the Arabs. Arab accounts mention Malibar (Malabar), a name synonymous with that of the land of pepper, which they cherished the most. In Arab accounts this land of pepper covered the whole of the western coast. Cardamom, ginger, cinnamon, cedar and sandalwood were other spices that the Arabs traded. They carried medicinal herbs, silk and porcelain too. It appears that the Malabar coast might have been a transit point for the Chinese goods. Chinese ships brought their cargoes to the ports on the seaboards of Malabar, and Arab ships carried these onward to northwest India and beyond.

Soon the Arabs succeeded in monopolising the trade between Kerala and the Persian coast. From the seventh to the eleventh centuries CE the gold dīnār continued to remain the medium of exchange in overseas trade. Though overseas merchants used money in their transactions, the exchange with the Kerala coast was based on barter, for it was exchange with societies under different economic conditions.* Therefore, it neither

---

* Forms of exchange varied according to economies of the regions. All economies did not use money as their medium, for they were non-monetised. When traders exchanged with non-monetised societies, they could only barter their coins as gold and silver objects and not as money because the receivers would understand coins merely as valuables. Only trading societies with notions of exchange value, price and profit would be able to use money as medium of exchange, means of payment and measure of value. Exchanges of Kerala before the thirteenth century were largely non-monetised. Nevertheless, there was a relatively stable gold–paddy ratio in the context of inter-goods exchange. Most goods in given measures were equated with fixed measures of paddy.

influenced nor transformed the existing productive system. In the tenth–eleventh centuries, most of the trade between India and the western lands was in the hands of the Arabs stationed at Morocco, Tripoli and Tunisia. Aydhab on the coast of the Red Sea was the terminal point of this sea route from where half of the ships sailed to the seaboards of Gujarat and Malabar. Historical documents, especially the Chinese travel accounts by Ma Huan and Fei-Hsin, mention trade contacts of the eastern Malaya archipelago Champa, Kalinga, Singala, Cōḻa and Karnataka with Kollam. In the accounts of Chinese travellers of the twelfth and thirteenth centuries CE, the ports of Kollam and Makotai (Mahōdayapuram) are mentioned. It was the foreign merchant bodies that carried on the exchange of goods and controlled the ports and marts (emporia or sale-stalls). Local merchants must have acted only as cargo suppliers and middlemen. Cāttan Vaṭukan and Iravi Cāttan mentioned in the Tāḻekāṭ inscription and the *maṇigrāmattār*—namely, Kōta Kumaran, Kumaran Kōta, Nākan Kaṇṇan and Kaṇṭan Kumaran—mentioned in the Bhāskarapuram inscription were probably such merchant middlemen. The names of these merchants apparently do not let us assume that they may have been Christians.

Some of the Tamil inscriptions of the eleventh and twelfth centuries CE contain references to merchants from Koṭunkōḷūr, obviously pointing to the commercial importance of the place. An undated inscription from Irinjālakuda, probably belonging to the period of Bhaskara Ravi Perumāḷ, refers to the renaming of Paṭinjāyiṛṛupōṭṭa as Bhāskarapuram and its turning into a market. Two of the inscriptions from Eramam and Pantalāyinikollam respectively, belonging to the same king, mention the chiefs of the places and a temple called Nagarēśvaram in Pantalāyinikollam. Trade centres in these places were geographically strategic and goods could be brought and despatched from these centres through waterways like rivers, canals and lakes. Exchange centres may have existed in the premises of all important temples which were themselves major consumer institutions. There is evidence of such centres in the eleventh and twelfth century CE maṇipravāḷam works. For instance, a maṇipravāḷam work called *Anantapuramvarṇam* describes the *cāla* market near the Padmanābhaswāmi temple, the various goods exchanged and the traders from other lands who had gathered there. Other poetic works from the thirteenth century CE onwards contain description of such markets with similar details.

Some of the inscriptions of Kerala mention various other merchant bodies such as nānādēśikaḷ, *patineṇbhūmi-tiśai-āyiratti-ainnūṟṟuvar* (literally, the one thousand and five hundred traders of eighteen lands), *nālpatteṇṇāyiravar* (the forty-eight thousand), *patineṭṭupaṭṭaṇattār* (itinerant merchants of eighteen towns) and vaḷanciyar, whose domain extended all over south India. In an Eramam inscription of the period of Bhaskara Ravi Perumāḷ, nānādēśikal along with vaḷanciyar are mentioned. An inscription of the eleventh century CE at Peruvempu mentions patineṇbhūmi-tiśai-āyiratti-ainūṟṟuvar and nānādēśikal. Nālpatteṇṇāyiravar appears in an inscription found at Ālathur near Palakkad and Tāḻekāvu near Pulpaḷḷi. Since these places are centres occupied by Jains, it points to the merchant body's relation to members of the Jain community and the latter's relation to trade. These merchant bodies appear in several inscriptions belonging to the eleventh and twelfth centuries CE in Tamil Nadu's Siva temples. The vaḷanchyiar organisation appears in the Juma Masjit inscription at Pantalāyinikollam of the period of Bhāskara Ravi. Since the local governments of the time were incapable of providing security throughout the route, the merchant bodies had to keep their own warriors with them. Some of the hero stones found along the borders of Karnataka and Tamil Nadu bear evidence of the movement of the merchant bodies and their encounters with thieves. Nālpatteṇṇāyiravar was entrusted with the protection of certain temples in Tamil Nadu, probably indicating their warrior power. It is significant that the Peruvempu inscription of the eleventh century that mentions the tiśai-āyiratti-ainnūṟṟuvar refers to Rajendra Cōḻa *samaya-sēnāpati* (chief of soldiers), which clarifies the warrior power of the merchant bodies.

Sources of the period point to the gradual monetisation of contemporary exchanges. Inscriptions mention *dināra*, *kāśu* and *pazhamkāśu* as terms referring to money by way of gold coins.

These coin names occur in contemporary records of other regions as well, indicating their circulation in a large area. Among these coin types, the dināra is well known as a Roman Coin, and finds mention in the Sanskrit portion of an early medieval Pāṇdya inscription. In the Tamil portion of the same record, the name kāśu is employed in the general sense of money. Earlier scholars have arrived at an equation of 1 dināra = 1 pazhamkāśu = 3 kaḻanju of gold. Regarding pazhamkāśu the name itself indicates the continuation of this coin from the past, a fact that is taken by scholars as a feature of the currency system of south India.

It appears that dīnāra was multi-purpose money with which payments of religious gifts, customary dues, taxes, fines, etc. could be made. As a means of exchange it could be used as a general equivalent. Here one is inclined to compare these functions of the dīnāra of the Perumāḷ period with those of the early historical period when the emphasis was on luxury and exotic items of exchange. Some scholars hold that Roman gold coins were received in early Tamiḻakam as prestige goods or primitive valuables. In this sense there is a basic change in the use of Roman gold coins during the two periods. Pazhankāśu (literally, an old coin) is mentioned in the inscriptions of the Perumāḷ period, but the actual references on such occasions are to the specified weight and fineness of the gold coin and not to the coin as such. Vāḻappaḷḷi copper plates of Rajashekhara Perumāḷ dated to c. 832 CE is the first inscription that mentions dināra. It is mentioned as coin in terms of number and not gold in terms of weight. There are a couple of instances more in inscriptions where the name of the coin figures as countable rather than weighable. Nevertheless, in the last instance it was gold valued in terms of its weight and fineness and usable but in exchange of given extents of land or a given measure of paddy. It is natural that the coin, as a specific weight of gold, was acting as good as money as well.

Kāśu figures as early as c. 849 CE in the context of a price-making market at Kollam in the form of a fixed amount of toll to be collected from the in-coming and out-going vehicles and boats. Each cart coming to and going out of the angāṭi had to pay eight kāśu, while each boat, big and small, had to pay four kāśus. In addition, a tax called *āḷkāśu* to be paid at the time of purchase of *aṭinmai* (slave) is also mentioned in the Kollam Tarisāppaḷḷi copper plate inscription. Here too the use of money is found in the circles of big merchants, ruling authority and land owners. Moreover, sometimes the term kāśu is used in the general sense of money without reference to any particular issue. This also adds to the confusion. However, scholars have observed that kāśu was struck in gold, silver and copper in different periods.

One finds it difficult to make statements with any amount of certainty about the indigenous nature of kāśu type of coins, because they are mentioned in the records of territories which are widely set apart from each other geographically. In short, dīnāra was called kāśu and pazhankāśu. Several records from the ninth to the twelfth centuries refer to a gold-paddy ratio which remained steady in different parts of Kerala. Dīnāra is known in Kerala from a single record, viz., the Vāḻapaḷḷi inscription dated to the twelfth regnal year of Rajasekhara (c. 832 CE), which mentions a fine of 100 dīnāras to be imposed on those who obstruct the daily offering in the temple of Tiruvārruvai. The context implies the use of money as a medium of exchange. A Pāṇḍya inscription mentioned above registers a grant of ten dīnāras for burning a perpetual lamp with the interest of the amount. This strongly suggests the investment of dīnāras in profit-oriented transactions, either as coin money or as gold.

This may be taken as indication of the fact that it was slowly falling out of circulation and would soon disappear altogether after the tenth century CE. It may be due to the value of gold as treasure. Its increased use as ornaments could be another reason. This is further strengthened by the fact that there is a sharp decrease in the use of coin money towards the end of the tenth century. Three of six records pertaining to the preceding century (820–898 CE) mention different coins in the contexts of actual remittance in coins, whereas three records out of forty-five records of the period 900–1000 CE only refer to coins and that too with reference to the equal weight of gold. On other occasions, gold of specified weight and fineness (*pon cuṭmuraiyum varavitu*) is mentioned in the context of exchange of paddy, remittance of fines, etc. Gradual disappearance of coins and the widespread use of gold as means of exchange is the notable feature of this period. A gold–paddy ratio of 1 kaḻanju of gold = 20 paṛas of paddy remained unchanged for quite a long period from Airanikkalam (869 CE) in the north to Kollur Maṭham (1189 CE) in the south, as clearly shown by epigraphical records. Inscriptions that are dated to the second half of the twelfth century CE present interesting information regarding a new set of coins: *accu*, *paṇam* and *calāka*. Kilimanur copper plates of 1168 CE refer to the accu–paddy ratio as 1:1, and thereby enable us to know that the value of one accu was equal to 1/20 of a kaḻanju or ½ *kāṇam* of gold.

Port Towns and Markets

A couple of the port towns (*paṭṭaṇams*) and markets (*ankāṭis*) of the early historical period—Muciṛi and Kollam (Quilon)—seems to have continued to the Perumāḷ period. New port towns like Kurakkeṇi Kollam (Quilon), Pantalāyinikollam near Kozhikode and Māḍāyi near Payyanur came up. Kurakkeṇi Kollam is the most famous among contemporary port towns. Temple centres were small townships where inland merchants converged. There were many markets at convenient points where trade routes intersected and these catered to the local needs. As we have already seen, this is well-attested by inscriptions, foreign notices and literary references. The Tharisapalli copper plate grant is the earliest inscription that mentions a full-fledged fortified ankāṭi at the port town of Quilon. References to carts and different types of boats coming to and going from Quilon indicate the inward and outward movement of merchandise, fixing up of their prices, collection of tolls and taxes, maintenance of the weights and measures, etc. This, in association with the market town, indicates that Quilon had the features of an urban centre.

Another salient feature of an urban centre was its multicultural confluence. All port towns of Kerala, right from the period of the Classical Roman Empire, were multicultural but of a lesser scale compared to what had come into being at Quilon after a millennium. Signatories of the Jewish copper plates of 999 CE included Persian, Arabic and Jewish merchants, showing the presence of multicultural communities at the port town. Subsequently, there were Jews, Christians and even Muslims in the most important port towns of Kerala such as Quilon, Koṭunkōḷūr, Pantalāyinikollam and Māḍāyi.

Local markets catering to the needs of the surrounding areas rose up during this period. Bhāskarapuram, Tāl̲ekāṭ and Kuṭavur in the middle tract of the agrarian settlements were some of them a little inland. Bhāskarapuram and Tāl̲ekāṭ present the genesis of formal trade centres. Inscriptional evidence at Tāl̲ekāṭ shows the allocation of land and setting up of shops there at the initiative of the maṇigrāmam under royal patronage. Association with religious centres was a feature of the local markets—the Syrian Christian control over maṇigrāmam is well known and the Tāl̲ekāt church has the inscription as well.

Literature, Art and Architecture

There has been a tradition of temple theatre and related literature in Kerala during this period. Some of the well known examples are the eighth-ninth century works *Āścharyachūḍāmaṇi* by Saktibhadran, a contemporary of Sri Sankara, and *Subhadrādhananjayam* by Kulaśēkhara Perumāḷ. Another important play of the same period was *Pradyumnābhyudayam*. As regards the architecture of the period, Kerala has only a few monuments, the oldest among which are the monolithic cave temples belonging to c. eighth and ninth centuries CE. The cave temples at Pūvār and Vizhinjam (Thiruvananthapuram district), Kaviyūr (Pathanamthitta district), Kallil (Ernakulam district), and Irunilankode and Thrikur (Thrissur district) are some examples. Pūvār and Vizhinjam on the coastal towns of the Āy rulers (c. seventh century CE) were on the fringes of the Pāṇdya empire and had the influence of Jain establishments like Chitaral—the famous centre of Jain Yakshi cult—and Tirunandikkara—the famous cave art site of c. eighth century—connected to kings like Vikramaditya Varguran and Jain monks like Achananti and Uttananti. At Kaviyūr the structure consists of a corridor, a quadrilateral chamber and a small rectangular cave. Similarly, at Kallil there are chambers with some sculptures. Thrikkur is a big rock-cut chamber-turned-sanctum sanctorum of a temple, obviously a later transformation. These caves show the influence of the architecture and sculpture in the Pallava–Pāṇḍya regions. However, none of these is comparable to the cave monuments of Tamil Nadu in terms of architectural and sculptural richness. We do not know anything about the artists or patrons behind the cave structures in Kerala.

There is archaeological evidence of the rise of temples in and out of the traditional brāhmaṇa settlements of Kerala, largely of the ninth–tenth centuries CE. A few examples are Thiruvananthapuram, Chengannur, Kaviyūr, Tiruvalla, Perunna, Trikadithānam, Tripūṇithuṛa, Paṛur, Trikkākkara, Tiruvanchikkaḷam, Tirumuḻikkaḷam, Irāṇikkaḷam, Tirumirrakōde and Trichambaram. All these temples have certain common architectural features such as the *garbhagṛham* (sanctum sanctorum), *mukhamanḍapam* (front pavilion), *currambalam* (structures on four quarters), *tiḍappally* (temple kitchen), *muḷayaṛa* (seedlings room), *vātilmāṭam* (gateway) and *kūttampalam* (temple's theatre hall). Kerala's temples are mostly small in size and least ornamental in style. They come with not many sculptures, except those of the *dwārapālaka* (watch and ward) icons, simple decorative motifs and the few representations on the balustrades. Two relief sculptures of Narasimha and Gajendra at the Kaviyūr temple are exceptions to this.

Apart from the brāhmaṇa temples there are other institutions of the period, such as the Tarisāppaḷḷi church in Kollam (not in existence or not identified as yet), and the Jain temples at Kallil (Perumbavūr), Ālathur (Palakkad), Trikaṇāmatilakam near Koṭunkōḷūr, Kinalur (Balusseri), Tiruvaṇṇūr (Kozhikode) and Tāḻekāvu (Wayanad). Kallil is a cave with Mahāvira and Sidhāyika as reliefs on the top and Pārśvanātha and Padmāvati as icons inside. It had a structure entirely different from what has survived as a mother goddess temple today. Alathur, another Jain temple, now as remains of a few statues of Mahāvira and Pārśvanātha, besides some broken pillars, has an inscription referring to the Jain temple of Tirukuṇavāi (Trikaṇāmatilakam) near Koṭunkōḷūr. Fragments of a wall, pillars and granite blocks of the monument remain scattered at the site, where excavations have revealed more parts of the wall, terracotta lamps and a few Cōḻa coins. Tirukuṇavāi Trikaṇāmatilakam is considered in *Śukasandēśam* and *Kōkasandēśam* as a Siva temple not desirable to be worshiped by brāhmaṇas, probably due to its erstwhile status as a Jain temple. Jain temples at Kinālūr and Tiruvaṇṇūr do not seem to have been architecturally far different from the brāhmaṇa temples. The Tāḻekāvu was a Jain *yaksha* (protector) temple that had depended on the long distance traders and local agriculturists. There are no remains of this temple except the inscription from which we know about it.

V

Formation of the State under the Perumāḷ Regime (c. 800 CE–1124 CE)

In the previous chapter we have seen how a relatively egalitarian agro-pastoral society dissolved itself into a stratified agrarian society of hierarchical relations based on differentiated land rights. And, as we make out from Keraḷōlpatti, a class-structured society, dominated by landlords who became an oligarchic body, obviously as a result of contests, emerged. It is widely accepted today that the state system in history owed its origins to the process of economic differentiation and social stratification. Theoretically speaking, the state would come into being in a society of asymmetrical relations as a result of contestations for domination among the elites. Contestations among the elites would depersonalise and institute the state. Writing and literacy would spread among the elites in societies of economic differentiation and enable documentation, which is a primary instrument of governance under the state system. The juridico-political apparatus of the state is enabled only in an elite-dominated society of writing and literacy. As already discussed, it was the temple-centred corporation of brāhmaṇa landlords who enjoyed proprietary control over productive land, and the enslaved workforce was subjected under the fetters of the evolving institution of caste. Oral traditions claim that these temple-centred oligarchs were the makers of the Perumāḷ state, which is quite tenable theoretically too.

The Perumāḷ Regime

Elamkulam Kunhan Pillai (hereafter, Elamkulam) calls the later Cēras as Kulaśēkharas, while M. G. S. Narayanan (hereafter, MGS) identifies these rulers as Perumāḷs, since 'Perumāḷ' was the honorific title inherited by them. There is no indication of a direct descent of the Perumāḷs from the old chiefly lineage of the Cēras, except a few remnants in the form of names, such as 'Cēramān', 'Mākōta' and 'Kōta'. The early ruling lineage of the chiefdom with Karur as headquarters does not seem to have continued beyond c. 300 CE to give rise to the kingdom of Perumāḷs with Mākōtai or Mahodayapuram as the capital during c. 800 CE. Mahodayapuram is the Sanskrit form of koṭum+koḷ+ūr. Koṭumkōḷūr in due course became Koṭunkōḷūr. It was known also as Muyirikōde (the 'kōde' of Muciṛi), the up-street of the old port, probably continued to the Age of the Perumāḷs. Mākōtai appears in the context of Cēra chieftains by way of an appellation signifying their personal name, as testified by a few coins. Nevertheless, the discontinuity marked by a period of transformation is a matter of tacit recognition because theoretically, the formation of the state takes place only in a stratified society. It is evident that the society got stratified as a result of the spread of plough agriculture along the alluvial plains, which was a process of the establishment of brāhmaṇa settlements by incorporating local people as hereditary occupation groups in their service. Subsequently, these occupation groups seem to have become endogamous caste groups. It is in the region integrated through brāhmaṇa settlements of economic differentiation and social stratification that state power, represented by the Perumāḷs emerged. Geographically, the 32 brāhmaṇa settlements and allied areas demarcated the kingdom of the Perumāḷs.

Unlike the case of the Pāṇdyas and Cōḻas, there is no genealogical order of patriarchal inheritance based on primogeniture in the case of the Perumāḷs, who seem to have followed the matrilineal system. While the Pāṇdyas and Cōḻas had their consistently alternated cognomen, their absence is conspicuous with the Perumāḷs. Elamkulam thought that Kulaśēkhara Āḻvār was the founder of this line of rulers. In the light of hints from the Keralōlpatti tradition, and corroborated by epigraphical evidence, Rama Rajasekhara—who MGS calls Cēramān Perumāḷ Nāyanār—is the first known king of the line. In the Vāḻapaḷḷi copper plate this Perumāḷ is addressed as '*rāja rājarājādhirāja paramesvara bhaṭṭāraka*'. According to *Periyapurāṇam* the first Perumāḷ was Cēramān Perumāḷ Nāyanār, whom the ministers of the last of the the last of the Cēras, Poraiyan, invited to the throne to overcome the predicament caused by the king's renunciation and retirement to the forest. Keralōlpatti mentions the tradition of the leaders of the brāhmaṇa settlements inviting the Perumāḷ for a period of twelve years from the ruling families outside Kerala. That the founder of the dynasty was Rāma Rājaśekhara, famously known as Cēramān Perumāḷ Nāyanār, is more or less a settled issue in the historiography of Kerala today. He must have ruled between c. 800 and 844 CE.

Rāma Rājaśekhara's successor was Sthāṇu Ravi Kulaśēkhara (844–c. 883 CE). His ascendance to the throne is precisely dated with the help of the definite mention of the Perumāḷ's coronation year in Sankaranārāyaṇa's *Laghubhāskarīya Vyākhya*, an astronomical text written in 870 CE. This Perumāḷ is well known through the Tarisāppaḷḷi copper plates that registered the Vēṇāṭu ruler's land grant to Maruvan Sapīr Īśo for founding the Teresa Church at Kollam. Sthāṇu Ravi Kulaśēkhara's last regnal year is not certain. However, the date of the succession of the next Perumāḷ, Kōta Ravi Vjayarāga (883–c. 913 CE), who figures in the copper plate as Koyil Aadhikarikal, has been established with inscriptional evidence. A stone inscription from Tirunandikkara mentions '*Vijayarāga tēvar tēviyār*', '*Kulaśēkhara tēvar makaḷār*' (king Vijayarāga's queen, king Kulaśēkhara's daughter) and a Tiruvorriyur inscription confirms Vijayarāga as a Cēra king. This shows that he was Sthāṇu Ravi Kulaśēkhara's son-in-law. Several stone inscriptions have shown that his actual name was Kōta Ravi. He was succeeded by Kōta Kōta Kerala Kesari (c. 913–c. 943 CE) about whom nothing much is known. There is no chronological certainty about the end of his rule and the beginning of the rule of his successor, Indu Kōta (c. 943–962 CE), whose terminal date is established through inscriptional analysis that has made his sequence with the next Perumāḷ, Bhāskara Ravi Manukulāditya (962–1021 CE), clear too.

Elamkulam had thought that there were two or more rulers with the name Bhāskara Ravi, which became famous through the Jewish copper plate. For quite some time his dates were disputed among historians for want of clinching evidence. Although there are several inscriptions of Bhāskara Ravi with dates mentioned, as usual only in terms of the position of Jupiter, the calculation of dates is not uniform. According to MGS the dating falls into two series—one starting with Jupiter in the month of Dhanu (December–January) showing 962 CE as the initial regnal year and ending with Jupiter in Cingam (August–September) showing 1020 CE as the fifty-eighth regnal year; and the other starting with Jupiter in Mēṭam (April–May) showing as 978 CE as the initial year and ending with Jupiter in Tulām (October–November) showing 1021 CE as the forty-third regnal year. It is evident that one series reckons the date from the enthronement (at the age of eight) and the other series reckons the date from the formal coronation (at the age of 17). MGS resolves the problem through his ingenious use of two synchronisms—one consisting of Bhāskara Ravi, Sree Vallabhan Kōta and Govardhana Mārthāṇḍan, and the other of Bhāskara Ravi, Kantankāri Varman and Rajendra Cōḻa. The former put an end to the possibility of pushing the upper limit anterior to the second half of the tenth century CE and the latter fixed the lower limit within the first half of the eleventh century CE.

Ravi Kōta Rāja Simha (c. 1021–c. 1036 CE) seems to have occupied the throne as the next Perumāḷ. His dates are tentative but reasonably fixed in relation to the fact that he was Rajendra Cōḻa's contemporary. Rājarāja, Ravi Rāma Rājāditya, Adityan Kōta and Ranāditya are the names of Perumāḷs mentioned in a few inscriptions of the post-Bhāskara Ravi period (c. 1036–1089 CE). We do not know the succession sequence of these kings. Nevertheless, Rāma Kulaśēkhara (1089 CE–1122 CE) was the next Perumāḷ after the last of the lot. Though this Perumāḷ's accession date is uncertain, the exit date is definite, thanks to the Kollam Ramesvarattu Koil inscription that mentions the thirteenth year of Rāma Kulaśēkhara, both by way of the position of Jupiter and in the Kollam Era. It is learnt from the inscription that Rama

Kulaśēkhara had an inglorious exit marking the end of the Mākōtai rule, due to the wrath of the brāhmaṇa oligarchs.

Juridico-Political Aspects

The circulation of resources served as the material basis of the social hierarchy of dependent relations. Social relations were based on customary obligations engendered by the hierarchical obligations (kaṭama) from the bottom to the top and from the top to the bottom, which constituted the foundation of the contemporary juridical system. Customary obligations integrated the social order through a system of self-regulated relationships. *Ūrmuṛa* (the village convention) is the term used in the Tiruvārruvai copper plates to mean the customary social code of conduct. These customs essentially related to the hierarchical social relations and served the smooth functioning of every transaction. On the basis of the general customs, specific regulations were formulated and made known by inscribing them on stone in open spaces. These regulations related to the fixing up of rent for a particular type of land, the expenses to be incurred out of the rent, the conditions thereof, the punitive measures on default, etc. Such regulations were specifically made under the customary sanction of ūrmuṛa. Unanimous decisions by the sabha with other authorities of the village would become the code of the regulation. Such regulatory codes were called *kaccams*. These codes regularise and reinforce the customs based on social relations, valid as long as the respective institutions endure.

Perhaps the best example of such a regulatory code is the Mūḻikkaḷam kaccam. Mūḻikkaḷam was one of the most prominent among the traditional 32 brāhmaṇa settlements. It was one of the thirteen well known divine villages (*divyadēśam*) in Kerala and was situated near Mahodayapuram, the capital of the Perumāḷ. It was also one among the four congregations (*nālutaḷi*) that were important as the advisory councils of the Perumāḷ. According to the Keraḷōlpatti tradition, the four congregations were leading councils of the 32 brāhmaṇa villages. In fact, Mūḻikkaḷam code is not known in its entirety. Several inscriptions cite this code as an authenticating precedent and the crucial part of the code is known from these inscriptions. In the Chōkūr inscription of the fifteenth regnal year of Kōta Ravi (898 CE) we see the first invocation of this code. Inscriptions invoking this code are also found in temples from Narayan Kaṇṇūr in Ēzhimala in the north to Arampoli in the south, including Maṇiyūr, Tirunelli, Chembra, Poṛangāṭṭiri, Rāmanāṭṭukara, Pūkōṭṭūr, Nāvāyikuḷam, Alanallūr, Tirumirrakode, Tripṛayār, Tāḻekāṭ, Aviṭṭattur, Kumāranellūr and Kaviyūr.

Since the context of inscriptional invocations to the Mūḻikkaḷam kaccam is invariably that of offences committed by individual brāhmaṇa landlords and the punitive measures to be imposed on them, the cited passages across these inscriptions remain the same. It is clear that the code contains what punitive measures should be imposed and against which offence of the individual brāhmaṇa landlords of the settlement (ūrāḷar) who made the assembly (sabha) that governed the settlement. Inscriptions mention that the ūrāḷar who violates the sabha's unanimous decisions would be considered as equal to the sinners of the *pancamahāpātaka*s (five great sins; such as marrying the mother after killing the father, killing the teacher, etc.) as per the Mūḻikkaḷam code. This implies the offender's inevitable excommunication, depriving the accused of the caste status, power and the entire material belongings. Any major decision of the sabha, regarding landed property and the rights of the settlers therein or rights granted to non-brāhmaṇas, was also reinforced and perpetuated by stating that the ūrāḷar who defy it would be considered to have committed the *pancamahāpātaka.*

Elamkulam believed that the Mūḻikkaḷam code was adopted under the king's initiative for safeguarding the interests of the tenants cultivating the temple lands. It is true that the provisions in the code were against the ūrār who obstructed cultivation, misappropriated the crops, denied the rights of the settlers, made inroads into their households and so on. However, the main objective seems to have been to ensure the rent due from the tenants for meeting the day-to-day expenses of the temple. A Tiruvanvandūr inscription naming Sree Vallabhan Kōta (c. tenth century CE) stipulates under the authority of Mūḻikkaḷam code that no section of the people should cause any hindrance to the smooth running of the temple. Based on the Aviṭṭattūr document of 903 CE it may be inferred that most of the instances refer to the highhandedness of the brāhmaṇa landlords upon the non-brāhmaṇas in the village. MGS rejects Elamkulam's interpretation of the Mūḻikkaḷam kaccam as evidence of the king's initiative in protecting the peasants because the kaccam was not a royal imposition, but a set of regulations that the brāhmaṇa landlords unanimously resolved. Temple inscriptions of the period generally mention at the beginning the reigning king's name with the regnal year, as part of a long drawn out practice. This indeed shows the people's consciousness of the king and his reign, but not the involvement of the king. Elamkulam's use of the word 'śāsanam' with the identity of one king or the other at once gives the impression that these inscriptions were royal proclamations. In fact, the king might not have even known about them, for they related to the matters of the temple or the settlement. MGS, therefore, argues that Mūḻikkaḷam regulations were what the brāhmaṇa oligarchs imposed on themselves to check their highhandedness at the individual level for safeguarding their corporate strength, rather than the king's initiatives in the safeguard of peasants.

Inscriptions mention four other codes from the temple settlements—Kaḍankāṭṭū, Tavaranūr, Sankaramangalam and Kaitavāram. The Kaḍānkōṭṭu code is mentioned during the twentieth regnal year of Kōta Ravi in the context of annexing the royal land of Cērmān Mātēvi to the temple. Tavaranūr kaccam is mentioned in Triprangode and Sukapuram documents belong to the twenty-seventh regnal year of Kōta Ravi (910 CE). The kaccam is mentioned in the context of administering the land to meet the daily expenses of the temple. The Sukapuram inscription, which is undated, records the payment to the temple by Tiruvarangur village and prohibits the councillors (sabhaiyār) from stopping cultivation or thus obstructing the daily rituals in the temple.

Locating Power Centres: Dēśam and Taṛa

A careful examination of the survey reports, settlement registers and the sociological and geographical studies of the time help us identify the *dēśam* settlement and its regional variants as the basic unit of economic production. These production units were responsible for building a sustainable life pattern as a salient feature of traditional village settlements. They were not self-sufficient settlements in terms of meeting their economic and social needs. In order to mete out these needs each settlement had to extend to an area larger than itself and this was how the *taṛa* units came into being. Very often, members of the village community extended their kin base to an area larger not only than the dēśam but also the taṛa. This area that was larger than the taṛa was called the *nāṭu*. In short, the dēśam, the taṛa and the nāṭu were spontaneously evolved units. They were not imposed by any political authority as part of the territorial division for the convenience of administration. As basic units of economic production that came into being spontaneously in response to the needs and potentials of a locality, they are more or less geographical in nature.

Nāṭus and Nāṭuvāḻis

There were several nāṭus, small and big, all over Kerala, ruled by chieftains (nāṭuvāḻis). Vēnāṭu, Kiḻumalaināṭu, Puṛakiḻānāṭu, Kalkkaraināṭu, Valluvanāṭu, Ēṛāḷanāṭu, Kurumporaināṭu, Nanruḻaināṭu, Kolattunāṭu, Netumpurayurnāṭu, Vempalanāṭu and Munjināṭu were prominent nāṭus during this period. Nāṭus are naturally-evolved settlements socio-culturally integrated and consolidated over centuries. Each nāṭu was a manifestation of local-level economic and socio-cultural development over a long period. Nāṭu, as a term, either derived from the root '*naṭu*' (to plant) or '*naṭa*' (to walk in) means an agrarian settlement.

Its Sanskrit equivalent is *janapada*. In the Dravidian region 'nāṭu' is an ūr writ large. In short, nāṭu has a historical background of natural evolution from below, although it is often forgotten under the general presumption that territorial units are administrative units created from above.

This historical status accounts for their long persistent regional identity. Every nāṭu had its own ruler addressed as *nāṭuṭayavar* (owner of the nāṭu) and its own warrior contingent in units of hundred (*nurruvakkuttam*). The nāṭuvāḻi of Nanṟuḻaināṭu had munnūṟṟuvar (the three hundred), Vēnāṭu had aṟunūṟṟuvar (the six hundred), Kiḻumalaināṭu had eḻunūṟṟuvar (the seven hundred) and so on. The warrior strength was determined by factors such as the extent of wealth, cultural strength and leadership, which were invariably uneven. As part of the power game, the Perumāḷ, the most resourceful in terms of all this, especially the cultural power acquired through their alliance with the brāhmaṇas, had domination over them with his warrior contingent, the āyiravar (the thousand). This is continuation of an early practice mentioned in the *Arthaśāsthra* by *mūlaparisha* (the intimate body guards or the companions of honour) translated as *uṭankūṭṭam* (the intimate body guards). Textbooks mistakenly take it for an assembly that helped the ruler in administration.

A few nāṭus like Vēnāṭu and Kiḻumalaināṭu were wealthy and powerful. Vēnāṭu was prosperous in agriculture and trade, which accounted for their political strength, evidenced by the copper plate charters granting land and people. Tarisāppaḷḷi and Māmpaḷḷi plates are examples. Kiḻumalaināṭu was rich in hill products that had overseas demand. It stimulated inland trade as well. In terms of the geographical extent Kōḷattunāṭu was the largest, but not quite rich in agriculture. It had commanded forest products as well as inland crops of exchange value, which accounted for their dependence on trade revenue. It appears that nāṭus had to pay their āṭṭaikkoḷ to the Perumāḷ. Inscriptional references to a variety of taxes paid by merchants vouch for the prevalence of a systematic appropriation of revenue from trade.

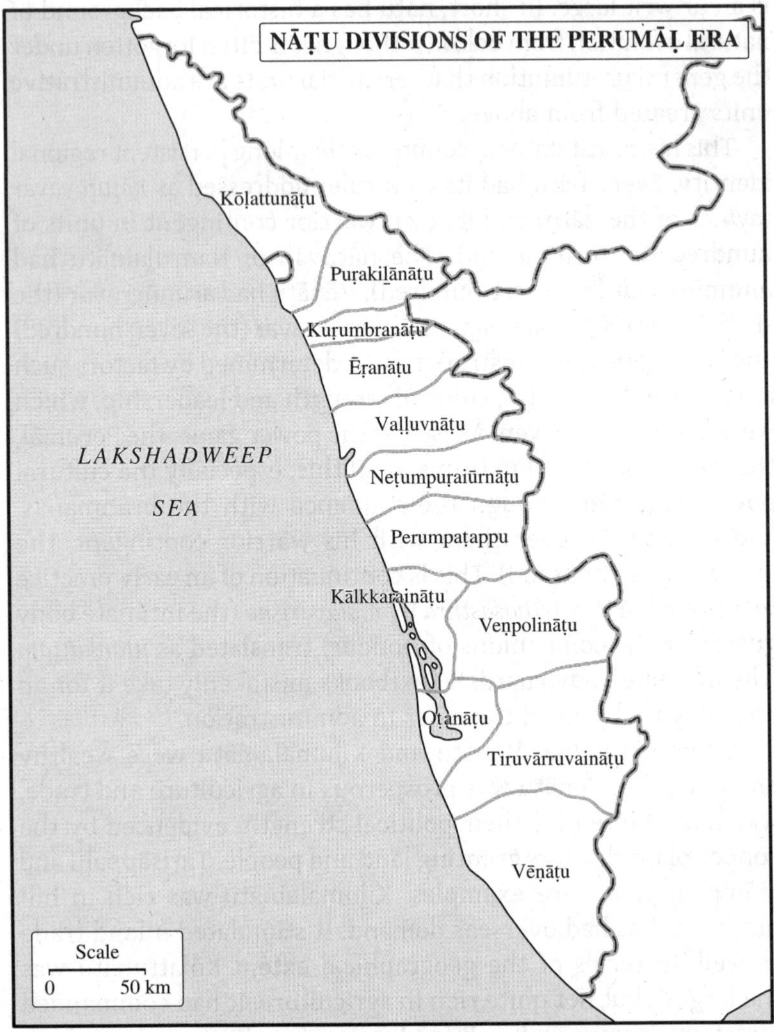

Note: 1. © Government of India, Copyright 2018.

2. The responsibility for the correctness of internal details rests with the publisher.
3. The territorial waters of India extend into the sea to a distance of twelve nautical miles measured from the appropriate base line.
4. The spellings of names in this map have been taken from various sources.

Among the nāṭus, Vēṇāṭu seems to have been relatively prominent. However, it is not possible to trace a complete list of rulers of Vēṇāṭu in chronological order for want of evidence. A ruler of Vēṇāṭu mentioned for the first time in the Tarisāppaḷḷi copper plates, dated to the fifth regnal year of Sthāṇu Ravi (c. 849 CE), is Ayyanaṭikaḷ, the donor of the grant. It is clear from the inscription that he enjoyed the power to grant land, to exempt from paying taxes and to alienate his juridical power over his subjects, indeed only with the knowledge of the Perumāḷ. Functionaries like *atikārar* (authority), *pṛakṛti* (clients), *pati* (lord) and ainnūṟṟuvar mentioned in the record indicate that the ruler commanded a whole system of local official infrastructure. Māmpaḷḷi copper plate, the earliest record discovered so far in the Kollam Era, refers to another ruler of Vēṇāṭu named Vallabhan Kōta (tenth century CE). Govardha Marthanda was the successor of Vallabhan Kōta. In the Jewish copper plate of Bhāskara Ravi (1000 CE) he appears to be one of the witnesses. The Trikkaṭithanam inscription also makes a reference to him.

Nāṭuṭayavar's power was regulated by the *kūṟu* system of inheritance and method of sharing the political rights and privileges. Literally, the kūṟu system means sharing of property and power through *sthānams* or positions of power in the order of seniority. This enabled the existence of several centres of power in one and the same territory. In the Tarisāppaḷḷi record the junior prince (*ilankūṟu*) was present when the deed was executed by Ayyanaṭikaḷ, the ruler or *mūttakūṟu* (the elder). In the northern parts of Kerala too the kūṟu system of inheritance was followed. It is clear from the Tirunelli temple inscription that registers the grant by the mūttakūṟu rulers of Kuṟumpoṟaināṭu and the Puṟakiḻanāṭu. A record of Bhāskara Ravi dated to 1000 CE mentions five nāṭuṭayavar as signatories in the charter issued to the Jewish merchant leader, Joseph Rabban. They are the nāṭuṭayavar of Vēnāṭu, Vempolināṭu, Ēṟāḷanaṭu, Vaḷḷuvanāṭu and Neṭumpuṟaiyurnāṭu. It is evident that these nāṭus were the historically-evolved localities of production and distribution. Their rulers were chieftains of very old lineages.

Monarchical Structure

The political structure of the Perumāḷ rule was of monarchy, as indicated by certain expressions in contemporary inscriptions. In the Vāḻapaḷḷi copper plates he is addressed as *rāja rāja rājādhirāja*, indicating the imposition of overlordship (*koima*) on local rulers, i.e., the nāṭuṭayavar whose authority was hereditary. There are other inscriptional mentions of overlordship in usages such as *konmai koṇtān* and *konoinmai koṇtān* (both literally meaning, 'having assumed overlordship'). In the Tarisāppaḷḷi copper plate and the Jewish copper plate, the Perumal's royal qualifications like *maṛukutalai ciṛantaṭippaṭuttālā* (having subdued the enemy) and *palanūṛāyirattāṇṭū cenkōl naṭattiyāḷā* (having wielded the sceptre for several hundreds of years) clearly show the sovereign power over the local chieftains. We come across a few instances of the Perumāḷ interfering with the inheritance of the nāṭuvāḻi and appointing the personage of his choice as the ruler. It is known from the inscription that the Perumāḷ had exacted āṭṭaikōḷ even from far-off areas like Pullūr Koṭavalam near Kanhangad. Inscriptional references show that the nāṭuvāḻis were not entitled to take major decisions such as the de facto transfer of resources or execution of contracts. Ayyanaṭikaḷ, the nāṭuvāḻi of Vēnāṭu, grants land and service personnel in the presence of the *koiladhikārkaḷ* (the junior prince). It is significant that the mention of the main sanction relating to the land grant with special rights and privileges is made jointly by the koyiladhikāri and the nāṭuvāḻi.

Nevertheless, the monarchical power was under the influence of the prominent brāhmaṇa landlords. The four most prominent brāhmaṇa settlements—Mulikkalam, Airanikkalam, Paravur and Irinjālakuḍa—constituted the core of the Perumāḷ's power structure. Authorities of these settlements constituted the royal council called *nālutaḷi* (four temples). Temple, being the headquarters of the brāhmaṇa settlement, the term *taḷi* (temple) is symbolic of the personnel of authority over the temple (*taḷiadhikārikal*), which meant the most prominent brāhmaṇa landlords. Prominent nāṭuvāḻis along with the nālutaḷi seem to have constituted the larger council of the king.

The idea of the Kautilyan monarchy was entrenched in the political system, as several inscriptions testify. Most parts under the concept of *saptāga* (the seven limbs) of the state mentioned in the *Arthaśāsthra*, such as *swāmi* (the king), *amātya* (the minister), *atikārar* (authorities or officers), *janapada* (territory), *durga* (fort, the *matil*), *kosa* (the treasury, the *paṇṭāram*), *daṇḍa* (the army) and *mitra* (friends) are mentioned in the inscriptions, especially copper plates. Perumāḷs enjoyed overlordship over the ruler (chieftain) of every nāṭu. There is at least one instance of the appointment of the ruler of a nāṭu over another nāṭu, as mentioned in one of the Trikadithānam inscriptions. It mentions the act of Bhāskara Ravi Perumāḷ making Govardhana Mārthāṇḍan of Vēnāṭu the ruler of Nanruḻaināṭu also. This is exercise of supreme authority by the Perumāḷ over the chief of a nāṭu.

It is significant to discuss the patronage given to the merchant bodies against the context of the Perumāḷ's power structure. The Tarisāppaḷḷi copper plates show that maṇigrāmam, the foreign merchant body, was powerful enough to secure a grant for a community settlement-cum-market town. Similarly, the Jewish copper plate charter of 1000 CE issued by Bhāskara Ravi Varma Perumāḷ granting aristocratic privileges much more directly to Joseph Rabban, the merchant leader of ancuvaṇṇam, the most prominent overseas trading organisation of the period, shows the political significance of the patronage. Overseas merchants would be powerful in the sea with vessels. MGS opines that conferring princely status upon the leader of an overseas trading group and granting him control over the port town close to Muyirikōde, the site of the Perumāḷ's palace, has an added political significance against the context of the threat of naval attack by the Cōḻas.

Of all the powers, the most decisive were the oligarchic corporations of the nālutaḷi-centred bṛāhmaṇa settlements in and the surrounds of Mahodayapuram, the headquarters of the Perumāḷ. These constituted the nuclei of contemporary power structure. They represented the rest of the traditional

32 temple-centred brāhmaṇa settlements and their corporate bodies. In course of time, the Perumāḷ's sovereign control which prevailed during the initial phase gradually declined and phased out completely by the time of Rāmavarma Kulaśēkhara, who had to abdicate his throne and go into exile.

Kollam Era

The dating system followed in the inscriptions of the period of Perumāḷs of Kerala was predominantly based on the course of Jupiter. Mentioning the king's regnal year in terms of the position of Jupiter against the star group or constellation was the practice. In a few cases the Kali Age is found as the point of reckoning for showing the date. Similarly, one or two instances of using the Hijera Era* and a few occasions of dating based on the foundation eras of certain Jain temples like Tirukuṇavāi and Kinālūr as well as brāhmaṇa temples like Trikkaṇḍiyūr, Trikkākkara and Trikkulaśēkharapuram can be seen.

However, the Kollam Era, also called the Malabar Era, is the most important and widely used Kerala's system of reckoning the date. As regards the inscriptions of the period of the Perumāḷ regime, this era has been found used only twice. In both the instances the expression, '*kollam tōnṛi āṇṭu*' (the year of the foundation of Kollam [Quilon]) is given. Obviously, it is the founding of Kollam as a prominent paṭṭaṇam or port town that the era commemorates. Its commencement date as 825 CE has been widely accepted by historians. Citing the mention of Koulam Māle, presumably the port town of Kollam, in Cosmas Indicopleustes' c. sixth century CE text, *The Christian Topography*, some historians seek to prove the existence of Kollam much before 825 CE. According to them, the basis of the era as the foundation of Kollam, therefore, makes no sense. MGS notes that Cosmas's Koulam Māle could be the Kōlamazhi (the port

* The Hijera Era is based on the Islamic lunar calendar, reckoned from 622 CE, the year in which prophet Muhammad and his followers left Mecca for Medina.

of Kōlam) of north Kerala (Kōlattunāṭu) and not Quilon. Another evidence to prove the existence of Kollam before 825 CE is present in the writings of Chinese traveller Ma Huan (c. 1380–1460 CE), who refers to mention of Kollam in the Chinese records of the Tang period (618–907 CE). MGS says that there is no evidence to show that the mention in the Tang records predates 825 CE and that it could be a mention dating after 825 CE.

Alternative explanations include linking the origins of the Kollam Era with the king Udyamarthanda (ninth century CE), who is said to have convened an assembly of astronomers and decided to commence the era; or to the exit of Cēramān Perumāḷ to Mecca (believed to have abdicated the throne and set on a pilgrimage to Mecca; identified with Rāma Kulaśēkhara of the Kollam Rameśvarattu koil inscription, who abdicated the throne in 1124 CE); or to the observance of Ōṇam; or to the ordaining by Śankarācārya are mere fabrications. The explanation associating the commencement of the era with the opening of the town of Kollam is well entrenched in historiography. A passage in the Tarisāppaḷḷi copper plates that states: '… *innagaram kaṇṭu nīrētta maruvan sapirīśo* …' makes it explicit that the market-town of Kollam was founded by Maruvan Sapīr Īśo, the leader of maṇigrāmam. However, the reckoning of the Kollam Era as 825 CE is a puzzle. K.V. Sarma says that it is a reckoning under the *kaṭapayādi* system with notations expressing astronomical constants and based on the solar calendar in which the year commences from Leo (*Simha*). Accordingly, the Kollam Era is reckoned from 15 August 825 CE.

VI

Agrarian Expansion and Trade (13th–16th centuries CE)

We have seen in the previous chapters, both agrarian expansion and exchange, including trade, were interrelated and continuous throughout the early historic period as well as during the consolidation of brāhmaṇa villages. Population grew steadily and under pressure agriculture exhausting the kari land expanded to the forested red soil tracts by turning them into household garden lands (*paṛampu purayiṭam*). Correspondingly, exchange networks also enlarged. Arabs, Nestorians, Jews and Chinese merchants, with their respective influential zones, coexisted. The earlier system of granting princely status to the head of the long-distance merchant body introduced in the case of maṇigrāmam and ancuvaṇṇam seems to have persisted. A charter of c. 1225 CE, namely the Vīra Rāghava copper plates, sanctions princely status to Iravi Kōrttān, then head of maṇigrāmam. It indicates that the market town of Mahodayapuram extended from the estuary (*aḻi*) of Koṭunkōḷūr to the gate (gōpuram) of the palace. Evidence points to the existence of full-fledged markets from the thirteenth century onwards. This chapter seeks to discuss the spread of agricultural settlements, the process of agricultural production, cropping patterns and exchange relations. It seeks to provide an outline of various other features of the period from the thirteenth to the sixteenth century CE. Several important developments such as the disappearance of the Perumāḷ rule, the ascendency of autonomous principalities, further expansion of agrarian settlements, increase in trade, proliferation of castes, emergence of Malayalam language and articulation of the region's cultural identity make this period distinct. The availability of several new types of source material in the form of travellers' accounts; royal records; archives of the Portuguese, the Dutch and the French; and household records of landlords, also adds to the discrete nature of the period.

Pattern of Settlement

Ecological uniqueness coupled with geographical peculiarities determined the pattern of settlement in the agrarian villages of Kerala. Since the landscape is undulating and dotted with hills and terraces, Kerala has its paddy fields scattered among depressions and garden lands confined to the red soil tracts. In almost all plots of land, irrespective of the altitude, water was available and enabled cultivation of multiple crops by every household. Individual agrarian households (*purayiṭams*) proliferated during the period, replicating the pre-existing pattern of the dispersed settlement. A dispersed settlement is a settlement in which houses are independent and isolated. The contemporary general pattern of housing in a village elsewhere in the subcontinent was a settlement made up of a cluster of houses congregated at a point or nucleated together, often around a water source. Kerala's pattern, a unique historical feature, was that of dispersed settlement with each house having a well of its own.

Basic occupational groups in all settlements consisted of agricultural workers, artisans and craftsmen. Various service personnel included the blacksmith, the goldsmith, the potter, and the washerman, the ritual-cum-medicine men, astrologers and so on. Coastal villages, where the main economic activity was fishing, had settlements exclusively of fishermen. Similarly, areas of coconut cultivation had īzhavas who were engaged in coconut plucking, toddy tapping, etc. A temple settlement was distinguished by the temple functionaries in addition to the basic occupational groups, while an urban settlement was characterised by various merchant groups who were members of the nagaram (town or marketing centre) organisation.

However, most of these villages were not self-sufficient in the strict sense because necessary occupational groups were not available in all settlements. For example, weavers were not present in all villages though cloth was a necessary item. Several needs converged on the marketing centres that integrated them. Such integrated larger zones were the nāṭus with marketing centres as their headquarters and nāṭuvāḻis as their political heads. Several nāṭus were satellites of a relatively old and great nāṭu that encompassed a major locality called a *swarūpam* (princely state). In fact, a nāṭu became a swarūpam by integrating a host of nāṭus that grew up as a result of economic growth, social expansion and wider exchange relations.

Expansion of Agriculture

Before discussing the expansion of agriculture, it is necessary to have an idea about the terrain and the soil. First, paddy fields were generally scattered among hills and hillocks. Second, the nature of the soil in many regions is usually sandy and loamy with very high sand content, resulting in rapid permeability of water. The roots of paddy do not go more than three to six inches deep and therefore cannot reach the underground water. So, cultivation was mostly dependent on the monsoon. Naturally, crops were often adversely affected by droughts. Third, the soil is infertile at various places. In fact, the colonial administrator Francis Buchanan reported in 1800 CE that the fields in north Malabar generally could produce only one crop. A Chinese text of the fourteenth century records that the paddy fields in southern Kerala gave poor yields and that rice was imported from Orissa every year. Finally, the forces of production remained outmoded and could not enhance the yield.

Agrarian expansion is best attested by the literary compositions of the period. Maṇipravāḷam texts refer to several new settlements of brāhmaṇas. Lakshmidasan's *Śukasandēśam*, a Sanskrit *kāvya* which is dated to the middle of the fourteenth century CE, describes a brāhmaṇa village named Veṅṅanāṭu, located in the territory of the Perumpaṭappu principality.

Uṇṇunīlisandeśam, which is dated to the last quarter of the fourteenth century CE, and *Śukasandēśam* mention the southern parts of Veṇpolināṭu as covered by forests. Some of the inscriptions and travellers' accounts also say the same, showing that there were still many areas not under the plough as yet. Foreigners often took the garden lands for forests. Friar Odoric of Pordenone observed that there were extensive forests to the north of Pantalāyinikollam. Actually, even from the Perumāḷ period, this area was full of agrarian villages with household garden lands of coconut and areca-nut palms interspersed by jack and mango trees. These villages were instrumental to the expansion of the agrarian society in Kerala.

Paddy

Cultivation of paddy was the major agricultural activity since paddy was the staple food of the people. This does not mean that cash crops were not so important. Our sources speak profusely about fields of sugarcane and extensive gardens of coconut and arecanut trees, and pepper gardens. There are also allusions to different fruit trees such as mango, jack, tamarind, etc. and vegetable plants of different varieties of onion, brinjal and yam. Plantains of various types were also cultivated. They are included in the food items to be supplied to the temple. Agrarian tracts of midland Kerala that yield two or three crops a year figure in almost all the śandeśakavyas as part of the description of the landscape between the messenger's starting point and destination. *Mūṣakavamśa Kāvya* mentions extensive paddy fields and highland tracts of cultivation forming part of the landscape of northern Kerala. Similarly, Keralōlpatti mentions the region of Pōḷanāṭu as rich in agriculture and as providing the resource base of trade and the income of the Sāmūtiris (Zamorins). Fields yielding two or three crops a year and the *punca* (summer crop or the third season crop of paddy) fields of Vaḷḷuvanāṭu in southern Malabar area are referred to in the literary texts of the period.

Accounts of foreign travellers to the coast of Malabar have some interesting references to the food crops of this part of the country. Several of them identify paddy as the most important food crop and rice as the staple food of the people. They notice that factors such as the nature of the terrain, texture of the soil, facilities for water management and so on, which determine the growth of paddy cultivation, varied from place to place in Kerala and, therefore, a uniform pattern never existed in agriculture. In the water-logged kari lands of Kuṭṭanāṭu water had to be drained out, whereas in the uplands of Vēnāṭu agriculture necessitated tank or canal irrigation. They mention a number of varieties of paddy, some of them indigenous and some others like *colan* from outside, reaching the market. Ma Huan (c. 1380–1460 CE), a Chinese traveller, who extensively visited the seaboards of southeast Asia and India during 1413 CE, 1421 CE and 1431 CE, had prepared notes on his visits and subsequently compiled them into a book titled *Ying-yai Shenglan* (1451 CE). In the work he notes, 'husked and unhusked rice heaped there for exchange'. Different types of millets, lentils and pulses, which complimented cultivation in the countryside, also reached the market. Chinese writings include them in the list of articles that were available in fairs and port towns. Sugarcane was grown in many fields and the jaggery industry flourished. Plantains were cultivated as part of post-harvest sub-crops in paddy fields. In addition to these there were several vegetables such as brinjal, cucumber, various gourds, yam, tubers, etc. all of which were grown mainly in the garden lands. Ma Huan reports to have seen them in markets among other items of sale, probably as seasonal crops brought for barter.

Cash Crops

Among the 'cash crops', pepper was perhaps the most important item and Malabar was known to foreigners as pepper country. For a pretty long time the Arabs enjoyed the near monopoly of the pepper trade with the port towns of Malabar. Arab merchants spread a lot of hearsay accounts of the pepper vine and its cultivation. According to most of their accounts pepper was a wild plant. Writing in the late twelfth century CE, Yaqut al-Hamawi (1179–1229 CE) says that pepper is a free plant without an owner and that it always bears fruit, both in summer and winter. Al Qazwini (1203–1283 CE) also repeats that there is no owner of pepper. Muhammad al-Idrisi's (c. 1100–1165 CE) account (*Tabula Rogeriana*; 1154 CE) seems to be more reliable and matter-of-fact. He records that pepper grows in Fandarina (the Arab rendering of Pantalāyinikollam), Māli or Kūlam Māli and Jurbattan (not identified convincingly but somewhere in the territory of Kōḷattunāṭu). At Jurbattan much pepper is said to have been cultivated on the mountains. About Kollam he says that five miles by sea from Kūlam Māli lies the island Māli, 'a large and beautiful spot, less hilly and covered with much vegetation. The pepper plant grows in this island as found nowhere else.' The Venetian traveller Marco Polo (1254–1324 CE) gives a beautiful account of his experiences in Asia during 1271–1295 CE in the *Book of the Marvels of the Worlds* or *The Travels of Marco Polo*. In this work, he makes mention of the pepper of Coilam (Kollam), Eli and Cannanur and of Malibar. He observes that pepper grows in abundance in Coilam and categorically states that the pepper trees are not wild but cultivated, being regularly planted and watered. Giovenni de' Marignolli (1338–1353 CE), a Catholic traveller from Europe, who passed through Malabar coast during his voyage to China in 1341 CE and back in 1347 CE, records that the whole world's pepper is produced at Kollam. Indigenous literary works also make mention of the cultivation of pepper in Kerala. Cardamom figures as an item of trade in the local market in addition to its demand from the foreign traders. Idrisi says that cardamom grows in the slopes of a mountain north of Fandarina.

The indigenous sources seldom mention the cultivation of ginger, though it is found included in the lists of articles of trade. Marco Polo includes ginger among other products of Malabar. Duarte Barbosa (c. 1480–1521 CE), a Portuguese mariner with experience of official assignments in Kochi, Kannur and Kozhikode, wrote the book called *Livro de Duarte Barbosa*

(*The Book of Duarte Baarbosa*) on his return to Lisbon in 1516. In this work, Barbosa speaks about different types of ginger cultivated in different parts of Kerala. According to him the territory of the Sāmūtiri and the northern part of Kōḷattunāṭu had ginger but that the Kozhikode variety was superior. Indigo was brought from Kollam as it was mostly cultivated in the southern parts of Kerala.

Turmeric was an extensively cultivated crop in the garden lands mainly for household consumption. Coconut and arecanut trees dominated the garden lands. They constituted a source of regular income in the erstwhile Puṛakiḻānāṭu between Kuṛumpoṛaināṭu and Kōḷattunāṭu. The *Daoyi Zhilue*, a Chinese text of the fourteenth century, describes that the coast of Malabar was flanked by coconut trees. By the sixteenth century, coconut had become an important item of trade. This is borne out by the fact that more than four hundred ships laden with coconuts left the coast of Malabar to different parts of the world. Fei Hsin (1436 CE) says that coconut was transported from the Malabar Coast among other articles such as pepper, fish and betel-nuts. Ma Huan notes that many wealthy people had coconut trees to the tune of a thousand or two thousand or three thousand as part of their property. He adds that the coconut tree was used for different domestic purposes. A steady increase in the cultivation of coconut trees on the Malabar Coast throughout the three centuries from the twelfth to the fifteenth is attested to by these contemporary records. From the regional sources we know that the coconut trees were grown not in monoculture plantations but in gardens where other trees like arecanut, mango and jack were also grown. *Śukasandēśam* mentions that pepper creepers were grown on the coconut trees. *Uṇṇunīlisandeśam* also refers to the multicultural garden where mango, jack, arecanut, plantains and sugarcane were grown. Arecanut was extensive in Kerala, as mentioned in the various literary compositions of the thirteenth and fourteenth centuries as well as the accounts of foreign travellers. Chinese travellers' accounts include betel-nut among the articles shipped from Malabar.

Forest Products

Forest areas were full of other resources as well. First, they provided timber for which there was demand from foreign merchants, especially the Arabs. Arab sources speak of the sappan wood or canella, also known as Brazil wood or red wood. According to Marco Polo, a great deal of the colomni was available at Kollam and it got its name from the country where it was grown. According to him, there were three varieties of sappan wood: colomni or colombino, ameri and seni. The name colomni or colombino is from kawlam or columbum. He also says that this variety was of very fine quality. The *Practica della mercatura* (or *Merchant's Handbook*) of Francesco Balducci Pegolotti (c. 1340 CE) records that the Brazil colomni or colombino was worth a sixth more than the *amen* (Polo's 'ameri'; *Caesalpinia sappan*) and three times as much as the *cini* (Polo's 'seni'; *Tetrameles nudiflora*). Rosewood, teak and cini were of great demand in foreign countries where teak and cini of Malabar were famous for ship-building and the term cini was popularised by Arabs who dealt with it. Ibn Battuta (1304–1369 CE) gives an account of the ship-building activities at the major Chinese port Zaitun (now known as Quanzhou) in great detail.

The Western Ghats was famous for its aromatic woods such as aloe and sandal, which were used for ritual purposes in temples and households of Kerala, and were in great demand as items of overseas trade as well. In the Tiruvalla copper plates there is a reference to the mutual exchange rate among aloe wood, sandalwood and paddy. It is said that a given measure of paddy was equal to 20 kāṇams of sandalwood or 10 kāṇams of aloe. Several other items such as honey, ivory and a number of medicinal herbs were also found in markets, obviously collected and brought by forest-dwellers.

In several areas on the coastal strip the fields are lower than the sea level. So, when the tide ebbs, it fills the fields with sea water. This facilitates salt panning, which was an important economic activity of the coastal regions, probably from ancient times. Salt panning in certain areas are reported directly or indirectly in some inscriptions pertaining to this period. Kollur Maṭham plates refer to the income from the areas of the salt-makers exacted by way of salt. Included among several rights and privileges to the merchant Iravi Kōrttān, as mentioned in the Vīra Rāghava copper plates, is the monopoly to make salt in Koṭunkōḷūr. Seawater was the only source of salt for the southern parts of the country and so the salt industry flourished in several places on coastal areas, until salt was declared a contraband article by British colonists. This age-old industry in Kerala was instrumental in developing exchange centres on the coast and it is reflected even to this day in a large number of place names along the coast—such as with suffixes like uppalam, paṭanna and kaḻi—that suggest that they were areas of brine water, salt panning or storing.

Process of Agricultural Production

Our sources are virtually silent about the process of agricultural production. What is possible in such a situation is to extend and extrapolate the facts of the immediately preceding and succeeding phases to the period under discussion. Judging from the inscriptions of the ninth to the twelfth centuries CE, fertile fields may have generally yielded two crops annually, the first crop being in Kanni (September–October) and the second in Makaram (January–February). A third crop, punca, was also raised in areas where water was available during the summer. The records of the seventeenth to the nineteenth century CE also make statements about the crops in the same way and so we can surmise that the pattern of the earlier phase continued in the period under study and even later. Between the major crops some interim crops were raised which included a variety of gingelly (*vayaleḷḷu*). Different texts like *Uṇṇiyāṭicaritam* and *Uṇṇunīlisandēśam* present different lists of seeds and some of the names are only local variations of one and the same variety. This also continued in the following centuries, as shown by the accounts of Buchanan, who visited the country in the year

1800 CE. According to Buchanan's description of Malabar, the mountain cultivation began in the month of March–April and ended with harvest in August–September. The parambu lands yielded a good crop only once in five years or so and therefore there was the necessity of shifting the field every year. Millets, lentils and pulses were also sown. The cultivation of sugarcane in the southern parts of Malabar and central Tiruvitāmkur is known from literary texts. Thus, the low-lying fields were utilised for both food crops and cash crops. Several varieties of paddy such as Kuṛuva, Cennel, Ponkāḷi, Ānakkōṭan, Cōḻian, Kāṭan, Mōṭan and Vīravittan are mentioned in the literary texts. During this period varities that would grow well on hill tracts, low-lying fields and other such conditions were developed. Different texts present different lists of seeds and some of the names are only local variations of one and the same variety.

The aforementioned pattern of agriculture implies a relatively improved technology and systematised knowledge about the climate, nature of soil and management of water resources. Agricultural tools and implements which were used in different parts of Kerala are mentioned in the maṇipravāḷam works, along with the articles which were exhibited for sale in the country-markets. The anonymous work *Anantapuravaṛṇnam*, attributed to the thirteenth or fourteenth century, mentions *tūmpa* (spade) and *arivai* (sickle). Damodara Cākkiyār's *Uṇṇiyāṭicaritam*, roughly belonging to the same period or slightly later, refers to *arivāḷ* (sickle) and also *muppalli* (a three-pronged fork used for up-turning the soil). In fact, the field was ploughed several times for each crop. Generally the plough-share was 6 to 8 inches long. Draught animals such as oxen and buffaloes were used for drawing the plough system. Transplantation of seed was of course kṇown, but in suitable places seeds were directly sown as well.

According to the geographical location and nature of the soil, water management raised various problems. In some places like Nāncināṭu, under the rulers of Vēṇāṭu, water had to be channelled from the rivers by means of sluices. Certain other places with waterlogged areas and wetlands of coastal tracts needed the water to be drained. Several inscriptions of Vēṇāṭu rulers of the fourteenth and fifteenth centuries mention channelling water to the paddy fields of Nāncināṭu through direct and indirect methods. Practices of building bunds and arresting water into small reservoirs for irrigating the fields were in vogue at least from the seventh century CE onwards. Such simple irrigation systems had existed in the eastern fringes of the Ēṛanāṭu taluk, as the evidence at Karulayi near Nilambur shows. A Tamil brāhmi label inscription of the sixth to seventh century characters informs about the existence of a *nīraṇa* (a small check dam) at Karulayi. Several place names with *kuḷam* (tank) as prefix or suffix suggest that there were human-made sources of water near agricultural fields, showing that tank irrigation was widespread in Kerala during this period.

Manuring was known and it was mainly of two kinds: green leaf and cow dung. Apparently, green leaf manure was considered very important. In land deeds, there are references to three types of lands, namely, *nilam* (fields), purayiṭam (house sites) and *kāṭu* (forest). Sometimes, kāṭu is qualified as belonging to the paddy field by the expression, '*atinoḷḷa kāṭum*'. These patches of forests were meant as the source of green leaf as manure to the nilams and purayiṭams. Virgin forests (*kanyāvanam*) also existed around the fields, as described in the literary texts.

Agriculture was dependent on natural facilities and supernatural beings rather than on technology. A whole system of beliefs, customs, practices, rites and rituals relating to agriculture existed. Knowledge of seasons was dependent on astronomy, which enabled prediction of seasonal changes. It gave rise to astrology and various methods of fortune-telling as well. As experts predicting the coming of monsoons and changes in climate, based on movements of the sun, the moon, etc., astrologers became indispensable in every village. In effect, the socio-cultural aspects of the village and the economic life thereof were agrarian in character.

Agrarian Relations

As mentioned earlier, agrarian relations and details of agricultural production do not figure as an item of any importance in the native literary sources. Travellers' accounts of Kerala contain some information about the cultivation of spices but many of them are mixed with hearsay evidence, fables and superstitions. Documents that speak of the various aspects of the agrarian system of the time are inscriptions of territorial rulers and family records of royal houses and local chiefs. Inscriptions pertaining to this period are extremely rare in central and northern parts of Kerala. They continued to be recorded on stone and copper in the territory under the rulers of Vēṇāṭu. Most of these epigraphs belong to the regions beyond the Western Ghats, and the agrarian practices of these regions differed a lot from those in Kerala. However, there are a few records that do furnish interesting information about the agricultural community in Vēṇāṭu. It is from these that we reconstruct the agrarian relations, but with many gaps. Family records, nevertheless, provide more details and these go a long way in filling the gaps in the inscriptional records. The history of the agrarian relations is attempted here within such limitations.

The available records show that the process of agricultural production hardly underwent any change immediately after the disappearance of the Cēras (Perumāḷs) in 1124 CE. Tools and implements remained more or less the same as in the preceding centuries. Facilities of water management and manuring also did not change much. Bonded labourers who were called *āḷ* provided the required agricultural labour for both food and cash crops. In the epigraphical sources, the āḷ labourers are always found attached to the arable lands, and in the contexts of transactions of land these labourers are also transferred along with the land. This seems to imply that they were the main source of agricultural labour. Theoretically they had no right over what they produced, but they seem to have been endowed with minimum requirements by the owner or holder of the land to which they were attached. Apparently, the āḷ workers received, in addition to the usual food, clothing, etc., some other articles such as grains and vegetables. It is not improbable that they raised some short-term crops like tubers and vegetables in the surroundings of their dwelling places for their own use. The presence of tubers and vegetables in the market places for exchange for articles of daily consumption can be explained only in this way. The āḷ groups consisted of pulayas, paṛayas, kaṇakkas, īzhavas and cānṛār who were engaged in various types of hard manual labour.

The āḷ bonded men produced food and cash crops for cultivators who were either the owners themselves or the *kuṭiyan* (tenants). Tenants, who received land in lease from the owners of land, paid for it a share of their produce which was known as *mēlvāram*, mēloṭi or pāṭṭam. When temple was the de jure owner of the land, the leaseholder was responsible for remitting dues for specified rituals and other expenses in the temple. Generally, the landed property of the temples was managed by the brāhmaṇas who were members of the governing body of the temples. In this period several brāhmaṇas received temple land as simple lease and acted as kārāḷar of the temples. Temple functionaries such as the priests, secretaries, drummers, garland-makers, sweepers, etc. received landed property on lease as service tenure called *virutti* or jīvitam for the services rendered by them. Various occupational groups such as the *jimiya* (oil mongers), kalavāṇiyan (potters), etc., who were settled in the purayiṭams owned by the temple were also responsible for remitting provisions to the temple.

Properties of brāhmaṇas and temples tended to become *sankētams* (rendezvous), already known from the preceding centuries. The institution of *sankētam* (enclaves) acquired much popularity during this period and most of the temples became *sankētams*. There were two kinds of them, viz., those instituted by the brāhmaṇa landowners and those established by the rulers as a sign of their devotion to gods and brāhmaṇas. Both were governed by brāhmaṇa landowners who enjoyed great powers within their limits. Many *sankētams* were governed by an assembly called *yogam*. Protection of the property of the *sankētam* was entrusted with the local warrior groups that existed as *nūttukkūṭṭam* (units in hundred) with varying strength, such as the aṛunūṟṟuvar of Vēṇāṭu and the munnūṟṟuvar of Nanruḻaināṭu. They seem to have continued for some time, as shown by a few inscriptions of Tiruvitāmkur. Later, in the fourteenth century CE, they seem to have been replaced by bodies like *ariśippaṭijanam*, *akampaṭijanam* and *cangātam* (armed companions of honour). They were entitled to receive a share of the produce as rakṣābhōga or *kāvalpalam* (protection fee). In the southern parts there were *manuṣyam* contingents, which consisted of the territorial warrior groups, the employees and the officials of the temple as shown by some of the Tiruvitāmkur inscriptions.

Apart from the individual owners and the institutions of the temple, the ruling houses and local chiefs too owned land in their respective areas. Right from the period of Perumāḷs of Mahodayapuram several of these territorial chiefdoms had already branched off to kūṛu lineages. Thus we hear about the elder and younger kūṛus of the ruling family of Vēṇāṭu as early as c. 849 CE. Similarly, the Kuṛumpoṛaināṭu and Puṛakiḻānāṭu chieftains also had at least two positions (sthānams): mūttakūṛu and ilankūṛu. Generally, the kūṛu lineages were stationed at different places in their jurisdiction, probably to receive the dues from their tenants in their locality itself. This lineage system obviated the burden of transportation of dues in kind to distant places in the absence of an efficient transport infrastructure. Some of the kūṛu branches of the territorial ruling houses had their own militia, as shown by their inscriptions. Each head of the ruling family was entitled to a share of the produce from the cultivators in addition to his share as rent from the cērikkal property. This was over and above the rent and it was realised along with the dues to the immediate landlord. The royal share or the king's customary due was known as *kōmuṛaipāṭu*, as seen in the records of the Vēṇāṭu rulers. It is interesting to note that the later records of the Sāmūtiris of Kozhikode contain a list of income to the ruler from the localities under their chiefs and this list has no item from agricultural produce. The territorial chiefs engaged their own men like the hundred organisations, such as munnūṟṟuvar and the eḻunūṟṟuvar. Later, this duty was taken up by the cangātam, akampaṭijanam or *lōkar* (armed fighters).

During the period, the agrarian order and the formation of economic ties were gradually becoming more and more complex with the emergence of new intermediaries. Old time regulations (kaccams) were replaced by new local customary laws and precedents which were known variously as *deśamaryāda* (local custom), *kīḻmaryāda* (precedence) and *kīḻiyakkam* (precedence). Most of the tenurial forms of the Perumāḷ regime did continue to persist and some of them such as the simple lease tenure and lease-cum-mortgage tenure became more prominent. As per the lease-cum-mortgage type of transaction, the leaseholder pays a lump sum in cash as *artham* (cash security) to the land owners in order to hold the land for cultivation. Landlords received a share of the produce after deducting the interest on the artham amount. It can be observed that the transaction usually took place between traditional landlords and the newly-growing intermediaries, like those who could expand their leaseholds through money lending against land mortgages. There was a steady increase in the number of lease-cum-mortgage transaction as a deal quite convenient to landlords as well as leaseholders. While the owner retained his rights over the land, he received a cash amount in the beginning and realised a regular income as rent as long as the deal was in force. In his turn the leaseholder got the interest of the lump sum as deducted from the rent. He could manage the land more effectively and raise profit. Involvement of money and interest on it are new features of this kind of deal which seems to indicate the ascendency of a moneyed intermediary group in the society.

Land relations in Kerala during twelfth to fifteenth centuries showed certain important changes such as increase of intermediaries as temporary landholders, increase in the role of money in obtaining leaseholds and transmutation of rent into cash. A significant development in land system was the rise of the intermediaries' *kuḻikkāṇam* right on the lease land, which gave them incentives for extension of agriculture in the lease land. Kuḻikkāṇam was the right to the long-yielding crops like coconut and arecanut trees that the leaseholders planted. This applied more to the new trees grown in the paṟampu lands and new plots of land brought under cultivation there. Under kuḻikkāṇam tenure, the share of produce for the *janmi* (landlords) was reduced because he had to compensate the cost incurred by the leaseholder for the improvement of land and crop. However, these changes were taking place within the customary law or kīḻmaryāda or *kīḻkaṭa* which ensured the old ties of dependence and service obligations. Kīḻmaryāda never allowed the sale of land leading to de facto alienation of the janmam right of the janmi, which retained the basic structure of the traditional agrarian relations without change. A Maṇalikkara inscription dated 1235 CE from the kingdom of Vēṇāṭu prescribes the dues to be paid by the tenants for each harvest every year and stipulates that in case of a natural failure of the crop, the dues could be waved.

Certain facts emerge from the foregoing discussion on the expansion of agrarian society in Kerala during this period. Production of food crops was extended to new areas after reclaiming forests in the eastern interior hill tracts and the waterlogged kari lands along the wetland and coastal areas. Simultaneously, there was an unprecedented growth in population. They consisted of the ruling families with their branches placed at different centres in their jurisdiction, their retainers, landed intermediaries, ritualists, artisanal/occupational groups, medicine-men and tradesmen. Those involved in the production of food grains were the kuṭi (settlers) and the āḷ (enslaved or bonded labourers). Inscriptions, literary texts and accounts of foreign travellers show that the non-cultivating groups and intermediaries had considerably increased by that time. There was, indeed, a corresponding growth of productivity and surplus as well. However, it should be noted that landlords and rich intermediaries owed the surplus to the system of exploitative expropriation of the poor tillers.

Jāti System

Jāti means 'that which one is born in' (*jāyatē asmin iti*), presupposing a trans-familial identity of relative status recognised by one's own families. Its widely used equivalent English word 'caste', adapted from the Portuguese '*casta*', is inappropriate because it approximates the meaning of jāti to a mere breed. Structurally, the jāti consisted of two sets of binaries viz., the pure × impure and the higher × lower, which each jāti sustained as the core of its identity. This became institutionalised with the integration of local descent groups as hereditary occupation groups in the wake of the reclamation of deltas for rice cultivation. Jāti came up as the most atrocious institution of social disciplining for exploitation of labour and its products.

It has been argued in the studies of Rajan Gurukkal that the historical context of the incidence of jāti was that of the opening up of deltas for agriculture, integration of agro-pastoral descent groups into hereditary specialists of occupational identity, and formation of stratified relations of production transcending kin labour. According to Gurukkal, it appears that the historically evolved coercive power of the seigniorial control had enabled integration of the agro-pastoral descent groups into full-time specialised labourers of hereditary identity, as required by the technology of iron plough which was inevitable for agriculture in the deltas. The emergence of hereditary occupation groups and promulgation of śāstraic norms must have been processes of mutuality and concurrence. This was the context of the jāti institution of coercive control and seigniorial jurisdiction over the labouring body for ideologically turning it into the impure, and hence inferior, in terms of the śāstraic norms, or as ordained by the brāhmaṇas in terms of purity × pollution. Organisational constituents of the jāti institution, already present in the *varṇa*-structured community (the primordial social division of functions without hereditary obligation, which subsequently turned into a rigid framework of four-fold social stratification ordering jātis into a hierarchy), seem to have gradually started acting as fetters on artisans, crafts-folk and tillers. Their *de facto* control was becoming increasingly inevitable in the wake of expansion of agriculture into the deltas.

Temple inscriptions give us some idea about the formation of the jāti system in Kerala. We have already discussed in Chapter Four, the various temple functionaries and their service tenures based on the system of rewards in land and land rights. Service tenure in land and land rights made the temple servants hereditary service personnel. However, there is no evidence to show that they had become endogamous jātis during the Perumāḷ regime. Some of them seem to have become jātis by the thirteenth century CE. For instance, the potuvāḷ and vāriyar are the two most important functional categories in the non-brāhmaṇa order, of which the first literally meant the common man (*madhyastha*) between the custodians of the temple and the devotees for all their transactions with the temple, and hence acted as the secretary of the temple, becoming a jāti. As a functionary shouldering managerial and executive responsibility, the potuvāḷ was relatively close to the brāhmaṇas and received virutti land as reward for his service to the temple. Evidently, the process was that of the turning of the service into hereditary occupation for retaining its reward in the form of land tenure; i.e., that occupational groups began being accommodated as endogamous jātis in the twelfth century CE. As groups of hereditary professions with economic stability, ritual status as the temple secretary and ranking due to close interaction with the brāhmaṇas, they could distance themselves from others through rules of intermarriage and interdining in order to constitute themselves into endogamous jātis.

Similarly, the drummers, dancers and musicians of the temple, paid through service tenure, have constituted themselves into separate jātis through the same process of becoming hereditary professionals first. Drummers of the temple are addressed in the inscriptions as *koṭṭikaḷ* or *uvaccakaḷ*, which as such have not survived as jāti names. Temple dancers, mentioned in the epigraphs as *cākkaimār* (male dancers) and *naññaimār* (dancing girls), became a jāti, namely cākkiyār, with the female members addressed by the old name, naññyar. These jātis are generally called the temple jātis (*ampalavāsis*) or the *antarāḷa* jātis, i.e., the jātis between the brāhmaṇas and the non-brāhmaṇas just below. It was convenient for the temple to make the services hereditary, for it ensured stability of service. Likewise, it was an added incentive for the family of the service personnel, for it brought stability of landed property through service tenure.

It is the same principle of service stability, material incentives and status that holds good in the case of others such as the merchants (vāṇiyar) and craftsmen/artisan groups (*kammāḷar*) too, whose trades became hereditary and the name of the trade became the jāti name. Inscriptions refer to groups such as taccar (carpenters), kollar (blacksmiths), kalavāṇiyar (potters), *vāṇiyar* (oil mongers) and vaṇṇār (washermen) as the main occupational groups of hereditary identity. In fact, as is evident from copper plate inscriptions, these essential occupational groups were brought and settled along the fringes of the villages with the obligation to render services to the temple as well as the landlords. Their reward was in the form of a land tenure (*kuṭiyāimai*), providing the entitlement to settle down in a plot of land for their unfailing services and at the pleasure of the landed. These people were caught up in an inescapable trap of immobility and functional obligations. At the slum of the bottom were the servile group (aṭiyāḷar) of varying names such as i͟lavas, pulayas and ceṛumas. Removed from the mainstream as untouchables, they formed the actual tillers, the most exploited group fated to be in perpetual servitude (*aṭiyāymai*). Attached to agricultural lands, they were transacted along with land as goods or livestock, as already mentioned in this book.

Thus service tenure that started during the ninth to tenth centuries CE was responsible for turning families of service personnel into hereditary occupational groups and subsequently into endogamous jātis. A higher service-tenement meant better economic status and proximity to the managers of the temple-centred village, the brāhmaṇas, implying a higher ritual status. Such a system of status differentiation in terms of economic as well as ritual value was instrumental to the naming of the hereditary occupational groups with the occupational name as a means of distinction. Subsequently, the occupational name became the name of an endogamous jāti integrated to the social hierarchy. With the primary producers at the base, the temple signified a gamut of social relations into which the principles of jāti were introduced for the first time in a full-fledged form by the eleventh century CE. Formation of a hierarchy was a natural consequence of the system of social differentiation, based as it was on varying levels of ritual status positions in the orbits around the brāhmaṇas. Those enjoying these varied entitlements in the hierarchical order seem to have begun the practice of undertaking their vocations on a hereditary basis, primarily for retaining the land rights as their family property.

Its extension into non-brāhmaṇa villages, and even to market towns, is attested by records. It was this system of service-tenure under the king and the local rulers, which gave rise to hereditary offices, generating jātis and sub-jātis with economy and royalty as determinants of status hierarchy. In short, jāti appeared as an institutional manifestation in the hierarchically-structured agrarian society in which services were paid for in the form of land rights. Other institutional formations like service tenements both in the domains of the temple and the king, crystallised hereditary occupations into jāti hierarchy. It is the aggregate of values and passions of the social formation. Naturally, the culture and ideological structures of the period reflected it. These made jātis a determinant force of political authority, enabling them to take precedence over the ruling power.

Rewarded under land tenure, the personnel in service to the king and local chieftains became hereditary for stability of service as well as permanence of family landholding. Exactly as in the case of the temple service, the names of hereditary offices in the royal and chiefly services became jāti names of varying status, as determined by their socio-economic and politico-cultural importance, as several instances from the Kerala region demonstrate. This is attested by inscriptions of twelfth to fourteenth centuries CE. The most significant offices in the royal and chiefly services were that of the warrior-chief (*paṭai nair* or subsequently *kuṛup* and *paṇikkar*) and of the supervisory accountant (*mēnon*). Nair was a generic term for headship, but the nair who signified the office of the warrior chief was of great importance not only politically but also economically. This is because the nair signified the largest leaseholder (kārāḷar) group. Most of the temple lands (dēvasvam), the individual brāhmaṇa holdings (brahmasvam), royal lands and chiefly holdings were leased out to nair families. Largest among intermediaries in land, with the entailing privileges of the nobility, the nair matrilineal families provided women for the nampūtiri brāhmaṇas under *sambandham* (a social arrangement for connubial relationship without being bound by any liability), which helped them acquire better status, although, they were considered part of the śudra varṇa.

Proliferation of jātis had been an ongoing process ever since jāti became the principal basis of identity for occupational groups and service personnel claiming socio-cultural distinction in terms of their relations to the three streams: brahmasvam and dēvasvam, the nāṭuvāḻi and the swarūpam. Every functionary in the service of the king, local ruler, the temple and the brāhmaṇa landlord was rewarded through land tenure. This turned the service hereditary under the incentive for the family to retain the land. As far as the land system was concerned, the practice in its turn ensured stability about supply of the workforce. Illustrating the historical experience of the Tamil south including Kerala, it can be argued that the proliferation of jātis happened as a result of the service tenure under the three seigniorial streams represented by the king, the chieftain and the landed temple–Brāhmaṇa combine.

Some of the personnel in royal service of swarūpams, who eventually became local chieftains, distinguished themselves from the rest of the nairs by adopting a kshatriya title such as 'vaṛma'. Likewise, the warrior-heads in the royal service called paṇikkar, who acquired land control through service tenure, distinguished themselves from the nair and became an endogamous jāti. In the same way, the office of the supervisory accountant, mēnon, was in the service of the ruling aristocracy as well as nampūtiri landlords, distinguished from the nair, and became an endogamous jāti of land control, socio-political power and ritual status. Each jāti, depending upon the extent of land control and the status of the service (the king, the temple and the brāhmaṇa household), improvised dining conventions and marriage rules as strategies of status-building. This was rampant during the thirteenth to sixteenth centuries CE.

Proliferation of jātis within the brāhmaṇa varṇa was extensive all over the subcontinent during the thirteenth to sixteenth centuries CE. An interesting feature in the case of the Kerala region was internal divisiveness within the nampūtiri caste under the brāhmaṇa varṇa. There emerged many *upajātis* (subcaste) and was an ongoing process throughout the seventeenth to eighteenth centuries CE. Internal divisiveness among the nampūtiris was based on the difference in wealth, the ritual status, Vedic and śāstraic tradition of the families, and the history of the household. Such traditionally contingent attributes entrenched the status of the families. In most cases the status of the household became the determinant of the status of the inmates there. Nampūtiris of vedic tradition with big land control who distinguished themselves as *bhaṭṭatiri*, later vacillated between *āḍhya* (the most superior in status and ranking) and *āsya* (the inferior). This internal divisiveness among the nampūtiri brāhmaṇas was almost to the extent of constituting each as a separate jāti within the jāti and forming a hierarchy of themselves.

In fact, since jātis were occupational identities, those who were in the service of the larger society would automatically belong to one or the other of the occupational jātis. People outside specific service tenures were artisans, craftsmen, traders and other occupation groups, and they constituted the agrarian society and hence the core of the jāti system. Further, when economic differentiation increases there happens internal divisiveness in every jāti, provided it is susceptible to growth in terms of economic and non-economic resources. A significant point to be noted here is that the dynamic of jāti exclusiveness preventing accommodation of those pursuing occupations other than that which is traditionally given was an extraneous pressure on them to form themselves into endogamous jātis. Punthanam Namputiri's *Jnānappāna* of c. eighteenth century CE gives us an idea about the zeal of jāti differentiation and distinction among the people above the oppressed. This zeal of each jāti to boast its status as 'far above the lower though just below the higher,' has been the passion for distinction that sustained the jāti system, which helped the oppressive productive relations to remain as well-entrenched fetters.

Overland Trade Relations

Traditional exchange of goods for goods persisted as part of regular and seasonal fairs, where bargaining was the method of procurement. Hawkers and peddlers gathered at such places and engaged in higgling-haggling with the local people, as mentioned in the *Anantapuravarṇanam.* All sorts of people including the lower sections of society participated in the local exchange activities. Articles thus bartered were largely items of immediate consumption like rice, paddy, millets, vegetables, plantains, coconut oil, fish, etc. Formal profit-oriented transactions of goods using money as means of payment and measure of value became entrenched gradually during this period. This form of exchange is distinguished as trade and it co-existed with other forms of exchange even in villages. *Uṇṇiccirutevicaritam* describes the town of Ayanarcira as a local commercial centre in the Vaḷḷuvanāṭu region. *Uṇṇunīlisandeśam* refers to the flourishing market at Kariyanāṭu near Tiruvalla.

Regular demand for spices and various other artefacts of Kerala with a long history of exchange had already been part of a large network of overland as well as overseas trade. Merchant bodies of the previous regime, figuring in the epigraphs of the ninth to twelfth century period, such as ancuvaṇṇam, maṇigrāmam, nānādeśikaḷ, nārpatteṇṇāyiravar, patineṇbhumi, tiśai āyirattu ainnurruvar and vaḷanciyar continued their activities, cutting across the boundaries of the various political regions of south India. Maṇigrāmam is mentioned in the grant of Vīra Rāghava

(c. 1225 CE) along with its leader Iravi Kōrttān who held the monopoly of trade in Koṭunkōḷūr. Some of these bodies figure in the inscriptions and literary texts of the period. They find mention in a literary text called *Payyannurpāṭṭu* which is an oral tradition that belongs to this period. During the period, Tamil brāhmaṇas actively participated in trade in the regions of Tamil Nadu and Kerala. They brought rice, cotton and silk, fabrics, etc. to Kerala and returned with large quantity of spices, especially pepper. This trade relation continued up to about 1520 CE.

Several merchants from different parts of Kerala figure in a number of Cōḻa inscriptions as devotees making donations to various temples in the Cōḻa territory. A record dated 1249–50 CE (Saka 1172) refers to a certain Kanṭan Çāntirayya Ceṭṭiyār of Pantalāyinikollam, who constructed a Śanivāramanḍapam in the temple of Karumāṇikka Āḷwār at Viśakhapaṭṭinam, also known as Kulottungacōḷapaṭṭinam. Some sort of diversification in trading activities due to specialisation in trade has been noted as an important development in the contemporary south Indian trades. Separate groups of vāṇiya (oil mongers) and kalavāṇiya (pot merchants) are mentioned in the Kollur Maṭham plates.

There are many references in the Cōḻa inscriptions of the thirteenth and fourteenth centuries to a special group of horse-dealers called *kutiraiccettis* who are said to come from the Malaināṭu. They figure prominently in the inscriptions of Tanjavur, Tirucciṛappaḷḷi and South Arcot districts. Apparently, they imported horses from foreign countries like Arabia and supplied them to the south Indian princes and nobles. Horse trade is mentioned as a profitable enterprise for Kerala merchants in *Uṇṇiyaccīcaritam*. A spurt in the horse trade in these parts of the country is partly explained by the political developments in the south Indian territories which was characterised by constant warfare and rivalry among the regional and local powers. The princes in Kerala also maintained a cavalry, as alluded to by *Uṇṇiyaccīcaritam*. The Persian historian Wassaf al-Hadrat (1299–1323 CE) informs us that the price of each horse was fixed at 220 dīnār of red gold on condition that if any horse should happen to die *en route* the value of them should be paid from the royal treasury. Wassaf also gives the total value of the annual import of trade in horse as 10,000 animals worth, i.e., twenty-two lakhs of dīnārs of red gold. According to Wassaf, the imported horses, most strong, swift, fresh and active, become weak, slow, useless and stupid within a short time due to the wrong type of feeding and other treatment. Hence the necessity of getting new horses annually. Marco Polo also was of the same opinion, that the people of south India did not know how to take care of horses. Large amount of wealth acquired by those who were involved in the profitable long-distance overland trade is reflected in their donations to the distant regional centres in the form of structural buildings, large numbers of cattle, landed property and a big amount of money.

Besides luxury articles and food grains considerable amount of metals, medicinal herbs, silk cloths and other fabrics were brought to Kerala. Several merchants hailing from the regions of Tamil Nadu, Karnataka, Konkan, Andhra, Kalinga (Orissa), Māḷava (Ujjain) and Venga (Bengal) reached the interior markets of Kerala. These markets were situated mostly on the traditional trade routes and they were centres of operation of the long-distance trading groups. The rise and growth of towns and markets in the new areas and their linkages with the itinerant traders clearly shows that new areas of production were integrated with the wider networks of intraregional and interregional transactions. Commercial contacts of Kerala with the north were established not only by land but also by the sea. Blessed with a long coastline, Kerala was always accessible by coastal navigation. Therefore, the inland trade between Kerala and the regions beyond the Western Ghats and the Vindhyan ranges depended on sea routes as well, which were cheaper than the land routes.

Overseas Trade Relations

For a fairly long period, navigation in the Arabian Sea was along the coast. It was tedious, time-consuming and expensive. Malabar is referred to by all the Arab writers as the country of pepper.

As their knowledge of the coastal cities of India gradually increased, they started calling the sea-board country as Malibar, the land of Mall—a term they used synonymously with pepper and land because pepper was the chief article of their trade. It is from Idrisi of the twelfth century that we hear for the first time Malibar. Ibn Battuta calls it Mulaybar and states that it is the pepper country. He adds that the country extends for two months' journey along the coast from Sandabur (Chandrapur in Goa) to Kawlam (Kollam). AI-Qazwini (1203–1283) informs us that many people are benefited by pepper trade and that the Franks carry pepper in the Sea of Syria to the farthest west. According to the same authority there were pepper plantations in the country and pepper was shipped from one end of the east, i.e., from the seaboards of southern India, to the other end of the west, i.e., the Mediterranean and Europe.

Large amount of spices including pepper, ginger, cardamom, cinnabar and malabathrum, spikenard, etc. were exported from the ports of Malabar. According to Garcia da Orta, a Portuguese apothecary who had stayed at Calicut for quite a long time, Malacca has pepper which was not so good and therefore there was great demand for the pepper of Malabar. Cardamom was known to Arabian physicians and merchants. This item was grown in the area between Kozhikode and Kannur. The trade mechanism of the Arabs is not known from the geographers' accounts except for some stray references to the quality test of the pepper or to some groups involved in the spice trade. Arab traders must have been able to get the support of a locally-stationed group which had access to the regions of pepper and also to the cultivators. Sulaiman al-Tajir (ninth century CE) reported that he had never known anyone in Hind or in China who had embraced Islam. Idrisi in the twelfth century says that in all the countries of Hind and Sind there were Muslims. Ibn Battuta speaks of several mosques on the coast of Malabar from the Hill (Elimala) to Kawlam (Kollam). He refers to the *qazis* (judge) and *khatibs* (prayer leader) of those mosques who were foreigners from places like Oman, Mogoishu (Zanzibar Coast of East Africa) and Baghdad. These statements of the Arab geographers and travellers suggest that Arab trade relations had involved networking with local people, leading to the formation of Islamic communities. Kinship building through local spouses must have been fundamental to the relations between Arab traders and local people.

Chinese Trade Relations

In historiography, the four centuries between the decline of the Perumāḷs of Mahōdayapuram in about 1125 CE and the advent of Europeans on the coast of Malabar in 1498 remains less illumined compared to the preceding and succeeding periods. Raghava Varier's studies shed light on the history of Chinese trade relations with Kerala and unveil how influential they were in the economy, technology and culture. His studies percolate relatively recent scholarly observations based on corroboration of Chinese travelogues with the archaeology of Chinese ceramics. Varier provides a fresh assessment of the extent of Chinese influence on contemporary Kerala by examining the distributive pattern of their porcelain goods.

We understand various aspects of Chinese trade relations from the accounts of travellers and seamen of the period between the thirteenth and fifteenth centuries CE. Chou-ju-kua, a Chinese inspector of foreign trade, who compiled his work *Chu-fan-Chi* (c. 1225 CE) mentions porcelain goods as having been quite important among the items of trade with Ceylon and Malabar. Accounts of Marco Polo (1254–1324 CE) provide details of the goods the traders brought to and shipped from the Malabar coast. He mentions about his visit to the ports of Quilon, Calicut and Eli, and has made valuable observations regarding the economic life of the people, their artefacts and techniques of production. At the port of Zaitun, Marco Polo records seeing several Chinese ships from Malabar, laden with 5000 to 6000 baskets of pepper in each of them. In addition to pepper, the Chinese traders shipped a fine type of cotton fabric (*kacca*) available at Calicut in exchange of silk, gold, silver, copper, ceramics, clove, spikenard, etc. They brought such items to Quilon and carried ginger and indigo from there.

Ibn Battuta's accounts bear testimony to the bulk of trade at Calicut where he reports to have seen thirteen Chinese ships at the harbour during his brief sojourn. Battuta mentions huge Chinese ships with six hundred sailors and four hundred warriors on board in the Chinese Sea (now, South China sea). He records that Chinese sailors frequented the ports of Quilon, Calicut and Eli. He mentions coconut, areca-nut, pepper and banana as the products of these ports of Malabar. According to him, those ships that intended to pass the monsoon in India alone used to go to Fandarina.

Early in the fifteenth century, Cheng Ho, the great Chinese navigator started on a series of expeditions to the countries of the south sea and to India, Persia, Arabia, and as far as the east African coast. Cheng Ho's ships were so large, towering and majestic that none could rival them, as stated by Gong Zhen who had the experience of traveling with him. He reports that Chinese authorities were keen in establishing political, cultural and trade relations with the countries they visited. Cheng Ho's first expedition reached Calicut in 1407, after anchoring at Ceylon for a few days. His second expedition reached Quilon, Cochin and Calicut in 1409. It was to the Malabar ports that the third expedition went in the year 1410–11, after a brief stay at Malacca. During 1413–15 a part of his fourth expedition reached Bengal. After a gap of sixteen years, in 1431–33 Cheng Ho again went on expedition to Ceylon and Calicut, trading in porcelainware, silk textile, metal vessels, perfumes, spices, medicinal herbs, pearls, coral and gems.

Fei Hsin and Ma Huan who accompanied Cheng Ho in his travels provide first-hand information about the Chinese trade with Malabar. According to Fei Hsin, Calicut was the main port of call for the Chinese fleet, which was an entrepot for the ships bound to the Persian Gulf, Arabia and the East African coast. Fei Hsin records that the Chinese goods were gold, silver, copper, coloured satin, blue-and-white porcelain, beads, musk, quicksilver and camphor. Pepper, coconut, fish and betel nut were shipped from the ports of Malabar. Ma Huan describes the ports of Quilon, Cochin and Calicut. In addition, he gives valuable information of ethnographical importance pertaining to the social and economic life of the people. Effective measures were taken at Calicut port for the safety of the merchandise of foreigners, and royal agents were directly testing the quality of goods, weighing the items, fixing the prices, arranging facilities for storage, etc. There was direct involvement of the king and his officers in the trade. It was firmly founded on the formal treaty relations. Several envoys to and from China indicate the formal relations maintained by the governments on both sides.

Chinese trade is believed to have brought a lot of gold and silver coins to Kerala, though there is not much archaeological proof for this. A slightly later Chinese record informs that this trade caused large-scale drainage of Chinese gold and therefore the southern Sung government (1127–1279 CE) proscribed in 1219 CE, the use of gold, silver and bronze coins in foreign trade. It was also ordered that silk fabrics and porcelain were to be taken to foreign countries to be exchanged against foreign goods. This regulation placed the Chinese silk and porcelain in an advantageous position in China's trade with foreign countries. Administrative statutes of the Sung government include Malabar among many other countries as recipients of the Chinese goods.

What the Chinese travellers' accounts describe about the relation between Kerala and China is attested by the early maṇipravāḷam texts of the thirteenth and fourteenth centuries. Quilon's status as the most prosperous port town and its connection with Chinese contacts are prominent in them. Allusions to Chinese junk (ships) anchored at Quilon are integral to their description of the port town and its prosperity. Chinese contacts with other port towns and the sustained Chinese influence upon them are evident in the place names. At Calicut port town, a compound is still called Cīnakkōṭṭa, meaning Chinese fort. Garcia da Orta says that the fort at Cīnakkōṭṭa was intact during his time. Chinese trade had penetrated even into the village life as the crude iron cooking pans (*chīnachaṭṭi*) and ceramic jars (*chīnabharaṇi*) in varying sizes. Similarly, there is a vast compound at Kappad named Cīnaccēri, meaning a Chinese settlement. At Pantalāyinikollam, there is a Cīnappaḷḷi, meaning a mosque of the Chinese, which shows that most Chinese seamen were followers of Islam. Factors such as the Chinese fort, settlement and mosque prove that Chinese trade had their own community network at port towns. Literary references and place-name survivals are supported by the archaeological remains in the form of Chinese ceramics all along the port sites of Malabar.

It is of special significance to note that the items brought by the Chinese traders included tin, lead, quicksilver, porcelain and silk, besides copper, because they are constituents of alloy metallurgy, particularly bronze casting. Various sources indicate a regular supply of these metals and minerals to Kerala, which explicitly presupposes a steady demand for the items in the region. This demand has an amazingly long continuity, ever since the days of the Eastern Mediterranean exchanges with the west coast during the period of the Roman Empire. Writing in the beginning of the sixteenth century, Garcia da Orta includes copper and mercury among items coming to the coast of Malabar in Chinese ships. Kerala had a commendable tradition of making high quality bell metal and high-tin bronze. A pattern of wide distribution of the *mūśāris*, a traditional sub-sect of artisans who subsisted on bronze working, in Kerala is well attested by inscriptions and place names. Also, there is strong ethno-archaeological testimony for the long tradition of bronze casting in Kerala. Several temple inscriptions corroborate the travellers' accounts about the inflow of copper and copper alloys, which were extensively used in Kerala for making various vessels and utensils for temples. Certain temple inscriptions set apart a portion of the income to the temple for periodical repair and maintenance of the bronze vessels. Bronze vessels were used not by wealthy sections alone but it reached the lower levels also, as attested by some later sources. The bronze mirror of Kerala is perhaps a unique achievement of this technological perfection. This highly demanded rarity is supposed to be a monopoly of a family of bronze-smiths at Aranmula, a village in central Kerala, but the fact is that there are other families also who have developed their own formulae for manufacturing fine bronze mirrors. Similarly, the craft of inlay work on coconut shells attained high sophistication on the coast of Malabar during this period. The Hooka shells with the inlay-work of bronze, made at Pantalāyinikollam and in the surrounding areas had, until recently, a steady demand in the Arab and the western countries.

Chinese ships brought some other articles that were also in great demand in Kerala. One such rarity was camphor, a very good disinfectant. The main consumers of the camphor imported by the Chinese ships to the coast of Malabar were temples, due to the reason that the central shrines of these temples, which generally had very little ventilation, always needed some air-purifying agent. This seems to explain the importance of smoking of camphor, which was wrapped in cotton wick, before the deity. In addition to this, camphor was an ingredient in some Ayurvedic medicated oils. Mercury was another imported item used for preparing some *sindūras* (purified medicated ash of *rasa*, mercury). The use of chemicals in the Ayurvedic treatment marks a definite stage of change in the history of indigenous medicine and healthcare. The commercial aspect of that change cannot be overlooked and so it can be seen that the commercial contacts of medieval Kerala with China and other countries played an important role in bringing about a basic change in the conception of health and the preparation of medicines.

Impact of Chinese contact can be enumerated as follows. At the economic level, the Chinese trade goods like copper, tin and lead that reached the coast of Malabar led to the growth of alloy technology and excellent craftsmanship in bronze, brass and bell metal artefacts throughout the villages. At the social level, the bronze-working in Kerala, which was totally dependent on the imported copper, resulted in the formation of a sub-sect of mūśāris and provided them a livelihood to subsist on in the rural village settlements. At the cultural level, the Chinese contact of Kerala was crucial in more than one way. Camphor was an essential article in temple worship. Camphor and mercury were important ingredients in some Ayurvedic medicines. The use of chemicals such as mercury and camphor brought by the Chinese to the coast of Kerala resulted in a paradigmatic change in the native medical treatment.

Medieval Coins

Circulation of coins and use of money mark a definite change in the mechanism of exchange. Money as a form of value tends to develop wherever there appears the commodity mode of production, which is a crucial development from the economy of hand-to-mouth existence. Chinese sources of the mid-fifteenth century describe such a practice in Calicut in the context of silk trade.

Some remarkable changes in the coinage and the use of money had taken place in Kerala during the period of our discussion, the thirteenth to fifteenth centuries. Literary texts of this period furnish long lists of coins that were in use in the bazaars. Accu was the main gold coin of the period and it prevailed over a vast region, including the Kongu country of Tamil Nadu and Kerala. Different types of accu such as ānaiyaccu are known from the inscriptional and literary sources of the period. Among the more popular coins were kampi, kāśu, pākam, paṇam, śalāka, tāram and tiramam. Most of them were current in territories outside Kerala. The validity of coins of regional power centres outside their territories apparently suggests that there was some amount of standardisation in the fineness and weight of coins. The exact difference between these varieties of accu is not known from our sources. It has been observed by scholars that accu was the standard coin in the west (i.e., Kerala) but the systems obtaining in Kerala and Kongu country were different. Inscriptional evidences attest a ratio of 1 accu = 1 paṟa of paddy.

Ānaiyaccu was in circulation in the Kongu country and it was perhaps the standard coin of that region. Its use in transactions is registered by inscriptions of Tiruchirāpaḷḷi, Coimbatore and Tirunelveli in c. thirteenth century. The name ānaiyaccu was given to the coin probably because the coin bore the figure of an elephant on one of its faces. A maṇipravāḷam literary reference informs us that the ānaiyaccu was used in the profitable business of horse trade between Arabia and south India. An Arab horse fetched 2000 pieces of ānaiyaccu to its dealer. Literary references and foreign notices taken together gives us the equation of 220 dīnāra = 2000 ānaiyaccu (1:9.9). The use of this coin type was presumably in big businesses, as shown by its references in the context of medieval horse trade as well as grants of large amount of money for various offerings in temples. In the available records āḷkāśu occurs in the context of religious grants and in higher-level transactions.

Pākam (bhāgam), meaning a portion or part, is referred to in the literary text of the period in the context of dealings in markets, whereas the inscriptions are silent about it. The literal meaning of the name suggests that it was a fraction of a bigger denomination. Bhāga is a Vijayanagara gold coin, probably the same as pākam of the Malayalam literary text. This was quarter of a paṇam and was also called kākini. Pākam with its smaller denominations must have been used for smaller transactions in the bazaars of Kerala.

Ponnu (literally, gold) is referred to among coins in certain Malayalam literary texts. It is highly probable that this was a gold coin called gaḍyāṇa and varāha. Interchangeability of these terms has been noticed on the basis of inscriptional sources. It occurs in inscriptions of Karnataka as honnu to denote gadyāṇa. An equation of *pon* with Devarāya Pagoda, a varāha or ten paṇam, has been arrived at. The coin paṇam enjoyed currency in almost all regions of south India. In Karnataka, it was known as haṇa. Malayalam literary texts as well as inscriptions of the post-Perumāḷ period mention paṇam, its half (arapaṇam) and one-fourth (kāpaṇam). Inscriptional evidence makes it clear that a paṇam was one tenth of a gaḍyāṇa/varāha/pon. Ibn Battuta, John Marignoli and Abdur Razzak refer to paṇam. Ma Huan records in the first half of the fifteenth century that kings of little Ko-lan (Vēṇāṭu, Kollam), Co-chin (Kochi) and

Ku-li (Calicut) had their own paṇams. It can be learnt from the Chinese traveller's account that in different regions paṇams were cast in gold of varying purity and weight. Literary texts of the period mention silver paṇam. Originally, paṇam was a gold coin but it seems that later it was stuck in silver too to suit the requirements of smaller transactions. Copper paṇam was also known to some regions.

Circulation of coins of cheaper metals indicates that there was increased use of coin-money even in small-scale transactions. Further, it would also show the spread of money-use into the lower strata of society. Palace manuscripts of the Sāmūtiri (*matilakam granthavari*), which are dated to the sixteenth and seventeenth centuries, invariably recorded the income and expenditure of royal treasury in terms of paṇam. By that time paṇam seems to have become a small coin and they used to be counted by means of a small board with several pits on it. Hence, it was mentioned as the 'measuring' of paṇam instead of counting, which is alluded to in some folk narratives.

It seems that the term kāśu was also in use during the period, but in a different sense of value compared to what it meant during earlier times. Literary texts of the period refer to different types of kāśu such as cōḷiyar kāśu, turikkakāśu (Turuska or Muslim) and veḷḷikāśu (silver). These coins are mentioned in the context of dealings in medieval bazaar, thereby implying that they were involved in everyday transactions. It is important to note that both paṇam and kāśu subsequently became synonymous to money in a generic sense. That shows the wider currency of the coins.

A coin called tiramam is known from literary texts along with different denominations of it like half-a-tiramam and three-fourth of a tiramam (mukkāl tiramam). But inscriptions do not mention it. A reference to golden tiramam (ponnumtiramam) indicates that the coin was struck in gold. Similarly, there was another coin called tāram that was struck in silver. Kozhikode and Kochi had their separate tārams, as stated by the Chinese traveller Ma Huan. Tāram, probably of other regions of south India, is mentioned in the epigraphs of those regions. Various authorities are of different opinions about its relation to other coins. Abdur Razzak says that one fanam fetched 6 tāram, whereas Varthema gives an equation of 1 fanam = 16 tāram. They are, however, separated by slightly more than half a century. At the time of the arrival of the Portuguese, tāram was in currency in different parts of south India. In the beginning of the sixteenth century, some Portuguese sources alluded to tāram as something like the scale of a sardine. Ma Huan says that it was used for petty transactions in market streets. Ma Huan and Abdur Razzak differ from each other regarding the value relation between paṇam and tāram. Ma Huan records a ratio of 1:16 between paṇam and tāram, whereas Abdur Razzak gives the ratio of 1:15.

In addition to the coins mentioned here, there are references in the Malayalam literary texts to coins like guḷika, mākāṇi, mummuṛi, munḍiyavaṭṭu and śalāka. Among these, śalāka, mentioned in inscriptions of the twelfth and thirteenth centuries, literally means a wire as in the case of kampi, the direct translation of *śalāka* (a small piece of metal string). References to use of all these coins in the market and the currency of silver and copper coins suggest that there was a higher degree of monetisation of trade and commerce than that of the earlier periods. Monetisation at lower levels of transaction is clear from the minting of coins of smaller denominations with cheaper material. Widespread use of money in buying and selling at Calicut is attested by the Portuguese sources of the earlier sixteenth century. Matilakam granthavari contain some interesting information about their *kammaṭṭam* (mint) and also about minting coins at Calicut. A record dated to 842 KE (1667 CE) informs that tāram was minted at Calicut and the royal authorities and other high officials involved in the task received a share out of the minted coins. Various aspects like the amount of coins to be minted, the measures taken for fixing the purity of silver, etc. are also mentioned in the records.

From the context of their occurrence it may be understood that all these medieval coins were multipurpose money with different functions in addition to the use of a general equivalent.

The prevalence of a large variety of coins makes the value relationship between different coins a difficult problem. However, it has been already noted that references to money-changers and speculators occur repeatedly in the accounts of Barbosa and Varthema, which appeared immediately after our period of study. Coins themselves were articles of exchange.

Urban Experience

Historical writings on urbanisation in Kerala are too meagre in spite of the fact that a fairly good amount of source material is available. The period from the thirteenth to the sixteenth century is illumined by the three early campu poems and some sandeśakāvyas in the Malayalam and Sanskrit languages. These literary compositions supply a lot of interesting details about the towns, markets and fairs, articles of trade, modes of exchange, sellers and buyers, weights and measures, coins and money-use and so on. The campu poems are said to have been composed in praise of dancing women who are invariably associated with their native urban complexes. Thus, the poet gets an opportunity to describe the hometown of the heroine. While the campu compositions present magnified images of individual urban centres, each sandeśakāvya gives a panoramic view of the area between the hero and the residence of the parted heroine. Sandeśakāvyas are in the form of description of the route following which the messenger could reach the heroine's house. Descriptive accounts of royal palaces, religions centres, urban complexes, rivers, bridges, etc. are given in the form of beautiful verse, which are easy to memorise. Politically, this is the period which witnessed the growth of a number of independent principalities in the different sub-regions of Kerala after the disappearance of the Perumāḷs of Koṭunkōḷūr. This literature coincided with the long process of the evolution of a distinctive Kerala idiom. Urban growth has to be analysed against the expansion of the garden land economy of cash crops, internal long-distance trade and overseas exchanges, political power and cultural processes. While many of the centres mentioned in these texts are known for the first time, some others can be traced back to an earlier period.

Port towns, temple premises and inland markets seem to have acquired features of urban centres in Kerala during the thirteenth to sixteenth centuries, as foreign travel accounts and certain literary texts in Sanskrit and Malayalam mention. Some of the port towns heralded a relatively-developed stage with bazaars, commercial groups and linkage with inter- and intra-regional commercial networks. They became more extensive multicultural centres of trade, which attracted long-distance overland as well as overseas traders. Temple centres emerged as small townships where inland traders converged. Traditional markets catering to local needs increased and became structured during the period. Kurakkeṇikkollam (Quilon) of the earlier period became more prosperous and elaborate, attracting many foreign traders. These are attested by foreign travelogues by Arab, Islamic and Portuguese travellers and literary texts like campus and sandeśakāvyas in Sanskrit and Malayalam. All the major port towns with community settlements of Jews, Christians and Muslims such as Quilon, Koṭunkōḷūr, Pantalāyinikollam and Māḍāyi were prospering during the period.

Such prosperous centres were surrounded by villages of expanded agricultural production, wider social consumption and extensive trade networks constituted regions of socio-economic and politico-cultural importance. Generally, historians discuss this phenomenon of the rise of regions with political authority as disintegration of the kingdom, as if the process represented an overall decline. In fact, the process is not one of decline but of growth. Growth of population, agriculture, crafts production, consumption and exchange makes the region politically important and accounts for the transformation of the region into a ruling principality. The emergence of principalities characterised Kerala of the thirteenth century CE.

VII

Emergence of Principalities (c. 13th–16th centuries CE)

Agrarian expansion, economic growth, social differentiation and trade in a region correspond to the development and consolidation of political power there. It is these changes that had led to the emergence of independent principalities in the late thirteenth century CE. Generally, this process is considered in historiography as the disintegration of the kingdom, obviously due to the preoccupation with the primacy of the state, and not as local economic and political growth. Actually, it has to be understood as the process of economic growth necessitating and facilitating the development of autonomy and power of the locality called nāṭu. Nevertheless, their formal release from the suzerainty of the Perumāḷ must have had its historical context.

Elamkulam presented the conflict between the Cēras and Cōḻas as an episode of a 'hundred years war'. MGS rejects this by showing that there were several years of peace between invasions that were led by the various Cōḻa kings from Parantaka onwards. Invasions happened rather frequently during 998–1018 CE and that led to the Cōḻa hegemony over the Perumāḷ during the period between 1018–1066 CE. After 1066 CE there were a few invasions again until the end of the Perumāḷ rule in 1122 CE with the abdication of the throne by Rāma Kulaśēkhara. MGS considers the rest of the story of the Perumāḷ's partition of the kingdom, abdication, conversion and pilgrimage to Mecca acceptable on rational grounds and because they match the historical circumstance. Perumāḷ's remorse over the guilt and the ritual confession (*prāyaśchitta*) at the Kollam Rameśvarattu

Koil, as testified by the inscription of the thirteenth regnal year (1102 CE), is an indication of the displeasure the brāhmaṇas had towards him. Another episode of repentance says that he had felt guilty of harming one of his āyiravar. According to the Keraḷōlpatti tradition of partition, the entire kingdom (160 kātam of land) between Putuppaṭṭaṇam in the north and Kannerri in the south was divided among the seventeen nāṭus of which Kōlattunāṭu, Vēṇāṭu, Perumpaṭappu, Kuṛumpoṛanāṭu, Pōḷanāṭu, Vaḷḷuvanāṭu and Eṛanāṭu were the major ones.

Vēṇāṭu

Vēṇāṭu ranked foremost among the principalities in wealth, resourcefulness and long history, though Kōlattunāṭu was the most prominent in territorial extent as well as purāṇic, legendary and historical tradition. Kil̲perur near Kiḷimānur was the headquarters of the Vēṇāṭu ruling house. In records it was known as Kil̲perur illam, suggesting its status of a joint family. Gradually, a branch settled at Tripāpur near Tiruvananthapuram, which was growing into a major trade centre. Vēṇāṭu had commanded a vast extent of agrarian lands and it constituted the principal resource base of the ruling family. Land dues from the landlords (kōmuṛaipāṭu), taxes on trade goods, tolls from trade routes and customary dues constituted the main resource base. This resource strength accounted for the rise of the rulers as kings. Within a span of two centuries the king's family branched off into three lineages—Tripāpur, Ciṛva and Dēśinganāṭu. Ever since, it became the convention that the eldest male member of these three families would become the king of Vēṇāṭu, the extent of which was demarcated between Kollam in the north and Tirunelveli in the south, notwithstanding the fluidity of borders that fluctuated due to incessant conquests and expeditions. Prosperity of Kollam town is well attested by the notes of travellers like Benjamin, Al Kasvini and others. Maṇipravāḷam works like *Unnunīlisandeśam* and *Uṇṇiyacīcaritam* describe brisk transactions of Kollam. Pāṇdya kings had suzerainty over the Vēṇāṭu kings of the period.

Vēṇāṭu was the first to emerge as a full-fledged kingdom sustained by warriors who were called *ariśippaṭijanam*, as several inscriptions of Vēṇāṭu indicate. It is possible that after the disintegration of the Perumāḷ kingdom Vēṇāṭu started to rule independently like other nāṭus. Rāmavarma Kulaśēkhara is believed to be the first ruler of independent Vēṇāṭu. In order to legitimise the independent political existence, the rulers continued the royal title Kulaśēkhara to indicate their lineal descent from the Perumāḷs of Mahōdayapuram. Excepting a few inscriptional references to names like Vīra Kerala Varma (c. 1125–c. 1155 CE) and his successors Vīra Ravivarma, who ruled Vēṇāṭu between 1151 and 1164 CE as the subordinate of the Pāṇdya king, and Māravarman Sri Vallabha, according to the Caturvedimangalam inscription (1161 CE), we do not know much about the rulers of Vēṇāṭu in the post-Perumāḷ period. Vīra Ravivarma's successor was Aditya Varma (c. 1165–c. 1175 CE). There are references to armed expeditions in many literary works. *Unnunīlisandeśam* alludes to the cavalry of the king Aditya Varma. Another Pāṇdya inscription from Gosala, dated to 1183 CE, refers to the next ruler of Vēṇāṭu, Udaya Mārthāṇḍa Varma (1175–1195 CE). This king was followed by Vira Rama Varma (c. 1195–c. 1205 CE). He is acknowledged in the Veḷḷāyani inscription dating to 1196 CE as the ruler Sree Veera Rama Varma Tiruvaṭi, and as one who commands the aṛunurruvar warrior contingent of Vēṇāṭu. Virarama Kerala Varma (c. 1205–c. 1215 CE), Ravi Kerala Varma (c. 1215–c. 1240 CE), Padmanabha Marthanda Varma (c. 1240–c. 1253 CE) and Ravi Varma Kulaśēkhara (c. 1299–c. 1314 CE) are other rulers of Vēṇāṭu mentioned in certain inscriptions. Kaṇdiyur (1218 CE) and Maṇalikkara (1236 CE) inscriptions mention Ravi Kerala Varma. From the Kaṇdiyur inscription, it can be inferred that at least eight nāṭus, north of Vēṇāṭu, were under the influence of the kings of Vēṇāṭu.

The Pāṇdyas established their supremacy over the southern part of Vēṇāṭu during the second half of the thirteenth century. It was a period of political instability. There is no reliable source material to reconstruct the political history of this period. Kōta Marthanda Varma (1251–1299 CE) was the ruler of Vēṇāṭu at the time of Sundara Pāṇḍya's invasion. Kōta Marthanda Varma's successor was Ravi Varma Kulśēkhara (1299–1314 CE). He was the first Vēṇāṭu king to ascend the throne through the matrilineal system of succession. Historians of Vēṇāṭu consider him as a king quite proficient in rule and territorial defence. The Srirangam inscription of 1300 CE hails him as the protector of the Vedas. Sree Vīra Udaya Marthanda Varma succeeded Ravi Varma Kulśēkhara and ruled from 1313 to 1345. His successor was Vīra Kerala Varma whose terminal date is not known. We only know that towards the end of the fourteenth century Iravi Iravi Varma and Iravi Aticca Varma, who were brothers, had been the kings of Vēṇāṭu. Vīra Kerala Marthanda Varma, mentioned in the Padmanabhapuram inscription of 1402 CE, is the next known king of Vēṇāṭu. His twin brother Cēra Udaya Marthanda (1383–1444 CE) seems to have restored the southern part of Vēṇāṭu through expeditions against the Pāṇḍya kings. Vēṇāṭu went into a phase of unrest again due to the invasions from the Vijayanagara kingdom. Sree Vīra Udaya Marthanda (1516–1535 CE) was the king during the period of the Vijayanagara invasion. It is not known who succeeded him. A king called Sree Vīra Kerala Varma seems to have ruled between 1544 and 1545. Rama Varma was his successor. His terminal date is not known. Unnikkerala Varma (1544–1594 CE) is said to have succeeded him. Udaya Marthanda Varma who died in 1595 is the next king known. Vīra Ravi Varma ascended the throne after him.

Apart from this, there is no reliable genealogy or chronology of the Vēṇāṭu kings. It is quite uncertain whether these kings were partially independent or mere subordinates of the Pāṇḍya kings. Ma Huan's reference to the coinage of the Vēṇāṭu king, which included gold coins weighing one fen (5.75 grains) each, attests to the privilege of minting coins, which is a very important sign of royal power. However, we do not know anything more about the rulers of Vēṇāṭu, such as their power structure and royalty. The political history of a region is closely connected with the issue of formation of state in that region. As discussed earlier, the concept of the Kautilyan state was already entrenched during the Perumāḷ regime, as testified by several inscriptions through references to the attributes of the state mentioned in the *Arthśāsthra*. Nāṭus were under the Perumāḷ's overlordship and historians generally referred to their rulers as his governors. During the period under discussion, sources inform that the nāṭuvāḻis were seeking to accomplish themselves as independent state powers.

Ēṛanāṭu

The Sāmūtiris of Calicut are the descendents of the the Ēṛāḷanāṭuṭayavar, who figures as a witness in the Jewish grant of Bhaskararavi of 1000 CE along with the chiefs of Vēṇāṭu, Venpolināṭu and Vaḷḷuvanāṭu. Ēṛanāṭu, like other prominent nāṭus, came up as an independent territory after the legendary exit of the last Perumāḷ. Keralōlpatti accounts show that they managed to annex the areas of Pōḷanāṭu with Calicut as its capital and Vaḷḷuvanāṭu with its centres at Ayiranazhi, Kaṭannamaṇṇa, Mankṭa and Aripṛa. There is no reliable source to know the early history of Ēṛanāṭu, which hence remains largely depended on popular traditions and legends. Ēṛanāṭu chieftains of Neṭiyirippu, known as the Ēṛāṭis, were confined to the hinterlands with no outlet to the seaboard until they conquered the coastal chieftains in the thirteenth century CE. They defeated the Veḷḷāṭṭiris of Vaḷḷuvanāṭu and Porḷātiris of Pōḷanāṭu in the northwest. These conquests enabled the Ēṛāṭis to wield control over Kozhikode, a place rich in spices, and Pantalāyinikollam, the main natural port famous for spice overseas trade. It enabled the Ēṛāṭis who commanded the supply of hill products to control the trade benefits of the sea coast and emerge as Kunnalakkōnātiri (the rule of the region from the Sahyadri hills to the western sea). Most of the revenue of early Neṭiyirippu came from spice and salt trade. Other sources of revenue were *ankam* (duel), *cunkam* (toll), *eḻa* (fee for owning unclaimed cattle), *koḻa* (service charge), *vaḻi* (route tax), *piḻa* (fine) and *cangāta mukam nokku* (periodical gifts). Neṭiyirippu lacked rice and, using other resources, Ēṛāṭis grabbed Vaḷḷuvanāṭu and became the patron of *māmānkam* (*mahāmakam*, the grand *makam* festival), celebrated once in twelve years on the asterism of *makam* (the star cluster called *māgha*) in the month of Tulām. This festival was of great economic significance too, for it used to be a major fair attracting many merchants even from far off places. That accounts for the interest of Ēṛāṭis to be the patron of *māmānkam.* The Ēṛāṭis moved further to the paddy-rich southern Kerala by the end of the thirteenth century CE from when onwards the Arab and Chinese accounts provide clear documentary evidence of their political control as having extended up to Arūkutti in the south and Putupaṭṭaṇam in the north.

Ēṛāṭis seem to have a well mobilised contingent of warriors, who were the lokar stationed in different parts. Neṭiyirippu chronicles refer to them as Paṭinjārrummuri lokar, Vadakumpuram lokar, etc. They were archers and swordsmen, trained in martial arts as the widespread institution of the kaḷari and the practice of ankam suggest. It is quite possible that horses and elephants were used in contemporary battles, although we lack details thereof. In addition to the lokar, there were guards called *kāval cangātam* for maintenance of internal peace and security. With their power felt at all the major income centres in the region, Neṭiyirippu rulers began to deploy strategies for acquiring kshatriya status and emerge as kings.

One of the strategies to achieve this status was the ritual attribution of the sword, dagger and rapier as royal insignia to the warrior heads. This important rite is called *uṭavāḷaṇakkal* (attribution of the sword). Making services customary and obligatory through rituals was common in traditional societies all over the world. Warrior leaders were functionaries of hereditary status with familial and local identities. Interfering with the right of inheritance by introducing a ritual attribution of the status to the concerned by the ruler came into vogue obviously as a strategy. It is at once a strategy of reaffirming suzerainty of the ruler and reassuring the warrior leader's fealty to him. For example, Cempil Mūtta Paṇikkar was a hereditary status or position automatically passed on to its claimant. Interfering with this traditional practice, Ēṛāṭi introduced a new custom of conferring the status as his prerogative. Similarly, it was Tammel Paṇikkar's hereditary right to train boys of the ruling family in the martial arts. But Ēṛāṭi made it necessary that he should ritually confer this right upon the Panikkar. Yet another example of interference with the traditional system of inheritance was the introduction of the custom of the Ēṛāṭi directly putting the cap of authority (*talēkkeṭṭu*) on the head of the new leader of the fisherfolk. Kozhikode granthavari of daily events and accounts mention the expenditure incurred on the occasion of conferring rights on Taṇṇīṛvākkaṭe Kaimal, Taṛakkal Menon, Eranjōḷi Accan, Maṭattinkīzh Mūppil Nayar, Pantalur Urāḷan, etc. These accounts bring out the institutionalisation of the relationship between Neṭiyirippu ruling family and the respective chiefs. Investiture ceremonies consisted of attributing the sword, giving knots and rapier, or giving head dress. For example, the Mūtta Paṇikkar of Cempil and Eranjōḷi Accan were given robes and rapier. There is documentary evidence for the power wielded by the village headmen. It was their duty to collect taxes due to local chieftains. Ēṛāṭis authorised them to carry out these duties. In this respect they embody higher powers. Ēṛāṭis acquired the title of Sāmūtiri (*swāmisṛee*; 'swami' meaning king, and 'sree' being the honorary suffix) through wealth, power and ritual strategies of legitimacy.

Minting coins was a sign of royal authority that the Ēṛāṭis utilised. Details of the system of coinage introduced by the Neṭiyirippu rulers are available. We get details of coins minted in 1667 CE from the Kozhikode granthavari and the expenses incurred on that account. Coins were minted at the kammaṭṭam under royal supervision. Coins were distributed according to the norms prescribed by tradition and hereditary rights, and not according to the whims and fancies of the king.

Documentation was an important feature of contemporary polity. Everyday events were documented as items of expenditure and the source of income, constituting the basis of revenue administration. Some kind of land assessment and fixation of dues must have been part of it, however unsystematic and incomplete the procedures might have been. Travellers have testified that they had seen a row of writers with palm leaves and stylus in their hands at the palace of the Neṭiyirippu royal family.

Māmānkam: This may be a festival with a history dating back to the times of the Perumāḷs. Māmānkam was a big fair on the Tirunāvāya bank of the river Bharathapuzha where merchants even from faraway places converged to exchange goods. Due to the obvious economic significance of the fair and the strategic importance of the site, a Sāmūtiri captured Tirunāvāya from its traditional owner, the chief of Veḷḷāṭṭiri, and annexed it to the kingdom of Kōzhikōde. Since then, the Vaḷḷuvanāṭu chiefs started sending warriors as *cāver* (suicide squads) to kill the Sāmūtiri who presided over the fair. This naturally turned the fair into a site of bloodshed by warriors who rushed to the king who was seated on the special platform (*nilapāṭu tara*) in a suicidal attempt to behead the Sāmūtiri. According to William Logan, the last māmānkam was observed in 1743 CE. However, K. V. Krishna Iyer argues that the last māmānkam fair was held in 1755 CE, and it ceased with the conquest of Kōzhikōde by Hyder Ali, the Sultan of Mysore in 1776 CE.

Other Powers

It is evident that all other nāṭus were growing during this period. There are examples of the rise of new principalities like Vengunnāṭu and Veṭṭattunāṭu. As they were new principalities there were no traditional chieftains. Therefore, rulers for those lands were chosen by higher authorities. The Veṭṭattunāṭu ruler, Veṭṭamuṭaya Mūttakōil was crowned with the blessings of the Neṭiyirippu royal family. Kuṛumpiyātiri, Pōrlātiri, Veḷḷāṭṭiri or Aṛangōṭṭu, etc. were other examples of non-traditional rulers. Even a traditional swarupam like the Kōlam was made to accept the suzerainty of the Sāmūtiri in matters of sanctioning the right of inheritance. All centres of resources were brought under control by providing irrigation facilities and by employing agents for collection of revenue.

Power Structure

Theoretically, we know that the power structure of the nāṭu was an extension of the seigniorial jurisdiction of the landlord. Seigniorial heads (the nāṭuvāḻis) were non-brāhmaṇa landlords with distinct geographical areas of jurisdiction that involved proprietary control over land and the local inhabitants (tenants and occupants). A bigger landlord was a nāṭuvāḻi and a bigger chieftain was the head of a bigger nāṭu. He had some control over the small chieftains who had customary obligations to him. It was a hierarchy with the landlord (janmi) on the top, with the tenants (kārāḷar), the artisan and craftsmen settlers (kuṭiyanmār) placed below, and the slave-like tillers (aṭiyār) at the base. Brāhmaṇa landlords of the temple-centred oligarchic corporations had grown more powerful and formed themselves into sankētam. Throughout Kerala the power structure of the previous period remained fundamentally the same but politically segmented (i.e., power was divided into small units), and the chiefly heads of resourceful principalities were adopting strategies to become kings with suzerainty over prominent landlords, including brāhamaṇa oligarchs.

Though these village headmen could be the new version of the *kuṭipatis* of the earlier villages (ūr), the joint management of ūr and sabha in the agrarian villages is absent during this period. In brāhamaṇa villages sabha was replaced by sankētam and *yogam* (congregation [of nampūtiri landlords]), which were both more or less ritualistic in nature. Administration was carried out by the chief of villages (ūruṭayār). However, royal power was gradually intruding into the village administration, depriving them of their traditional prerogative. The king exercised control over the resources through the head of the village. Instead of āṭṭaikol, the annual rent collected by the collective authority of the village during the Perumāḷ rule, it began to be taken over by the headmen during this period. Thus, ūr and sabha were rendered unimportant and confined to ritualistic functions. The Vēṇāṭu king is mentioned in inscriptions as the Lord of Kollam; the Odanāṭu king is mentioned as the Lord of Townships;

and the Sāmūtiri is mentioned as the Lord of Kozhikode. This presupposes that in every town the respective kings were in control of law and order, protection of merchants and their warehouses, determination of prices, collecting taxes, etc.

Thus the power structure of the period shows certain signs of the state. Yet, there was no standing army, which is one of the fundamental signs of a perfect state. It was not a system in which sub-centres functioned as true copies of a centralised state system. On the contrary, it was in the process of taking control of sub-systems of traditional autonomy, as part of centralisation. Nevertheless, it was not a strategy of direct deployment of warrior power, but keeping that at the back. It was the tactic of manipulating high status into political authority and to interfere with the traditional rights of inheritance.

Administration of Justice

Administration of justice and punishments continued to follow local customs and precedents, which, however, reflected the changes in social relations and practices. Accordingly, certain conventions phased out as new ones came in vogue. A major change was the disappearance of the codified precedents like the Mūḻikkaḷam kaccams that discriminated wrongs and prescribed punishments against them. Another change was the introduction of trial by ordeal, which included ordeal based on water, poison and fire. Of these the most common was the ordeal of dipping the finger (*viralmukku*) in boiling oil. If the finger of the accused was found burnt, the accusation would be confirmed and due punishment would be inflicted. Sucindram in Kanyakumari district was famous for this ordeal by fire, details of which are found in Stone inscriptions dating to the ninth–thirteenth centuries CE. Several temple documents and palace chronicles contain references to the practice. Kaḷarivātukkal in the Kōlatiri's domain, Lokanārkāvu in the Kaṭathanāṭṭu Raja's domain, and the Tiruviḷayanāṭu kāvu in the Sāmūtiri's domain were famous sites for the fire ordeal. This trial involved deposition of a fixed sum of money by the accused to be shared by local authorities, temple servants and the washerman who supplied the cotton for covering the finger after dipping.

Settlement of Disputes

Ankam (duel) was the most common method used for the resolution of conflict. It represented a form of conflict resolution that involved fight between hired mercenaries unto death. Preparations for a duel start with the payment of dues to the local ruler for his sanction. Then the conflicting persons choose their fighters for the duel by paying their fees. It is the local ruler's responsibility to inform the public about the date, time and venue of the duel. Witnessed by people, the duel is fought till the defeat of one or the other and he who wins justifies his patron's claims. Usually the duel would end in the death of one of the warriors. Therefore, these professional warriors would demand enormous sums as reward. This might be the reason why preparations for duels attained ritualistic status.

There are no contemporary records of duels, but *Vaṭakkan Pāṭṭukaḷ* provide accounts of the institution of the duel in the course of their narrative. These songs narrate the whole story of certain duels from the origin of the dispute to the tragic end of the warrior. The best example of such a story is that of Aromal Cēkavar. A dispute on seniority arose between Uṇikkonār and Uṇichandror of Kuṛungāṭṭeṭam, who hired the fighters Arōmal Cēkavar of Puthuramvidu and Aringōṭaṛ respectively. Ballads cannot be paraphrased as history for they are oral compositions of stock expressions and stereotypes. We can only make certain inferences about the practice, its overall context, related ideas, values and passions of the heroic society of the period from the stories, and not a history of the events. It is natural that heroic passions, pride and values were strong enough to keep warriors at the beck and call of the prominent households which required their service. This practice of duels was prevalent in Sri Lanka too, where too the duel was called ankam. The fighters in Sri Lanka were known as *sēvakar*, similar to Malayalam's cēkavar. Among the weapons used in Kerala and Sri Lanka, *curika* (rapier) was the most important. Its institutional base was kaḷari in both places. Kaḷari was widespread in north Malabar. It is not accidental, therefore, that the Sāmūtiri's records mention the income from duels as the principal source of revenue.

Crime and Punishment under the Swarūpam

Ordeals as a means of producing evidence in legal matters are mentioned in several sources pertaining to different periods. Accounts of some foreign travellers provide us with descriptions of ordeals that the authors witnessed or collected from informants. The Synod of Diamper of 1599 contains references to ordeals prevailing among the native Christians in Kerala. It is interesting because this text presents the indigenous customs and practices as uncultured, decadent and objectionable from the perspective of a foreigner. Stone or copper inscriptions and archival records mention ordeal performances though incidentally as part of income and expenditure of temples or royal houses. Elamkulam refers to various types of ordeals in Kerala during the period.

Of the six documents on viralmukku ordeal at Sri Valayanāṭu temple in the suburbs of Kozhikode, two are about murder cases, two register instances of *māraṇakriya* (black magic for the death of the enemy), one refers to sorcery and the last refers to a theft of *bhaṇḍāram* (the treasure casket). In these documents, however, the details of the offence were not specified and the offender was not identified. A record from Lokanārkāvu refers to a certain Kumkamma of Kappaḷḷi, the *taṛavād* (house) of the famous hero Koman of *Vaṭakkan Pāṭṭukaḷ*. There are accounts of income and expenditure of viralmukku rituals in the temples of Valayanāṭu, Lokanārkāvu, Kudalikkāvu, etc. Various functionaries figure in the records along with officers and members of local committees like nagaram. From the various lists of functionaries, representatives and dignitaries we get some idea about the social section which assembles in the temple as audience-participants at the time of an ordeal performance.

The *Dharmaśāstra* texts and legal texts of later periods refer to other forms of ordeals such as *jalaparīkṣa* (ordeal by water), *viśaparīkṣa* (ordeal by poisoning), *agniparīkṣa* (ordeal by fire), etc. Every ordeal involves some amount of torture of the body. Of these, agniparīkṣa was practised in Kerala during the seventeenth century CE. Its ritual relation turns the entire procedure religious and sacred. This could remind one of the *Dharmaśāstra* concept of ordeal as *divya* (divine) and would persuade a modern student of history to describe justice as god's will in the context of medieval jurisprudence. Sources also document the presence of the king's representative, which shows a royal involvement in the juridical system. In this traditional penal mechanism, the investigation carried out by the royal officials was comingled with the methods of ordeals performed by the accused. That is, investigation is mixed with punishment, and this is a significant aspect of the performer's act of ordeal. It is clear that in contemporary society the person suspected of a crime was conceived as an offender deserving some amount of punishment.

In some cases the accused might refuse to undergo the ordeal. For example, when Kumkamma (sixteenth century CE) of the Kappaḷḷi family was asked to perform the ordeal of agniparīkṣa, she refused to obey the order and hence the authorities had to settle the issue by realising an amount as fine. These stray cases were perhaps indicators of dissent and protest against the existing juridical system. One is inclined here to take these authoritative acts of recording the events of protest or dissidence as a sign of the slow and gradual breakdown of the existing systems of social order and juridical practices. In other words, the traditional ideals and worldviews of social justice were weakening and the society was getting prepared for a change.

Ideology

Ideology is a collection of ideas and beliefs that distort and hide the truth about the conditions of human existence. It justifies exploitative social relations, inequality and domination.

For example, economic exploitation and oppression of the lower rungs of the social system and their accommodation under discriminatory caste practices. Ideology ensures social conformity and solidarity. Ideology is a phenomenon elaborate and enormously complex, and cannot be abridged. Ideology helped the polity of small principalities to counterbalance its relative powerlessness through the use of high-sounding titles and qualifications. For instance, the Vēṇāṭu kings took titles like Kulaśekhara Cakravarti, Venṭuman Konṭa Bhutalavīran, Samgramadhīran, Dharmānganāthan, Manne Sultan, etc. Similarly, Neṭiyirippu called himself Sailabdhiswaran, Sāmūtiri, Mana Vikraman, Puntura-kon, etc. Kōlattiri took such titles as Karipat Unuttiri, Udayavarman Kōlattiri Vadakan Perumāḷ. There are evidence for the continuation of ancient rites which were used to make kshatriyas out of rulers who were not kshatriya by birth, such as *tulāpuruṣadānam* (gift of gold equal to a man's weight) and *hiraṇyagarbham* (golden womb).

It was during the time of swarūpams that the ideology of devotion (bhakti), continuing from the previous period, became more popular. In fact, the cult of devotion teaches people to accept the contradictions in the social system in a fatalistic perspective. However, rages and rebellions arising out of these contradictions manifested through devotional movements. Though these were aborted rebellions, they echoed the popular voice of rebellion. They generated a flare for popular linguistic and cultural freedom. It is this cultural background in which Malayalam freed itself from the neighbouring languages and became an independent language with grammatical distinction, as exemplified in the treatise *Līlātilakam*. Establishing Malayalam as clearly distinguished from the Cōḻa-Pāṇdya languages was an effort inspired by regional identity.

Parallel to the written tradition there was also a popular stream of oral literature. It had many offshoots like heroic ballads, *toḻil pāṭṭukaḷ* (workers' lore), ritual songs, etc. Heroic poetry was pregnant with the vitality and spirit of physical culture and heroism that grew around the schools of martial arts. In composition they all followed the oral tradition. *Putturampāṭṭukaḷ* in the *Vaṭakkan Pāṭṭukaḷ* and *Chengannurātipāṭṭukaḷ* in the *Tekkan Pāṭṭukaḷ* (southern ballads) come under this category. They express particular and common tendencies in social life, which segregate as well as congregate, i.e., the attitude to be divisive as well as to go together as a collective. It is noteworthy that in all these song traditions it is the Keraḷōlpatti legends that are narrated along with elements of the greater tradition (*mārgi*). By examining the ballads and ritual songs of northern style of Malayalam, we can get an idea of how the greater tradition percolated into the different layers of the culture of the region.

Thorrampāṭṭukaḷ constitute an important category of literary source for the folk theatre that existed parallel to the temple theatre. The literary part of this text follows the techniques of oral tradition and its central idea revolves round the well-being of social life. Its invocations are almost the same for all deities, as the prayers—'Let the seeds sown and plants planted be fruitful manifold'; 'Let disease and poverty exit'; 'Let the cows give plenty of milk'—exemplify. There was no worry about heaven or hell in the prayers and they by and large refrain from the desire for wealth and splendour. They show no anxiety about social security either. Places where people gathered for the ritual were sacred spots of the gods' incarnation on the earth. Every community had its own gods and their abodes. Through these spots people came into contact with their kith and kin who were scattered all over the region. It was customary for them to participate in the rituals at all these spots to ensure the well-being of every member of the community. One aspect quite central to the ritual was the collection of voluntary *kālum arayum* (quarters and halves of paṇam) contributions from all according to his or her ability.

The *Teyyam* Ritual

Teyyam (*daivam*; deity) is the most prominent ritual performance in north Malabar, in which the performers assume themselves as the god. Some people characterise it as part of the tribal ritual art. Indeed, it may be an old ritual anterior to the period under discussion. However, as it survives today, it is a systematised performance of aesthetic perfection in the facial painting and decorative costumes. Each jāti such as the vāṇiyar, maṇiyāṇi, cāliyar, tiyya, vela and pulaya, had its own teyyam shrine. On occasions of the teyyam ritual of each jāti, the kith and kin of the jāti congregated. According to belief, after descending on the earth, the teyyam proceeded from one spot to another and retained a network of the *mumpusthānam* (the previous spots of presence). This network of sacred spots of each jāti shows the migration pattern of its kindred descendants. Every ritual occasion required the presence of the fellow members of the jāti and they made kālum arayum contributions. Irrespective of the differences of the jāti, kinship among the teyyams existed. For instance, the teyyam of vāṇiyar is conceived as the elder sister of the deity of a maṇiyāṇi or a tiyya teyyam. This facilitates a ritual enabling of solidarity in a society of differentiated jāti composition.

Literature and Culture

Localisation of culture and formation of regional identity were prominent in the works of art and literature during the fourteenth and fifteenth centuries CE. These works belonged to various literary genres such as poetry, commentaries, plays, tantric texts, astronomy and mathematics. A number of works were written in Sanskrit and maṇipravāḷam. An important but incomplete poetic work in Sanskrit is *Srikrishṇa Vilāsam* by Sukumara dated to the twelfth century CE. It is still disputed whether Sukumara was a native of Kerala or not. Divakara's *Amogharāghava* (1299 CE) deals with the first canto of *Rāmāyaṇam*, attesting to the contemporary popularity of the story of Rāmā. Some scholars take it as the first *campu* poetry, which is a mixed genre of poetry and prose. Malayalam works also followed the same tradition, the first of which is *Rāmacaritam* by Cirāman (thirteenth century CE), who was probably a member of the Vēṇāṭu ruling family. Uḷḷur S. Paramesvara Iyer, eminent poet, scholar and historian, notes that Cirāman is Vīra Mārthāṇḍa, also known as Maṇikanṭha, who ruled Tiruvitāmkūr from 1195 to 1208 CE. *Rāmacaritam* basically narrates the events in 'Yuddha Kāṇḍa' of the *Rāmāyaṇam*. The historical importance of this work is that the narrative marks the shift from the Sanskrit poetic tradition by abandoning Sanskrit meters in favour of the regional narrative tradition of Malayalam meters.

Following the tradition of *Rāmacaritam* (fifteenth century CE), three poets of the Kaṇṇaśśa family at Niraṇam (also called Niraṇam poets)—Madhava, Sankara and their nephew Rama (fourteenth–fifteenth century CE)—wrote several works which, according to Puthussery Ramachandran, are the first major attempts at liberating the Malayalam language from the influence of maṇipravāḷam. Madava Panikkar wrote the first Malayalam version of *Bhagavat Gita*. Sankara Panikkar's major work *Bhāratamāla* is the first Malayalam version of the *Mahābhārata*. Rama Panikkar, the most illustrious among the Kaṇṇaśśa poets, wrote *Rāmāyaṇam*, *Bhārtam*, *Bhāgavatam*, *Brahmāṇḍapurāṇam* and *Sivarātri Māhātmyam* in Malayalam. Rama Panikkar's works marked the culmination of the historic liberation of Malayalam from the linguistic texture and poetic diction of maṇipravāḷam. His *Brahmāṇḍapurāṇam* is particularly important, for it represents an early example of writing literary works in prose. Ulloor S. Paramesvara Iyer observes that Rama Panikkar's contribution to Malayalam is akin to Spencer's for English. The Niraṇam poets adopted a distinct metre (later known as the Niraṇam metre) for their composition, which subsequently became popular in the poems of *tullal* (a vibrant, satirical dramatic performance).

Tuncattu Rāmānujan Eḻuttacchan (sixteenth century CE) of Trikkanṭiyur near Tirur continued in the tradition of the Niraṇam poets, enriching the literature of Malayalam language. Eḻuttacchan wrote his *Adhyātmārāmāyaṇam* and *Sri Bhārtam* in Malayalam. Puthussery Ramachandran has shown a direct relation between Rama Panikkar's *Rāmāyaṇam* and Eḻuttacchan's *Adhyātmārāmāyaṇam*, though the latter follows a different metre. Eḻuttacchan was the first great Malayalam poet who popularised the *kiḷippāṭṭu* (parrot song) mode of versification, which imagines as if a parrot sings the whole story. Another widely believed major contribution of Eḻuttacchan to the Malayalam language is the standardisation of its alphabet. This has earned him the epithet 'father of Malayalam'. His writings are considered sacred due to their explicit passion for the cult of bhakti to Lord Nārāyaṇa and are entrenched as part of the sacred culture of Kerala.

There are a few other works as well, such as *Śukasandēśam*, *Uṇṇunīlisandeśam*, *Mayurasandēśam*, *Kōkasandēśam*, *Uṇṇiyaccīcaritam*, *Uṇṇiccirutēvīcaritam* and *Uṇṇiyāṭicaritam*. *Śukasandēśam* by Lakshmidasan, supposedly a member of the Karingampally family in the Kanayanur taluk in Kochi and *Uṇṇiyāṭicaritam* by Damodara Chakkiar were the great works of the time. Nothing is known about the authors of *Uṇṇunīlisandeśam*, *Kōkasandēśam*, *Uṇṇiyaccīcaritam* and *Uṇṇiccirutēvīcaritam*. These works give importance to agriculture, trade and worldliness around the temple with an aura of devotion. These sandēśakāvyas begin with an unreal event in which the hero is separated from the heroine and is in a place far away. He sends a message to the heroine, which becomes incidental in comparison to the realistic description of his native when he recounts the route connecting temples, markets and fairs; the goods exhibited there; the houses of dancing girls, etc. There are such love poems in almost all Indian languages, but they deal with an unearthly domain and bizarre themes, unlike those of maṇipravāḷam works which are realistic, especially with regard to the geography and routes connecting various centres. Naturally, these narratives reflect the material culture of surplus, exchange and spatial mobility, all of which account for the prevalence of a sensuous culture that courtesans represent. This cultural environment served as the basis for the praise of famous courtesans such as Iḷayacci, Ceṛiyacci, Māralēkha, Mārajamantika, Mēdinī Veṇṇilāvu, Kauṇōttara, Ceṛukara Kuṭṭatti, Tachappiḷḷy Iṭṭy Uma, Manavimēnaka and Uttarācandrika. There were other literary works like *Vasudevasthavam* as well in maṇipravāḷam.

The social themes in the maṇipravāḷam works that deal with independent plots have a special relevance to this discussion. Written in the style of ballads, these works exhibit the gradual development of certain idioms of linguistic identity. It is this identity which *Līlātilakam*, a grammatical treatise by Lakshmidasa, systematically builds and provides linguistic justification. This work can be taken as a major attempt in the construction of Kerala's linguistic and cultural identity by freeing its language, Malayalam, from other Dravidian languages, including Tamil.

Kerala's poetic tradition is best expressed as a distinct turn of pristine linguistic identity in *Krisṇagātha*, the celebrated work of Cherusseri, a courtier of Udayavarman Kōlattiri, the ruler of Kōḷattunāṭu, c. fifteenth century CE. Although *Krisṇagātha* also follows the great tradition of *Rāmāyaṇam* or *Bhagavata* in terms of selection of themes, we see here the poetic distinction typical of the Malayalam language best expressed for the first time. Its influence is leavening even to poets of recent times, such as Vallathol, Balamani Amma, Vailoppally and others.

A number of works of codified knowledge in different branches, such as history, politics, tantra, astrology, medicine, architecture and grammar, appeared during this period in Sanskrit and maṇipravāḷam. *Mūṣakavamśam*, which eulogises the illustrious genealogy of the Kōḷattunāṭu rulers, is the earliest known historical narrative. *Bhāṣākauṭalīyam*, an old Malayalam rendering of the *Arthaśāstra*, was the first major work that appeared in the regional language. *Prayogamanjari* by Iravi Namputiri of Cokiram village, *Īśānaśivagurudevapaddhati* whose author is presumed to be either Īśānaśivagurudeva or the teacher of Īśānaśiva, and the anonymous work *Kṛiyāsāram* are tantric works belonging to this period. A work of similar nature but more popular was *Krisṇīyam*, by the tantric and astronomer Krishnacharya. *Muhurtaratnam* and *Daśādhyāyi* by Talakkulathu Bhattatiri were two major works in astrology. *Tantrasamuchayam* by Chennas Nampoothiri, the Sāmūtiri's courtier in the second half of the fifteenth century CE, is a text that combines tantric and astrological ideas with architecture. Works of codified knowledge were written in the regional language too, as exemplified by Thamaranallur Bhattathiri's *Tāmaranallur Bhāṣa* in maṇipravāḷam and Alathur Nampi's *Ālattūr Maṇipravāḷam*, representing astrology and ayurveda respectively. *Uṇṇunīlisandeśam* refers to architectural features of houses such as *tekkini* (the southern), *vaṭakkini* (the northern), *kiḻakkini* (the eastern) and *paṭinjātta* (the western). *Manuṣyālayacandrika* by Tirumangalattu Nilakantan is the first example of an architectural text in maṇipravāḷam, but it appeared slightly later than *Uṇṇunīlisandeśam*. There are more caste-based social prescriptions about who deserved to build house and where, rather than any principles of architectural knowledge in the *vāstu* (architectural) text. *Tantra Samuccaya* and *Manushyālaya Candrika* are the main vāstu texts of this period.

There were several panegyrics and other literary compositions belonging to the period. Most important of these were works of scholars in the Sāmūtiri's court, well known as *patineṭṭarakkavikaḷ* (the eighteen-and-a-half poets). It is said that the phrase '*ara*', translated as 'half', was in fact a corruption of the Malayalam word *arca* (king). Therefore, the expression could also only mean eighteen court poets. Great scholars and poets like Payyur Paṭṭēri, Mullapaḷḷi Namputiri, Kakkasseri Bhattathiri, Chennas Nampoothiri, Uddanda Sastrikal and Punam Namputiri were members of this royal court that witnessed the composition and spread of numerous works in various branches such as poetry, drama, grammar and philosophy. Similarly, there were scholars in the court of Samgrāmadhīra Ravi Varma (1299–1314 CE) of Vēṇāṭu, such as Samudrabandha who wrote the commentary of Mankhukan's *Alankāraśarvaswam* and Kavibhushaṇa who wrote commentaries of Kalidasa's *Raghuvamśam* and *Kumārasambhavam*.

The use of prose in literary works had a vitalising effect. *Bhāṣākauṭalīyam* is the first prominent example of prose, and remains distinct for the wide use of local style. Other prose works such as *Āṭṭaprakāram* and *Kramadīpika* contain detailed instructions for actors about settings, make-up, gestures, acting and so on. *Āṭṭaprakāram* deals with the acting of each character, and *Kramadīpika* describes other theatrical devices such as the prologue and formalities to be followed by actors. These works proclaim the skill and excellence that Kerala had achieved in the theatrical arts and testifies to the development of prose suited to the needs of the time. All this refutes the common assumption that Malayalam owed prose to the Christian missionaries.

Codified Knowledge

Codification of knowledge refers to the organisation and systematisation of knowledge into codes or abstraction or theory. Codification becomes necessary for a society that needs to store, easily access and widely transmit knowledge. Every society has its knowledge but not all of it is codified. For instance, societies of oral tradition seldom codify their knowledge. Economic differentiation, social stratification, formation of the state and growth of literacy necessitate as well as enable codification of knowledge.

In the case of Kerala, further expansion of the agrarian system paved way for the growth of material culture but without any new technology, because of the opening up of new areas of agriculture and accumulation of increased surplus. Metallurgy was the chief technology that spread with adaptations. There were three communities of artisans connected to metallurgy—blacksmith, coppersmith and goldsmith. Out of the metal smelting community certain families specialising in the craft of making bronze emerged as an endogamous jāti called the mūśāri. A few families engaged in metal crafts at places like Āṛammuḷa and Aṭakkāputhur acquired expertise in manufacturing high-tin bronze mirrors. What appears as a matter of surprise is the amazing growth of bronze metallurgy in Kerala where copper and tin had to be procured from overseas traders. Literary works of the period mention gold and silver ornaments, metal wares and iron implements kept for sale in markets.

As in the case of metallurgy another branch of higher knowledge that spread locally was astronomy. Two systems of astronomical calculations, theoretical and practical, spread in Kerala as elsewhere. Practical systems in astronomy refer to methods and devices used for reckoning. Preparation of calendar is an example of a practical system of astronomy. Most of these ways have their theoretical basis. Estimation of the value of pi or formulation of theorems for higher trigonometric functions are a few examples of theoretical astronomical knowledge.

An important aspect of the period is the passage of higher knowledge to the Malayalam language. Works like *Tāmaranallur Bhāṣa* represent this trend. Pure mathematics had become necessary in the measurement of seasons relating to planetary motions. Agricultural expansion and increased transactions necessitated the spread of the knowledge of arithmetic. Introduction of coins, increased fairs and exchange of goods intensified the need for arithmetic applications. Merchants, landlords and astrologers were, therefore, much in need of arithmetical knowledge in a codified form.

Another branch of knowledge that got codified was healthcare. Medical books in Sanskrit spread throughout Kerala during this period. Medical works also began to appear in the regional language, as exemplified by the writing of *Alathur Maṇipravāḷam*. Literary works of the time also mention physicians such as Ālathur Nambi. In addition to the greater tradition of medicine, there existed the little tradition of popular healthcare. In village settlements families of Maṇṇān, Velan and Pāṇan represented this popular tradition. Their womenfolk were hereditary custodians of the traditional knowledge of midwifery.

Of the systems of specialised knowledge mathematical astronomy ranks foremost as the most advanced in Kerala. Kerala's contribution of calculus, a system based on the summation of infinitesimal differences, which is used for finding areas or volumes of unusual shapes and for measuring rates of change, deserves special mention here. We are indebted to several scholars of this period who were instrumental in sustaining information about this tradition of advanced mathematics in Kerala. However, the role of K. V. Sarma is remarkable. A scholar in manuscripts, Sharma was responsible for the worldwide attention that mathematical astronomy could attract. George Geevarghese Joseph, a specialist in the history of mathematics in India, presumes the possibility of overseas transmission of the new mathematics from Kerala. Thanks to Geevarghese Joseph's work, it is a matter of worldwide recognition today that the concept of infinity and knowledge of the power series goes back to Mādhava of Sangamagrāma (Irinjālakuda) (c. 1340–1425 CE), a village in Thrissur district. Mādhava's lasting contribution to mathematical astronomy is infinite series approximations detailed in his work *Veṇuāroham*, which was a development on the inferential items in *Āryabhaṭīyam*. Since G. W. Leibniz (1646–1716 CE) had published his notation and differential method after Mādhava, the power series in the initial phase of calculus has been referred to these days as Mādhava-Leibniz series. There was a perceptible epistemic shift in traditional Indian knowledge production in general and Kerala astronomy in particular since the time of Mādhava. Inferences drawn from Mādhava were subjected to scrutiny and correction by Paramēśvaran (c. 1360–1425 CE) and his sons Dāmodara (c. 1390–1470 CE) and Govinda (c. 1385–1460 CE), Putumana Somayājī (c. 1410–1490 CE), Nīlakaṇṭha Somayājī (c. 1444–1544 CE), Jyeṣṭadeva (c. 1500–1610 CE), Mahiṣamangalam Nārāyaṇa (c. 1540–1610 CE) and Melppattūr Nārāyana Bhattathiri (1559–1645 CE).

Kerala is a region marked by a long protracted tradition of vedic sacrifices, and therefore the region had many vedic priests who were making remarkable contributions to mathematical astronomy during this period. The belief that the conduct of sacrificial rituals would go futile in case of the incidence of an eclipse during their performance was the primary compulsion behind acquiring the knowledge and competency to predict the occurrence of eclipses. Since they were elaborate, long-lasting and expensive in terms of goods, services and rewards, it was quite important for the vedic sacrificial rituals to have their successful completion once they have begun. Losing a sacrifice on the incidence of an eclipse was ignominious to the priest who officiated and the king who patronised its performance. Therefore, the ability to predict eclipses was a crucial need for both the priest and the king. Mathematics began to grow as the fundamental tool of astronomy that had ritual pressure in producing predictive knowledge about planetary positions and movements. Putumana Somayājī, well known for his *Karaṇapadhatī* that has contributed to improving Mādhava's series, was a prominent scholar in astronomy. He wrote two works, *Grahaṇāṣṭakam* and *Grahaṇagaṇitam*, exclusively on eclipses, seeking to develop and sustain the faculty to predict. Interestingly, Nīlakanṭha Somayājī's *Tantrasangraha* that theorises the epicyclic and eccentric models of planetary motion devotes two chapters (*Chandragrahaṇaprakaraṇa* in 53 *slokas* and *Ravigrahaṇaprakaraṇa* in 63 slokas) almost entirely to the discussion of various trigonometric techniques and algebraic means of reckoning the incidence of the eclipse of the moon as well as the sun.

Paramēśvaran seems to have done direct astronomical observations for fifty-five years, systematically recorded the results, and wrote a treatise called *Drggaṇita*, a mathematical model of astronomy, an example par excellence for the epistemic tradition. His mastery over the extant knowledge and sizeable contribution to it in the form of new theorems are embodied by the commentaries he wrote on the *Mahābhāskarīya*, *Āryabhaṭīya* and *Līlāvatī* of Bhaskara II. The mean value theorem propounded by him is considered quite crucial and essential to proving the fundamental theorem of calculus. Similarly, his mean value type formula for inverse interpolation of the sine function, a one-point iterative technique for calculating the sine of a given angle, and a more efficient approximation that works using a two-point iterative algorithm, is now understood to be essentially the same as the modern secant method. He is said to be the first mathematician to provide the radius of a circle with an inscribed cyclic quadrilateral.

Likewise Nīlakanṭha Somayājī in his *Tantrasamgraha* carried the process further producing more clarity to pre-existing theories, particularly the expansion of the sine-cosine series of Mādhava. He is acclaimed for expanding the methods and theories of Mādhava, particularly by elaborating his derivations, improving proofs for his series of the arctangent trigonometric function, and other infinite series. *Tantrasamgraha* is composed in eight chapters and 432 sḷokas in Sanskrit, generally on the epicyclic and eccentric models of planetary motion, but specifically dealing with the motions and longitudes of the planets, various problems related with the sun's position on the celestial sphere, including the relationships of its expressions in the three systems of coordinates—namely ecliptic, equatorial and horizontal coordinates—the lunar and the solar eclipses, the deviation of the longitudes of the sun and the moon, the rising and setting of the moon and planets, and a graphical representation of the size of the sunshine part of the moon.

Nīlakanṭha's study is a clear indication of how new knowledge is created lineally by developing on the results of the previous studies. He is an example worth citing in the context of epistemic universals about traditional Indian knowledge production, such as rationality, analytical comprehension of the extant knowledge, new tools of observations, methodological modifications, systematic recording of observational results, mustering of inductive mathematical proofs for previous theorems, hermeneutic additions and scholarly integration. *Tantrasamgraha* embodies these epistemic distinctions, which one of its contemporary bhāṣyas, *Yukthidīpika*, is said to have highlighted. His *Grahaparīkṣākrama* is a methodological manual of observations in astronomy and the use of observational tools. *Sidhāntadaṛpaṇa* is Nīlakanṭha's other significant work, often noted for the interest he exhibited in methodological instructions. Nīlakanṭha's masterpiece, *Āryabhaṭīyabhāṣya*, provides a heliocentric model of the solar system and many results on calculus. He is said to have significantly improved Āryabhaṭa's model for Mercury and Venus. His methodological rationality is best highlighted and pursued further by Jyeṣṭadeva who has given many rational approximations based on continued fractions, which scholars have not made out as yet.

The insistence of the production of proof as a primary epistemic requirement is best manifest perhaps for the first time in the works of Jyeṣṭadeva. It is interesting to note that proofs for Mādhava's series expanded by Nīlakanṭha into sine, cosine and inverse tangent series were given only after a century by Jyeṣṭadeva in his *Yuktibhāṣā*, a Malayalam text and the world's first book on calculus. In spite of the constitution of the three crucial power series heading towards the invention of calculus, a comprehensive theory of differentiation or integration was not achieved by him. *Yuktibhāṣā* is his bhāṣya of *Tantrasamgraha*, but embodies fresh mathematical proofs of the theorems of Mādhava and Nīlakanṭha. What is totally new here is a convergent infinite process capable of attributing the value of π to arbitrary accuracy. Jyeṣṭadeva shows that several such processes were known to the astronomers of Kerala. *Yuktibhāṣa* gives two methods for the calculation of the circumference: (*a*) an algebraic recursion relation involving a square-root that converges to the exact value; and (*b*) a way to avoid square-roots in the calculation. What turns out as a matter of epistemic significance in *Yuktibhāṣā* is the onset of the practice of providing proofs rather than just statements of results. Another significance of the text is its use of the regional language (Malayalam) instead of Sanskrit and replacement of the poetic genre with prose. Jyeṣṭadeva's formula showing a passage to infinity, which facilitates calculation of areas under parabolas, is an essential constituent of the theory of calculus. It is the same formula that contemporary European scholars such as Pierre Fermat, Blaise Pascal and John Wallis also used. Interestingly, the planetary model of Nīlakanṭha and Tycho Brahe is one and the same. George Geevarghese Joseph, who has played a major role in securing international recognition of Kerala's contributions to mathematics, presumes the possibility of overseas transmission of the new mathematics from Kerala.

It appears from the genealogy of astronomers that transmission of knowledge was evidently personal and part of the system of *gurukulam* (traditional method of learning by living with the teacher). There is the instance of Melpattūr Nārāyaṇa Bhaṭṭatiri learning astronomy from Achyuta Piṣāroṭy (1550–1621 CE), a student of Jyeṣṭadeva. Anyway, the non-nampūtiris, of course those with upper-caste status, could go to a nampūtiri to learn astronomy, as evident from the case of Sankara Varier (c. 1500–c. 1560 CE) being a student of Nīlakanṭha or Piṣāroṭy being a student of Jyeṣṭadeva. However, acceptance of this as a common practice precludes the possibility of the nampūtiri orthodoxy to have taken astronomy as a part of vedic scholarship and to have allowed immunity to nampūtiri scholars from *pātityadoṣa* (losing the caste status and ranking consequent on doing the forbidden for the brāhmaṇa varna). Teaching and learning higher mathematics by non-nampūtiris is a clear indication of pure academic interest transcending the jāti-based discrimination and prejudice, which were very strong during this period.

In short, Kerala's midland became a land of Malayalam-speaking people, brāhmaṇical hegemony, Sanskritic intellectualism, hereditary occupations, caste-based hierarchy, agrarian economy, and independent principalities with cosmopolitan ports and inland marketing centres inhabited by Jews, Christians, Islamic Arabs and Chinese traders. It was to this spice-rich land of enormous trade potential that European trading companies arrived in the sixteenth century CE.

VIII

Arrival of the Europeans (16th–17th centuries CE)

The arrival of the Portuguese, the Dutch, the French and the English on the west coast as traders made a difference in the exchange relations of the period. Till the close of the fifteenth century, the Arab, the Jew, the Christian and the Chinese overseas merchants were the main participants in maritime exchanges and their relationship was based on cooperation and co-existence, i.e., the competition was seldom aggressive. The advent of Europeans upset this balance, for their aim was to establish monopoly, which led to conflict of interest and rivalry among the merchants. Moreover, a striking feature of the trade relations that some of the European countries built up during the period involved colonisation through aggressive means. A brief review of trade by the Arabs, Jews, Christians and Chinese will clarify the difference.

Trade Before the Arrival of the Europeans

We have already discussed the early history of the Arab, Jewish, Christian and Chinese trade relations with Kerala. Over the centuries the Arabs, Jews and Christians had become locally routed in different parts of Kerala under the patronage of the local rulers. The Chinese hardly seem to have become part of the local people, although Chinese trade relations with Kerala—especially with Kozhikode and Pantalāyinikollam—was flourishing since the thirteenth century CE.

According to Odoric of Pordenone, in the beginning of the fourteenth century CE, there were settlements of Christians and

Jews at Pantalāyinikollam, a major pepper trading centre. Such settlements were there in most ports on the west coast as well. Historian Basil Gray certifies that the Jewish merchants played a significant role in the trade between the East and the West with the support of their relatives in Yemen. Duarte Barbosa, in the sixteenth century CE, says that there was a flourishing Jewish settlement at Māḍāyi towards the north of Vaḷarpaṭṭaṇam. Māḍāyi seems to have been a settlement of overseas traders, particularly of Jews and Arabs who might have occupied the place till late sixteenth century CE. Al-Idrisi mentions this port town along with Puthupaṭaṇam, Vaḷarpaṭṭaṇam and Cherupaṭṭaṇam. This is corroborated by the archaeological remains of Persian ceramics and a pond, still called after the Jews (Jutakkuḷam), found at the site identified as Māḍāyi.

Some of the strategic places like port towns, ferries, temple premises and junctions where multiple routes converged had become big exchange centres and townships by this time. Ma Huan, the French mariner Francois Pyrard de Laval and several others mention these busy centres of exchange. Among them it is the Arab traveller Ibn Battuta who first describes what a contemporary port town of Kerala looked like at the instance of Pantalāyinikollam. He refers to it as a township surrounded by beautiful coconut garden-lands. Another example of a big port town and market described is Quilon in Vēṇāṭu. We have already discussed the references of foreign travellers to Quilon as the most prominent centre of exchange of the period, and as the town that attracted people from far off places and different cultures. As shown earlier in detail, several literary works in contemporary Malayalam contain beautiful descriptions of such port towns, markets and fairs, replete with almost all kinds of goods for ordinary daily life and luxurious living. Goods piled up in these markets included food grains, textiles, implements, ornaments, fruits, fish, herbs, etc. Descriptions of Thiruvananthapuram, Kollam, Mattam and Kozhikode show that most townships had separate streets for each item of exchange. All the markets in these towns were more or less similar, with the din and bustle of people speaking various languages and the babble of crowds of traders exchanging a variety of goods. Brāhmaṇas and slaves, traders and versifiers, jostled against one another in the crowd that thronged the market. All this was in full swing at the time of the arrival of European traders.

Transport and communication had hardly witnessed any change during the period. Horse, the symbol of speed, was an important object of trade since thirteenth century, but only as a transit item. It had no use in the plains of Kerala, where trade routes passed mostly through marshy villages. There were no roads, only pedestrian tracks along midland Kerala, often connecting the ferries. Even bullock carts were of limited use, for they were unsuitable to the tracks along the marshy plains as well as the undulating uplands. Ma Huan has recorded the practice of carrying pepper and various other goods as head-load for short distances and on pack animals for longer distances. *Uṇṇunīlisandeśam* mentions the transport of goods on pack animals between Tamil Nadu and Kerala through the Chenkoṭṭai pass. Coastal trafficking of goods via vessels was also prevalent. Settlement registers of Pantalāyinikollam and Kozhikode mention certain plot names in the royal land of the Sāmūtiri suggestive of the existence of a community called oṭāyis, who were engaged in the construction of sea-going vessels. The Italian traveller Ludovico di Varthema, in the beginning of the sixteenth century CE, praised the craftsmanship of the oṭāyis in planking the hull leak-proof without the use of nails.

On the eve of the arrival of Europeans, Kerala was characterised by a social formation with paddy cultivation continuing as the dominant industry. A significant change was the growth of the economy of garden crops that had exchange value overseas. Garden lands (paṛampu) are cultivated red soil terraces (*punam*) adjacent to paddy fields; they are mostly covered by wild flora and domestic fruit-bearing trees along with coconut and arecanut palms. In the same land tracts, a variety of seasonal millets, pulses and spices, such as ginger, pepper and turmeric, were grown. There was a relative increase in the reclamation of punam lands as garden lands of cash crops by those who had held them as their household (purayiṭam) and traditional property (kāṇam). This accounted for the rise of dealers in cash crops and stationary merchants with permanent godowns (*pāṇḍikaśāla*), retail shops (*kaṭa* and *pīṭika*) and monetisation of exchanges. Money had made transmutation of land dues into cash and a relatively systematised imposition of ferry tolls and tariffs possible in the resource-rich principalities of Vēṇāṭu and Ēṟanāṭu, which had become full-fledged state powers by this time. However, monetisation did not replace the conventional system of transaction based on inter-goods exchange rates. Even in big centres of exchange like ports, the price of merchandises was fixed in terms of money, but the actual exchange was in barter mode. Gold was the basic metal of value in higher transactions and paṇam was its form of currency. Silver was the next valuable metal and tāram was its currency. In Kozhikode, the purity of gold was 60 per cent according to its chronicles. There were established inter-currency exchange rates among the coins of gold and silver of different countries. For instance, each silver tāram was equal to 3 Chinese li. There were copper coins as well, but these were used only in small transactions. Both paṇam and tāram were very small in size. Ma Huan and Portuguese travellers describe them as looking like fish scales.

According to accounts of the Arab and Chinese travellers, trade was bustling on the seaboards of Kerala. According to Fei Hsin, coconut was an important item of demand in China along with pepper, fish and areca. One estimate shows that annually more than 400 ships sailed from the Malabar coast with coconut. Ma Huan's accounts also contain references to the cultivation and yield of coconut palms. He mentions that some of the rich landholders owned 3000 coconut trees, while others had garden lands with coconut palms varying between 2000 and 1000 in number. Travel accounts show that the Malabar coast was extensively covered with coconut garden lands by the turn of the fourteenth century CE. Chinese, Jewish, Arab and Syrian Christian overseas trade declined in the beginning of the sixteenth century with the formalisation of the Portuguese trade relations with the Sāmūtiri and others.

Merchants were the possessors of money. Local Christian merchants (*tarakan*) were very influential as the chief money lenders. They were the suppliers of silver and copper to royal mints. In a way, they minted coins for the rulers of the two major principalities. Holders of kāṇam lands also had access to money. Traditional landlords, who were mainly holders of paddy lands, had to borrow money from merchants by leasing pieces of their paddy fields, at interest that was to be deducted out of the dues (pāṭṭam) from the leased land.

Contemporary social formation was characterised by the hierarchy of land-rights headed by janmi or urāḷan and the rest viz., kāṇakkāran, kārāḷan, kuṭiyan and aṭiyāḷar in the descending order. It was hierarchy of hereditary occupation castes (*kulattoḻil jāti*) as well. Arts, crafts and unskilled labour were obligatory and attached to the land held by prominent swarūpams and brāhmaṇas. The two most prominent swarūpams of the period were Vēṇāṭu in the south and Ēṛanāṭu in the north, as we have already discussed. They were not full-fledged states as yet, though some institutional and bureaucratic mechanisms were in place for the collection of dues, self defence and revenue administration. Big powers were busy extending their sphere of control, into which penetration was difficult for the alien trade monopolists. They had evolved a system for such aliens to enter into formal relations of exchange. However, small ruling powers, contesting, conspiring, betraying and cheating against one another, were amenable to influences of alien trading forces.

Arabs, Jews and Christians of the Persian tradition were culturally adapted to the local people and had little in common with the religious identities of their foreign counterparts. Those who came to Kerala from different parts were religiously more rigid and conscious of their identities. But, the Persian tradition was of pre-Christian and pre-Islamic way of life, and hence more akin to the Hebrew. Many of its elements were present in the Islamic Arabs, the Jews and Christians as part of the common cultural binding factor among them. However, settlements of these localised Arabs, Jews and Christians, who were in control of the coastal and inland trade networks, had functioned as the main contact of overseas merchants belonging to the religious communities concerned. The Christians of Syrian and Persian connections dominated Quilon under the rulers of Vēṇāṭu. Arab Mussalmans of Malabar, called Kunhali Marakkars, were linked to the spice trade network of Mamluk Sultans and Al-Karimi merchants whose control had extended up to the Mediterranean. They were the cargo suppliers of the Muslim traders coming from this vast region, especially from Egypt and Tunisia, and coastal traders engaged in the zone from Nāgapaṭṭaṇam to Kunimedu. The Marakkar Mussalmans and Jews were the cargo suppliers in Kochi, Kannur and Māḍāyi. Kozhikode was the most prosperous coastal town of the period, not a convenient port though, due to the rock barriers that prevented ships from going closer to the seaboard. Therefore, Pantalāyinikollam, that had suitable landscape features and a bay for the ships to anchor, was the favoured port.

European trading companies arrived one after the other following the Portuguese who pioneered the voyage to the Malabar coast. They rivalled each other for monopoly and in due course each lost their dominance to another. Nevertheless, dominance did not mean disappearance of the other. They co-existed rivalling against one another and intriguing with the local rulers. We discuss here the history of their trading companies in Kerala keeping the order of arrival and the sequence of dominance in mind. With the victory over Tipu Sultan in 1792, the establishment of English hegemony became complete. Therefore, that date is considered the virtual end period of the other companies in Kerala in this discussion.

The Portuguese

King Immanuel of Portugal had obtained the Pope's sanction to explore new areas of trade and own them. This papal sanction added to the king's ambition to reach the west coast of India and own the Indian Ocean trade zone through conquest. Accordingly, he had acquired prior knowledge about the sea route to the west coast with the help of Bartolomeu Dias, the well-known explorer of sea routes between eastern Africa and India. He had gathered knowledge about the land and people of the land by sending spies as well. The selection of Vasco da Gama as the captain was an accidental coincidence. Vasco da Gama set out from Lisbon on 8 July 1497 with 170 persons on board, who were mostly criminals, and sailed along the African seaboards of Mozambique, Mombasa, Malindi, etc. It is said that a Gujarati mariner sent by the Sultan of Malindi navigated his ship through the waters of the west coast of India and to the seaboard of Kozhikode. Along the way, several of his people died of scurvy. He reached the seaboard of Kozhikode on 18 May 1498. Once he came to know about it from the fishermen, the Sāmūtiri advised the captain to get his ship moored off-shore at Kappad, a safer point at the onset of the monsoon. Vasco da Gama consulted his co-navigator Nicolas Koel Hoe about the ways and means of meeting the Sāmūtiri. He waited for three days to get a formal sanction to meet the Sāmūtiri. Meanwhile, the Marakkar Mussalmans, who were aware of how Portuguese trade would adversely affect their trade prospects on the Malabar coast, informed the Sāmūtiri that da Gama's goal was the conquest of Kozhikode and not trade. Naturally, the Sāmūtiri received da Gama with apprehension and kept him under the custody of the soldiers for a few days, apparently as a protective measure against a possible attack on him by Marakkars. Vasco da Gama is said to have gone back to Portugal humiliated.

In 1500 the Portuguese traders came again as a huge contingent of 1200 mariners of Europe, especially from Italy and Germany, in 13 ships led by Pedro Álvares Cabral. They gave the message of aggressive trade under monopoly by attacking sailors and fishermen on the Malabar coast. Cabral returned with pepper and other spices collected through forced negotiations and imposed relations. In 1502, Vasco da Gama came back with a vindictive mind. He arrived flanked by a huge naval contingent of 20 ships full of armed fighters, including several German and Italian gunmen. Killing several people off-shore, his contingent spread horror and demanded 20,000 crusado (the standard currency of Portugal) by way of compensation for the loss during his first visit and assurance for ousting the Marakkars from the Malabar coast. But the Sāmūtiri declined and da Gama's men ravaged the port town of Kozhikode. Vasco da Gama cut the hands, ears and lips of envoys sent by the Sāmūtiri. He took several people, including women and children, as captives and mutilated or killed them. Many Mussalman traders and fishermen were brutally murdered.

According to convention, the ruler had control over the sea adjacent to his territory. The Arabic term *carthas* refers to the ruler's sanction to sail in his sea. This term shows that Arab rulers had imposed this practice on mariners sailing through their sea. Mamluk Sultans and Chinese rulers also followed this practice. Sāmūtiris and the Ali Rajas too had the system of according formal sanction for sailing in their waters. Portuguese rulers, however, claimed control over the vast ocean far beyond their territory on the basis of Papal authority and aggressively imposed carthas wherever their ships reached. They took the carthas system as an excuse for attacking the traders sailing in the Arabian Sea. This upset the traders as well as the local rulers, who were the authorities in their waters. Conflicts became inevitable under these circumstances. Sailors approached the Sāmūtiri and demanded immediate action against the Portuguese.

Portuguese Alliance with Kōlattiris

It was not possible for the Kōlattiri to depend on Kunhali Marakkars, who always preferred the patronage of the Sāmūtiri. Following the second voyage of Vasco da Gama, the Portuguese became more prominent than the Kunhali Marakkars. This advantageous position of the Portuguese as enterprising overseas traders and a formidable naval force encouraged the Kōlattiri to draw closer to them. Keeping in view the Sāmūtiri's trade revenue and state power, an alliance with the Portuguese was of great strategic importance for the Kōlattiri. A ruling power without features of a state system, the Kōlattiri, whose land was rich in pepper and other spices, had no institutional or organisational means to take the benefits of trade directly. Therefore, the Kōlattiri was waiting for an opportunity to gain friendship with the Portuguese so that he may reap the revenue benefits from trade. The Portuguese, knowing fully well that the relationship with the Sāmūtiri would be always unsteady, wanted to secure a relatively stable alliance with an alternative political power. The Kōlattiri ruling house was an ideal alternative. Thus, a mutual agreement of help and cooperation was reached between the Portuguese and the Kōlattiri. While the needs of the Portuguese trade were met with the help of the Kōlattiri, the Kōlattiri's economic and political needs were met by the Portuguese. The Portuguese relation with the Kōlattiris was stable and continuous till the former's final defeat in the hands of the Dutch in 1663 CE and exit from Kerala.

Marakkar–Portuguese Conflicts

After the initial encounters the Kunhali Marakkars grew friendly with the Portuguese. They were good supporters of the Portuguese in their early years. Despite the conflicts over carthas, Portuguese relations with the Marakkars on the Malabar coast was not always one of enmity. In fact, the Marakkars required the support of the Portuguese too. As coastal traders and cargo suppliers, the Kunhali Marakkars always needed a stable group of overseas traders and the Portuguese who had taken precedence over the Arab Al Karimi traders constrained the Marakkars to shift their dependency from the latter to the former. At one point in time, the Kunhali Marakkars helped the Portuguese by providing 1500 seamen to confront the Sāmūtiri.

Nevertheless, the Kunhali Marakkars and Portuguese were frequently in conflict over issues apparently various but fundamentally one, i.e., economic rivalry. One of the serious issues was the rise of the *cassados*. Cassados were offsprings of Portuguese men who took local spouses. By the latter half of the sixteenth century CE, cassados emerged as an organised trading group on the Malabar coast under Portuguese protection. The Kunhali Marakkars revolted against the Portuguese with vengeance when the cassados began to push Kunhali Marakkars out from their costal trade monopoly at various places on the Malabar coast. Therefore, the Marakkars strongly confronted both the Portuguese and the cassados. However, as usual, this conflict also subsided through compromise for economic reasons.

At times Marakkar conflicts with Portuguese have been characterised as communal. Accordingly, Kunhali Marakkars and many Mussalman fishermen are said to have fought against the Portuguese with the spirit of the *jihadis* (the religious duty of holy fight against the infidels). It is possible that Islamic religious sentiments may have been used to strengthen the solidarity of Mussalmans. *Tuhfat Ul Mujjahiddin* by Shaik Zainuddin (c. 1510–1583 CE), an Islamic scholar of Ponnani, is the famous contemporary source on the subject. It excites Islamic solidarity through a narration of the history of Mussalmans of Malabar, highlighting their miserable life with the arrival of the Portuguese.

Kunhali Marakkars constituted a formidable force that resisted the Portuguese from establishing themselves on the Malabar coast till the close of the sixteenth century CE. It was at Ponnani that they fought the Portuguese for the first time and lost. Routed from Ponnani, Kunhali Marakkars established themselves at Kottakkal and became known as Kottakkal Kunhali Marakkars. However, as mentioned already, the Portuguese could not afford permanent enmity with Kunhali Marakkars, who were their cargo suppliers.

While the Portuguese permanently fought the Al Karimi merchants as their rivals in spice trade, they always patched up their rifts with the Kunhali Marakkars, whose support was crucial in coastal transactions. With the Al Karimi merchants losing grip in the network of spice trade and cassado kinsmen becoming prominent in the coastal transactions, the Portuguese were attempting to stabilise their control over all trade activities on the Malabar coast. They approached the Sāmūtiri for permission to build forts at Chaliyam and Ponnani, but the Sāmūtiri declined. Their forceful attempt at building a fort at Chaliyam was foiled by the strong resistance of the armed contingent of the Kunhali Marakkars. The Portuguese were not able to establish control over the Malabar coast despite their aggressive moves during 1597–99 due to the formidable attacks by the Kunhali Marakkars. Finally, the Portuguese gained an upper hand only through the treacherous murder of the most assertive Kunhali Marakkar of the time. The paradox is that it was the Sāmūtiri, who in retaliation to a humiliation meted out to him, deceitfully trapped this Kunhali Marakkar and handed him over to the Portuguese. By the end of the sixteenth century CE, however, the Portuguese succeeded in establishing themselves at Kollam, Kochi, Koṭunkōḷūr, Kozhikode and Kannur by building their forts at strategic centres.

The Sāmūtiris and Kunhali Marakkars

Sāmūtiris and the Kunhali Marakkars had a long relationship of mutual support and collaboration but with ups and downs. As we have already seen, the basis of their collaboration as well as conflict was economic. The Sāmūtiris patronised Kunhali Marakkars for the strong naval force they provided and the good revenue benefits from their trade. Similarly, Kunhali Marakkars supported Sāmūtiris for their trade interests. The Kunhali Marakkars were the main fighters of the Sāmūtiris in all their encounters with the Portuguese. For the Marakkars, friendship with the Sāmūtiri, who had sovereign control over Kozhikode, was indispensable. This mutual relationship between the Sāmūtiri and the Kunhali Marakkar, after the arrival of the Portuguese, was centred and opportunistic. Portuguese traders were both the hope and despair for them. Whenever there was a better economic opportunity, however, the Sāmūtiris and the Kunhali Marakkars betrayed each other. Often the Sāmūtiris thought that the Portuguese trade would be more profitable to them and, therefore, helped the Portugese against the Kunhali Marakkars. In spite of such betrayals, the Marakkars patched up with the Sāmūtiri because his port of Pantalāyinikollam and the market town of Kozhikode were their main strategic centres of trade.

In 1584 the Sāmūtiri conceded a Portuguese request to build a factory at Ponnani on condition that they would allow the Kunhali Marakkars to conduct trade along the seaboards of Gujarat, Persia and Arabia. However, when the Portuguese tried to build a fort at Chaliyam, the Sāmūtiri prevented it with the help of the Kunhali Marakkars led by the indomitable fighter Pattu Marakkar. Pleased by his leadership, the Sāmūtiri permitted him to build a fort at Iringal. After Pattu Marakkar's death, his brother's son, very assertive and over-ambitious, became the leader of the Kunhali Marakkars. He expanded the fort with a moat around it and behaved like the Māppiḷa Sultan of the Arabian Sea, much to the displeasure of the Sāmūtiri. In 1599, he defeated even the Sāmūtiri's own soldiers in a clash. Before he could take any action against him, unfortunately, the Sāmūtiri died. The Kunhali provoked the next Sāmūtiri by slicing the tail of the royal elephant that entered the premises of his fort. Adding to the wrath of the new Sāmūtiri, he humiliated the soldiers who questioned his action. Soon the Sāmūtiri, through the mediation of two Jesuit priests, made an alliance with the Portuguese to wreak vengeance upon the Kunhali Marrakkars, by accepting the condition that the Kunhali would be captured and handed over. However, the Sāmūtiri is said to have sought the Portuguese to promise that they would treat Kunhali nobly.

Surrounded by a joint contingent of the Sāmūtiri soldiers on land and the Portuguese navy, the Marakkar is said to have helplessly begged for pardon. Accordingly, the Sāmūtiri, pretending to be friendly, invited the Kunhali to his palace. Pyrard de Laval gives an eyewitness description of what really happened as follows: The Kunhali reached the palace and walked towards the Sāmūtiri who was flanked by nair soldiers and Portuguese soldiers on either side. The Sāmūtiri quietly moved closer to Kunhali, dispossessed him of his sword, patted him and said, 'Kunhali, you brought me a lot of suffering and loss.' The Sāmūtiri then turned to the Portuguese leader Andre and said,

'Here you are. Now Kunhali is yours.' The Portuguese soldiers took him away. They not only killed him brutally but also exhibited his corpse in public. This brought the Sāmūtiri intense remorse and severe distress. He fell out with the Portuguese after this incident.

The Germans

The Germans reached Malabar along with the Portuguese as their security personnel and soldiers. The Germans were close to the Portuguese as merchants and canon workers, and had the royal sanction for trade. They had a settlement in Lisbon and a foundation called Bartholomew Fraternity with a hospital under it. Several German merchant families had settled in Iberian islands as well. It was these Germans who joined the Portuguese fleets as traders and canon workers. Some of the Germans were good geographers and mathematical astronomers. Martin Behaim, the astronomer and mathematician, who guided the African voyage of the Portuguese (1482–1488 CE), is a famous example.

Several rich German merchant families had reached Malabar in 1505 CE independently along with the fleet of Almeida (the fleet of 22 vessels with 1,500 men led by Francisco de Almeida, who was appointed as the Portuguese Viceroy of India). It is seen in the records that a family called Welser was rich enough to invest a total of 20,000 crusados for the trade. We get details about the German merchants of the time from the travelogue of Balthaser Spanker, who was the agent of Almeda's ship. We understand from his writings that as the Portuguese control of trade with Malabar grew, the German population also saw a rise. The Germans had a settlement at Cochin with a church in the name of St Bartholomew.

Being the main consumers of Indian spices, Germans owned and controlled all the major spice markets in Europe. They were able to reap huge profit as retailers, middlemen and bulk dealers in spices like pepper, ginger, cloves, cinnamon, chappangam, etc. Since Germany was a land of copper and silver, it was easy and more profitable for German merchants to barter these metals for spices or trade in them by using metallic money. In a way, it provided a situation of trade monopoly for them. This created excited opposition from the Lutherans who were against trade monopoly. However, the Lutheran criticism of trade monopoly subsided after the onset of agrarian revolt in Germany (1524–1525 CE) against peasant oppression under feudal lords. Luther's protest movement and its call for the poor to claim divine law against exploitation was the inspiration for the peasants. But it bothered the middleclass Lutherans who were least interested in the peasant revolt. This encouraged German merchants to seek monopoly in the spice trade. Meanwhile, the rise of Portuguese private trade with Kerala upset the ambitions of German monopoly over spice trade and created opportunities for others.

Some of the very rich German merchants forged ahead, exploring chances of monopolising spice trade. Conrad Rot, a fabulously rich German merchant, acquired pepper trade monopoly in Asia and Europe through two contracts in 1578 under the patronage of King Sebastian I of Portugal. He reaped enormous profit through spice trade by transporting huge quantities of it from the west coast of India in Portuguese ships. His enterprise declined after the death of the king in a battle and due to the economic depression of the 1580s. However, he recouped his pepper trade during 1587–92 with the end of the recession and remained the main supplier of copper to the coast of south India and particularly Kerala. Earlier copper was brought by the Chinese traders. With the onset of European monopoly over eastern trade, the Chinese withdrew from the field. After this, it was Rot who prevailed as the main supplier of copper to the Indian seaboards.

German trade in the eastern world declined with the fall of the Portuguese. The Germans were heavily depended on them as traders as well as their service personnel. Some of them entered the service of the swarūpams. For example, the King of Cochin had a German as his advisor, which accounted for his firm decisions in matters of trade relations with European powers.

The Germans had introduced guns, gun powder and canons in Kerala. The Sāmūtiri was perhaps the first in the region to secretly obtain the service of a German canon worker in developing local guns. The Sāmūtiri was able to institutionalise the technology of firing by making one of his soldiers as the *vetikkurukkal* (gun-man). Soon several Germans became canon workers under the local rulers in Kerala. It was not the technology of battles alone that they developed here. They were also responsible for the improvement of handicrafts technology, especially of the textile sector. Many of them turned to religious missionary enterprises. German missionaries were the first to combine religious activities with community healthcare and livelihood improvement. As part of their missionary work, several of them were genuinely interested in the history, society, language and culture of the people of Kerala. It is a continuation of this scholarly interest that we see in the works of Hermann Gundert. Germans were critical of the superstitious beliefs and irrational practices, such as the caste system, prevalent in the region. However, they distinguished themselves as a noble people and always kept a distance from the local people.

The Dutch in Malabar

The Dutch appeared on the Malabar coast in 1604. On 14 November 1604, the Dutch naval captain Vander Gohen entered into a trade agreement with the Sāmūtiri that accorded sanction for the Dutch to transact their business at Ponnani and Kozhikode. However, this hardly created significant results for Dutch trade. In 1608 a Dutch fleet consisting of 15 ships came and moored off-shore in the Kozhikode sea. The captain of the fleet Vir Hoven presented two canons captured from the Portuguese and certain other valuables to the Sāmūtiri. Thus began their trade with Kerala. They soon encountered various swarūpams. Spices, especially pepper, attracted their attention. But they also dealt with other items like cotton, arecanut, conch, indigo, timber, lime, bricks, coir, rice, coconut oil, salt, firewood, etc. In these initial years the Dutch had no other interest but trade.

However, they soon began interfering with the political power relations by taking sides during internal dissentions among local rulers. A traditional source material called *Patappattu* (collection of poems in Malayalam using Persian and Arabic words) deals with episodes relating to such interventions and they belong to the category of heroic songs. They are part of the oral tradition of the māppiḷas of Malabar, whose songs deal with themes such as religion, love, satire and heroism and are recited on festive occasions celebrating birth, marriage and death.

In Europe the Dutch and the Portuguese were inimical to each other. Naturally, they also fought on the Malabar coast because trade rivalry was an added provocation here. In 1661, the Dutch captain Van Goyans was instructed to capture all the strongholds of the Portuguese on the west coast from Kanyakumari in the south to places such as Quilon, Cochin, Kannur and Goa in the north. The captain reached Quilon in December 1661 with a fleet of 24 ships. After a clash involving serious collateral damage, the Portuguese withdrew from Quilon. Goyans chased the Portuguese and attacked them at their seat in Cochin. In support of the Portuguese the Sāmūtiri sent his soldiers, but his support was in vain. Despite a strong Portuguese defence, the Dutch captured the Koṭunkōḷūr fort and the factory at Cochin.

The Sāmūtiris and the Dutch

The Sāmūtiris had neither any permanent enemies nor any stable friends. Naturally, when the Portuguese began to phase out, the Sāmūtiri drew closer to the Dutch. His intention was to conquer the Perumpaṭappu with the support of the Dutch. If that was not likely, the Sāmūtiri desired that the power of the Neṭiyirippu should be extended at least up to Vaippinkara. The Sāmūtiri could not achieve any of these because the main objective of the Dutch after the defeat of the Portuguese was to establish their monopoly in spice trade. In order to achieve this, the Dutch sometimes allied with the Neṭiyirippu and at other times with the Perumpaṭappu. When the Dutch extended their

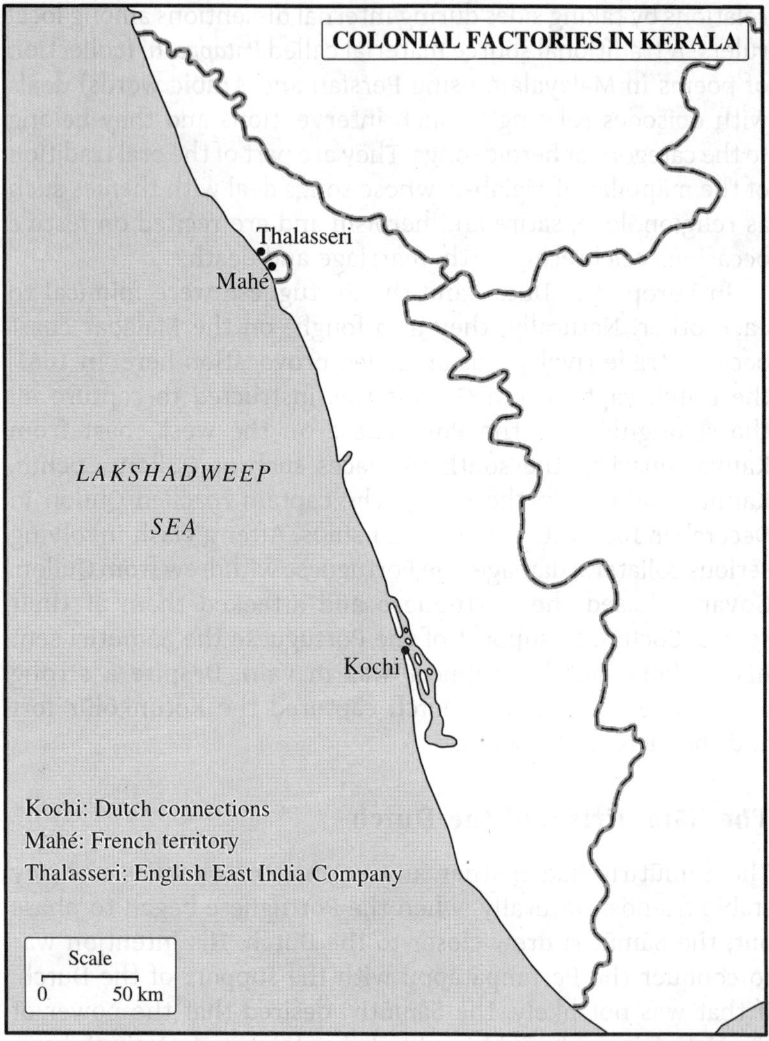

Note:

1. © Government of India, Copyright 2018.
2. The responsibility for the correctness of internal details rests with the publisher.
3. The territorial waters of India extend into the sea to a distance of twelve nautical miles measured from the appropriate base line.
4. The spellings of names in this map have been taken from various sources.

control to Cochin, the Sāmūtiri who had helped them demanded the Dutch to cede Koṭunkōḷūr and Vaippinkara to him. But the Dutch refused because the Sāmūtiri had allowed the English to build their fort at Kozhikode. The Dutch were alert to prevent the establishment of the English on the Malabar coast at any cost. Now the Portuguese navy came to the help of Sāmūtiri. However, there was no use because the combined force of the Portugese and the Sāmūtiri was no match for the Dutch. In 1670 the Sāmūtiri fought against the Dutch and lost. Such ups and downs were not unusual in the history of the Sāmūtiris.

In 1678 Hendrik Adriaan van Rheede tot Drakenstein, the Governor of the Dutch East India Company, went to Ponnani palace and met the Sāmūtiri with gold and other valuables as gifts to patch up. This visit of van Rheede had great diplomatic importance in the context of the Dutch rivalry with the English East India Company. Sāmūtiri, growing apprehensive of the rise of the English, thought that the Dutch help would be better. Accordingly, an agreement was reached between the two. Soon there arose a conflict over the heir of succession in the Perumpaṭappu and the Dutch interfered in it much to the displeasure of several local rulers in Malabar. First, the ruler of Veṭṭattunāṭu (Tānur), a small coastal principality, expressed dissent and joined the side of the English East India Company. Various local rulers of other small principalities between Cochin and Palakkad, such as Paravur, Mangād, Maṇakkuḷam, Ayanikkūṟu and Kavaḷappāṟa, also turned against the Dutch. This made the position of the Dutch in Malabar quite vulnerable. They became unsafe in the region south of Cochin as well due to the threat of Tiruvitāmkur. Naturally, the Dutch appealed to the help of the Sāmūtiri and made their earlier agreement more formal as a treaty of mutual support against their enemies for twelve years and that sustained them in Malabar for over a decade. The treaty enhanced the Sāmūtiri's power as well. The Sāmūtiri who came to the throne in 1684 had an efficient advisor called Bavan Pattar, a Konkani brāhmaṇa. He cast an extensive network of spies penetrating into all the ruling families in Malabar.

Some of the senior personnel in the service of the Perumpaṭappu were also said to have been his spies.

Attingal Revolt (April–October 1721): Attingal Revolt was a significant political event in Tiruvitāmkur during this period. Attingal was part of the kingdom of Vēṇāṭu, which comprised Nedumangad (Perakam), Tiruvitāmkur, Kollam, Karunagappalli, Kottarakkara (Elayidam), Karthikappalli and Kaymkulam. Attingal was the seat of the queens of Vēṇāṭu kings and the queens, in the order of the seniority, ruled the place. Over the years, the tradition gave Attingal the relatively autonomous status of a principality. Among the several queens of Attingal, Rani Aswathi Tirunal Umayamma Rani (1677–98 CE) was the most prominent. She ascended the throne of Attingal as the successor of Makayiram Tirunal Rani.

It was a time when the Dutch and the English East India Companies were rivalling each other for monopoly in spice trade. Both the Dutch and the English had their factories at strategic points in Malabar and Tiruvitāmkur. There were internecine conflicts between the Dutch and the English over the trade in pepper. Britain, France, Scotland, Ireland and the Netherlands reached a peace agreement in 1679 CE accepting the colonial monopoly of any of them on raising their flag at the fort site. The English were the first to establish a fort and get their monopoly accepted. Accordingly, the Rani was to sell pepper and spices from Anjuthengu (Anjengo) only to the English. The Dutch had a factory at Thengapaṭṭaṇam in Kanyakumari district and the English had their factory at Anjengo. Umayamma became more powerful as the head of a confederation of the principalities of Tiruvitāmkur, Nedumangad, Kottarakkara, Kollam, Karunagapalli and Kayamkulam from 1682 CE onwards. She was tactful in her dealings with the foreign trading companies as well as the local landlords, called pillais and māṭampis, who constituted the decisive elements of contemporary power structure. In 1684 she subdued Kerala Varma of Nedumangad, a member of the collateral family and suppressed the landed aristocracy that supported him.

In 1684 CE John Childe of the English East India Company decided to purchase maximum quantity of pepper from Attingal and the surrounding principalities, which displeased the Dutch because of the mutual competition and rivalry among the overseas trading companies. Naturally, the Rani was in favour of the English East India Company. However, the rivalry between the English and the Dutch continued, and as part of it the pillais destroyed the Dutch factory at Thengapaṭṭaṇam, set their ships on fire, and executed its captain in 1684. Though the Rani of Attingal tended to compensate the loss of the Dutch, the pillais prevented it.

By way of strengthening the friendship with the English, Umayamma Rani accorded sanction for the establishment of the English settlement at Anjengo in 1694 CE. Soon the company wanted the Rani's permission to fortify the settlement and the factory. Initially, pillais and māṭampis were not in agreement with the idea of allowing the English to fortify their factory. Later some of the pillais and māṭampis, along with the Rani, yielded to bribes and granted permission to the company in 1694. Due to various reasons, however, the company could not start the construction of the fort immediately.

Meanwhile some of the māṭampis and pillais secretly allied with the Dutch and exerted heavy pressure on the Rani to withdraw the royal sanction given for the company's fortification. Two prominent māṭampis, Kudaman Pillai and Vanjimuṭṭom Pillai, who used to rival each other on state affairs, apparently united against the fortification scheme of the English. This forced the Rani to be apprehensive about the possibility of the English as a fortified power, in defiance of the royal orders, and abstaining from paying the tax. Accordingly, the Rani nullified her earlier sanction and asked the English not to fortify their factory. Ignoring the royal orders, the company went ahead with the project of fortification in 1696 CE. Annoyed by the action, the Rani sent a contingent of nairs and Muslims to attack the English, but Vanjimuṭṭom Pillai failed the move by secretly passing prior information to the English as a way of securing their favour. Issues with the company aggravated further when the Court of Directors in England refused to accept the conditions put forward by the Rani. Nevertheless, the Rani let the English continue their trade ties with Attingal, Anjengo and Vizhinjam. Until Umayamma Rani's death in 1698 CE, the English trade with Attingal prospered. It is a matter of conjecture on who succeeded as the Rani of Attingal after Umayamma. Left with no heirs, Umayamma had adopted Aditya Varma and his two sisters of Kōḷattunāṭu. In her study of this period, Leena More opines that of the adopted sisters, the younger alone survived, and that the pillais conspired against her and made Ammu Tampuran, who would later become the heroine of the ensuing revolt, the Rani of Attingal.

In 1707 England and Scotland were unified under a single crown. That same year the Court of Directors issued orders permitting private trade by officials of the English East India Company. Several traders in the Company used the opportunity to make profits. However, they were cautious about their dealings with the local merchants and landlords. None of the chiefs had any serious problems in the exchange relations with the rulers. In 1719, the new chief of the Company, John Kyffin, was too enthusiastic about profit from private trade. Naturally, his relations with the local dealers worsened and he was dismissed from the Company's service. His successor, Willam Gyfford, was equally motivated by the profit from private trade. He made huge profits by shipping additional cargos of pepper to Europe in the ship owned by his brother-in-law, the famous Thomas Cook. Gyfford's behavioural oddities added to the growing popular discontentment against the English who had become notorious for their disobedience of the Rani. Gyfford would often cast aspersions on people belonging to different communities. Once he publicly insulted a brāhmaṇa and forced him to shave the beard of a person belonging to an untouchable caste. Poking fun at Muslims was part of Gyfford's odd behaviour and he encouraged others to do the same. He and his wife took pleasure in splashing dirty water upon Muslims who passed by the fort. There were several instances of caste-based insult and discrimination of the local spice dealers by company officials.

Moreover, Gyfford's men were in the habit of exploiting the local people. Corruption was rampant among the company officials. The anger of the pillais and māṭampis was rising due to non-payment of dues to them.

A provocation for what subsequently became a revolt was an illegal purchase of a plot of a temple land by Ignacio, an interpreter of the company, and the forcible occupation of the land at the displeasure of the local people. Another provocative incident was the ill-treatment of a few traders who went to the fort, which was plotted by Gyfford vindictively against those who had refused to trade with him. On 26 February 1721, a few pepper merchants belonging to the nair caste who met Gyfford and his translator were so badly insulted that it became a serious issue of discontentment. The immediate provocation was Gyfford's rejection of the demand by pillais and māṭampis to hand over the annual dues and customary gifts to the Rani through them. Gyfford insisted that he and his soldiers would directly handover the dues and gifts to the Rani. This position worsened the relationship between the officials of the company and the locals. In what ensued, Gyfford was asked by the Court of Directors to pacify the local people and restore warmth in the company's relationship with them. Accordingly, Gyfford bribed and sought the help of Vanjimuṭṭom Pillai to sort out the differences of the local people with the company.

Vanjimuttom Pillai arranged to crown Ammu Thampuran, whose royal descent is unknown, as the Rani and invited Gyfford to the coronation ceremony. Gyfford was also asked to clear all dues to the royal treasury and payments to the pillais, and renew his trade by pleasing the Rani. Accordingly, Gyfford set out from the fort of Anjengo for the palace of Attingal on 14 April 1721 with 140 men carrying the dues for seven years and gifts for the queen and the pillais. Only women, children, the old and the sick besides four men attending to their affairs were left in the fort. Kudaman Pillai and a contingent of armed nairs welcomed Gyfford and his people to the palace. In order to clear the dues, the English had only the new currency of the East India Company with them, but the pillais insisted payment in the traditional Venetian currency. It appeared that the pillais were delaying the transaction and Gyfford expressed his desire to meet the Rani. Since it was getting dark Kudaman Pillai advised the English men to stay back till the morning to meet the Rani. Accordingly, Gyfford and his men relaxed in the premises of the palace. Casey, Gyfford's deputy, suspected some treachery and advised Gyfford to finish the payment and leave, for he felt it unsafe to stay in the palace, but Gyfford ignored this warning. Sensing danger, however, Gifford soon sent a messenger to the fort at Anjengo, six kilometres away and quickly finished the transactions. The soldiers fired a couple of rounds in completion of their business in the palace (a sign for all the soldiers scattered at different points to get ready to leave the station). The nairs suddenly collected the arms of the English soldiers and killed all of them one after the other. Gyfford, Malhiero and Fleming, leaders of the English, were butchered and thrown into the Vamanapuram river.

Samuel Ince, the English gunner who remained, heard of the tragedy and adopted measures to defend the fort against possible subsequent attacks. Ince shifted the women, children and the aged along with all valuables and food resources to a ship moored off-shore. He also set fire to the gunpowder stock in the premises. The nairs attacked the fort immediately after the massacre but they failed to breach its walls. Moreover, a couple of canons were firing at them and the gun powder was burning in the premises. As anticipated, the fort was attacked again in a few days, but by this time Ince had secured more reinforcement through the sea and the nairs suffered serious losses. Nevertheless, the attack went on intermittently for six months causing collateral damages on both sides.

On hearing about the massacre, the Rani expressed regret and held Kudaman Pillai responsible for everything. She wrote to the king of Vēṇāṭu, withdrew to the palace at Kollam with the determination not to return to Attingal until peace was restored. She would never return to Attingal. Reacting to the situation, the king of Vēṇāṭu accused the Rani for everything.

The Attingal Revolt of April to October 1721, was the first armed uprising of local landlords, traders and local peasants, against social discrimination, misbehaviour, corrupt practices and untrustworthiness of the English East India Company. It was a revolt planned and executed by the landlords and the Rani. Their grievances were entirely economic and power related. Ordinary soldiers had no direct involvement in the revolt and they just obeyed the command of their leaders. However, in the attack of the fort there was the participation of the local people, especially of those belonging to the lower castes and Muslims, who had serious grievances against Gyfford and his officials. At the bottom of the revolt was the ruthless competition and rivalry among indigenous and foreign beneficiaries of the pepper trade. A series of events that followed made the English East India Company more and more powerful under Adams who tactfully intervened in the disputes of succession in the Tiruvitāmkur royal family and manipulated adoptions. Rama Varma, adopted from Kōḷattunāṭu at his behest, quite obligingly allowed the company to build its fort at Colachel and Idava. He granted the company total monopoly in pepper trade and gave license to mint coins. Rama Varma's two nephews, who were made princes at Neyyattinkara and Iraniel respectively, helped the English establish further in the region. In 1728 the prince of Neyyattinkara marched to Attingal with the help of the Naiks of Madurai and made his relative Karthika Thirunal the Rani after suppressing the pillais. Soon, the prince of Iraniel played a much more decisive role in curbing the pillais and māṭampis who were the main enemies of the company. It was this prince of Iraniel who ascended the throne of Tiruvitāmkur as the famous Anizham Tirunal Mārthāṇḍa Varma (1729–1758 CE), after the death of Rama Varma in 1729.

In one of his reports, Van Goyans mentions that Vēṇāṭu had been a small principality between Kanyakumari and the Vilavankode taluk when the Dutch reached the Malabar coast. Regions further north, such as Attingal, Dēśinganāṭu and Kayamkulam, were under the control of Eledathu Swarūpam and Perunthallur Swarūpam. Besides the Sāmūtiri, the Dutch had transactions with other swarūpams, such as Trippapur, Dēśinganāṭu, Perunthelli, Kayamkulam, Perumpaṭappu, etc. According to a Thalasseri record of 1726, the swarūpams were not in harmony with one another.

Tiruvitāmkur began to emerge as a great kingdom with the accession of Anizham Tirunal Mārthāṇḍa Varma who subjugated the *eṭṭuvīṭṭil pillais*, the eight prominent landed households of traditional dominance, and the māṭampis, integrated the collateral swarūpams and conquered the neighbouring kingdoms. This was the period when the Dutch were trying to expand towards the south of Cochin as part of their ambition to acquire monopoly over pepper trade. Mārthāṇḍa Varma's expansion was along the pepper routes as well. Naturally, the two came into conflict with each other and the first major encounter took place at Kayamkulam. A Dutch fleet returning from Sri Lanka attacked Tiruvitāmkur (1730–1731 CE). Encroaching upon the villages at Thengapaṭṭaṇam, Kadiyapaṭṭaṇam, etc. the Dutch inflicted loss of life and property. Hearing that they have sacked a few villages and have advanced towards Eraniyal in Kanyakumari district, Ramayyan Dalawa marched ahead with a troop. The Dutch were heading towards taking control of the Padmanabhapuram palace. Mārthāṇḍa Varma rushed to the spot where Ramayyan's force also converged, enabling the combined forces to contain the Dutch force in time.

On 31 July 1741 the famous battle of Colachel was fought. Mārthāṇḍa Varma defeated the Dutch at Colachel, marking the first defeat of a European country in Asian soil. Leaving the dead and the wounded in the battlefield, the Dutch soldiers withdrew to their ships. Several of them were taken as captives. Many canons and swords were recovered from them. It took the Dutch government seven years to recognise the defeat. Mārthāṇḍa Varma and Ramayyan Dalawa were noble and generous to the Dutch soldiers. Some of them were employed in the royal service. Yustecius De Lenoy and Dona de were given high positions in the king's defence. De Lenoy was made the chief captain (*valiya kappittān*). These Dutch naval officers were responsible for modernising the Tiruvitāmkur navy. De Lenoy was entrusted with the task of building forts and armory at strategic points.

It is often pointed out that much more than might and mien of the nair soldiers, the Dutch preoccupation with the affairs in the islands of East Asia was responsible for the Dutch defeat. Since they were busy establishing their strong hold in Java, it was not possible for the Dutch to send the required naval force to Kerala. Compared to the rich resources of Sri Lanka and Java, Kerala's ports were a source of poor revenue. Realising the fact that enmity with Mārthāṇda Varma would only bring loss to them, the Dutch expressed their desire to be on peaceful terms with Tiruvitāmkur. The Dutch leaders Essekkiel Rabbi and Silvester Mendez signed a treaty with Tiruvitāmkur at Mavelikkara whereby they agreed to several provisions drawn after long discussions with Ramayyan Dalawa and Thalavati Kunhu Mūttatu Kāryakkār. The main provision was that the Dutch would give weapons worth Rs 12,000 in return for sufficient quantity of pepper and clothes.

Besides local converts (lascorins), the Dutch had also employed in their trade offices Europeans and their local off-springs (topasses). The Topasses imitated the European culture in dress and language. All of them lived around their stations on the coast. This enabled effective transactions between the Dutch and the local traders as well as between themselves and other Europeans. In addition to these workers, there were also missionaries, who had wider social contacts in the region in connection with their religious activities. The missionaries were, in fact, the real intermediaries between European traders and the local people. Some of these missionaries were scholars deeply interested in the local knowledge systems such as astronomy, mathematics, medicinal plants and grammar. *Hortus Malabaricus*, an elaborate compendium of medicinal plants that was prepared with the help of local scholars, is an example of the scholarly contributions of the missionaries.

The French

The French East India Company was a royal enterprise with direct investment by the king himself. It began its activities in Malabar in 1664 under the direction of Jean-Baptiste Colbert, who was the finance minister of King Louis XIV. In 1666 the company established its first factory in India at Surat. Its representatives reached the eastern coast of south India, as permitted by the Mughal Emperor Aurangazeb. They established their trade station at Puthussery, also called Pandissery by the local people. In French Pandissery became Pondicherry, obviously due to a spelling mistake. However, it is now a well-established place name. The trade station and settlement at Pondicherry were built exactly according to contemporary French architecture and town planning. Mayyazhi (called as Mahe by the French) was the only station that the French could establish in Kerala.

In 1721, the French East India Company established its settlement at Mahe, a strategically important place. By 1765, Mahe became a major trade centre and community settlement of the French people. During the initial phase, the French sphere of influence stretched about 26 km inland along the Mayyazhi river up to Vatakkekkara, Peringathur and Poythara. Subsequently, their main activities were confined to the area from the coast to the hinterlands between Azhiyur in the south and Pallur in the north. Surrounding this station were local rulers like the ruler of Mayyazhi, Kuṛungōṭṭu Nair and Iruvai Nāṭu Nambiar, who had rifts with each other. All of them were under the overlordship of the Kōlattiris. As the soldiers of Kōḷattunāṭu, the ṇairs of the region held tax-free land while the mussalman māppiḷas and tiyyas had to pay tax for the land they held. Taking advantage of this explicit discrimination, the French drew the tiyyas and māppiḷas to their side by employing them in their military and other services.

Like other European trading companies, the French company also had its missionaries with extensive social relations. Missionaries became influential in the society through their healthcare service at the time of the small pox epidemic that frequented Malabar during this period. They made use of traditional herbal medicines like neem, chenthamari and turmeric in combating the epidemic and established a hospital at Mahe. Several missionaries, such as Clement, Innocent, Rokh, Poulinose and Germanian, who were actively involved in healthcare at Varappuzha near Cochin, reached Mahe and boldly engaged in the risky service of the epidemic victims. This tremendously enhanced the trustworthiness and acceptability of the missionaries in the eyes of the general public. An immediate result was large-scale conversion of the local people to Christianity, which brought in significant changes in the social composition of Mahe. Along with the nairs, tiyyas, māppiḷas and others like the castes of kammāḷar, the French people and converted Christians constituted an important segment of distinct culture in this place. A small church, built out of mud and roofed with coconut leaves, was the main institution where the French and their converts congregated. Subsequently, in 1736, the church was rebuilt with stone and lime.

Once the company was established, the French also followed the Portuguese and the Dutch strategies of taking advantage by interfering in the local power relations by taking sides in their rifts and rivalries. Often, they took part in the conflicts of local rulers and intrigued with them to aggravate their mutual antagonism. Kurungottu Nair was a very close associate of the French and he used this friendship against his enemy Iruvainattu Nambiar. Even big swarūpams sought the company's help in times of external threat. At times the French officials did not hesitate to even encroach upon the political rights of the rulers. For instance, they once drove away the toll collectors of the Kadathanāṭu rulers from the toll post of Mahe. Nevertheless, the French expansion and activties of self-aggrandisement encountered a major threat from the English who were getting established in a big way on the Malabar coast. As part of the French people's self-defence against the English, they drew closer to Hyder Ali, a military chief of the Mysore King.

Expansion to Lakshadweep

The Lakshadweep islands and the coastal mainland of Malabar must have come in contact at an early date but the history of those days is unclear. Some clues are available in legends relating to the occupation of the islands. A legend they share refers to some sailors who met with a shipwreck and happened to be ashore in one of the islands, as the first settlers. They were voyaging in search of their Perumāḷ, who had presumably gone to Mecca but never returned. These first settlers, as per the legends, occupied Amini, Kalpeni, Androth, Kavaratti and Agatti, and these islands are called the taṛavād islands as distinguished from the other islands which are known as melacheri islands. This story suggests that human life in the islands began with the arrival of the mainlanders.

The peaceful life on the islands was disturbed when Portuguese traders appeared in the Arabian Sea. Their cruel acts and harshness forced the islanders to seek the help of the Kōlattiris. First, the westerners were driven away, but soon they took bloody revenge in the form of large-scale massacres more than once. There are a few popular heroic folksongs from the islands that celebrate a certain Abu Bakr Khazi, who was killed by the Portuguese in 1549–50. It appears that the islands were ruled by the Kōlattiris for long. A historical Sanskrit kāvya called *Mūṣakavamśa* by Atula, dated to the eleventh century CE, says that the 'eighteen islands' in the ocean were under the Mushakas, traditional ancestors of the Kōlattiris. It is known from records that the Kōlattiris were collecting some dues from the islanders. Subsequently, the Raja of Chiṛakkal transferred his authority over the islands to the Ali Raja of Kannur for a regular payment of 6000 paṇams annually. It appears that this contract was in force until mid-eighteenth century CE. With the decline of the Chiṛakkal Rajas, the Ali Rajas stopped the payment of annual dues. This led to conflicts between the two ruling families.

As a part of the conflict over the revenue from Lakshadweep, the Ali Raja of Kannur invited Hyder Ali for a military intervention.

Accordingly, Hyder Ali invaded north Malabar in 1765–66, which almost ruined the Rajas of Chiṛakkal. These political events on the mainland had some effect on the islands too. The Ali Rajas of Kannur held sway over the islands with a view to enjoying their riches. They introduced coir monopoly leading to over-exploitation, and this resulted in a revolt of the northern islands against the Raja. On one occasion, it so happened that some boats laden with the products of the islands bound for Kannur sailed to Mangalore and they disposed of their goods there. This act of the sailors of the island infuriated Aṛakkal Beevi of Kannur, the queen of the Ali Raja of Aṛakkal, who sent her personnel to the island, confiscated the headman's property, emptied his houses and took several people as captives. Before the ships could leave, however, the people rose against the Bibi's personnel and overpowered them. They caught the personnel and released their fellow islanders who were in chains. Then they took the personnel to Mangalore and produced them before Tippu with a request to take action against the Bibi of Kannur. Tippu refused to act against the Bibi, who was friendly with him.

The Ali Rajas pretended to be protectors of the island and imposed regular tolls on the people. They made an effective arrangement for exaction of revenue to the royal treasury, rather than satisfying the needs of their people. The islanders felt the presence of royal power in the form of the legal-cum-revenue officer who represented the Ali Rajas. The Rajas first managed the island as per traditional practice, but later appointed their own *kāryakkār*, who had under him three or four assistants. In the absence of the king, the local assistants of the kāryakkār became exploitative in the islands. There were instances of some of the prominent islanders themselves being appointed as kāryakkār. On such occasions their official remuneration was reduced to half the amount. Therefore, they freely levied their dues from fellow-islanders. Naturally, the islanders hated the kāryakkār, who had become so cruel and harsh that the islanders had in their minds a dreadful image of these royal agents.

The English

The arrival of the English on the Malabar coast is marked by the landing of the English East India Company's Captain Keeling at Kozhikode in 1615 CE. At that time the Sāmūtiri was at Koṭunkōḷūr, engaged in fighting the Portuguese. Keeling proceeded to Koṭunkōḷūr and met the Sāmūtiri. It was agreed upon in the meeting that the English would offer all help to the Sāmūtiri for ousting the Portuguese out of Cochin. It was also agreed that the expenses of the battle would be shared equally by the Sāmūtiri and the English. A crucial benefit that the English secured through this agreement was complete freedom to conduct trade within the Sāmūtiri's kingdom. Accordingly, Keeling arranged for building two forts at Ponnani and Kozhikode. On 22 March 1615 the English opened a warehouse at Kozhikode, but the enterprise did not succeed and the English disappeared from the scene.

In 1664 the English reappeared on the Malabar coast. The Sāmūtiri was aggressively retorting to the Dutch for the repetition of the Portuguese treachery by them as well. It provided an appropriate occasion for the English to win the support of the Sāmūtiri. As anticipated, the Sāmūtiri relaxed the entire export tariff except for pepper, in favour of the English. In and around Kozhikode English soldiers became a big nuisance for the Dutch. They tried every means possible to expel the English from Kozhikode but all were in vain. Their clever schemes to mutually antagonise the Sāmūtiri and the English were counterproductive. Whatever they did to please the Sāmūtiri also failed to win his favour. For example, in 1691 the Dutch ceded Chettuva to the Sāmūtiri, who in turn gave the English sanction to build a warehouse there.

It was north Malabar that produced high quality pepper. Therefore, the English turned their attention towards the north. They chose to develop Thalasseri as their principal trading centre. During this period, local rulers of Kerala were emerging as swarūpams and the swarūpams were branching off into factions, quarrelling over the revenue shares. Each faction was trying to establish authority in its own space. Every swarūpam wanted to retain its authority. All of them fought against one another for more power and wealth. Kuṛumpoṛaināṭu, Kadathanāṭu, Puṛavaḻināṭu, Kōḷattunāṭu, Allarathunāṭu, etc. fought against one another. Lineages quarrelled over the division of returns. It was in this conflict-ridden political scenario that the English made their entry. Initially, the policy of the English was to keep off from the mutually-conflicting local powers. However, they soon followed the strategy of interference, which the other East India Companies had pursued. Self-aggrandisement and economic gains were the benefits that they wanted. Many of the quarrelling branches and factions invited the English to interfere. This gave them plenty of opportunities to make material benefits. They took sides and the political circumstances justified their involvement. Internal dissensions among the swarūpams and their collateral branches aggravated over the course of time. Strangely, this hardly affected the alliance between the English and the Sāmūtiri. Their relationship was only getting stronger. The Sāmūtiri sanctioned 25 per cent reduction in the export tariff of pepper in about 1670 CE.

In Europe also it was a period of incessant battles among ruling lineages. The English had led major battles against the French, the Spaniards and the Dutch. The American War of Independence broke out during this period. All this had serious repercussions in the trade relations and activities of the English East India Company in Kerala. The English had to fight several battles in Kerala against various European companies to establish monopoly in the spice trade. Apart from internal discord and incessant quarrels among the petty principalities and their minor ruling powers, the onset of the Mysorean invasions of Kerala (1766–1792 CE) provided suitable circumstances for the English to emerge as the most powerful.

IX

Mysore Raids and the English Ascendancy (1766 CE–1792 CE)

Mysore's military might, which could descend into north Malabar from Mysore or breach the southern boundary from Tirunelveli, terrorised the swarūpams of Kerala. Even the kingdom of Vēṇāṭu which was further south from Malabar was in constant fear of Mysore. These forays of the Mysore army into Kerala must be viewed against the backdrop of the long-standing rivalry between Mysore and the Marathas. Whenever the Maratha threat slackened Hyder Ali would invade Malabar, and when the Marathas resumed hostilities Hyder Ali would pull out his army from Malabar and redeploy them to counter the Marathas. Thus, these unpredictable intermittent attacks created a sense of anxiety and insecurity among the kings and the ruling families of Kerala. The Sāmūtiri's exasperation is evident in the following statement in a granthavari: 'Even though we have adhered in full faith, to the instructions of the Portuguese King, it is not possible to live in peace anywhere in the country.' Similarly, the ruling family of Aḷḷaṛathu swarūpam expressed its anxiety thus: 'It seems the Nawab's next target will be Aḷḷaṛathunāṭu. Since quite a few local families are against me, I do not expect to be able to continue here for long.' This shows how disunited the local rulers of Kerala were even when they were under intense insecurity.

The main aim of the army of Mysore seems to have been to replenish their supplies. Unfortunately, the local rulers themselves had paved the way for it. For example, the Sāmūtiri would always heckle the Palakkad Tarur swarūpam and extract as much as possible from them in cash and kind. In 1756–57

Sāmūtiri had attacked Palakkad. Just before this onslaught he had subjugated Valluvanāṭu and extended his power up to Neḍunganāṭu. Then he turned his attention to Palakkad and grabbed Naḍuvaṭṭom. This resulted in a vertical split in the Tarur ruling family. To escape the clutches of Pūnthuṛakkon (another name for the Sāmūtiri or the Zamorin), the head of the Palakkad ruling family, Komi Achan, sought help from Mysore, which in return demanded an annuity of 12,000 paṇam. Komi Achan agreed. During these conflicts Hyder Ali (1720–1782 CE) was the *foujdar* (a military commander) of the Mysorean army stationed at Dindigal. In accordance with the instructions of the Raja of Mysore, Hyder Ali dispatched a large battalion under Makhdum Ali to Palakkad. When the Sāmūtiri got wind of this, he refrained from an encounter with the Mysorean army, and instead bought peace by agreeing to pay a lump sum of 12 lakh rupees to the Raja of Mysore. This indeed was a big victory and spurred Hyder Ali to attack other petty kingdoms in Kerala who, he speculated, had enriched themselves through trade with foreign merchants. Immensely pleased with Hyder Ali over the checkmate of Sāmūtiri and facilitating a huge payment, the Raja of Mysore rewarded him with a *jagir* (a person who was granted revenue rights with the responsibility of maintaining military contingents).

Hyder Ali's Campaigns

The Sāmūtiri, however, failed to pay up the promised sum and the Raja of Mysore was enraged. Meanwhile Hyder Ali, who was growing in power and stature, deposed the Raja of Mysore and consolidated administration in his own hands by 1761 CE. He renewed the demand for money from the Sāmūtiri. When the Sāmūtiri refused to relent, Hyder Ali led an army to Malabar. Though the Sāmūtiri marched north to encounter the army of Mysore at Kōḷattunāṭu, he had to soon retreat. At Kaṭathanāṭu, he resisted valiantly, but the Mysore army defeated him and pushed him further south. The Sāmūtiri's efforts to counter the enemy forces at Kottakkatavil also failed. Finally, Hyder Ali's army reached Kozhikode and camped outside the south-eastern corner of the *kovilakam* (the royal quarters). The area where the Mysore army pitched its camp is still known as Pāḷayam (military camp). East of the main palace stood its subsidiary, Kiḻakke Kovilakam, spread over the present Thaḻeppāḷayam and Chinthāvaḷappu. This was the residence of the Ēṛāḷppad, the heir to the throne, and other important members of the royal family.

Since Hyder Ali's military camp was in dangerous proximity to the main Kovilakam, plans were made to transfer women and children to more secure places in the south. All the residents of Kiḻakke Kovilakam were sent to Ponnani. Manorama Thampuratty, who would later become a renowned scholar of Sanskrit, was still a child and was among those who were shifted to safe quarters. Hyder Ali's military held the Kovilakam under siege and blocked the supply of all essential goods. Left with no other option, the Sāmūtiri pleaded for conciliation. Hyder Ali now demanded a purse of 10 million gold coins. The Sāmūtiri did not have the resources to raise that sum of money. On 27 April 1765, a full moon day (Kollam Era 961, Mēṭam 14 Chitra Pournami), the Sāmūtiri shut himself in the armoury and blew it up killing himself and destroying the palace completely. Following this, Hyder Ali stationed two of his people at Kozhikode—Raza Ali, to take care of the military operations; and Mathanna, to collect tax—and withdrew to Coimbatore via Palakkad. All along the way the local people revolted against Hyder Ali's military march. Hyder Ali quelled all these uprisings, because of which he had to bear heavy losses. In 1766 CE, he led the army in a counter-offensive against the nair troops at Puthiyangāṭi of Veṭṭathunāṭu.

Though the Sāmūtiris had grown to be a force to reckon with in terms of manpower, weaponry and military strategy, their expansionist policies failed miserably not only because of their rivalry with the Perumpaṭappu swarūpam and skirmishes with the English, also but because of the military raids by the Rajas of Mysore. Also, it would not be wrong to say that the new generation of royal kinsmen inducted from the Nileswaram Kovilakam lacked experience, though they were not ready to admit the same (induction of kinsmen from another royal house was very common across the Tiruvitāmkur, Perumpaṭappu, Sāmūtiri and Kōlattiri kovilakams through the institution of *dattu* [adoption]). Besides, Mangattachan, the minister of the royal militia, and others who occupied ministerial and other high offices treated these kinsmen as the new additions through adoption. All these led to friction between the royal power and the cabinet. As a result, the royalty depended more and more on the advisors who had accompanied them from Nileswaram.

When the 1766 battle was over and the situation eased, members of the Kiḻakke Kovilakam returned. They occupied Venkiṭṭakkōṭṭa which was earlier acquired from the Kottakkal Vellattiri. The story goes that Venkiṭṭakkōṭṭa was the quarters of Montambalathu Moose, who was a military leader under Vellattiri. Moose connived and murdered the Sāmūtiri's military leader Tenayancheri Eḷayathu. In retaliation, the Ēṛāḷpād, under the Sāmūtiri's instructions, killed Moose and Venkiṭṭakkōṭṭa fell into the possession of the Sāmūtiri, who made it the new Kiḻakke Kovilakam. Later, the Sāmūtiri drove away several of Hyder Ali's tax collectors and military leaders and reclaimed portions of the lost territory.

Aṛakkal and Chiṛakkal dynasties sided with Hyder Ali for various reasons. Hyder Ali had captured Bidanur in 1763 and the Aṛakkal royalty had had diplomatic relations with Mysore ever since. Aṛakkal's sole aim was to coax Hyder Ali to invade Chiṛakkal. But the Chiṛakkal royalty wanted Hyder Ali to fight the English. In 1767, Hyder Ali marched from Mysore till Koṭunkōḷūr. He had plans to attack Vēṇāṭu but that did not materialise. In 1773, a large battalion, led jointly by Sayyid Sahib—Hyder Ali's favourite commander—and Srinivasa Rao—a powerful commander of Mysore—came via Tamarasseri Churam (pass). They looted and plundered the regions they captured. And thus, many parts of Malabar came into the possession of Mysore.

In 1776, Hyder Ali made one more attempt to invade Vēṇāṭu. This was to settle a score: Vēṇāṭu had given asylum to refugees from Malabar. Moreover, he intended to claim at least part of the expenses incurred during his Malabar campaign during the last decade. Hyder Ali demanded that the ruler of Vēṇāṭu pay a sum of 15 lakh rupees to avoid war. The ruler of Vēṇāṭu floated a counter-proposal that if Hyder Ali would return the captured territories to their lawful owners, he would consider Hyder Ali's demand. Hyder Ali marched towards Vēṇāṭu. Thrissur and Koṭunkōḷūr Kovilakams surrendered. Kochi Kovilakam bought peace and subsidiary status with four lakh rupees and 10 elephants. Kochi also facilitated the march of the army of Mysore to Vēṇāṭu. But the Dutch frustrated Hyder Ali's plans. They not only attacked Koṭunkōḷūr Kovilakam but also resisted the progress of the Mysore army. Besides this, the English also made it difficult for Hyder Ali to march forward. However, the French volunteered to help Hyder Ali but it was in vain. Hyder Ali had to give up his plans to invade Vēṇāṭu and his ire turned towards the English.

In the Thalasseri documents, there is a brief mention of the king of Chiṛakkal in 1779–80 (Kollam Era 995) capturing Ranṭuthaṛa in Kōḷattunāṭu, on instructions from Tipu Sultan (1750–1799 CE). From 1780 onwards, Hyder Ali ran offensives against the Dutch and the English. In 1782, while countering the forces of the English Major Abington, Hyder Ali's military leader Sardar Khan was fatally injured, taken prisoner and died shortly afterwards. With that, several of the territories captured by Sardar Khan, including Palakkad, Dharmadam, Mahe and Neṭṭur, fell into the hands of the English East India Company. The company forces also captured a large booty of canons and other fire arms. In Kerala, Mysore could retain just one piece of territory called Palakkattuseri. Makhdum Ali led the regiment stationed at Palakkattuseri to Chavakkad. After capturing Chavakkad, the regiment moved north to Kozhikode. On 13 February 1782, the English forces marched from Thalasseri to Kozhikode to aid the Sāmūtiri. The English regiment, jointly led by Abington and Colonel Humberstone, took hold of the city and the fort. Then they launched a counter-offensive against the Mysore forces. They chased Makhdum Ali and his regiment camping at Thrikkalayur. Makhdum Ali retreated to Ponnani. Humberstone pursued him but torrential rains forced him to retreat to Kozhikode. Though he renewed his campaign later, the situation had changed by then. Hyder Ali had returned to Srirangapattanam, and had entrusted the regiment at Palakkattuseri to his son Tipu Sultan. On 7 December 1782, Hyder Ali died suddenly, and this necessitated Tipu too to return to Srirangapattanam and assume power.

Tipu Sultan's Campaigns

Tipu Sultan continued the forays of the Mysore army into Malabar. Tipu's officers camped in Malabar to estimate and impose revenues and collect taxes. But unpaid taxes accumulated in arrears because the people of Malabar didn't accept Hyder Ali and Tipu Sultan as their lawful rulers. There were other hitches too—neither had Hyder Ali evolved into an administrative head from a military leader nor did the society have a well-established revenue system or policy. Hence the process of tax collection was, in reality, a combination of looting and plunder. Tipu Sultan took cognisance of this fact and, being an able administrator, made arrangements to measure the land, classify it according to type, assess the yield and impose proportionate taxes. There was widespread resistance from the landlords due to their apprehensions about the imposition of heavy dues and even land alienation. Under the instigation of the landlords many settlers and peasants put up resistance. Tipu swooped in with full military might and unleashed the most ravaging raids Malabar had ever experienced, with loot, plunder, arson and massacre in 1789 CE. Of course, there were a few instances of forced religious conversions as well. However, as an administrator, Tipu's sole aim was to set up a process to collect taxes due to him.

The military raids created insecurity and fear among the locals, irrespective of their social standing vis-à-vis status, caste or creed. The army could barge into private houses or official institutions and loot and burn as it pleased. Hence members of the royal houses of Chiṛakkal, Kuṛumpoṛaināṭu, Parappanāṭu, Nilambur Kavaḷapppaṛa and the like, and landlords and commoners made an exodus to far-flung southern territories in search of asylum.

One regiment of Tipu's army under the command of Srinivasarayar marched north from Palakkad through Mankara and Cherpulassery to Kozhikode. There they camped south of the new Kovilakam. The new Sāmūtiri tried to ward off Tipu's onslaught in multiple ways. He sought help from the French outpost at Mahe. Comte du Prath, the officer-in-charge at Mahe, was sympathetic to the Sāmūtiri's cause and extended as much help as he could. He was even ready to loan a battalion of the French army. However, this was not a feasible step because the French were in alliance with Tipu Sultan. Hence Comte du Prath's superiors vehemently opposed this move and, in fact, recalled him. The Sāmūtiri hoisted French flags in Kozhikode to exploit Tipu Sultan's friendship with the French, but the Sultan did not budge.

Meanwhile, the English were reeling under a double whammy. Never-ending wars were depleting the profits of the East India Company and since trade was dull, profits were deplorably low. The finances of the English East India Company were in dire straits and company officials were worried. This financial crisis of the 1770s compelled the English to end the war with Tipu Sultan and the French and make peace. By then the power equation in Europe had changed as well, the English and the French had negotiated a peace treaty. When peace negotiations with Tipu Sultan were progressing, the English attempted to destroy Tipu's military camps in covert operations.

Aṛakkal Beevi of northern Kerala was a close ally of Mysore. In December 1782, the English force under General Macleod had subjugated Aṛakkal Beevi and imprisoned her. She was forced to sign an agreement by which the Aṛakkal family had to pay an indemnity of 1.5 lakh rupees annually and a further annuity of one lakh rupees to the Bombay province. Tipu Sultan was still at war. Finally, the English were ready for a treaty. But during the negotiations Tipu and his ministers were not prepared for any compromise. Tipu insisted that he must have sovereignty over the rulers of Malabar who had been allies of the English for a long time. The English relented and deserted their allies to the mercy of Tipu Sultan. Later, the English General Macleod would lament: 'In a hurry to achieve peace, deserting our allies who fought with us side by side, will be interpreted as a bad policy.' The peace treaty stipulated that the English would control north Malabar and Tipu would have sway over south Malabar. General Macleod withdrew his army from Aṛakkal. There were uprisings against Tipu in several places but he quickly put them down.

On 14 November 1783 Colonel Fullerton subdued Palakkattuseri and captured the fort. Company officials stationed at London instructed the East India Company to agree for an armistice with Tipu and restore all the captured properties and territories. But claiming that Tipu had violated the conditions of the treaty, Fullerton refused to return the fort, instead passing it on to the Sāmūtiri. Nevertheless, Tipu's forces defeated Sāmūtiri and recaptured the fort within a few days.

An entry in Pazhassi documents, dated 2 December 1796, can be summarised at this juncture: In 1783 CE, in accordance with the instructions of Tipu Sultan, while Arshad Beg Khan was controlling the hilly territories, Kadathanāṭṭu Porlathiri Godavarma agreed in writing to surrender Wayanad to Tipu Sultan. The Sultan in return agreed to confer a jagir of 15,000 rupees on Godavarma. By the time the agreement was finalised in 1785, Godavarma had lost possession of Wayanad.

In 1788, preparatory to a well-planned Malabar invasion, Tipu Sultan invaded Iruvaināṭu and subjugated Kuṛungoṭṭu Nair. This time Tipu targeted ports and roads along the way. Allying with the French, he wanted full authority over the Malabar coast from Chiṛakkal to Dharmadam and control of its strategic ports and roads. Aṛakkal Beevi sought help from the English. Dharmadam changed hands between the Kōlattiri and the English a couple of times, but in 1789 the English reclaimed it. The Kōlattiri sided with Tipu Sultan and invited him to Kannur. Tipu's forces descended on north Malabar and the populace fled south.

Once again, the ruler of Vēṇāṭu gave asylum to the refugees. This angered Tipu who had set his eyes on the rich treasury and trade of Vēṇāṭu. But the English put up strong resistance. Even Kochi, traditionally bullied into submission by Mysore, sided with Vēṇāṭu this time. On 20 December 1789, Tipu invaded one of the bastions of Vēṇāṭu, the Neungotta. However, the English forces forced Tipu to retreat. Tipu turned his attention now to Kozhikode. His large battalion wreaked havoc there—the city and its surroundings were burnt down, several people lost their lives and several were maimed.

In December 1790, the English recaptured Kozhikode. Colonel James Hartley's regiment inflicted heavy losses on Tipu's army at Thirurangadi. The same story was repeated by Robert Abercromby at Kannur. Though the English had made peace with the French in Europe, the English had to fight the French in India because of the latter's collusion with Tipu. The English blocked French ships at Mangalapuram and the land movement of arms and supplies to Mysore. This greatly weakened the military strategy of Mysore. Finally, in 1792, with the signing of the Treaty of Srirangapatnam the dominance of Mysore ended. In accordance with the stipulations of this treaty, Malabar, Salem, Bellary and Anantapur were annexed to Madras Presidency. A letter written in August 1795, by a private citizen named Chuḻali Kelappa Nambiar, states: In 1788–89 (Kollam Era 964), after Tipu's forces devastated the place, a General from Bengal came with his regiment, chased Tipu to Srirangaptanam, defeated him and then returned to Kannur.

Wayanad's Trauma

Tipu persisted in battering Wayanad till the very end of his life. People of Wayanad had to put up with great hardship. We know about this trauma of Wayanad from the letters and petitions in the Thalasseri records. In a private correspondence, dated 6 September 1797, it is mentioned that cattle and people were rounded up and captured by Tipu's soldiers. Another letter, dated 9 September 1797, by Kuṛumpoṛaināṭu Vīravarma Rāja addressed to Christopher Peile, the deputy superintendent of the Thalasseri factory of the East India Company, mentions the menacing presence of Tipu's soldiers in the neighbourhood. In a subsequent letter, dated 30 September, he wrote that the pounding of Wayanad by Tipu's army had become a routine affair. On 28 June 1798, he wrote to James Stevens, the superintendent of the Thalasseri factory, that Tipu's raids had created untold miseries for brāhmaṇas and ordinary citizens alike. In the letter he thanked the English for defeating Tipu and restoring order. He also mentions two of the *tampurāns* (royal men) being hanged and *tampurāṭṭis* (royal women) being taken as prisoners. One Kachirayan, in a petition submitted in the same year, states that during Tipu's raids many people had to flee leaving their homes.

The East India Company had employed several people as their informants. We get a lot of interesting instances of their communication from the archives of the Company at Thalasseri. A few excerpts from their messages pertaining to Tipu and his invasions are relevant here. Messages in the Company records generally praise Tipu's agreeable disposition. There are several letters referring to his disagreeable characteristics. A letter by a certain Kanagovi Baburayan addressed to James Stevens throws light on the friendship between Tipu Sultan and Pazhassi Raja. Kaitheri Ambu, a dependent-turned-enemy of Pazhassi, figures in the records as a secret informant passing information about Tipu Sultan's dispatch of guns and cartridges to Pazhassi Raja. He also gives strategic information about Edachena Kunkan, a close friend of Pazhassi Raja, managing to reach Thalassrri, obviously to spy the Company's plans. One of the informants refers to the Nileswaram Raja demanding a bribe of 3000 *varahan* (gold coins) from one Raman of Thalasseri, and the latter in turn appeals about it to Pazhassi Raja, who asks Tipu Sultan to issue a *firman* (decree) to the Nileswaram Raja not to trouble Raman. It says that Tipu Sultan indeed complied with it in 1799. Three letters, dated 8, 9 and 21 May 1799, by some anonymous informants convey three important messages respectively: (*a*) that the English army has set out to capture Tipu;

(*b*) Tipu has begun his attack, and (*c*) rumour spreads that Tipu has lost Srirangapattanam. An informant's letter dated 11 January 1800 conveys the message that on the murder of Tipu by the English force all his territories have come under the possession of the English. Several relevant petitions are also there among the Thalasseri records. A joint petition, dated 2 February 1800, by the Christian population of Goa complains about the atrocities committed by Hyder Ali and Tipu Sultan. It states that Tipu, in an effort to eradicate Christianity from the coastal regions, had rounded up, imprisoned and sent to Srirangapattanam about 70,000 children and adults from regions south of Goa.

Consequences of Tipu's Campaigns

Tipu's military raids greatly affected the social fabric of the entire length and breadth of Kerala coast in general and Malabar in particular. Like any army raid, Tipu's forays also resulted in heavy losses of life and property. Territorial chieftains and landlords were looted and killed. Such brutal activities more often than not ended in arson. There were also instances of religious conversion and plunder of temple property. Granthavari at several places makes direct references of such incidents. They mention that Tipu's troops under Sardar Ahmed in 1790 and under Saikatpaṭṭy Sardar in 1791 ransacked Eṭattaṛa, Koliyāṭi Dēśam, Tirumangalattu Kōṭṭa Dēśam, Gaṇapativaṭṭom, Kiṭanganāṭṭu Dēśam, Wayanad, Pulpaḷḷi, Pūtāṭi, etc. Men were taken prisoners or killed, cattle were driven away and grains, including seeds, were looted. Some places, including Wayanad and surrounding localities, were set on fire.

Superior weapons and strategic warfare enable victory in war and facilitate concentration of power. Tipu was an able administrator, and his military campaigns could also be viewed as the interventions of an administrator. During Tipu's time, Malabar was a conglomeration of diffuse independent territories, such as Kuṛumpoṛaināṭu, Veṭṭattunāṭu, Chiṛakkal and Aṛakkal. The administrative apparatus hadn't evolved in any of these territories. A strong ruler, centralised administration, rule of law, well laid out sustainable revenue recovery process—none of these existed in any of these native states of Malabar. Even the Sāmūtiri's Kozhikode, which was undoubtedly acclaimed to be one of the best, lacked such structures. The feudalistic and hereditary *zamindari* system prevailed in the exclusively agrarian society where produce was the birthright of the upper caste. Besides annuity, the feudal lords could demand cash or kind in multiple ways: ankam (mandatory tax for resolving disputes by duel), cunkam (kind of Octroi), el̲a (payments received from confiscated property), kol̲a (bribe), val̲i (fee for permissions), pil̲a (fine), etc. But there were no proper documentation for any of these sums, because the concept of taxation was virtually nonexistent. Tipu Sultan encroached upon this chaotic ambience to introduce and consolidate an administrative process. His objective was to set up an effective revenue collection machinery.

Till then it had been an unregulated regime and the sovereignty over the land, its people and the produce or resources was vested with the territorial rulers and the zamindars, who played friends or foes among themselves as the situation demanded. Naturally, to set up a centralised and regulated administrative apparatus, territorial lords and zamindars must be suppressed or eliminated. That is what Tipu Sultan did. Many of the landlords and zamindars fled to Vēṇāṭu during his campaigns, and several were captured or killed in the process. Tipu also tried to eliminate the Nair regiments which owed allegiance to their lords. Since the upper castes claimed produce/resource as a birthright, Tipu dared to annul such rights as well. Thus he built the foundation for a centralised administration. To sustain such a set up and run it efficiently, additional checks and balances—such as assessment of revenue, arrangement for its systematic appropriation, some officials, defense system, markets and roads—were necessary. Tipu assessed the land in terms of fertility-crop-yield and levied proportionate tax and ensured regular collection of taxes.

With a view to improving trade, he made arrangements for the protection of ports and markets. Tipu stationed armed men at all ports and markets in order to ensure peace and order in transactions. He made some structural reinforcements with wharfs and dockyards at Ponnani and Beypore. It was Tipu who made Feroke a market with built-in structures and expanded it. Similarly, several important roads linking resource centres with ports and markets were creations by the troops of Tipu. The main route connecting Malabar with Mysore through the Wayanad pass was made a full-fledged road under Tipu for the movement of his soldiers and battery men. Most roads were built for commercial as well as defense purposes. Tipu brought his state monopoly for coconut, pepper, sandalwood, tobacco, teak, etc. In short, for the first time, Malabar witnessed the manifestation of all the fundamental attributes of a modern state with a systematised revenue administration, trade policy, defense and infrastructure development.

Pazhassi Episodes

Descriptive accounts of the Pazhassi episodes are available in two versions. One of them contains the official views of the British colonial authorities, whose aims were evidently to present the local chief as a rebel and unlawful. At the same time, they wanted to explain the prolonged fight between the company and the local chiefs. The colonial version, however, does not fail to explain the native force as inferior both technically and in terms of efficiency. The other version, presented by the nationalist historians under the influence of the Indian national movement, understandably depicted Kerala Varma Pazhassi Raja (1774–1805 CE) as a hero and a freedom fighter, who had the support of the kurichya guerilla fighters of Wayanad. His failure was, however, explained as a result of the advanced technical weapons of the western forces. It has to be noted that both the versions are generally based on the British official documents. A set of documents collected by the Basel Mission Missionaries, including Dr Hermann Gundert, and preserved in The University of Tübingen in Germany, brought out comparatively recently compel us to look at the whole affair from a different viewpoint, and all Pazhassi letters mentioned in this section are from these archives.

The ever-increasing dearth of resources, aggravated by the infighting among the native royal families, the insecurity and fear caused by the repeated inroads of the Mysorean forces and the competing commercial strategies of the monopolist groups of the western mercantilist interests form the historical background of the Pazhassi episodes. These documents, mainly correspondences among various groups—including the native royal families, officials of the East India Companies, local magnates and members of various native groups—belong roughly to the period 1796–1800, but many of them shed light on some events earlier than that period as well. On the basis of these documents it is evident that the relation between Kerala Varma Pazhassi Raja and the different British officials was highly complicated.

Kuṛumpoṛaināṭu and Puṛaḷi were the two swarūpams of north Malabar. They were related to each other with certain property relations and, naturally, this ensured constant dispute with regard to power. Pazhassi belonged to the Puṛaḷi swarūpam. Both the swarūpams submitted to the British power, surrendering their sceptres and crowns at the feet of the company authorities. It is on this occasion, when these local chiefs acted as the collection agents of the East India Company that the whole affair took a different turn, due mainly to the wrong and inefficient policy of the authorities of the Thalasseri Factory. Pazhassi was a supporter and good friend of the company. During the time of the Mysorean inroads, he did not run away like the other rajas of north Malabar and seek refuge under the Vēṇāṭu rulers. Instead, Pazhassi remained in the region and supported the company in arresting the advancement of Tipu. These events are referred to in a letter written by Kerala Varma Pazhassi Raja on the tenth of Tulām 1796. This relation was disturbed by a misdeed on the part of the company authorities. This is the subject matter of a letter written by Pazhassi to the company authorities at Thalasseri on the twelfth of Dhanu 1797. This letter states that Kerala Varma was enjoying the rights over a territory which he got hereditarily. This territory was given to the chief of Kuṛumpoṛaināṭu by James Stevens without the knowledge and permission of Kerala Varma saying that the right over the territory will be shared by the chiefs of Kuṛumpoṛaināṭu, Kottayam and Parappanāṭu and the existing arrangements would continue. Kerala Varma did not enter into any excess action but simply complained to the company authorities. This was followed by another excess on the part of the foreigners. In fact, people had started approaching the Company officials at Thalasseri for redressing their grievances. Thalasseri records contain many petitions and complaints by people regarding their grievances against landlords, local rulers and kings. Interestingly, the Company officers negotiated disputes, resolved issues and even adopted punitive measures against the offenders. This is mentioned in a pair of letters.

On the tenth of Mēṭam 1797 CE, military men of the company entered the Pazhassi palace through the eastern door, destroying it. Knowing that the intruders were company people, Kerala Varma told them that he would open the door but they did not wait. The entered the palace, caught hold of three persons who were there, including Kerala Varma, tied them with a rope, looted the precious articles kept in the safe custody and went out.

What can be gathered from the company correspondence is that this was not an act sponsored by the company authorities. The atrocity finds mention in several letters, which show that the response of Kerala Varma to this incident was disciplined and lawful. He informed the authorities of the East India Company at Bombay and Bengal about the matter, since Malabar was in the Bombay Presidency. On 13 June 1797, Kerala Varma wrote to the Bombay Governor:

> I may be allowed to come and see you to inform you about the incident. I have nobody else other than the company to rescue me. My assistant (*Pandāri*) will inform you about the incident in detail.

In another letter, Kerala Varma wrote that he helped the company remove the cantonment of Tipu and settled people in the areas after felling the forest. Further, he says, 'I borrowed money from Thalassery to help the people.' This is further repeated in a letter written by some private individuals. Immediately, after receiving the complaints from Kerala Varma, the authorities said that the articles stolen by the soldiers would be returned. But, they could not keep their word and the fact is referred to in a letter written by Christopher Piele. All these letters throw light on the impairing discipline and the growing inefficiency of the Thalasseri Factory.

Kerala Varma Pazhassi Raja's letters reminded the English East India Company of how he remained fighting Tipu, unlike the Kuṛumpoṛaināṭu Rajas who escaped to Vēṇāṭu, leaving the task of fighting entirely to their Nairs. Letters from officials in the company repeatedly mention Pazhassi's support to the company in its efforts to ensure the retreat of Tipu's soldiers in order to ensure security to the life and property of people. In a letter to James Ishtimin, Pazhassi mentions that he went to Vēṇāṭu only after retaining enough soldiers to combat the recurrence of the raid. On 9 December 1796, he writes to Peale that he has faith in the company because neither has anybody told him that the company would cheat nor has he heard of the company to have cheated any. In a letter to Jonathan Duncan, written on 12 June 1797, he says that he has not thought about any other security, for he had no security other than the company. This is not to mean that Kerala Varma was permanently against the Sultan of Mysore. There are letters showing his alliance with Tipu during 1796–97 in fighting the Company. A letter mentions Tipu's military support to Pazhassi in 1797 by way of arms and soldiers. It is clear that the relationship of Pazhassi with both Tipu and the English East India Company was based on the needs of his own territorial power. By 1800 Kerala Varma became almost entirely inimical to the English East India Company. He withdrew to Wayanad and mobilised the kurichyas into a fighter contingent. For about five years he fought the English until he was shot dead on 30 November 1805 at Mavilathodu in Wayanad. What ultimately helped the English in their victory was the disunity among the local rulers and their lack of state power, rather than their arms and military prowess, as the correspondences in the Thalasseri records indicate.

Towards English Hegemony

Like other European trading companies, the English company too was interested in trade monopoly. The company's initial attempts were at gaining control over trade routes and capturing ferries for monopolising spice trade, which gave gradual access to rights over tolls and tariffs. They fortified their factory and adopted various measures to reinforce the set up, which included intrigues with conflicts among local rulers. This fetched them good revenue in the form of rewards, tributes and compensations. Allying with some of them in times of external threat and fighting to subdue them in times of internal peace, the English steadily advanced towards territorial control. They began to claim control over the territories conquered or restored by the local rulers with the company's military support.

After the defeat of Tipu Sultan and the scattering of the local rulers, people began to approach the English for the redressal of their grievances. The Thalasseri records contain several instances of the victims of Mysore raids going to the authorities of the company with various complaints regarding loss of persons, property, rights and privileges. Most complaints about Tipu are by way of explanation for the default of dues to the company. Local people realised that it was of no use to depend on the local rulers who had no power. The company took advantage of the public need for some kind of juridical and political order, and imposed their state power through revenue assessments and fixation of dues. In fact, it was Tipu who had initiated land settlements and assessments. The English sought to build on the system introduced by the Sultan.

The company's tax assessment was extremely exploitative and often beyond the capacity of the assessed. According to a record dating back to 31 August 1796, the tax assessed in the Malayam Province (Kerala) was such that the landholders had to pay 1 paṇam per 2 coconut palms or per 4 arecanut palms, 2 paṇams per jackfruit tree and 2 paṇams per pepper vine. In certain other records it is as high as 3 paṇams per coconut palm. It is evident that the people could've grown tired of the taxation under the company's self-imposed rule, because the amount is over and above the traditional claims by the local rulers.

By the end of the eighteenth century Malabar witnessed the ascendancy of the English rule to a hegemonic position. This domination of Malabar by the English extended itself to Lakshadweep as well. Traditionally, Kōḷattunāṭu was the owner of the Lakshadweep islands. With the emergence of Chiṛakkal, Kannur and Aṛakkal ruling houses, the revenue ownership of Kōḷattunāṭu got divided among them. Thus the Chiṛakkal Raja, the Ali Raja and the Aṛakkal Beevi enjoyed revenue rights on the Lakshadweep islands, notwithstanding the problem of the absence of a clear settlement in the areas over which they had jurisdiction. As the queen of Ali Raja, Aṛakkal Beevi had control over all those islands that were significant in terms of trade. In alliance with the Aṛakkal Beevi, and by ceding a few parts of what he had grabbed from Kōḷattunāṭu to the Chiṛakkal kingdom, Tipu imposed his direct rule over the islands of Ammeni, Kaṭamam, Kilthan, Chethilath and Bhithra in 1783. Aṛakkal Beevi was administering the trade there under an alliance with the English East India Company, and shared the profits equally with them. With the defeat of Tipu at Srirangapattanam in 1792 and according to the treaty thereof, all the territories of Malabar conquered by Tipu came under the control of the English. The English had already entered into an alliance with the Aṛakkal Beevi, according to which, Aṛakkal Beevi was paying Rs 15,000 to the company annually. Aṛakkal Beevi was least regular about the payment and the company was increasingly ever more exploitative. As a result, the English moved closer to the Chiṛakkal rulers. In 1847, the island of Anthroth was badly affected by a hurricane. William Robinson, the chief of the English East India Company, sailed to Lakshadweep along with the Chiṛakkal king, who was on a mission to mitigate the misery of the victims. Robinson promised the Chiṛakkal king necessary financial help for the reconstruction. This loan, together with the interest accrued for four years, was too huge for the Chiṛakkal king to pay back. In 1854, the Chiṛakkal king ceded the Lakshadweep to the English.

The English hardly stepped in to rule the islands for over two decades, because the traditional ruling houses of Chiṛakkal, Kannur and Aṛakkal that controlled the revenue thereof were paying them their dues. Finally, in 1875, the Company took over the territorial control of the Lakshadweep islands, after accusing both the Chiṛakkal king and the Aṛakkal Beevi of non-payment of dues and misrule. However, even after this, excepting a biannual visit to the islands, the English seldom directly intervened in the administration of Lakshadweep. The Amien, who was appointed by the English, governed the islands on the basis of customary laws and the pleasure of the *kāraṇavakkūṭṭam* (the elders of the island community).

Impact of the Colonial Relation

It is relevant to recapitulate the major results of the three hundred years of competition for overseas trade monopoly by European companies, and the entailing rivalry and conflicts in which local rulers, the people, and their land and resources suffered. The institution of state-controlled overseas trade under non-conventional terms and conditions; the establishment of factory outposts at strategic points by the foreign trading companies; the introduction of a new technology of ship-building and sailing; an altogether different concept of navy with unprecedented arms, ammunition and strategies of battle; steady encroachments into the traditional authority of local rulers; and subsequent control of resources, the land and people in Kerala were the main changes that marked this period. The regular use of the mariner's magnetic compass, gunpowder invented by the ancient Chinese, the Latin sail invented by medieval Arabs, and the practice of building forts were outstanding among them.

There were changes in the technology of subsistence and survival of the local people, which had socio-economic manifestations. The Germans introduced new handicrafts technology in spinning and weaving. There were several changes in architecture, town planning, healthcare and household utensils. Words with Portugese origin, such as *kasēra* (chair), *mēśa* (table), *aḷumāri* (shelf) and *janal* (window); French, such as *fanas* (lantern); and English, such as *rantal* (lantern) and *arikkilamp* (hurricane lamp), were introduced into the common tongue. A lot of new ideas and practices came in as a result of the interaction and co-existence of people from distant lands and different worldviews. New communities of religious identities emerged based on distinct beliefs, institutions, customs, rites, rituals and practices. They entered into connubial relations with the communities outside and persuaded them to accept the new religious life. European and Malayali hybrid populations, such as the cassados and Anglo-Indians, came up at places on the coast where the respective foreigners had their sway. Foreign merchant communities had become distinct for their religious identities, such as Jews, Islamic Arabs and Christians. They were linked to their early settlements of Persian traditions of religious flexibility. There was a remarkable expansion of the people of Islamic faith along the coastal belt due to the Arabs taking local spouses during this period. Similarly, there were many Mussalman converts in the rural areas, especially along the routes and stations of the Mysore raids.

However, all this hardly made any fundamental change in the predominantly agrarian socio-economic relations and structure based on the caste system. People were integrated mainly by occupations and functions of agriculture, mainly of paddy cultivation. Other occupations like those of the artisans and craftsmen were also integral to the agrarian relations. All occupations were hereditary and attached to the agrarian settlements, of course with different degrees of rigidity. Human resources were largely owned and controlled by the land owners as part of their property. This precluded the possibility of the existence of a class of labourers unencumbered by the agrarian socio-economic system. Naturally, any foreign trading company and their settlement had to enter into negotiations with the local rulers for the allocation of artisans and craftsmen to them for ensuring their services.

Nevertheless, there was a steady growth of trade and commerce, which presupposed monetisation of all transactions. A good quantity of foreign coins and currency, both as a measure of value as well as means of payment, entered the field of exchange. The Portuguese were the first to introduce paper currency, called Rupia, in Kerala. Many of the Portuguese, Dutch, French and English paper currencies had entered the domain of multiple transactions of goods and services. In imitation of the Mughal and European coins, the major swarūpams began issuing their own coins. Kaliyugarāyan paṇam, anantharāyan paṇam, orrapputhen, eraṭṭapputhen and kochi puthen were names of a few of the coins in Malabar. Tiruvitāmkūr minted its own paṇams. It had minted silver coins, called chakrams, of different denominations. Rupee became the most significant form of money and it was adapted by the swarūpams as well as the English in Kerala as well as elsewhere.

Since there were no basic changes in the economy, the institutions and ideas at the juridical and political levels broadly remained the same. But, swarūpams such as Vēṇāṭu and Neṭiyirippu, which were nearing the entrenchment of themselves as full-fledged state systems, were assimilating various institutional arrangements and practices of systematic land assessment, taxation, bureaucratic revenue administration and organised militia. However, soon they were subsumed by the English during their long rule over the subsequent one hundred and fifty years.

The Making of Colonialism

The nature of the interaction of the Portuguese, the Dutch and the French with the Malabar coast registered the beginnings of colonialism. This historical epoch of colonialism could be understood differently as a long process with various levels and strategies of subjection of indigenous people, physically, economically and intellectually, until they were totally conquered. The police, army and other available repressive instruments, including newly introduced laws, rules and regulations, were extensively used for this. Colonies were conquered economically by denying the people of the land access to the natural economic resources and by discouraging traditional skills and strategies of using their resources in maintaining a sustainable livelihood. This could be achieved either by purchasing the right to use the natural resource or by forcefully proscribing the use of such natural wealth by means of rules and regulations.

The cases of leasing out local iron-ore deposits for ninety-nine years to the East India Company by the local rulers of Vaḷḷuvanāṭu and Kadathanāṭu could be taken as examples of the former type of conquest. Iron ore was not simply a natural resource which was owned by the ruler of the territory, but a form of livelihood for the community of blacksmiths. It was this livelihood that was snatched away by alienating one of the basic natural resources which was essential for several activities in an agrarian society. Salt was another essential article on which the colonists wanted to exercise control. Francis Buchanan reports in 1800 that a large number of salt-pans were working on the coast of Malabar. He informs that the salt produced locally was enough for local consumption and that a surplus was used for export. Francis Buchanan notes that during the period of his visit (1800 CE) local production of salt was not prohibited, but by an order of the kings of Tiruvitāmkūr, Cochin, Kozhikode and Kolattunatu the salt produced at local centres could be sold only to the ruler. Thus, virtually, the salt trade became a monopoly of the government. However, salt production on the coast of Malabar declined, as it could not compete with the salt imported by authorities from Bombay through government contractors. Weaving and other village industries also were put under great pressure due to the import of mill products from the West and the ousting of native products from the market, which could not compete with the imported products.

The present corpus of correspondence has at least one letter referring to a case of interference of the French authorities at Mahe in the economic resources of the local ruler. The fragmentary letter, whose last portion is missing, informs us that the Raja of Kadathanāṭu had employed an agent to collect toll from Mahe. Obstructing the Raja's agent, the Captain of the French settlement at Mahe posted his own men at the toll point and collected tolls. In the letter, the Raja requests the Captain of the fort at Mahe to be kind enough to restore the previous position so that he could collect the toll as before. It is also submitted that the Captain's obstruction caused much sorrow since it affected his status as well as income. The document clearly indicates the nature of bondage of even rulers of native principalities, not to speak of ordinary people.

It is too early at this stage of political development in Malabar to investigate into the strategies of the company administrators that secured intellectual bondage and ensured the ultimate surrender of the colonial subjects. One of the major threats to the European colonists was from tropical diseases and in the beginning the foreigners were advised by the company administrators to take native medicine and treatment. There was also some effort at the level of medical education to integrate the indigenous as well as the western systems of medicine and healthcare. Indian astronomy and mathematics were other forms of knowledge which attracted the westerners during the seventeenth and eighteenth centuries. The European Jesuit missionaries, who were keenly interested in Oriental systems of knowledge, worked in various eastern cultures, including Tamil Nadu and Kerala, and collected several texts pertaining to these branches of knowledge. Recently, it has been observed by scholars and mathematicians that the attitude of the western scholars to Indian systems of scientific knowledge in the eighteenth century was that of recognition and admiration.

In their correspondence with the foreigners, some local rulers pretended to be of equal status with the royal houses of '*ingaress*' (the English) and '*paranthiress*' (the French), and allude to the mutual benefits of the political 'alliance' between their swarūpams or extended ruling families and the foreign *vamsas* (dynasties). However, it is evident from a large number of letters of the local Rajas and their agents to the authorities of the French and the English settlements in Malabar towards the turn of the eighteenth century that the white men were not only held in high esteem but were also taken to be their protectors. One of the repeated requests of the local Rajas was to protect them and their families from their enemies. At the same time, some of the sources help us maintain that the French had known and recognised the 'excellent quality' of the Indian artefacts.

It could be inferred from the available sources that the European attitude towards the quality of intellectual achievements and technical skills of the native culture was pragmatic, empirical and one that was developed out of direct contact. The rulers of the northern principalities in Kerala, on the other hand, saw a real saviour in the European colonists. As a result, they tended to depend on the English and the French factories in their neighbourhood even for petty things. On a certain occasion when the Raja of Chirakkal had to go to Thalasseri by boat he approached Comte Duprat, the French Captain at Mahe, and requested him to send a special kind of boat to Kappuzha with sufficient number of fishermen.

The dependence of the Rajas of Malabar on western colonists could be understood only against the background of historical developments. First, the geographical and geological peculiarities of the region have played an important role in shaping the contours of human life in this region. In many places, the coastline is below the sea level and therefore the area has long stretches of waterlogged tracts and marshy lands. During the ebb tide, saline water reaches about 15 km up the river. In the interior, the land goes up to form the paṛampu uplands and the paddy fields are scattered among the undulated grounds. These features render the cultivation of paddy, the staple food of the people, unprofitable. At the same time, the land on the coastal strip could be used differently for salt panning, shell mining, etc. and the extensive uplands in the interior favoured cultivation of crash crops, especially spices. It is interesting to note in this context that cash crops like coconut, arecanut and pepper are included as important items of regular income to some brāhmaṇa temples in the region under consideration as early as the tenth century CE. The information available in Chinese travel accounts also suggests that there was always a shortage of food grains and a surplus of cash crops in Malabar. This is supported by the maṇipravāḷam texts that provide the names of several varieties of imported paddy in the markets and bazaars of Kerala. Right from the early medieval period there was always a scarcity of resources and the only solution was either extension of one's own territory to areas without effective resistance or appropriation by force for which adequate resources was essential. Puṟakiḻār swarūpam which figure in the present corpus of records as seeking support from an alliance with the French authorities had already started extending their economic interests to the fertile soil of the northern parts of Wayanad plateau, as is clear from the Tirunelli copper plates. Kuṟumpoṟaināṭu was another traditional power centre from the time of the Perumāḷs of Koṭunkōḷūr who wielded control in Wayanad simultaneously with the Puṟakiḻār. The letters written by the local rajas and chieftains to authorities of the French and English companies bear testimony to this situation.

This state of affairs did contribute to a feeling of insecurity on the part of the local rulers. Infighting was a regular feature not only among the several principalities and their subordinate local chieftains, but also between the heads of the families and the heirs-apparent of the ruling swarūpams. There are several literary accounts on the legendary rivalry between the Sāmūtiris of Calicut, the Porḷātiri who was the previous owner of Calicut, and the Veḷḷāṭṭiris of the erstwhile principality of Vaḷḷvanāṭu. One of the invocatory *thorrampāṭṭukaḷ*, which narrates the story of a hero named Karikkurikkal, refers to a dispute between the elder and younger members of the Alladam swarūpam of Nileswaram, situated to the north of the erstwhile Kōḷattunāṭu. Some letters written by the elder Raja of Pazhassi, and the Raja of Kuṟumpoṟaināṭu to the administers of the Thalasseri Factory underline some dispute in the royal house of Pazhassi. Further, we know that the historic hostility of Kerala Varma Pazhassi Raja towards the English was not due to any patriotic reason but to the fact that his petition to the company authorities to consider him as the claimant of the Privy Purse was turned down.

One of the letters, written by some local agent (it does not carry the sender's name, but was in all probability written by the Raja of Chiṛakkal) to the company officials refer to acts of hostilities by the dissident younger Raja of Kottayam. In a situation like this, the local rulers had no other means to suppress their own ambitious descendents but to seek support from foreigners who had already proved their strength and efficiency in dealing with crises. Against this background, the political meaning of that letter becomes clearer. In such situations it is even not improbable that the friendship and the support of the company was considered a social capital that went a long way in punctuating one's own social and political status.

By and large the tribal people, midland farmers, nāṭuvāḻis and rulers of principalities in Malabar passed through trauma during the invasions by the Sultans of Mysore. European trading companies aggravated the situation through their intrigues. Moreover, their cultures, practices and ways of life began spreading among the people along the coast and around the trading centres. Their religious worldviews attracted several people and they became converts. Many, under impelling circumstances, had to accept them. Such situations of violent cultural interactions excite social and religious reform movements among people. Not only Kerala, but virtually all parts of the Indian subcontinent witnessed such movements led by a series of saintly leaders.

X

Socio-religious and Caste Reform Movements (19th–20th centuries CE)

Socio-religious reforms in medieval India had heralded some of the ideas that would be considered radical even today. Several movements exposing the unethical and irrational in the orthodox beliefs and priestly rituals were articulated in ancient and medieval India. Most of these movements, though rooted in traditional social institutions and cultural practices, were genuinely radical in their objectives and procedures. Anti-slavery movements, anti-caste movements, anti-untouchability movements, caste-reform movements, caste-based self-respect movements and so on are examples. When European passions, values and worldviews entered the orthodox, upper-caste/class youth through education, they triggered movements of similar nature. This is not to give the impression that reformists emerged only from the upper caste/class alone. There were a few reformists of lower caste and lower class origins. Most reformers, however, were not rooted in tradition and, as a result, uprooted and westernised the educated and intelligent youth. Very few remained rooted without being swept off by the western current of modernity. Such reformists faced the current of modernity in a relationship of confrontation. In the process, they absorbed the dynamic of modernity in its entirety but infused it with the culturally contingent insights of the Indian variant. Such reformists of rootedness had emerged in many Indian states during the nineteenth and early twentieth centuries. This chapter briefly reviews the example of such socio-religious and caste-reform movements that happened in Kerala.

Generally, the causality of socio-religious movements is discussed at the instance of new ideas. Actually, it is not the spread of new ideas that trigger fundamental social movements. Movements for changing the juridical, political and religious practices spring up under economic pressure. Agricultural expansion, growth of garden-land economy, arrival of European trading companies, rise of markets, urban development, increased monetisation, transmutation of agrarian dues into cash, and emergence of a class of moneyed intermediaries were the prime forces behind the movements.

The opening up of schools under the initiative of Christian missionaries, as part of social preparation for facilitating religious conversion, played a major role in the spread of new ideas. Protestant missionaries under the London Mission and the Church Mission Society had started working in Tiruvitāmkur for the spread of education during the early decades of the nineteenth century. They established several English schools in different parts of the kingdom. Rev. Fr William Tobias Ringeltaube, an early German Protestant missionary, had established several English schools in and around Nagercoil. The Tiruvitāmkur kings were inspired by the education initiatives of the missionaries. Rani Parvathi Bayi gave a donation of Rs 21,200 to the Church Missionary Society for spreading education in Tiruvitāmkur. In 1834, the first government school was established at Trivandrum. Another government school was established in Thrissur in 1837. Rev. Fr Mead of the Church Mission Society, Rev. Fr Norton and Rev. Fr Henry Becker were founders of schools in Alleppey and Kottayam. The first college and seminary in Kerala were established in Kottayam. The Basel Evangelical Mission led educational enterprises in the Malabar region during this period. In 1841, Rev. Fr Habic started an English school at Kannur and appointed Ampu, an īḻava scholar of Malayalam, as a teacher. In 1848, the Basel Mission established a primary school at Kallai near Kozhikode and one at Thalasseri. The service of Hermann Gundert to the field of education is immensely rich. In the field of industry also the Basel Mission made significant contribution.

The Maharaja's College of Thiruvananthapuram and of Ernakulam were established by the Tiruvitāmkur royal family in 1866 and 1875 respectively.

German missionaries of the Basel Mission were responsible for technological development in the manufacturing sector of Kerala. As mentioned earlier, their interest was in the improvement of the handicrafts technology. A sector that they focused on the most was weaving. In the mid 1860s they established textile factories at Kozhikode and Kannur. In 1873, they started a tile factory at Kozhikode. This marked the beginning of the factory system, the symbol of the emerging new mode of production, in Kerala. During this period, the economy necessitated the liberation of the workforce from the clutches of the social system. There were several institutional fetters that tied the worker and the most inescapable of all was that of caste. The worker had no right over his/her body, and was subjected to atrocious forms of bondage for the perpetuation of landlords' proprietary control over the workforce *de facto*, such as untouchability and inapproachability. Religious beliefs, rites and rituals reinforced this wretchedness. In short, the socio-cultural conditions badly demanded movements capable of challenging the heinous customs, institutions and practices.

Socio-Religious and Caste Reformers

An ethical rethinking of the social conditions of human existence was necessitated by the material matrix of the nineteenth century. It is the intellectuals, often sages, who insightfully respond to the challenges of their times. Sages like Aiyya Vaikunda Swamy (1809–1851), Thaikkattu Aiyya Swamy (1814–1909), Chattampi Swami (1853–1924) and Sree Narayana Guru (1856–1928) are examples of such respondents in the case of Kerala. Sensitive to the ethical needs of their times and making sense of new worldviews spreading around with the arrival of European religions, they began rethinking religious beliefs and social practices. All of them ridiculed superstitious beliefs, such as idol worship, defied priestly domination and exposed the emptiness of expensive religious ceremonies. They questioned the caste system and went about mobilising people to be in defiance of caste restrictions.

A common feature among these four sages is rootedness in tradition and the relationship of resistance to the European worldviews, which they withstood without being swept off. In the process, they seem to have grasped the spirit and sobriety of the alien worldviews. Like most reform leaders elsewhere in India in the nineteenth and early twentieth centuries, these sages of Kerala too seem to have articulated the passion and values akin to the nineteenth century European progressivism represented by the Protestant Christian missionaries. These sages, apparently very orthodox, were the architects of what has come to be known as the Kerala Renaissance Movement, a movement that propagated universal humanism, rationalism, democracy and social equality. Vaikunda Swami was its pioneer.

Aiyya Vaikunda Swami (1809–1851)

As in the case of any of the past personages, the details of Vaikunda Swami's life are not entirely known. Apart from tradition, we know about him authentically through the accounts left by Thaikattu Aiyya Swami, his chief disciple and companion; references made by Rev. Fr Samuel Mateer and Rev. Fr Mead; and from the archives of the London Mission Society.

Vaikunda Swami was born in a poor cānnār family of Sāmitōppu near Kanyakumari in southern Tiruvitāmkur on 12 March 1809. His parents named him Mudichudum Perummal (literally, the crowned king) but changed it to Muthukkutty under opposition from the upper castes. He was initiated by a traditional teacher of his village in texts like the *Ramayana*, *Mahabharata*, some of the *Puranas* and a few Tamil works like *Tirukkural* and *Tiruvachakam*. It seems that Rev. Fr Mead taught him the fundamentals of the Bible. Rev. Samuel Mateer was in touch with him too. He was initiated in the Quran as well. However, after the traditional education, he took to toddy tapping, the hereditary occupation of his caste. Better informed and very sensitive towards social practices, he could not lead the life of his fellow members. Soon he went out roaming around as a mendicant and became a *sanyasi*. That was when he came to be addressed as Vaikunda Swami.

Vaikunda Swami was significantly influenced by the values and passions of Christianity. It seems to have given him an altogether different worldview. He became a critic of various social and religious practices in Tiruvitāmkur. Unlike most sages, he never withdrew to a space of meditative seclusion. Instead he incessantly communicated with his people on the futility of idol worship, the meaninglessness of expensive rituals, the social misconceptions about god, the injustice of the caste system, upper-caste oppression of the poor, the need to abolish servitude and the importance of social equality. It is liberation of the untouchable, unseeable, lower-caste body from bondage, that he stressed the most. His mobilisation of the cānnār women into a rebellious march in 1813 CE wearing the upper garment was, in fact, a collective assertion of the women's right to cover their chest. It was a prolonged struggle that lasted several decades until a final settlement of the issue in 1859 CE. He led the cānnār peasants into a revolt against oppression. His leading of the cānnār into a temple in agitation is another instance of assertion of the subjected. He had opposed all taxes imposed on the lower-caste agriculturists and led the cānnār peasants into a revolt against oppression. Through the popularisation of *samapanti bhojanam* (inter-caste dining) he fought against caste divisiveness. He tried to materialise his dream of social equality through the socialisation of the concept of *samatva samajam* (society of equality). He tried to represent the entirety of the *avarṇa** castes and called upon them to converge.

* In Kerala all castes except the nampūtiris and *antarāḷajātis* (ampalavāsis) were *avarṇas*. Nampūtiris never recognised the existence of kshatriyas and vaiśyas in Kerala and, according to them, there were only brāhmaṇas and śūdras. Hence, the ruling class and rich merchants have been attempting to live as the *savarṇas* by imitating various customs, rituals, dining practices and marriage rules. Ruling castes including the nairs and various temple castes had already succeeded in asserting themselves as savarṇas.

He attracted a following who obeyed his exhortations. He appealed to them to give up meaningless rituals and expensive ceremonies. A sage who took all religions as human creations, Vaikunda Swami condemned the practice of communal divisiveness that fragmented the society. His criticisms and public appeals often invited the wrath of the Tiruvitāmkur king. The upper-caste landlords, who turned inimical to him for his anti-caste exhortations and efforts towards the unification of avarṇas, tried to poison him to death. Under their pressure, the king got him imprisoned for refusing to confine his activities to his own caste. He was in jail for a while until Swāti Tirunāḷ Rama Varma (1813–1846 CE), the king of Tiruvitāmkur, intervened to set him free. He continued to work towards uniting all the lower castes to fight for achieving a life of security and self-esteem. He was the first social reformer who raised the slogan: 'One caste, one religion, one god, one language, one world, for humanity.' In 1851, before his death, he had consecrated a mirror as the deity in the temple at Sāmitōppu, his village. He asked the people to be worshipful in front of the mirror after removing their upper cloth and turban, to look at themselves in the mirror and salute. This was perhaps the most powerful ritual strategy that anyone used to boost self-respect among frustrated castes.

Vaikunda Swami's followers addressed him as Aiyya (father). He has gone down in history as one of the earliest leaders of the nineteenth century socio-religious reform movement in India. After his death, his followers called their way of life *aiyya vaḻi*, the path of Aiyya. They continue to be a distinct sect till date.

Thaikkattu Aiyya Swami (1814–1909)

Thaikkattu Ayya Swami, also known as Sadananda Swami, was the chief disciple and companion of Vaikunda Swami. Aiyya Swami was named Subbarayan when he was born in a family of Siva Yoga and Siddha tradition in Nakalapuram in Tamil Nadu in 1814. At the age 12 he was initiated in Siddha and with his teachers he travelled to various places in northern India and places in Burma, Singapore, Penang and Africa. During his extensive journey, he gained knowledge in various fields and acquired proficiency in English.

In 1839, he happened to meet Vaikunda Swami at Sāmitōppu and sat on penance at Maruthamalai for several days. Ever since, he maintained frequent contact with the Swami till the latter passed away. He pursued aiyya vaḻi and carried forward the social reform movement of his guru against the caste system, untouchablity, unapproachability, idol worship and unjust taxes imposed on the lower castes. Women's right to wear upper cloth was pursued as part of his commitments to aiyya vaḻi. Aiyya Swami used to be very active in organising inter-caste dining at Sāmitōppu and efforts in uniting the avarṇas.

In 1873, he was appointed the superintendent under the Resident McGregor and came to be called Superintendent Aiyya. He became a close associate of Manonmaniyam Sundaram Pillai and with him he founded the Saiva Prakasha Sabha at Trivandrum. He spent a lot of time initiating his disciples in Yoga, giving them spiritual lessons, imparting lessons in Advaita and exhorting them to mobilise people to fight against social evils. Soon he became famous as Aiyya Swami. He reiterated the famous proclamation of his guru with the words: 'One Religion, One Caste and One God.' He delivered several lectures on bhakti, yoga and vedanta at Jnanaprajagaram, where eminent personages assembled for deliberations, in Trivandrum. He also wrote several books on these subjects in Tamil, Malayalam and Sanskrit, some of which were published posthumously by his disciples. Aiyya Swami had many disciples; some were very rich and some extremely poor, some belonging to different religions like Islam and Christianity, and various castes, upper and lower. Chattampi Swami, Narayana Guru and Swayam Prakasini Amma were the most illustrious of his disciples.

Swathi Tirunal and Raja Ravi Varma were devoted to Aiyya Swami. He was the teacher who inspired most of the progressive thinkers and social reformers of nineteenth- and twentieth-century Tiruvitāmkur. His teachings led to the establishment of several socio-religious, literary and politico-cultural movements in Kerala, with concerns for the downtrodden, Sri Narayana Guru's movement, for instance. Aiyya Swami attained *samadhi* (sacred death) on 20 July 1909 as a Siva Yogi. In 1943, a Sivalinga was consecrated over his samadhi at Thaikkatu, and is now known as the Thaikkatu Siva temple.

Chattampi Swami (1853–1924)

Chattampi Swami was born on 25 August 1853 at Kollur in southern Tiruvitāmkur. He was named Ayyappan and called Kunjan at home. He had his education under Pettayil Raman Pillai Asan, a well-known scholar. Kunjan was the monitor of his class and that is how he got the name Chattampi (he who maintains *chattam* or norms). In the early 1870s Raman Pillai founded Jnanaprajagaram, which we've referred to earlier. The Jnanaprajagaram gave Chattampi opportunities to acquaint with several scholars. He learnt Tamil from Swaminatha Desikar, philosophy from Professor Manonmaniyam Sundaram Pillai and Yoga from Thaikkatu Aiyya Swami during their association with Jnanaprajagaram. Chattampi met Subba Jatapatikal in a Philosophical Conference at the Tiruvitāmkur palace complex and became his student for several years, learning Tarka, Vyakarana, Mimamsa and Vedanta. He also studied Siddha medicine, martial arts and music during these years.

Chattampi's next phase of learning was under a Christian priest in a monastery in Tamil Nadu, where he acquired knowledge of the Christian religion, its philosophy and spirituality. Later he learnt the Quran under a scholar of Islam and got acquainted with Sufi mysticism. He then roamed all over India, met several sages and obtained insights into the worldviews of many of the world's religions. Chattampi came to be referred to as 'Swami' following his realisation and sermons that the essence of all religions remains the same and that religious conflicts stem from ignorant interpretations. According to him, distorted notions turn religions into tools of oppression and subjugation.

Subsequently, he learnt more about the Siddha perception of God and after having become an accomplished sage, he returned to Mavelikkara.

Chattampi Swami had great insights into the socio-religious conditions of Kerala. He criticised superstitious and ritualistic religion. He formulated the right kind of rituals and religious rites for the people. He opposed the monopolisation of traditional knowledge by a minority and the priestly control of religious texts. His interest was in exploring how religious texts could be made accessible to the ordinary people. He was against unjust social institutions, customs and practices such as caste. The emancipation of women was a major concern of Chattampi Swami's discourses and he worked towards bringing them to the forefront. Pointing out the fact that the *sastras* prescribe equal status to women, he argued that women owe their enslaved position to the misinterpretation of the traditional texts by arrogant men.

Chattampi Swami has written many books in various fields of knowledge, mostly in Malayalam. Some of these works were published posthumously. His intention was to take the knowledge of Siddha and Advaita to the common people. *Vedadhikara Nirupanam* is considered to be one of his most insightful books. He wrote on Christian religious thoughts as well. Religious philosophy was not the only subject he dealt with in his writing. *Prachina Malayalam* is a classic example of his interest in language and culture. He believed that people's awareness of such subjects of scholarship that unveiled the history of ethnic and cultural unity would remove divisiveness among them.

Narayana Guru, Neelakanta Thirthapada and Thirthapada Parmahamsa were his main disciples. All of them influenced the Swami as much as he influenced them. Chattampi Swami had great regard for his disciples, admired their ideas and worked with them, championing their social cause as well. Chattampi Swami died in 1921. On his burial at Panmana in Quilon district a Sivalinga was consecrated and it is a Siva temple today.

Sree Narayana Guru (c. 1856–1928)

Nanu was born perhaps in 1856, as the son of a poor īḻava peasant, at Chempaḻanthy in Thiruvananthapuram district. He spent his childhood as a cowherd for a rich household. Kummanpallil Raman Pillai Asan, the headmaster of a Sanskrit school at Kayamkulam, opened the door to Nanu's education and changed the course of his entire life. He sent Nanu to Moottha Pillai Asan, a Nair teacher at Kaḻakkuttam, and Moottha Pillai Asan initiated the boy. Later Raman Pillai Asan himself educated him for six years in the basics of Malayalam and Sanskrit literature. During this period Nanu stayed at Raman Pillai's house. Nanu took interest in Vedanta and started helping the neighbouring children learn the basics of Malayalam and Sanskrit. Thus, Nanu grew up to be known as Nanu Asan.

In 1882, Nanu Asan met Chattampi Swami and lived with him for several months discussing and learning Siddha, Yoga and Vedanta. They travelled together to different parts of the country. During this period, he developed a critical attitude towards social evils such as the caste system and participated in the reform initiatives of his guru. Chattampi Swami introduced Nanu Asan to Aiyya Swami who received him as a disciple and taught him for several months. Nanu Asan seems to have had a brief period of *grahsthashrama* (a phase of life preoccupied with home), but wanted to become a sanyasi. It was Chattampi Swami who took him to Aruvippuram, where he meditated and practised Yoga for several months. Local people began meeting him for advice and guidance in matters of everyday life. He dissuaded them from superstitious beliefs, meaningless rituals, expensive ceremonies and notorious caste practices. More and more people went to him and he reiterated the proclamation of Vaikunda Swami: 'One caste, One religion and One God.' Nanu Asan came to be known as Narayana Guru around this time.

A burning youth who was utterly impatient of the upper caste dominance, Narayana Guru picked a stone from the river and installed it as God Siva at Aruvippuram in 1888, challenging the nampūtiri caste's ritual monopoly of consecrating the idol.

This act shook the upper-caste society. To the infuriated, his reaction was that he had consecrated only an īḻava Siva. It was this historic self-proclamation of Narayana Guru as an anti-caste radical that revolutionised the character of Kerala's socio-religious reform movement.

This was the time when Dr Padmanabhan Palpu—the first īḻava bacteriologist, trained in London and a great political leader—was petitioning and mobilising support to achieve civic rights for the īḻavas who, along with other downtrodden castes, were denied access to public places and positions in the royal service, despite their being educated. Following the Malayalee Memorial Petition of 1891 that sought jobs for educated Malayalis in the Tiruvitāmkur Civil Services, Dr Palpu took the lead in mobilising the īḻava community into an organisation called the īḻava Sabha. However, it did not pick up despite his efforts. It is said that Dr Palpu managed to speak about caste-based ostracism in Kerala with Swami Vivekananda at Bangalore in 1893 for a few minutes while he plied his hand-pulled rickshaw with the Swami on it. Vivekananda is said to have advised him to depend on a sage to lead the anti-caste agitation by spiritualising and industrialising the people. This probably led Dr Palpu to realise the necessity of seeking the blessings of Narayana Guru to mobilise the īḻava community. After the submission of his īḻava Memorial Petition of 1896 to the king of Tiruvitāmkur, signed by over 13,000 īḻavas, Dr Palpu grew closer to Narayana Guru.

Narayana Guru, though busy interacting with people who used to gather as Vavoottu Yogam (a formal social gathering) at Aruvippuram, was in deep introspection at rest, debating over his own thoughts and aims. The outcome of this reflection was *Atmopadesa Satakam* (a hundred hymns in self-instruction), an eminently readable philosophical poetry in Malayalam that he composed in 1897. In 1898, Narayana Guru expanded his Vavoottu Yogam into the Aruvippuram Kshetra Yogam. A special meeting of the Aruvippuram Kshetra Yogam was held in 1903. The gathering, led by Dr Palpu, required the Yogam to work for the progress of īḻavas both in spiritual and material affairs.

Accordingly, in the same year, Aruvippuram Kshetra Yogam was registered under the Indian Companies Act, No. 6, 1882, as Aruvippuram Sree Narayana Dharma Paripalana Yogam with Narayana Guru as its President.

In 1904, Guru settled at Sivagiri for his spiritual pursuits, but with even more involvement in social-reform activities. A temple was built for Sarada Devi in 1912 at Sivagiri. He started a Sanskrit school at Varkala with an orphanage under his personal care, providing education for destitutes belonging to any caste. Guru asked the pilgrims who reached Sivagiri to understand pilgrimage as a movement for the promotion of education and devotion to God as self-awareness. His exhortation to them was to educate, enlighten and become strong through organisation. He expected the pilgrimage to help them realise that it is agriculture, trade, handicrafts and technical skill that make people independent. Another advice that he gave them was to carry the message of cleanliness all over the country. Several temples were built at places such as Mangalapuram, Kannur, Thalasseri, Kozhikode, Thrissur and Anchuthengu and consecrated by him. In 1913, he established the Advaita Ashramam, conceived as a Brahma Vidyalaya for the comparative study of religions and propagation of universal brotherhood (*Om Sahodaryam Sarvatra*), at Aluva. Rabindranath Tagore had met Narayana Guru at his Sivagiri Ashram in November 1922. Tagore is said to have remarked that he had met no sage more accomplished in spiritual attainments than Narayana Guru.

Since 1916 Guru's relation with Sree Narayana Dharma Paripalana Sangham (SNDP) involved differences over what should be the priority of the Yogam. Guru seems to have felt serious incompatibility between his concept of *dharma paripalanam* (maintenance of *dharma* or ethics) and what SNDP had been practicing. It finally reached a point where Guru had to make it clear that his aim was not the welfare of any particular caste through a caste organisation but the emancipation of all the lower castes through an anti-caste organisation. He even made a public statement about his inability to be a part of any caste organisation. However, despite differences, he attended the SNDP annual meet at Palluruthy held in 1927. He died on 20 September 1928.

Social Movements

There are certain characteristics that distinguish social movements from socio-religious reform movements, although the latter also acquires social dimension subsequently. First, social movements are neither religious and nor are they inspired by spiritual leaders. This is not to say that social movements had no leaders to inspire and that none of them had a spiritual outlook. Indeed, there were leaders behind social movements but mainly as the source of inspiration rather than leading in action. By and large social movements were spontaneous and self-directed popular movements addressed to state power. All of them were, therefore, rebellious and explicitly demanded personal freedom. Each one of them was a collective utterance of truth to power in the voice of the agitated.

Cānnār Agitation (1813–1859 ce)

We have already made a mention of the cānnār women agitation that had its inception in 1813 under the inspiration of Aiyya Vaikunda Swami. It was a fairly long and protracted social movement by cānnār women who were Christian converts. Wearing upper cloth was the dress code through which upper-caste women distinguished themselves from the rest. When cānnār women walked on public roads dressed like an upper-caste woman, it provoked upper-caste men and they assaulted them. In response to the agitation of 1813, the Dewan of Tiruvitāmkur Colonel John Munro granted permission to Christian cānnār women to wear upper clothes. However, this was revoked under pressure of the king's council. The council declined the Dewan's decision saying that it would obliterate the age-old caste differences.

Inspired by this movement by Christian cānnār women, nādār and ī<u>l</u>ava women also agitated for the right to wear upper clothes. As a result, they were allowed to wear a type of jacket (*chaṭṭa*) worn by Syrian Christian women and the body-cloth (*kuppāyam*) worn by Muslim women. The nādār and īḻava communities continued their agitation till the right to wear upper clothes was sanctioned unconditionally in 1820. Following attacks on nādār women, churches and schools, the Government of Tiruvitāmkur revoked the sanction order in 1828. Agitation continued and several lower-caste women began to dress like upper-caste women in protest. In 1858, the agitation acquired the dimension of a violent upsurge in different parts of Tiruvitāmkur. Finally, on 26 July 1859, the Governor of Madras Charles Trevelyan persuaded the king of Tiruvitāmkur to issue a proclamation granting all lower-caste women the right to wear upper clothes of their choice.

Mūkkutti Agitation

Although not a similar movement of wider social dimension and sustained struggle, the *mūkkutti* (nose stud) agitation deserves mention here. In fact, mūkkutti agitation was probably a late nineteenth century event that unexpectedly acquired the dimension of a movement. An upper-caste landlord pulled out the nose stud of an īḻava woman at Kayamkulam market and injured her. He did so because lower-caste women were not allowed to wear nose studs. Upon hearing about this event, Arāṭṭupuzha Velayudha Panicker, a local thug with some scrupules, became furious and rushed to the market with several nose studs. He distributed them among the lower-caste women and asked them to wear it. Unlike the violation of the dress code, the wearing of nose stud seems to have had no sustained opposition, probably because it was not an ornament typical of upper-caste identity. Also, there was no widespread pressure from the women to wear it, unlike the upper cloth.

Even though wearing of nose stud was not significant in the context of caste marker of identity, the assault of the īḻava woman by the landlord has social structural implications. Wearing of the nose stud by the woman meant assertion of her right over her own body, which was violative of the age-old system of the landlord holding proprietary right over the body of the lower-caste person. Both the act of wearing as well as the resistance are significant as an attempt at the liberation of the bonded body through self-assertion and the attempt at preventing it for safeguarding the social system.

Kallumāla and Irumpuvaḷa Agitation (1915 CE)

If the mūkkutti agitation was for the right to wear an ornament, the *kallumāla* (stone bead-chain) and *irumpuvaḷa* (iron bangle) agitation was for the right to discard certain ornaments. Pulaya women of the untouchable slave caste made this agitation into a movement. The kallumāla and irumpuvaḷa were typical ornaments of the pulaya women, while gold and silver ornaments distinguished the upper-caste women. Like other women the pulaya women too wanted to wear ornaments made of other materials and metals that they could afford. Various low cost ornaments reached their fairs and festivals. Nevertheless, fearful of inviting the wrath of their owners, none of them dared to buy and wear these substitutes to their traditional ornaments.

Some of the educated middle classes would advise the pulaya women to discard their traditional ornaments that were marks of slavery. They told the women to see the irumpuvaḷa as relics of the chains of slaves. Inspired by this the women attempted to discard their kallumāla and irumpuvaḷa, but were ruthlessly prevented by their landlords from doing so. A few times such events became rebellious and the Tiruvitāmkur police had to interfere. It was Ayyankali, the great radical social reformer, who gave the pulaya women of Perinad in Quilon district the courage to discard these disliked ornaments. In Perinad and nearby villages the women discarded the traditional ornaments in October–December 1915. In a meeting chaired by Ayyankali on 21 December 1915 at Perinad, several pulaya women threw away their kallumāla and irumpuvaḷa, proclaiming that like others they would also wear other ornaments.

Other Reformers

Social reform movements were an ongoing process and several others had figured as reformers in the early decades of the twentieth century. A notable difference is the civilian status of the reformers. Largely, they do not seem to have assumed the garb of a sage, except a few like Vagbhatananda (1885–1939) and Nataraja Guru (1895–1973). Spiritual matters apart, these reformers did not enter the channel of religion to communicate their ideas of reform. A great social reformer who is ranked among the four major personages, Aiyya Vaikunda Swami, Thaikkattu Ayya Swami, Chattampi Swami and Sri Narayana Guru is Ayyankali (1863–1941), who never became a sage though. We include Poikayil Appachan (1879–1939) for discussion, for he started off as a social reformer with spiritual clout, though subsequently he became Kumara Gurudeva and the sage of a distinct cult.

Ayyankali (1863–1941)

Ayyankali was born on 28 August 1863 in Venganur in Thiruvananthapuram district. He was the eldest of eight children and was born to parents of the pulaya caste. In those days it was extremely difficult for pulaya children to receive formal education and all of them had to get involved in livelihood activities at an early age. Ayyankali, therefore, had no formal education. He was a very intelligent and courageous boy, who grew up positioning himself in a relationship of resistance and confrontation. Never to have anything to do with the pulaya behaviour of obeying as if born only to obey, Ayyankali questioned orders and invariably disobeyed them as a child. Strangely, he was a self freed by none and placed himself above social fetters, enabling to objectively understand human existence without being subsumed by the enslaved condition of his caste. He remained most unperturbed, but equally infuriated to retaliate.

In the late 1880s he attracted a few followers and their number increased as he turned his protest to singing and dancing.

This fraternity led to the formation of a group that could put up resistance against upper-caste atrocities. Ayyankali came to be known as *urpillai*, the leader of the pulaya settlement, or *moothapullai*, the headman. In 1893, Ayyankali dressed up like a nair landlord with a golden turban and took a ride to the Nedumangad market through the public road, seated in a bullock-cart he had purchased, boldly in defiance of all upper-caste impositions. This was a major demonstration of himself as the lord of his own people, a scene purposely enacted so that his people would take pride in themselves. This rare historic event sowed the seeds of self-esteem in his people, perhaps for the first time. It was a very powerful act of dissent and protest, and assertion of a subjected body of its ownership and the right to exist in public space. Ayyankali's demonstration triggered a series of protests by the oppressed castes of Tiruvitāmkur. By 1900, the Government of Tiruvitāmkur was forced to grant pulayas the right to use all the public roads in the state, except those that led to the temple.

In 1904, Ayyankali happened to listen to an inspiring speech of Aiyya Swami, who called upon the people to put a stop to caste practices such as untouchability and unapproachability. Aiyya Swami's exhortations to bring unity among the downtrodden castes attracted Ayyankali. Similarly, the teachings of Narayana Guru immensely influenced him. Guru's stress on education was most convincing to Ayyankali. Ayyankali took sustained efforts to spread education among his people by exerting pressure on the government to make public schools accessible to children of the untouchable communities. Subsequently, in 1907, the government ordered public schools to admit children of the untouchable castes. The upper castes opposed this order. They burnt the school at Ooruttambalam that had admitted a pulaya girl. Ayyankali had to fight this fall out through open confrontation. He had to warn the landlords that the pulayas would not work in their fields if they continued to oppose the education of their children. In 1907, Ayyankali founded the Sadhu Jana Paripalana Sangham (SJPS), an association for the protection of the poor. Through SJPS, he mobilised resources for establishing schools for the pulayas. That same year he started a pulaya school at Venganur.

Among the social reformers of the period, Ayyankali remains distinct for not adding a religious dimension to his work. Although in admiration of Aiyya Swami, Ayyankali had established a Brahma Nishta Matam at Venganur, the Yoga taught there was not a path acceptable to him for his action. This was also true in his relationship with Narayana Guru. Ayyankali was not interested in Guru's teachings of Siddha or Yoga or *brahmavidya* (the knowledge of Brahma; i.e., the self-realisation of the inseparability between the individual consciousness [*ātman*] and the super consciousness [*bhrahman*]). A towering figure capable of influencing affirmative action in government, Ayyankali became a member of the Sree Mulam Praja Sabha of Tiruvitāmkur from 1914 onwards.

In 1915 Ayyankali was involved in the kallumāla and irumpuvaḷa agitation, also called the Perinad agitation by pulayas, as we have already seen in the previous section. As a representative of his people in the Sree Mulam Praja Sabha, Ayyankali was largely focused on pressing affirmative action into service through the government. However, he was also involved in all the movements led by his people. During the second half of his career, Ayyankali spent much of his time advocating for the rights of the depressed classes within the government. A committed and active leader of his community, he continued his efforts to ensure opportunities in education to the downtrodden until he died on 18 June 1941. Ayyankali's importance as a radical who strived for social change through collective action and emancipation of the depressed is becoming increasingly important in the wake of the different shades of Dalit movements in the country today.

Poikayil Appachan (1879–1939)

Poikayil Appachan was born on 17 February 1879 to a paraya family that was attached as slaves to a Syrian Christian family called Sankaramangalam at Eraviperur in Pathanamthitta district. His parents named him Komaran, but he was raised as

Yohannan and taught to read and write. Though a slave, literacy and exposure to the Bible had helped him liberate his mind from his subjected position. He was acquainted with works by missionaries as well. As an intelligent man with critical consciousness, Yohannan could go beyond religiosity and grasp the bare truth of real life. Commonalities of the slave castes became clear to him as he grew up and wanted to unify them rather than going around spreading the gospel. In 1900, Yohannan left the Sankaramangalam family, seeking his roots and brethren communities aimed at organising them into a new one.

With the belief that a liberal Christian sect will help him, he joined the Marthoma Church, but soon realised that an untouchable caste had no status there and tried his luck with the Brethren Mission, which was a much more reformed sect, but in vain. He was soon convinced that the Christian religion was no alternative to escape caste-based bondage and discrimination. He badly missed the basic tenets of Christianity in the Christian religion that he came across. In 1907, he joined Ayyankali's SJPS and became actively involved in the pulaya movements. But he was being dragged more towards the spiritual and mystical ways of attaining the world of equality through imaginary relations during this time. In 1909, he started his own religious commune of dissent and protest called the Prathyaksha Raksha Daiva Sabha (PRDS). It was from here on that Yohannan came to be known as Appachan, who advocated values and passions of equality that were not too distant from Protestant humanism.

Poikayil Appachan was nominated to the Sree Mulam Praja Sabha in 1921 and 1931. He died on 29 June 1939 at the age of 61, revered by his disciples as Kumara Gurudevan, the immortal one. Sanal Mohan, an analyst of the dalit experience and memory of slavery, has studied the movement and cult of Kumara Gurudevan. He goes into the historical process of the making of the PRDS community by studying the experience of slave castes in ninteenth and twentieth century Kerala. He examines their struggles against inequalities and dreaming of equality in the making of the PRDS community. This study of PRDS has drawn the attention of scholars the world over. Another important study relevant to the context is by Joan P. Mencher, who has looked at the slave life as experienced by the dalits in Kerala. She has seen it against the self-imagination of their own life as juxtaposed against that of the upper castes.

Community Movements

After the movements led by socio-religious reformers and with the establishment of SNDP, several community-based reform movements were heralded under great leaders like Pandit Karuppan and Vakkam Moulavi. Some of the leaders like Vagbhatananda and Nataraja Guru continued the spiritual tradition of Sree Narayana Guru, while others like Sahodaran Ayyappan led hardcore social movements based on rationality and atheism. Various communities began to organise themselves into bodies for initiating reform movements within themselves. The nampūtiris formed their community organisation called Yogakshema Sabha under Desamangalam Valiya Sankaran Nampūtiri and Kurur Unni Nampūtiri. Similarly, the nairs formed Nair Service Society (NSS) under the leadership of Mannathu Padmanabha Pillai. Some of the leading figures and their contributions to community organisation and caste-based social reforms are reviewed below.

Pandit Karuppan (1885–1938)

Kandathiparambil Papu Karuppan, called Sankaran during his childhood, was born into a lower-middle class family of the dheevara fishermen community on 24 May 1885 at Cheranelloor near Ernakulam. He was given the name Karuppan, derived from the Tamil word *karpan* (wise), by a Tamil mendicant who found in the boy signs of greatness. After his initiation in Malayalam, he had his education in Sanskrit kāvyas under Mangalappillil Krishnan Asan of Cherai. Later, he further studied the kāvyas under Annamanada Rama Pothuval. Then he joined the Koṭunkōḷūr Gurukulam, where he was trained under great scholars, for higher studies.

Karuppan was already a poet by the time he reached Koṭunkōḷūr. As a twelve year old boy, he had excited his early teachers by composing *Lankamardanam* in beautiful Sanskrit. In 1904, as a nineteen year old at Koṭunkōḷūr Gurukulam, he wrote *Jathikummi*, a Malayalam composition that criticised the caste system and untouchability. When the king of Cochin visited Koṭunkōḷūr Gurukulam during his pilgrimage to Tiruvanchikkalam, he was informed of the prodigious student. Impressed by Karuppan's rare talent and scholarship, the king took him along to his palace at Cochin and made arrangements for his learning in Sanskrit under Rama Pisharody, the chief preceptor of the Tripūṇithuṛa royal family. After his advanced lessons, Karuppan became a pandit in Sanskrit and was appointed as the Sanskrit teacher in the Caste Girls' High School at Ernakulam in 1912. Eventually, Pandit Karuppan would publish may works of poetry and drama. Pandit Karuppan also wrote *Aacharabhushanam* that was aimed at generating awareness against superstitions among the depressed classes. As early as in 1913, the king of Cochin honoured him with the title *Kavithilakam* (star poet).

Karuppan became a social activist and organised the Cochin Pulaya Maha Sabhā in 1913. Karuppan called a *kayal sammēḷanam* (meeting by the lake) that same year. He organised the people of his own community into regional groups called sabhās for fighting ignorance and superstitions. He was equally involved in organising other communities as well. In 1915, Karuppan persuaded other communities like velas, sambavas, ulladas and kudumbis to form similar sabhās to give momentum to their fight against social evils and discrimination.

Pandit Karuppan's appointment in the Caste Girls' High School, an institution exclusively for upper-caste girls, excited strong opposition from the upper castes. They expressed their reluctance to send their girls to be taught by a teacher belonging to a lower caste. However, the king of Cochin came heavily on the issue and ordered that girls who refused to be taught by Pandit Karuppan would be ousted from the school. The opposition fizzled following this order. Six years after this event, Pandit Karuppan moved to Victoria Girls' High School at Thrissur as the Sanskrit teacher. Later he also taught at the Thrissur Teacher Training School. In 1921, he went back to the Caste Girls' High School at Ernakulam, which had by then become a college for girls of all castes.

In 1925, Pandit Karuppan was nominated to the Cochin Legislative Council as a representative of the downtrodden for whose emancipation he had struggled through the movements and his writings. This was indeed in recognition of his services to the oppressed. As a member of the Council, Karuppan was extremely helpful to the constituency that he represented. He was successful in influencing the government to establish a separate Department for the Protection of the Depressed Classes. As Assistant Protector of the department, Karuppan introduced several schemes for the welfare of the depressed classes, such as establishing settlements, opening separate schools, instituting scholarships and extending various concessions. This department was later renamed the Harijan Welfare Department, and it still functions under the Government of Kerala. He also started schools of fisheries at Cochin. He was responsible for establishing fish-curing yards as an industry for the welfare of the fishing community. Pandit Karuppan held various important positions during his time as member of the council, such as Secretary of the Elementary Education Committee and the Bhashaparishkarana Committee, and Superintendent of the Department of Vernacular Education of Cochin State. In 1932, he became lecturer in Sanskrit at the Maharaja's College, Ernakulam.

Karuppan voluntarily retired from jobs in 1934 to devote more attention to be active in social reforms. On 23 March 1938, he became seriously ill with pleuritis and passed away.

Vakkam Moulavi (1873–1932)

Abdul Khader was born in 1873 to a prominent merchant in Vakkam, a village in Chirayinkizh taluk of Thiruvananthapuram district. His parents ensured that he received excellent education under several eminent scholars from various parts of the country. These teachers included an itinerant Arab scholar, who made the brilliant boy proficient in Arabic, Persian, Urdu, Tamil, Sanskrit and English besides any knowledge he aspired to learn.

Abdul Khader started the historic newspaper *Swadeshabhimani* on 19 January 1905, with Ramakrishna Pillai as the editor. They were openly committed to speaking the truth to people and unveiling all injustices that prevailed. Simultaneously, Abdul Khader also began his efforts in community welfare by founding the Islam Dharma Paripalana Sangham in 1906. His newspaper did not last long due to its critical stand against British imperialism. On 26 September 1910, the British banned the newspaper, confiscated the press, and arrested and expelled Ramakrishna Pillai from Tiruvitāmkur. However, this hardly affected the social reform enthusiast and cultural activist in Abdul Khader.

Abdul Khader wrote several books on Islamic thought and brought out Malayalam translations of works in Persian and Arabic. This made him famous and soon he came to be known as Vakkam Abdul Khader Moulavi. As a humanist who advocated democratic values and expressed his insights into society, religion and culture, he was very much engaged in bringing about progressive reforms within the Muslim community of Kerala by distinguishing genuine religious teachings from superstitious beliefs and customs. He is hailed today as the first socio-religious reformer of Kerala who tried to uplift the Islamic community through modern education. He extensively campaigned among his people to make them realise the importance of education, and tirelessly worked for the promotion of modern education among women.

He published Arabi-Malayalam periodicals that were aimed at improving public education and social awareness among the Muslim community. The periodicals *Al-Islam* that he began in 1918 and *Deepika* in 1931 played a pivotal role in educating the Muslim community about the fundamentals of the Islamic religion. He set up the Islamia Publishing House in 1931 and made publication of books in this regard effective. The progressive outlook of his publications that exposed the meaninglessness of *nercca* (donations by devotees) rituals and Uroos festivals, death anniversaries of Sufi saints, celebrated at their tombs (*dargahs*), invited the wrath of the orthodox leaders of the Muslim community. The *ulema* (a body of experts in Islamic theology) issued a *fatwa* (ruling) dissuading the Muslim public from reading the publication. Many *mullahs* (scholars in Islamic theology) turned against him, branding him a *kafir* (a derogatory Arab word for an anti-Islamic person) or a Wahabi (an orthodox Sunni Muslim belonging to the sect of Muhammad ibn Abd al-Wahhab). However, these journals generated strong waves of reform among the Kerala Muslims. Unfortunately, their publication was short-lived due to the absence of enough people to take the enterprise forward.

Introduction of Arabic teaching in all public schools with Muslim children was the sheer result of his sustained pressure on the Government of Tiruvitāmkur. Moulavi got the girls taught free and boys with fee concessions and scholarships. He wrote textbooks in Arabic and prepared a manual for training teachers of Arabic in primary schools. Soon the government standardised the qualification for teachers of Arabic under his masterly stipulations. He was made the chairman of the Muslim Board of the Government of Tiruvitāmkur in recognition of his efforts in uniting the Muslims of the Tiruvitāmkur, Cochin and Malabar regions through his work in the Muslim Aikya Sangamam in 1922 that aimed towards integrated development and modernisation of the Muslim community through education. Regional community organisation was his central institutional strategy of social mobilisation for literacy and modernisation. He had already emerged top in community leadership by establishing the All Travancore Muslim Mahajanasabha and Chirayinkizh Taluk Muslim Samagam. Abdul Khader Moulavi died on 23 August 1932.

Sahodaran Ayyappan (1889–1968)

Sahodaran Ayyappan was born in an īḻava family at Cherai in Vyppin island of Ernakulam district on 21 August 1889. He lost his father in childhood, and was raised by his elder brother Achuthan Vaidyar. After his school education in Cherai and North Paravoor, Ayyappan pursued further studies at Malabar Christian College, Kozhikode. During his student days he showed great talent in public speeches on socio-political affairs and this gained him the acquaintance of Sree Narayana Guru. Under Guru's guidance he continued his education at Maharaja's College, Ernakulam, from where he graduated in 1916. His meeting with Kumaran Asan added fire to his thoughts on working towards a social revolution that would put an end to the caste system and untouchability.

Ayyappan began his social activism by forming an organisation called Sahodara Sangamam (Confluence of Brotherhood), because of which he came to be known as Sahodaran Ayyappan. Under the aegis of this organisation he organised a *misra bhojanam* (inter-caste dining) at Cherai in 1917. About 200 people belonging to various lower and upper castes gathered and dined together, ignoring the strong opposition from orthodox nairs. Even prominent i̱lava households objected to this event. They even ridiculed him as 'Pulayan Ayyappan', as if it could be abusive, but he hailed it as an honour bestowed on him. On 15 May 1921, Narayana Guru blessed him through a message in support of his inter-dining and inter-caste marriage initiatives under Sahodara Sangham. Along with social activism he worked towards and secured a degree in Law from Government Law College, Thiruvananthapuram.

Nevertheless, his drive for social reform persisted and he launched a periodical called *Sahodaran* from Mattancherry. *Sahodaran* carried progressive articles and poems, appropriate for nurturing social awareness that combated superstitious beliefs and social evils such as untouchability. An accomplished rational thinker of renaissance humanism, Ayyappan firmly believed that progressive social development would not materialise without uprooting the bizarre notions of people. Thus, in 1928, he started the *Yukthivadi*, a magazine for the promotion of rational thinking in society. He proclaimed: '*Jati venda, matham venda, daivam venda manushyanu*' ('Human beings need no caste, no religion and no god'). Ayyappan had great devotion for Sree Narayana Guru without any sense of contradiction, obviously because he knew that deep in Guru's thoughts and social actions was the leavening influence of Vedantic atheism.

Ayyappan pioneered working-class politics and trade union leadership. In 1928, he was elected as member in the Cochin Legislative Council, which he retained for over two decades. He became minister in the Cochin Legislative Assembly twice and once in the Thiru-Kochi Assembly. An above-board and hardworking social worker with no selfish motives, Ayyappan commanded great respect from all sections of the society. On 6 March 1968 he breathed his last.

V. T. Bhattathirippad (1896–1982)

Vellithuruthi Thazhathu Karutha Patteri Raman Bhattathiripad was born on 26 March 1896 in Kaippilly Mana at Mezhathur, which is situated on a bank of the Nila river. Like many nampūtiris of the period, Raman remained illiterate. He grew up critical of the orthodox practices of the nampūtiri caste. A person of sharp intellect, he felt the need to reform the community. What excited his empathy was the miserable plight of the nampūtiri women who mostly encountered the predicament of early marriage to an old man. Naturally, many young women became widows and had to lead a wretched life. A nampūtiri woman was almost in an imprisoned state within the *mana* (house) and existed as a chattel. Outside she was under the cover of a *marakkuta* (a palm leaf umbrella) and *ghosha* (a shawl wrapping the torso). Patriarchal domination was of an extreme degree, although there were exceptions.

A nampūtiri woman charged with infidelity was subjected to a special trial of caste exclusiveness, called *smarthavicharam*. The woman would be wrapped in a mat and rolled down the roof. They were invariably permanently ousted from the mana. All the men involved in immoral relations with the accused were excommunicated too. In 1905, a woman named

Kuriyetathu Thathri was accused of infidelity and subjected to smarthavicharam. During the trial she disclosed the names of several men who she was involved with, included some persons of high status, and produced proof of the same. It literally shook the nampūtiri patriarchs and they appealed to the king of Cochin to sanction a *purushavicharam* (cross-examination by the accused men), which the king conceded, despite the absence of precedence. Some of the men even hired the professional service of barristers and the whole institution of smathavicharam involved unprecedented procedures in this case. Nevertheless, all this proved in vain and all the men who were accused were excommunicated. This event was subsequently viewed by V. T. Bhattathirippad as a major protest of women of the community against the patriarchal hegemony of their nampūtiri landlords.

V. T. Bhattathirippad was very critical of atrocities against the *antharjanam* (literally, those inside) and he saw it as an extension of caste discrimination, because nampūtiris treated their women as sudras. His efforts were focused on developing awareness among nampūtiri women. He relied on theatre as an effective channel of communication for social reform and women's empowerment. His play *Atukkalayilninnum Arangathekku* was a turning point in Malayalam theatrical tradition. It unleashed a wave of criticism within the hegemonic system of nampūtiri patriarchy.

Many nampūtiris congregated at the mana of Cherumukku Vaidikan on the Periyar River during the Sivarathri of 1908 and resolved to establish the Namputhiri Yogakshema Mahasabha, a community welfare organisation oriented towards the nampūtiris. Its main objective was the spread of modern education and improving literacy within the nampūtiri community. In order to circulate progressive ideas and convince the people of the need for social reform, the sabha began publishing a monthly called *Yogakshemam*. Kurur Unni Namputhirippad gave the leadership in deliberations about the reforms. This marked the first organised move to introduce reforms within the community.

Adoption of promotion of education in the 1928 annual meeting of the sabha at Edakkunni and the subsequent opening of Namputhiri Vidyalayams in different parts of the state remained the all-time major achievement of the sabha. Similarly, among social reforms, abolition of *ghosha* (the purdah) was systematically implemented following its adoption at another annual meeting held at Edakkunni in 1930. This provided an occasion for V. T. Bhattathiripad to prove his leadership qualities. His staging of the play had far-reaching impact on nampūtiri women, especially young girls. M. R. Bhattathiripad's *Marakkutakkullile Mahaa Narakam* (Hell Inside the Palm Leaf Umbrella) encouraged women to discard the umbrella behind which they had to hide.

V. T. Bhattathirippad argued for the introduction of inter-caste marriages in his deliberations in the Yogakshema Mahasabha. As a demonstration, he gave his sister, who was a student of a Vidyalayam, in marriage to a nair youth. However, the Vidyalayam Committee moved court against him for violation of the contract between the Committee and the parent for compliance of the school's norms and code of conduct, and emerged successful.

As an organisation that represented the nampūtiri community, the sabha could get two of its leaders elected to the first Legislative Council of the Cochin State in 1925. These members introduced the Namboothiri Bill in the Council and, despite strong opposition by orthodox members, got the Bill passed. In the Travancore Legislature the Bill was passed without much difficulty, but it failed thrice in Cochin. Subsequently, it was accepted after the realisation of the futility of preventing it. It was adopted as Namboothiri Law in Malabar through legislation in the Assembly of the Madras Presidency. The Mahasabha brought about changes in the property laws of the nampūtiris, which were customarily based on primogeniture (the eldest male as the sole legal heir to the family property). The passing of the Namboothiri Law made each member of the family entitled to an equal share of the property. All this sequential development that brought about fundamental transformation of property relations of the nampūtiris was the result of V. T. Battathirippad's initiatives.

In 1934, at the annual meeting of the sabha held at Peramangalam, a resolution for widow marriage was introduced, but this was strongly resisted. Nevertheless, it was passed when some advocates pointed out the passing of a similar Bill by the Government of India earlier. Its implementation was inaugurated by V. T. Bhattathirippad who arranged for Mullamangalath Raman Bhattathiripad (1908–2001), famously known as MRB, to marry a widow. Other activities like *sudhham* (purity) and misra bhojanam were also carried out by Bhattathirippad. Some years later an organisation of nampūtiri women, Antharjana Samajam, was formed.

General Socio-Political Awakening

Foregone discussions of spiritual leaders, social reformers and various movements vouch for a general socio-political awakening in Kerala during the nineteenth and the first quarter of the twentieth century. Colonial trade, European juridico-political interference, the Mysorean invasion, socio-religious reforms, land reforms by the Tiruvitāmkur kings, missionary educational social preparation, royal patronage of general education through schools, women's social movements, anti-caste as well as caste-based self-respect movements, and so on significantly impacted Kerala. An educated and agitated middle class with a critical consciousness, anti-feudal/anti-imperialist resentments, democratic values and political activism was becoming increasingly influential. They began to question landlordism and the oppression of peasants under them. All this was heading towards a phase of organised movements of peasants in different parts of Kerala.

XI

Peasant Movements and Nationalism (1921–1947)

The exploitation of peasants only intensified with the self-imposition of the British over the traditional system of revenue appropriation. In the traditional agrarian system, i.e., the janmi (landlord) system, landless tillers who constituted the untouchable castes, were exploited the most. Landless tillers were subjected, almost like slaves, with the bondage of caste and the fetters of untouchability; they were attached to land as chattels and were largely unable to rise in revolt. So, peasant movements, in general, did not comprise this most oppressed class of landless tillers.

Background

Intermediaries in the janmi system were people of various hereditary occupation castes with differing levels of land rights. They constituted the category called tenants and held lease lands, wetlands for paddy cultivation or garden lands for cash crops or both. Artisanal castes were the lowest category of tenants who merely possessed their hutment. The intermediate castes practised agriculture and were small and big farmers. The janmi system was an ensemble of multiple rights and claims of hereditary nature, independent of the janmi's volition, as we have discussed in an earlier chapter. It was not possible to alienate a tenant of his holdings at the janmi's will. The tenancy was a traditional right that the tenant had to forfeit only on default of obligations, such as payment of periodic dues.

Since the establishment of the British on the top, two major changes were arbitrarily imposed on the janmi system: first, turning the janmi into an absolute landlord with the right to evict tenants; and, second, making tenants directly liable to the British. It was a combination of the *zamindari* (treating zamindars as the absolute owners of land) and *ryotwari* (treating peasants as holders of the land that they cultivate and hence responsible to pay tax directly to the British) systems. This upset the traditional agrarian relations in Tiruvitāmkur, Kochi and Malabar. Peasants were forced to pay dues far beyond their capacity; the dues were assessed in kind as well as cash by the janmis, who were under the pressure of the British. Under British compulsion, the janmis alienated the traditional rights of many tenants by evicting them from their lands and leasing the land to new tenants. These measures made peasant life extremely miserable and they turned against the janmis, who were those who executed the colonial imposition and were the immediate and visible masters for peasants. In turn, the janmis became inimical to the British who appropriated a lion's share of the janmis' surplus.

Under the influence of the British officials, the local rulers of Tiruvitāmkur and Kochi could introduce certain tenancy reforms in the latter half of the nineteenth century, ensuring fixity of tenure, fairness in rent and freedom to transfer. This provided for a certain amount of peasant mobility too. In fact, it was meant to facilitate the opening up of the plantation estates of coffee and tea by the British Company. In general the British land reforms and regulations made the ruling aristocracy and the nair landlords relatively less powerful. These were new regulations that replaced traditional means of appropriation for effective revenue administration. They turned traditional agents of appropriation into revenue officials. In the process, traditional nair intermediaries of the janmis became almost like the colonial revenue officials. It deprived them of their independent status and power as warrior heads under the janmi system. In fact, the British government was only using peasant grievances as an opportunity to interfere with the traditional system of appropriation of dues by janmis. These interferences are called reforms and regulations. Actually the word 'reform' was just part of the British rhetoric, for it meant change in the traditional practices, which was invariably unfavourable to peasants. Changes enabled or in certain cases forced the landlords to exploit peasants more intensely.

Such a move was unnecessary for the British in Malabar where they could acquire, through escheat and confiscation, enough plantation lands in the Ghats region like Wayanad. Therefore, they let the janmis of the plains in Malabar free to exploit the peasants with no fixity of tenure and no fair rent. Unlike in the regions of Tiruvitāmkur and Kochi, they forced the landlords of Malabar to evict peasants from their settlements and deprive settlers of their hereditary lease-rights for failure of payment of dues in time or in assessed quantity. In most cases the default was due to inability to pay the dues that were not affordable. Such cases of eviction and alienation of tenancy rights through tenancy super ordination (*melccārtṭu*) and arbitrary revamping of tenancy conditions (*policcucārttu*) became common in Malabar. These were open violations of the land-tenure conventions of the period. Naturally, the peasants in the south and north Malabar regions revolted against them several times through the nineteenth and twentieth centuries. Peasant revolts were more frequent in north Malabar, with a concentration in Kasargod. They aggravated all over north Malabar in the initial decades of the twentieth century.

Vaḻunnor janmis, the local and regional ruling lineage who also comprised the class of juridical and political power, revolted against the British in the beginning of the nineteenth century. Velu Thampi in Tiruvitāmkur, Paliath Achan in Cochin and Pazhassi in Malabar are some vaḻunnor janmis who rose in revolt. Among peasants, the māppiḷa share croppers (*verum pattakkar*) of south Malabar rose in a series of armed movements in the nineteenth and early decades of the twentieth centuries. The British responded to these movements by reforming the janmi × kuṭiyān (landlord × tenant) relation, but without compromising with the economic gains accruing to them or to the janmis. Naturally, the British efforts, incapable of addressing the real cause, only aggravated the tension of the peasantry. Central to the reform was the imposition of control over the janmi's proprietary right over peasants by asserting the British as the ultimate power even for the peasants. This apparently enabled the peasants to approach the British for redressing their grievances. In reality, it only worsened their condition. Reforms were by way of reducing the peasants' customary obligations to their janmis. They in no way affected the amount of dues to be paid to the British. Naturally, the British efforts, incapable of addressing the real cause, could only aggravate the tension of the peasantry.

Velu Thampi Dalawa

Velayudhan Chempakaraman Thampi (1765–1809), popularly known as Velu Thampi, was the *dalawa* (prime minister) of Tiruvitāmkur kingdom during 1802–1809 under Maharajah Bala Rama Varma Kulśēkhara. This was a tumultuous period with intrigues in the royal family, cliques, conspiracies, seditions and popular uprisings and the officials of the English East India Company were central to all these. Popular uprisings were caused by the greed for more revenue among the British traders and the entailing oppression of the primary producers. Other issues were due to the grievances of the local people against the misbehaviour of the British traders. Equally important was the resentment of the local chieftains, big landlords and merchants, whose economic interests were adversely affected by the Company's influence on the king. Velu Thampi represented this upper-class rivalry against the growing dominance of the English East India Company in the economic and political matters of the kingdom.

Velayudhan Thampi belonged to an aristocratic family of Kalkulam near Nagercoil, which had close connection with the Tiruvitāmkur royal family. Elders of this family were conferred the title of 'Chempakaraman' for their services to the kingdom during the reign of Marthanda Varma. Velayudhan Thampi began his career in the Tiruvitāmkur royal service as the kāryakkār (or tahsildar) of Mavelikkara during the reign of Bala Rama Varma, an inefficient ruler who was susceptible to influences of the greedy cliques in the palace. Jayantan Sankaran Namputiri who headed the clique became the *dewan* (prime minister) after the murder of Dewan Raja Kesavadas. Extravagant and corrupt, the new dewan depleted the royal treasury and ordered the dalawas to pay huge amounts disproportionate to the revenue due from their district. Velu Thampi Dalawa was ordered to pay Rs 3000. He sought a couple of days' time to pay the amount and mobilised the people against the corrupt dewan and his two ministers. People marched to the palace and demanded instant removal and deportation of Jayantan Sankaran Namputiri. Further, the agitated people demanded two ministers to be whipped in public and their ears chopped off. Accordingly, the king was forced to inflict the punishments and put them in jail.

Following this, Velu Thampi became the next dalawa of Tiruvitāmkur. He had to encounter various problems and the depletion of the royal treasury was foremost among them. Since he lacked insight into statecraft, Velu Thampi was unable to prove himself a successful dalawa. He was more a warrior chief than a diplomatic minister. However, Velu Thampi effectively confronted corruption that had by then become rampant. Thampi imposed severe punishments like open flogging of the dishonest, nailing the corrupt to trees, chopping of the ears and the nose of those accused of bribery. Soon Thampi's supporters in the royal service, tired of his ruthless and rebellious nature, turned against him. Kunjunilam Pillai, a senior official in the palace conspired and got the king to order the arrest of the dalawa on charges of sedition. On hearing about the conspiracy of Kunjunilam Pillai, Velu Thampi, who was then staying then in Alappuzha, went and met the British Resident at Kochi, Lord Macaulay. Pillai's role in the assassination of Raja Kesavadas was known to Macaulay and, therefore, he sent a small troop of British soldiers headed by Velu Thampi to Tiruvitāmkur to investigate Kunjunilam Pillai's conspiracy against Raja Kesavadas. Thampi proved Pillai's role in the murder of the dalawa and got him ousted.

In 1804, as part of reducing expenditure, Velu Thampi proposed a cut in the remuneration of the nair troops in the royal army, causing resentment among the nair soldiers. Presuming that the British Resident Macaulay was behind Thampi's proposal, they conspired to kill both Macaulay and Thampi. They gathered in thousands and marched to the palace, demanding the immediate dismissal of the dalawa and severing all ties with the English East India Company. Meanwhile, Velu Thampi rushed to Kochi and met Macaulay to evolve a strategy to overcome the threat. Accordingly, Macaulay and Thampi mobilised a huge contingent of soldiers from the Carnatic Brigade, marched to Tiruvitāmkur and suppressed the nair mutiny. The leaders of the mutiny were mercilessly executed. Krishna Pillai, the commander of one of the mutinous regiments, had his legs pulled apart by two elephants. All those who were identified as being disloyal were ousted from the royal army.

At the instance of the nair mutiny, Macaulay proposed a revision of the treaty of 1795 signed between Dharmaraja and the English East India Company in the light of the latter's policy of 'Subordinate Isolation'. This was the policy of enhancing the tributes of the native rulers to the English East India Company as well as the Company's military control over the kingdom. Accordingly, the treaty got amended in 1805 and the size of the British Indian army stationed in Tiruvitāmkur and the tributes to be paid to the British got virtually doubled. This caused a drastic cut in the expenditure of the royal militia. The kingdom already owed a large sum of money to the British by way of the expenditure incurred in suppressing the nair mutiny. Liabilities imposed by the 1805 treaty began to add to this and plunged the royal treasury into a crisis.

Velu Thampi's friendship with Macaulay did not last long. Macaulay began demanding for the debt to be cleared immediately. On the dalawa's advice, the king of Tiruvitāmkur required the Madras headquarters of the Company to replace Macaulay by a new Resident. This infuriated Macaulay and made him all the more adamant about insisting on the debt payment. The rebellious Velu Thampi went about mobilising a formidable force to confront Macaulay. In the meanwhile, in 1807, Macaulay conspired and cleverly persuaded the king to oust Velu Thampi from power. Nevertheless, thanks to one of the queens, Thampi got the news of the king's move to replace him.

Velu Thampi and Govindan Menon, the Paliath Achan (prime minister of the king of Kochi), planned to make a united move against Macaulay and put an end to the British dominance over the native kingdoms. They mobilised their forces and, in 1808, sought help from the Sāmūtiri and the French East India Company to supplement their forces. Realising that the help sought would not be forthcoming, they went ahead with the plan to jointly attack the Kochi Fort and kill Macaulay in 1809. Simultaneously, they made also arrangements for an attack of the British force at Kollam. In 1809, as a prelude to his battle against the English East India Company, Velu Thampi made his famous anti-British proclamation at Kundara in Kollam district. The Kundara Proclamation, as it came to be known, was a call to the people to fight against British dominance and safeguard their land and their tradition. Without support from the king and the people, the movement failed and Velu Thampi had to leave Tiruvitāmkur crestfallen. In utter disappointment and shame, Thampi committed suicide in the Mannadi temple and the British soldiers exhibited his severed head at a few places.

Paliath Achan: Paliath Achan was the head of the aristocratic Paliam family of nair chieftains, located at Chendamangalam in Ernakulam district. These heads were hereditary prime ministers in the kingdom of Kochi from 1632 to 1809. The Paliam household had extensive land control, which was virtually half of the landed property of the kingdom. The *achans* (headmen) of the family were traditionally the authority second only to the king. In 1731, the Paliath Komi Achan, the then headman of the family, was conferred the position of the Prime Minister of the Kochi Raja. Several of them figure in the political deeds and documents of the times. Some of them joined the revolts against the Europeans and their allies.

Kurichya Revolt (1812)

Most prominent among the tribal people of Wayanad were the kurichyas. According to popular tradition, 'kurichyar' was the name given by Kerala Varma Pazhassi Raja (the king of Kottayam of north Malabar) to a group of people who accompanied him to the Wayanad forest during the days of his conflict with the English East India Company. According to popular tradition, the kurichyas were nairs of a particular lineage called *tekke kari nair* (the nairs of the south). They may have originally belonged to the southern part of Kuṛumpoṛaināṭu in north Malabar. Like nairs, the kurichyas too followed the matrilineal system of inheritance (*marumakkattāyam*). Rating themselves highest in status among the tribes and castes of Wayanad, the kurichyas considered even the nampūtiris as a polluting caste. They served Pazhassi Raja as his loyal personal army. These expert archers were responsible for much of the loss that the English East India Company incurred during the days of its conflicts with Pazhassi.

After Pazhassi's death on 30 November 1805, in an encounter with the British soldiers, the East India Company became vindictive towards the tribals, particularly the kurichyas. The Company militia often intruded into tribal settlements, destroyed their farms and routed them deeper into the forests. The British soldiers became a menace to the life and property of the tribal people. Thomas Warden, the collector of Malabar, introduced many restrictions on the tribal people as part of his revenue administration. Under the pretext of these restrictions, the Company's revenue officers routinely harassed the people of the forests and plundered their crops. Arbitrarily revised tax rates severely oppressed the tribals and the check on their transactions of forest resources shattered their livelihoods. Insistence upon payment in cash made the tribals permanent defaulters, because their transactions were based on barter.

Many of these tribal people were taken as captives and abused as slaves. Teased and frustrated, several tribal families withdrew to safer zones within the forest, but the kurichyas reacted strongly against these atrocities. The kurumpas, who were another tribe in the region, also strongly confronted the British.

There was widespread discontentment among farmers, merchants, landlords and local rulers in other parts of Malabar as well as against the exploitation and humiliating attitude by the British. In Kochi and Tiruvitāmkur also the ruling aristocracy, landlords, merchants, traditional revenue officials and farmers resented the Company's over-exploitation and oppression. Some of them even rose in revolt, such as the mutiny of 1812 in Tiruvitāmkur in which a few European officers and soldiers were killed.

The kurichyas and the kurumpas took preparations for an armed fight with the British by manufacturing iron-tipped arrows using the railings pulled out from bridges. They sought to mobilise support of the traditional village revenue staff and even of the police constables in their fight against the British. In order to ensure the total participation of the kurichyas and kurumpas, the fight was projected as decreed by God. Everything was planned under extreme secrecy, and the Malabar contingent of the British militia under Colonel James Tagg hardly had any information about it. On 25 March 1812 the revolt broke out under the leadership of the kurichyas, and hence the name kurichya revolt. The tribal armies attacked officials of the East India Company and their armed security police. In a couple of days the insurgence spread like wildfire, blockading all routes to Wayanad and preventing the movement of enemy troops.

Many in the police and revenue service joined the rebellion. Within a short span of time, the kurichya revolt became a mass movement against the British. James Tagg's military contingent failed to contain the revolt and Thomas Baber, a Company official, sought additional forces from Canara. Soon a force of 2000 soldiers dispatched by the British Resident in Mysore reached the riot-hit forest areas of Malabar. Several contingents from Kannur also joined them.

The combined British forces was able to kill and imprison many of the armed kurichyas. In a couple of days, Baber restored law and order through repressive measures. Several were pardoned on the basis of requests submitted under pressure of the police. Most leaders of the revolt were either not caught or could not be persuaded to surrender and seek exoneration. As a result, rebelliousness persisted among many of the kurichyas and caused intermittent outbursts of violence in Wayanad for about two months. However, the kurichya revolt was indeed a major revolutionary movement. In his *Military Reminiscence*, James Welsh (1930), a General in the army of the East India Company, recollected that none of his servants lived to return with him after the suppression of the kurichya revolt. Several of his officers in Wayanad passed away soon after the rebellion. According to him, the consequences of the kurichya revolt among the British were so distressing that it turned out to be an eye opener to the East India Company.

Beginnings of Nationalism

With the establishment of British paramountcy in Kerala and the systematisation of the colonial mode of exploitation by the turn of the twentieth century, the agrarian unrest and the beginnings of nationalism converged. In 1885, G. P. Pillai, editor of the *Madras Standard* and the first nationalist leader of Kerala, initiated agitations for civil rights in Tiruvitāmkur state, which was was more political than Cochin or Malabar. The Travancore Legislative Council, which was formed in 1888, is the first democratic legislative in India. The Malayalee Memorial and the Īḻava Memorial, two major popular representations submitted to the government, give us an idea of the dimension of political activity in Tiruvitāmkur.

Towards the end of the nineteenth century, Kerala welcomed the Indian National Congress (INC) which was formed in 1885.

C. Sankaran Nair, a nationalist leader from Kerala, even became the president of the INC. The formation of a district committee of INC in 1908 was the main political event of contemporary Malabar, where in different parts during the subsequent years began the Home Rule Movement. In 1916 and 1917, the annual meetings of the district Congress committee were held at Kozhikode. In Tiruvitāmkur and Kochi too Congress committees were formed and political activities increased. In 1921, the Kerala Provincial Congress Committee (KPCC) was formed by integrating all the Congress activities in Kerala. And this integrated committee organised the first All-Kerala Political Conference in that same year.

Malabar Rebellion (1921)

The Khilafat Movement (1919–22) was a pan-Islamic Indian political protest that aimed at influencing the British government against abolishing the Ottoman Caliphate. It happened along with the Non-cooperation Movement as a mark of fraternity among the Hindu and Muslim religious communities. Naturally, the British government declared the Congress and Khilafat meetings illegal all over the country. This declaration, and the subsequent repression of Khilafat meetings in Ēṛanāṭu and Vaḷḷuvanāṭu taluks, triggered the māppiḷa rebellion or the Malabar rebellion in 1921. It was the culmination of a series of revolts since the late nineteenth century. Its course started in August 1921 and lasted about six months. Several Khilafat activists excited communal feelings to strengthen the movement. Communal violence went out of control. The māppiḷas seized several police stations, law courts and government treasuries.

Most active among this violent mob were the landless Muslim sharecroppers, who were a severely exploited and depressed class in the agrarian system. They had strong grievances related to impermanency of tenure, unbearable renewal fees, high rents and other oppressive appropriations. In fact, they had revolted against the landlord several times in the nineteenth century. The rebellion of 1921 was, however, significantly different in magnitude due to its communal mobilisation. With the pent up fury flared up, they looted granaries and killed several of their oppressive landlords. This rebellion was led by Vāriyamkunnath Kunjahammed Haji, Seethi Koya Thangal and Kumaranpathor Ali Musaliyar. Several brāhmaṇa janmis fled towards the coast where they were protected by the local Muslims.

Muhammad Abdurahaman, a progressive leader from Koṭunkōḷūr was active in peace-making campaigns. Similarly, K. Madhavan Nair—a Congress activist of Malabar who was closely associated with the Home Rule League and imprisoned during Non-Cooperation Movement—was the leader of the relief work in Kozhikode for the refugees of the māppiḷa rebellion. As a Congress leader who was critical of British imperialism, Abdurahaman was already an irritant to the British. They were apprehensive of Muhammad Abdurahaman's influence among those of the māppiḷa community and other people in the region. A leader of communal harmony like him was a hindrance to the British strategy of dividing people into conflicting religions. Conspiring and cooking-up charges of communal mobilisation against him, the police arrested and imprisoned him for two years in October 1921.

Historians have viewed the movement in various ways, some purely as a communal riot, several others as a peasant movement and a few as part of resistance against the British. K. N. Panikkar has analysed it as a movement against the landlord and the British government. Māppiḷas who rebelled were the *veṛumpāṭṭakkār* (landless tillers) under the nampūtiri landlords. As a contrast, it has been noted that such uprisings did not take place among the veṛumpāṭṭakkār like cerumas and pulayas in the same region, despite the fact that they were under more subjected conditions. Panikkar argues that such an uprising became possible among the māppiḷas due to their religious identity and the distinct worldview. Further, they were not under the fetters of caste and untouchability, unlike the cerumas and pulayas.

Gandhi's attitude towards the māppiḷa revolt has been a matter of debate among the Congress and several others. They expressed reservations against Gandhi's policy of Muslim appeasement, quite explicit in his defence of the Khilafat movement. Gandhi viewed everything against the higher goal of liberating the country and he found communal harmony extremely important for it. Nevertheless, Gandhi was seriously perturbed by the māppiḷa rebellion and the aftermath. He mobilised funds for relief operations by various voluntary agencies in the riot-affected areas for over six months. As a sad impact of the British tyranny, for almost a decade, resistance became largely confined to the problem relating to caste and untouchability. This accounted for the shift of Congress' thrust from problems of political freedom to social issues, which enabled convergence of all groups of people for collective operations for social equality. It was in this background that movements like Vaikom Sathyagraha became important.

Vaikom Satyagraha (1924–25)

Vaikom satyagraha was the culmination of a long sustained struggle for freedom to walk through roads irrespective of one's caste. It was an anti-untouchability movement centered on roads leading to the Mahadeva temple at Vaikom in the kingdom of Tiruvitāmkur. There were a series of attempts to break the laws preventing avaṛṇas from using the roads ever since 1803–04 when 200 īḻavas ventured to walk through the temple road, but in vain. Vaikom Satyagraha was organised during 1924–25 by eminent leaders of SNDP and Congress activists. It acquired nation-wide attention through the involvement of Gandhi and Periyar.

The satyagraha was organised on 30 March 1924 under the leadership of eminent people like K. P. Kesava Menon and T. K. Madhavan, demanding freedom for lower castes to use the road. Lower-caste people were not permitted to walk through the road to Mahadeva temple. According to the Travancore Royal notification of 1865, reaffirmed in 1884, public roads in the state would be open to all castes. After a judicial review, the High Court of Tiruvitāmkur in 1887 distinguished village roads from public roads and clarified that the notifications applied only to the latter. Since the roads around the temple at Vaikom were village roads, they need not be kept open to the lower castes along the lines of the notification.

During the Congress session at Tirunelveli on 23 September 1921, T. K. Madhavan had informed Mahatma Gandhi about the sad plight of the lower castes, including that of the i̱lavas, in spite of the collective efforts by the SNDP. At the Kakinada session in 1923 T. K. Madhavan, Sardar Panikkar and K. P. Kesava Menon persuaded the Congress leaders to include eradication of untouchability in the All India Congress Committee (AICC) agenda. It was conceded. Accordingly, the Provincial Congress met at Ernakulam on 24 January 1924 and formed an Untouchability Abolition Committee (UAC) consisting of K. Kelappan as convener, and T. K. Madhavan, Kurur Nilakantan Namboothiri and others.

It is said that the immediate provocation for the Vaikom movement was the stopping of Narayana Guru and his disciple Kumaran Asan from passing through the temple road. Even otherwise, on 28 February 1924, the UAC resolved to take a procession of lower castes through the roads on 30 March. However, the local magistrate was apprehensive of a communal clash and banned the procession. Eventually, the UAC decided to march only up to the point of the prohibited road and let only three of their members to enter and court arrest.

This continued for over a month and explored the possibility of compromise between the upper caste leaders and the Congress, but in vain. T. K. Madhavan and K. P. Kesava Menon courted arrest on 7 April. The Satyagraha soon caught nationwide attention and many offered support. Sikhs, Christians and Muslims volunteered to go on a fast. Gandhi asked them to leave the matter to the Hindus and told the satyagrahis to rely on local resources. E. V. Ramasami Naikar (famously known as Periyar) joined the Satyagraha on 14 April and courted arrest with his wife. Gandhi was upset about the development but could not resolve the issue. Rani Sethu Lakshmi Bhayi, who succeeded Moolam Thirunal as ruler of Tiruvitāmkur, finally ended the agitation by according sanction to open the temple roads to all castes and releasing the prisoners.

Civil Disobedience

Kerala widely responded to Gandhi's call for participation in the second phase of the civil disobedience movement, distinct for its famous Salt March at Dandi in March 1930. People violated salt laws at various places in Kerala and courted arrest. In Kozhikode the salt satyagraha became violent and leaders like Muhammad Abdurahaman were injured in the ensuing lathi-charge. Abdurahaman was sentenced to nine months' rigorous imprisonment at Kannur Central Jail. The civil disobedience movement ended with the signing of the Gandhi-Irwin pact of 4 March 1931. In the wake of the disobedience movement, a movement for responsible government was organised in Tiruvitamkur and Kochi during 1938-39, which demanded the dismissal of Dewan Sir C. P. Ramaswamy Iyer.

In 1931, the Guruvayur satyagraha was staged. The satyagraha which lasted till 1932 was organised under the leadership of K. Kelappan, an eminent Congress leader, to remove the caste discrimination against untouchables, who were prevented from entering the Guruvayur temple. Another significant movement in Tiruvitāmkur was the Nivartana Prakshobham (Abstention Movement) under the leadership of C. Kesavan. This movement was against the limitations of the constitutional reforms of 1932, such as restricted franchise, which stipulated that franchise had to be extended on the basis of possession of property and other qualifications. Īḻavas, Christians and Muslims feared that restricted franchise would result in pushing their number of seats in the legislature below that of the nairs. Therefore, they demanded for seats proportional to the strength of their respective populations. But this demand was not conceded and the AICC left the matter to the region. The abstentionists formed the Joint Political Congress and appealed to the voters to abstain from voting in the local government elections of 1937, that was to be conducted as stipulated by the Government of India Act of 1935. After the initial refusal the government yielded to their demand and the abstention call was withdrawn.

However, most of the candidates of the Joint Political Congress got elected.

With the appointment of C. P. Ramaswami Iyer as the dewan of Tiruvitāmkur (1936–47), several progressive reforms were adopted in the state. One such reform was the decision to allow temple entry to all the lower castes. In November 1936, the King Chithira Thirunal Balarama Varma issued the Temple Entry Proclamation. Similarly, the progressive reforms of Shanmukham Chetty, the dewan of the Cochin state, added political rigour to democratic movements in the state. In 1936, Chetty brought about a political reform through which an assembly member who secured the top majority could become a minister. Another important development in this state during this period was the founding of the Kochi Praja Mandalam in 1940 under the initiative of leaders like C. Achutha Menon.

Congress Socialist Movements

In 1934, a section of young activists of the Provincial Congress formed the Congress Socialist Party (CSP) under the leadership of P. Krishna Pillai and E. M. S. Namboodiripad. This emergence of the CSP was encouraged by the increasing participation of peasants and workers who had participated in the Civil Disobedience Movement. A progressive group of Congress men among the Muslims in Malabar and many others joined the Socialists and made CSP dominant within the Provincial Congress. However, CSP remained integral to Provincial Congress and AICC till a split during World War II. By 1938 Kerala had become very active in the national struggle for freedom. Simultaneously, they also struggled for responsible government in the princely state of Tiruvitāmkur.

In 1936, the All-India Kisan Sabha was organised with a view to achieving total liberation from the exploitative socio-economic system. As an extension of the All-India Kisan Sabha, the peasants of Malabar were organised into the All-Malabar Karshaka Sangham, with constituent units from the district and taluk levels to the villages. The Sangham included even landless tillers. Naturally, it was an ensemble of differentiated tenants who belonged to different castes. However, peasants of the lowest category had no fixity of tenure, and they remained at the mercy of the landlords. So, organising them into a body was difficult, for many of them feared punitive retaliatory measures of their landlords. However, the leaders of the All-India Kisan Sabha were anti-caste activists, and empathetic and committed to the poor, and tried to be closer to the peasants by visiting their huts and eating their food. Soon the Sabha became a body of political pressure and bargaining power.

The Sabha demanded abolition of all illegal exactions like customary dues by the landlords. On the formation of the Congress Ministry in Madras Presidency in 1937, the Kisan Sabha demanded for Malabar the tenancy legislation ensuring fixity of the tenure and fair rent, which was already in vogue in Tiruvitāmkur. Further, the Sabha exerted pressure on the ministry to implement the Karachi resolutions of the Congress, which contained a list of fundamental human rights.

During 1937–39, the peasant activists in Kerala were preoccupied with anti-feudal struggles. They were frantically trying to resolve the problem of abject poverty and widespread famine among artisans, craftsmen and landless tillers. Their activities were treated as part of the Left Civil Disobedience Movement and activists belonging to both the Congress and the CSP were imprisoned under the Defence of India Rules. A general charge was that these people organised movements on militant lines, involving criminal intimidation, social boycott, no-rent, no-tax campaigns and taking law in their own hands to run a parallel government.

Communist Party

During World War II, Provincial Congress was dominated by the Socialists and refused to comply with the AICC's call to individual Satyagraha. They wanted to campaign against the War and organise a stir against imperialism. This caused a split, and led to the formation of the Communist Party. In December 1939, a secret group consisting of P. Krishna Pillai, E. M. S. Namboodiripad, N. C. Sekhar and K. Damodaran met at Pinarayi and formed the Communist Party unit of Kerala, as authorised by S. V. Ghate of the Communist Party of India. AICC's call made no impact on most peasants who had by then become convinced of the need for radical political action. The Communist Party, in collaboration with the All-Malabar Karshaka Sangham, resolved to observe an Anti-Repression Day on 15 September 1940. Despite the ban on processions and meetings on the day, peasants and workers gathered in large numbers to demonstrate against repression. At Thalasseri, Mattanur and Morazha the police ill-treated the protesting peasants who in turn became violent, necessitating firing. Soon the British government declared the All-Malabar Karshaka Sangham and its local units illegal, and enabled the police to impose repressive measures on them. All peasant activists and nationalists of north Malabar were treated as Communists by the government. As a result, the anti-landlord and anti-imperialist struggles became strongly rooted and secretive in Malabar. In the meantime, the police arrested and imprisoned the senior Congress leader Abdurahaman, who had by then had association with Subhash Chandra Bose's All India Forward Block.

During those days, the Communist Movement meant peasant mobilisation for radical action against landlords and the British government. Provincial Congress activists tried to mobilise people for the Quit India Movement in August 1941. However, most peasants and Communists refused to be active in that movement. In March 1941, peasants of Kayyur, a tiny village, staged a demonstration under the leadership of the local Communist unit against the repressive measures of the police. They raised slogans cursing British imperialism and upper-caste landlordism. Through their speeches, leaders of the Kayyur Communist unit exhorted them not to pay dues to the janmis, not to contribute to the war-fund of the government and not to join the army. Inspired by these exhortations, peasants raised slogans cursing the British imperialism and upper-caste landlordism.

Angry farmers in the protest demonstration became rebellious against the two prominent janmis in the village, causing the death of several people. Soon the police arrested the peasant leaders and in one such encounter a police constable was drowned to death. This incident is known in history as the Kayyur Revolt. All of them who were suspected to be peasant leaders or Communists were arrested and imprisoned with the murder case imposed on them. Meanwhile, peasant uprisings and anti-imperialist struggles were disrupted by USSR's alliance with Great Britain in World War II. The Communists withdrew from the anti-imperialist movement and the British government lifted the ban on them as well as their peasant organisation on 26 July 1942. However, the trial of the accused in the Kayyur Revolt ended with the sentencing of four to death. They were hanged at Cannanore Central Jail in 1943.

Communists resumed their anti-feudal and anti-imperialist struggles as soon as the War ended. Their Central Committee resolved to start a mass movement for the incorporation of the princely states into the Indian Union. In Malabar, the peasants and agricultural workers had become all the more impoverished. The peasants had to pressurise the government to expand the means of production and open up more opportunities for agricultural labour. This could be done by reclaiming wastelands, which either the government or the landlord had to permit.

A janmi of Karivellur donated the dues collected from peasants to the local temple. Members of the Karshaka Sangham put up an organised protest against the janmi's action and this led to police firing that killed two persons. In Kavumbayi, activists of the Karshaka Sangham made a united move to cultivate the land that was left fallow by the janmi. This incident too led to police firing that caused the death of five peasants. In a few places the Karshaka Sangham mobilised peasants to cultivate the government land that was left uncultivated. All these collective actions were ruthlessly dealt with by the government who put peasant activists and Communists behind bars.

Punnapra-Vayalar Revolt (1946)

C. P. Ramaswami Iyer's progressive measures, based on the values of democracy in the initial years, were conspicuous for their absence during the later years of his rule, which were noted for his attempts at centralising power. Naturally, there was a series of Congress-led movements against his autocratic reforms. Pattam Thanu Pilla, C. Kesavan and T. M. Varghese organised protest meetings all over Tiruvitāmkur. Congress activists submitted a mass petition to the Tiruvitāmkur king for urging him to act against the diwan. But the furious diwan adopted repressive measures to suppress these movements. In many places the police took to lathicharge and firing. C. P. banned the Congress and the Youth League in Tiruvitāmkur. On Gandhi's advice, the Congress withdrew the petition submitted to the king and the agitation subsided. This resulted in widespread resentment among the agitating youth and led to their eventual joining in the Communist Movement.

Under the leadership of the Communists the peasants and agricultural labourers launched on a war path against C. P.'s scheme to turn Tiruvitāmkur into an independent state with a Constitution modelled on the American Constitution. Conflicts between the government and the working classes came to a head and resulted in an armed struggle against the police. Alleppey was the stronghold of the Communists in Tiruvitāmkur. Opposed to C. P.'s regime, they were virtually running a parallel government there, suppressing administrative officials and even the police.

In Alleppey and Cherthala agricultural workers and peasants rose in revolt under the guidance of the Communists on 23 October 1946. The workers declared a strike until their urgent labour demands were satisfied and political freedom was restored. C. P. clamped martial law in Alleppey on 25 October and arrested leaders like R. Sugathan. The marching peasants encountered the armed police at Punnapra, leading to casualties on either side. On 26 October, the military attacked the peasant workers' training camp at Vayalar. On 27 October, peasants and workers marched with wooden spears (*vārikuntam*; made of areca palm) in hand to confront the Tiruvitāmkur militia that had already surrounded Vayalar. Futher, a naval contingent made its presence in the water body nearby, isolating the village. Still the peasants fought helplessly and killed several military men before they became victims to the firing. In different parts of Alleppey people confronted the armed police and became martyrs. Over 800 people were killed in the incident and many more injured. It was a distinct historic sacrifice that the working classes made for the cause of the integration of Tiruvitāmkur with the Indian Union.

A lot of people came forward to help the victims. In Malabar, under the initiative of the Communists, many peasants and workers constituted a Travancore Aid Committee to help the riot victims. Politically, the Punnapra-Vayalar Revolt had a serious impact on the masses by way of arousing nationalism with the values of socialism and secularism, as opposed to janmi landlordism and British imperialism. Consequently, on 23 January 1947, the Government of Madras passed an ordinance banning such peasant movements. Using that as the legal excuse, many Communists were imprisoned. In several places in Malabar the anti-feudal movements continued encouraging anti-caste agitations and struggles for freedom to use public roads and the right to enter the temple.

The most significant development in Tiruvitāmkur was the declaration of independence by the princely state of Tiruvitāmkur. With the support of C. P. Ramaswami Iyer, Chithira Tirunal, the king of Tiruvitāmkur, made his Declaration of Independence from British rule on 18 June 1947. AICC rejected it and a compromise was reached between C. P. and the Congress leaders by which Tiruvitāmkur accepted the offer of greater autonomy in return for joining the Indian Union. Nevertheless, C. P.'s American Model remained a lurking danger in the minds of both the Congress as well as the Communists. A crucial event at a concert in commemoration of Swathi Tirunal's first anniversary brought an end to this danger. On 25 July 1947, K. C. S. Mani, a Communist activist, attempted to assassinate C. P. who escaped with serious injuries. Meanwhile, conferences and negotiations between the AICC and the British government had advanced to the point of India securing independence on 15 August 1947. The attack on C. P. accentuated the accession of Tiruvitāmkur to the Indian Union. On 19 August 1947, C. P. resigned from the Tiruvitāmkur service and left for England.

In Cochin the king Paarikshit Tampuran, as advised by Pandit Jawaharlal Nehru, declared that all ministries, except External Affairs, would be handed over to the people's elected representatives. Feeling resentment with this decision, the dewan of Cochin, Sankara Varier, resigned and a new ministry headed by Panampally Govinda Menon took over. As desired by the king, T. K. Nair was made the Minister for External Affairs, but the general public disapproved it. A public meeting held at Rajendra Maidanam on 18 October 1947 ended up in lathicharge, causing injury to many, including some of the Praja Mandalam leaders. Following the incident, the Panampally ministry resigned and through the election of October 1948, a new Praja Mandalam ministry headed by Ikkanda Varrier came to power and formed an accomplished provincial assembly that was founded on democracy and nationalism.

Freedom Fighters of Kerala

K. Madhavan Nair (1882–1933), a Congress activist from Kozhikode and the first Secretary of the Provincial Congress, was one of the earliest freedom fighters from Kerala. In agitations such as the Civil Disobedience Movement, boycott of foreign cloth and boycott of Simon Commission, he was a leading figure. In the Vaikom Satyagraha his role was important. He was one of the leaders of the Guruvayur Satyagraha and the Director of Guruvayur Temple Entry Referendum. For a term he had also served as a member of the Central Legislative Assembly of the Madras Presidency. Madhavan Nair was one of the founders of *Mathrubhumi* and led the publication as its first managing director.

George Joseph (1887–1938) was one of the earliest Congress activists from the Christian community. His involvement with

Provincial Congress began with the Home Rule League and through participation in the Non-cooperation Movement. He was part of the Home Rule League Deputation to England, which had to return from Gibraltar under the orders of the British government. Motilal Nehru had made him his successor to the editorship of the *Independent*, a newspaper issued from Allahabad. George Joseph was arrested for his editorial criticism of the British government during his time at the *Independent* and put in jail for a brief period. Later, when Gandhi was imprisoned, George Joseph had served as the Editor of *Young India*. He thus became a national figure. As a freedom fighter who was imprisoned for his participation in Vaikom Satyagraha and as an elected member of the Central Legislative Assembly of the Madras Presidency, his presence was widely felt in Kerala. A key player in the movement for responsible government and a leader of the Abstention Movement, George Joseph remains one of the earliest figures in the politics of Tiruvitāmkur.

Another important freedom fighter was K. P. Kesava Menon (1886–1978), who started his activities in Provincial Congress as early as in 1915. He was the Secretary of the Malabar branch of Home Rule League and was a member of the Home Rule League Deputation, which presented in 1917 the memorandum to the Secretary of State in London under the leadership of Annie Besant. In 1921, he was elected as Secretary of Provincial Congress and during the māppiḷa rebellion he worked in peace-making campaigns and relief camps. One of the founders of *Mathrubhumi*, Menon was its first Editor. One of the organisers of the Vaikom Satyagraha, he had courted arrested in 1924 and was lodged in Trivandrum Central Jail for six months. Menon then moved to Malaysia in 1927, where he served as barrister for the cause of Indian workers. In 1942, Kesava Menon joined the action committee of the Indian Independence League formed by Ras Behari Bose. With the formation of the Azad Hind Government by Subhas Chandra Bose, who was the leader of the Indian Independence League and Indian National Army (INA), Kesava Menon left the League due to difference of opinion. He opposed the Japanese move to exploit Indian freedom fighters in Malaya and the Japanese police arrested him in Singapore. Till the end of World War II he was in solitary confinement. In October 1946, he returned to India and became the editor of *Mathrubhumi* once again. After Independence, he was appointed the Indian High Commissioner to Ceylon, but he did not continue in service due to difference of opinion with the Government of India.

K. Kelappan (1889–1971), famously referred to as Kerala Gandhi, was a social worker and the Founder-President of the Nair Service Society. He joined the Non-cooperation Movement by quitting his education at the Bombay Law College and returning to Malabar to start active work with the Congress. During the māppiḷa rebellion, he was the leader of Congress' mission for peace and communal harmony. He courted arrest during Vaikom Satyagraha and was sent to jail. A committed Gandhian, his main involvement was in the uplift of the downtrodden. He was a leader of Guruvayur Satyagraha as well. For his active involvement in the Quit India Movement, he was imprisoned. On his return from prison be became President of the Provincial Congress. Later, he he left AICC for ideological reasons and became part of Acharya Kripalani's Kisan Masdoor Praja Party (KMPP).

A. V. Kuttimalu Amma (1905–1985), who hailed from the Anakkara Vadakkath family of Ponnani in south Malabar, ranks foremost among the women freedom fighters of Kerala. She entered the freedom movement at a very early age and participated in the main activities of the Congress. She was deeply involved in the Khadi and Swadeshi movement, and led the picketing of foreign cloth-shops in Kozhikode in 1931. Her participation in the Civil Disobedience Movement at Kozhikode, with her two-month-old baby in hand, is famous in the history of the freedom struggle. She was arrested and put in jail for two years. She took her baby too into the jail in defiance of the authorities who objected. Kuttimalu Amma was elected to the Madras Legislative Assembly in 1936. For her participation in the individual Satyagraha she was imprisoned for a year in 1940. Soon she was imprisoned for two years for her involvement in the Quit India Movement. Following her release from jail in 1944, she was elected the president of the Provincial Congress. She was a member of AICC and the Congress Working Committee as well. In 1946, once again she became a member of the Madras Legislative Assembly.

Muhammad Abdurahaman (1898–1945) of Azhikode, Koṭunkōḷūr, was mostly in Kozhikode as an eminent Congress activist. He joined the Non-cooperation Movement after quitting studies at Aligarh University and became active in the Khilafat agitations in Malabar. During the post-rebellion days in Malabar, he was a lead personage in the mission for peace and communal harmony throughout the affected areas. Nevertheless, the police arrested him in October 1921 and imprisoned him for two years. For his participation in the Salt Satyagraha at the Kozhikode beach on 14 April 1930, as we have already mentioned, he was lathicharged by the police and the court sentenced him to nine months' rigorous imprisonment, which he spent at Kannur Central Jail. Abdurahaman was the editor of a patriotic newspaper called *Al-Ameen*, which was printed from Kozhikode during 1929–1939. He was frequently bullied by the police for his work as editor, and he had to close down the newspaper due to such governmental pressure. Abdurahaman was a member of the Kozhikode Municipal Council during 1931–34. He was in the Malabar District Board in 1932. In 1937, he became a member of the Madras Legislative Assembly. Abdurahaman was elected as President of the Provincial Congress in 1939. An activist of Forward Block formed by Subhas Chandra Bose and ardent opponent of the partition of India, Abdurahaman was detained in jail during 1940–45. Back from jail, he became once again active in the Congress, but died on 22 November in the same year.

C. Kesavan (1891–1969), an active organiser of Travancore State Congress and a Working Committee Member, is remembered in the history of modern Tiruvitāmkur along with Pattom Thanu Pillai and T. M. Varghese. A lawyer-politician of critical social consciousness, Kesavan was mentored by the thoughts of Karl Marx, Sree Narayana Guru and Gandhi. He was actively involved in anti-caste movements and agitations against untouchability, and became the General Secretary of SNDP Yogam. He was one of the prominent leaders of the Abstention Movement of Tiruvitāmkur since 1932. A powerful speaker and strong advocate of Responsible Government, he was arrested on 7 June 1935 for his famous public speech at Kozencherry and sentenced to two years' imprisonment. For his participation in Quit India Movement in 1942, Kesavan was sentenced to imprisonment again for a year. In 1947, Kesavan was elected to the Travancore Legislative Assembly and he served as a Minister in the cabinet of Pattom Thanu Pillai for a few months.

T. M. Varghese (1886–1961), another eminent freedom fighter of Tiruvitāmkur, was an active leader of the movement for Responsible Government and the Abstention Movement of Travancore. His contributions for the making of the Responsible Government in Tiruvitāmkur Assembly during his tenure were remarkable. He was active in the drafting of the Joint Political Party demands, promulgation of a new Constitution for Tiruvitāmkur state in 1936, the state assembly election campaigns in 1937, contesting in the election as a candidate of Joint Political Party, assumption of the office of the deputy president in the Sree Mulam Assembly, moving of the adjournment resolution for the establishment of Responsible Government in Tiruvitāmkur, sustained struggle against the Dewan C. P. Ramaswamy Iyer, preparation of a comprehensive memorandum seeking the vesting of the dewan's powers in a cabinet of ministers, expansion of legislature, establishment of universal franchise, sustenance of an independent judiciary and institution of an inquiry into C. P. Ramaswamy's administrative and financial actions. During the period between 1938 and 1943 he was arrested several times for his involvement in various agitations. He was elected from the Pathanamthiṭṭa Constituency to the Legislative Assembly of Tiruvitāmkur and became its deputy speaker. A founding member of the Working Committee of the State Congress, Varghese designed its programmes for a decade. After Independence, Varghese became a minister in the cabinet of Pattom Thanu Pillai. In the integrated Tiruvitāmkur-Kochi Assembly, he was made speaker in 1949.

One of the most enterprising and influential political leaders of Cochin was Edakkunni Ikkanda Varrier (1889–1977). He was the grand-nephew of Diwan Sankara Varrier, the architect of modern Cochin. Ikkanda Varrier became a lawyer in Trichur and later Chairman of the Trichur Municipal Council, ably leading the measures to improve the civic amenities of the township. He was elected to the State Legislative Council of Cochin for four terms. He was the second President of the Cochin State Praja Mandalam and, during his term, he contributed a lot towards turning the state into a Responsible Government. For his participation in the Quit India Movement, he was arrested and sentenced to imprisonment for two years. After the 1948 elections, Ikkanda Varrier, as head of the Legislative Party, became the Chief Minister of Cochin. Agrarian regions of Cochin State owe their development in irrigation water network to Ikkanda Varrier. Following his chief ministership, he was the Minister of Food and Agriculture of the state for some time.

Neelakanta Iyer (1899–1971), a Gandhian politician and graduate teacher, who served in various schools in Cochin and Malabar was a notable freedom fighter in Cochin State. In 1930, he was arrested for participating in the Salt Satyagraha at Kozhikode and sentenced to imprisonment for six months. Neelakanta Iyer was the first President of Cochin Praja Mandalam for several years. He was arrested and imprisoned at Viyyur Central jail for participating in the Quit India Movement in 1941. He was the Secretary of Harijan Seva Sangh and had participated in the anti-caste movements and agitations for temple entry.

Accamma Cherian (1909–1982) was another prominent woman freedom fighter. She entered active politics by leading a very huge public procession against C. P. Ramaswamy Iyer's ban on the Travancore State Congress. This was one of the most prominent processions that the Congress ever led. It attracted participants from Kanyakumari to North Parur. Accamma led the procession to the Kowdiar palace of Sree Chithira Tirunal to submit the memorandum demanding removal of the ban on the State Congress and the release of prisoners. She achieved the goal of the procession.

Accamma's accession to the presidential chair of the Congress was unexpected and contingent upon a series of developments relating to the Civil Disobedience Movement. In the first Civil Disobedience Movement of 12 March 1930 all the Congress leaders including the President of Provincial Congress, Pattom Thanu Pillai, were arrested. It was decided that the arrested president would nominate the successor and accordingly the government arrested eleven presidents one by one. When Kuttanad Ramakrishna Pillai, the eleventh president was arrested, he nominated Accamma Cherian as his successor. In October 1938, Accamma Cherian travelled from one end to the other, visiting all the local units of the Congress and appealed to women to join as members of the *Desasevika Sangh*. It is said that Accamma's call resulted in a massive entry of women volunteers to the local bodies of the state Congress. On 24 December 1939 Accamma was arrested for participating in the first annual conference of the State Congress and sentenced to one year of imprisonment. After her release, she was involved in the activities of the State Congress much more vigorously and rose to the position of the president again. In her presidential address on 8 August 1942 Accamma Cherian celebrated the Quit India Resolution of the Bombay Session of the Indian National Congress. Consequently, she encountered several arrests for the violation of the ban orders.

All these personages, their enterprises and campaigns shaped the politics of Tiruvitāmkūr, Kochi and Malabar in the strong mould of anti-imperialism, democracy, social justice, egalitarianism and nationalism. They turned the three territories into integral constituents of the Kerala state and put it on the track of modernisation, anticipating the making of modern Kerala.

XII

The Making of Modern Kerala

This chapter is a discussion of the brief history of the integration of the two princely states of Kerala—Tiruvitāmkur and Kochi—with the area directly governed by the British as part of the Indian Union. Such a discussion is possible only by recapitulating the backdrop of economic and social development. By 'modern Kerala', we mean the state of Kerala that was formed under the provisions of the States Reorganisation Act of 1956, which introduced the linguistic criterion to determine state boundaries. This integration was preceded by the Aikya Kerala Prasthanam, a popular movement that advocated formation of a state of Kerala. This chapter is primarily an overview of the history of Kerala's political modernisation and socio-cultural development, which goes back to the techno-economic and socio-cultural modernisation of the nineteenth century, which have been discussed in the tenth and eleventh chapters. Most of the ideas discussed in this chapter have to be read in association with the backdrop discussed there.

Economic Development

Kerala's economy continued to be predominantly agrarian with its hierarchically-structured land relations. There were some changes, such as the introduction of fixity of tenure and stability of rent rate, as a result of organised peasant movements and political initiatives in land reforms. However, the *pāṭṭa viḷambaram* (Royal Proclamation of Leasing Regulations) of the kings of Tiruvitāmkur deserves special mention at this juncture. During the second half of the nineteenth century, the kings of

Tiruvitāmkur issued a few proclamations granting lower castes the right to cultivate small plots of *pandāravaka* (crown lands) lands. Accordingly, several families of agricultural workers and landless tillers, particularly the īḻavas, received small strips of crown lands leased to them for cultivation. This improved their livelihood and let them send their children to schools. It emancipated several children from the bondage of labour and the trap of kulathoḻil (the caste-based occupation) and let them seek jobs based on their educational qualification. Protests against caste system and untouchability had somewhat mitigated the related misery. Nevertheless, most problems of caste and contradictory land relations persisted.

Introduction of Western technology and the beginnings of the industrial mode of production were notable changes in the colonial economy. Its foundation was laid by German missionaries. The Basel Mission was responsible for bringing about technological transformation in the traditional handloom industry of Kerala. Kannur emerged as the main centre of textile production in the nineteenth century. In the wake of World War I, the British people appropriated all the major textile establishments and turned them into powerloom factories by selling semi-mechanised units to local entrepreneurs. Samuel Santhosh, a Christian convert, started a textile mill at Pappinissery near Kannur as early as in 1890. His son renamed it as Aaron Spinning and Weaving Mills Ltd. and owned several spinning and weaving mills in Kannur during 1944–45. Kannur flourished as the capital of textile looms and designs in Kerala State.

Similarly, the East India Companies were responsible for the beginnings of technological transformation in coir production. Coir products of Alleppey had reached all over the world as products of the age-long handicrafts tradition. In 1859, James Darragh, an American-Irish industrialist, and Henry Smail, a prominent overseas trader, made the beginnings of modernisation of coir production technology. Subsequently, coir factories were established in Alleppey, Kollam, Kozhikode and other parts of Kerala. Darragh, Smail & Co. was followed by a series of industries such as Pierce Lesley & Co., William Goodcare & Sons, Madura Co., Coir Yarn Textiles, Bombay Co., Volkart Brothers and Aspinwall & Co. Soon the royal family of Holland opened its Royal United Carpet Factory at Aroor. The royal family of Tiruvitāmkur had major shares in Aspinwall & Co. The British people appropriated the major establishments in the wake of World War I and with Independence the British owners sold their factories to Indians. Several Indian companies like Alleppey Co., C. George Peter & Sons, Pitchu Iyer & Sons, Coir Floor Furnishing Co., Empire Coir Works, Commercial Emporium, Charankattu Coir Mfg. Co, Travancore Mats & Matting Co., Devaswomchira Coir Fabrics, Kochu Pillai & Sons and Koncherry Coir Factories also came up during this period. These companies flourished and contributed to the economic development of Kerala in the twentieth century. Industrial economic development was the material basis of Kerala's modernisation as well.

Plantations

Plantation agriculture was a new industry that started growing under British colonial rule. Coffee and tea were introduced extensively at high- and higher-altitude forests respectively. The history of coffee plantations in India goes back to 1670 with the planting of seedlings at Baba Budangiri at Chikmagalur in Karnataka. In 1840, in the same hill surrounds a plantation estate was opened. It was from there the coffee cultivation spread to Wayanad hills in Kerala, where they were grown in shadowy estates of Malabar. British colonial traders had taken interest in coffee estates and the export of the yield from there. The variety Arabica, which reached India from Yemen, became popular in Malabar during the colonial period.

Tea was cultivated much more extensively in high-altitude evergreen forest hills and the nineteenth century witnessed a burst of tea plantations in the highland forests of Kerala. Munnar that remained pristine forestlands till the late eighteenth century began to be opened up as the haven of tea gardeners by the late nineteenth century. The Duke of Wellington was the first to identify Munnar as an ideal plantation landscape. John Daniel Munro (1778–1858), the British Resident of the kingdom of Tiruvitāmkur, was responsible for formally opening up Munnar for tea plantation during the 1870s. Munro happened to see the high ranges of Munnar during his visit to the region to resolve a boundary dispute between Tiruvitāmkur and Madras. Traditionally, Munnar belonged to the Poonjar royal family as its *janmam* (hereditary possession of absolute ownership) land. It came under the control of Tiruvitāmkur during the course of the expansion of the kingdom. Munro persuaded the Tiruvitāmkur royal family to lease 588 sq. km of the Munnar hillocks and grassland to him to transform it into tea estates and spice gardens. Accordingly, in 1879, Munro founded the North Travancore Land Planting and Agricultural Society. The society began tea, coffee, cardamom, cinchona and sisal plantations in various parts of Munnar, but soon tea dominated as the most successful plantation of Munnar. Several high-altitude forestlands in the region were converted into over fifty tea estates. A. W. Turner, an adventurous plantation enthusiast, established his tea estate in Munnar in 1877. A. H. Sharp, who entered the field in 1880, became the leading proprietor of tea estates in the 1890s. Soon Finlay Muir & Company emerged at the top by buying many estates. The major tea industry that managed these estates was Kannan Devan Hills (named after the then adivasi headman of the area) Produce Company, established in 1897.

During the immediate postcolonial period, the Tata Group took over most tea plantations in the region. Today Harrison Malayalam, AVT tea, Michael's tea and Brooke Bond are the main tea plantation industries in Munnar. The tea industry has had its ups and downs, but ever since its inception it has decided the fortunes of the plantation economy in Kerala.

Transport and Communication

Main Central Road, popularly called MC road, was the first major road communication of Tiruvitāmkur and it was established during the period of Raja Kesavadas in the late eighteenth century. However, the modernisation of roads began only in the twentieth century. The Travancore State Transport Corporation, constituted in 1937 during the reign of Chithira Tirunal, was the first major landmark in the history of the development of transport infrastructure in Kerala. In 1938, the king ordered the commissioning of the State Motor Company and inaugurated the state motor service in Tiruvitāmkur. The king and his kinsmen and the companions of honour were the first passengers in the transport bus that was driven by the British Superintendent named Salter. Along with this thirty-three other buses were made to ply between the headquarters and suburbs. Another development was the passing of the Road Transport Corporation Act of 1950. Subsequently, the Kerala State Road Transport Corporation was established on 15 March 1965.

The British built the first major bridge in Kerala, the hanging bridge at Punalur, around 1878. Subsequently, several arch bridges were constructed across major rivers in Kerala. Marthanda Varma Ilaya Raja, the architect of modern Tiruvitāmkur, was the first king of Tiruvitāmkur who began the project of building river bridges in Kerala. The Marthanda Varma Bridge at Aluva is a notable example built under his initiative. It was at Muvattupuzha, the first concrete bridge of Asia was made in 1914.

The Bepur–Tirur Line of Malabar, opened way back in 1861, was the first rail transport in Kerala. In 1902, a narrow-gauge railway line linked Shoranur with Ernakulam. Rail transport began in Tiruvitāmkur only in 1904, with the establishment of the Chengotta–Punalur track. Railway transport got extended to Thiruvananthapuram when the Central Railway station was built in 1931. During the time of the integration of the state, the various regions of the state were not connected by a single road or railway line. Perhaps the relatively well-frequented were the waterways. Ernakulam–Kottayam and Kollam railway lines were built later, during the period 1956–58.

The Anchal post was the earliest mode of communication. In this mode, the postman would to run from one point to another with the message. This postal service began in the kingdoms of Tiruvitāmkur and Kochi in the first half of the eighteenth century. It was started by Anizham Tirunal Marthanda Varma in 1729 in Tiruvitāmkur and it was established in the 1770s in Cochin. The first anchal post office of Alleppey was opened in 1852 by Uthram Tirunal Marthanda Varma. In 1863, the first telegraph communication was introduced in Tiruvitāmkur. Money Order Service, the door delivery system of money, began in India in 1888 and reached Kerala only with its introduction in Tiruvitāmkur in 1901.

The Aikya Kerala Movement

The making of the modern Kerala was a long and protracted historical process, the actual constituents of which evolved during the eighteenth and nineteenth centuries. They related to the collective movements of the people in the upper as well as the lower strata, mostly organised by upper-caste/class activists belonging to the KPCC and the Socialists. Integrating Kerala was the primary agenda of the Congress in the 1920s. In 1928, the Nehru Committee approved the idea of the formation of Kerala on the ground of linguistic identity. Ever since, the KPCC had been pressing for the integration of the Kerala state and mobilising people to endorse it. In 1945, the Congress made it the main promise to the people during the provincial assembly election.

As we have already discussed, the Communists were busy with peasant movements against exploitation as well as for distributive justice during the post-War depression of 1946–48. The Communist-led movements invariably ended up in violence and police action. Thus, the Government of India imposed a ban on the Communist Party and its trade unions. Consequently, the Communists by and large shifted from violent movements to democratic protests. They began to focus on preparatory exercises by way of campaigns for the mobilisation of people into politically-aware citizens fit for parliamentary democracy. Electoral contests for ascending to power became their primary political agenda.

The Provincial Congress forcefully put up the demand through an Aikya Kerala movement to realise the goal of forming the linguistic state of Kerala. A meeting was held at Cheruthuruthi in 1946, under the leadership of K. P. Kesava Menon, to press for the demand. Kerala Varma VII (1870–1948), a Cochin king, who ruled during 1946–47, was the main leader of the movement and it earned him the title 'Aikya Keralam Thampuran'. He was the first to propose the idea of a united Tiruvitāmkur-Kochi State under the inspiration of the national policy of integration. In 1947, the historic Aikya Kerala Conference was convened under the Chairmanship of K. Kelappan. AICC, in its Jaipur session of 1948, constituted a high-power committee to study the recommendations submitted by the Dhar Committee for the formation of linguistic states. The Aikya Kerala movement further gained strength on 1 July 1949 with the merger of the states of Kochi and Tiruvitāmkur into the Tiruvitāmkur-Kochi State with the king of Tiruvitāmkur as its head (*rajapramukh*).

T. K. Narayana Pillai, the chief minister of Tiruvitāmkur in 1949, headed the first popular assembly of the integrated Tiruvitāmkur-Kochi State. Panampalli Govinda Menon was the last Chief Minister of Tiruvitāmkur-Kochi State. Following the fall of the ministry in 1956, Tiruvitāmkur-Kochi came under President's rule. Soon, when the States Reorganisation Commission recommended language as the basis of the determination of the state boundary, it was decided that Malabar and Kasargode would be integrated with Tiruvitāmkur-Kochi. Accordingly, the state of Kerala was formed on 1 November 1956 by uniting the princely states of Tiruvitāmkur and Kochi, the Malabar District of Madras Presidency, and the Kasargod area of South Canara as a territory of Malayalam language.

Political Development

In 1951 the Communist Party began its people's movement against the Congress Party as an organisation of feudal and capitalist interests. Mobilisation of small peasants and landless agricultural labourers provided great social base for the Communists of Kerala.

Many of the freedom fighters of the Congress continued in the Congress Party of independent India. Some of them remained Gandhians. K. Kelappan contested in the general elections of 1952 and was elected from Ponnani parliamentary seat through Kisan Mazdoor Praja Party. After his five-year term in the Lok Sabha, he left active politics and became a Sarvodaya leader and founded a rural Institute at Tavanur. He was also involved in the Bhoodan movement in Kerala. T. M. Varghese, a prominent Congress leader became a minister in the cabinet headed by A. J. John. Accamma Cherian retired from the Congress party when she was denied a ticket to contest the 1952 elections. However, she contested as an independent candidate from Muvatupuzha constituency. She contested again in 1967 but lost and left party politics.

The first Assembly Election of the state of Kerala was held in March 1957 when the state was under President's rule. It was mainly a contest between the Congress and the Communists. Out of 126 constituencies the Communist Party won 60 seats. With the support of a few independent legislators, the Communist Party formed the government on 5 April 1957 with E. M. S. Nampudiripad (hereafter, EMS) as chief minister. The 11-member cabinet headed by EMS is celebrated as the first-ever democratically elected Communist ministry in the history of the world. On 18 December 1957 the minister K. R. Gowri presented the Agrarian Relations Bill in the Assembly. It aimed at ending the janmi system in Kerala by removing the exploitative land relations.

Such radical socio-economic reform legislations of the ministry provoked the Congress, and all anti-Communist upper-caste/class and religious establishments converged to lead a state-wide agitation for liberation from Communist rule. The opposition spread turbulences in the state that lasted several months. The Agrarian Relations Bill was vehemently opposed by the landlords and their interests were represented in the Legislative Assembly by the Congress and its allies. Among the general public the major bodies that opposed the ministry were the Catholic Church in Kerala, the Nair Service Society and the Indian Union Muslim League. After prolonged discussions, the Bill was passed on 10 June 1959. Dissent and protest aggravated and finally, on the basis of the Prime Minister Nehru's advice, the President of India dissolved the state Legislature by applying Article 356 of the Constitution on 31 July 1959.

In the mid-term election of February 1960, a coalition of the Congress, the Praja Socialist Party (PSP) and the Muslim League came to power with Pattom A. Thanu Pillai of the PSP as the Chief Minister and R. Sankar of the Congress as the Deputy Chief Minister. However, Pattom Thanu Pillai had to resign on 25 September 1962 over a controversial appointment. R. Sankar took over as Chief Minister and during his term a diluted version of the Land Reforms Bill was passed in 1963. Sankar's ministry remained in power till it succumbed to a Congress-led no-confidence motion in September 1964. After an abortive election that failed to avert President's rule, a coalition of the Communist Party of India (Marxist), Communist Party of India, Muslim League, Revolutionary Socialist Party, Karshaka Thozhilali Party and Kerala Socialist Party won the general election of March 1967 and formed a government with EMS (of CPI-M) as chief minister. During this period, the Land Reforms Bill was whetted and legislated afresh in 1969. The coalition failed and the EMS ministry resigned in October 1969, giving way to a fresh coalition headed by C. Achutha Menon (of CPI). It was Achutha Menon's ministry that successfully implemented the Land Reforms Act of 1969. In January 1970, the ministry abolished the janmi system in Kerala, and liberated about seven lakh tenants from the clutches of landlordism. However, the extant national juridical system prevented the extension of the application of Acts to the redistribution of agricultural land to the tillers. As a result, the slogan, 'land to the tillers,' a long-sustained dream of the small peasantry could not be realised. Menon resigned and the Assembly was dissolved on 26 June 1970.

The CPI-led coalition consisting of the Congress, the RSP, the Muslim League and the Praja Socialist Party came to power in 1970 with a considerable majority, under the headship of C. Achutha Menon. Extended twice with the Congress in and out, the ministry lasted for almost six years. In March 1977, the general election led to the formation of the Congress-led coalition ministry headed by K. Karunakaran. Karunakaran resigned on 25 April 1977 on an adverse finding by the high court on the Rajan case. This was the case of the custodial death of Rajan, a brilliant student at Regional Engineering College, Kozhikode, who was arrested from the hostel during the days of Emergency of 1976 on suspicion of involvement in extremist activities. In its verdict over a *habeas corpus* writ filed by Rajan's father, Eechara Varier, the high court accused the government of being irresponsible. A. K. Antony (Congress) took over as the next chief minister. However, on 27 October 1978, Antony also resigned on a political issue, and this led to P. K. Vasudevan Nair (of CPI) to take over as the next Chief Minister in a couple of days. Nair stayed in power for hardly a year. He had to resign because of CPI's decision to join the Left Democratic Front (LDF) consisting of CPM, Revolutionary Socialist Party (RSP) and the Congress faction led by A. K. Antony. Following the resignation of Vasudevan Nair, C. H. Muhammad Koya, the leader of the Muslim League and the head of the United Democratic Front (UDF), became chief minister. However, the UDF ministry failed to prove majority in the House and had to resign. The LDF government was formed in Kerala on 12 October 1979 and a new ministry headed by C. H. Muhammad Koya came to power but it lasted only for less than two months.

In the next election of 1980 the structure and composition of the political coalition in Kerala underwent some changes with the All India Muslim League and a faction of the Congress led by A. K. Antony becoming part of the LDF. On 25 January 1980, E. K. Nayanar became the chief minister in an LDF-led government and ruled till 20 October 1981. The A. K. Antony faction of the Congress left LDF and, consequently, K. Karunakaran came back to power on 28 December 1981 and ruled till 17 March 1982. In the meantime, Karunakaran had to resign again due to his implication in a verdict in connection with the palm oil case. As a result, A. K. Antony became chief minister on 22 March and continued till 9 May 1996. In the following election, LDF came to power and E. K. Nayanar was made chief minister for the period between 20 May 1996 and 13 May 2001. This was followed by the UDF ministry headed by A. K. Antony as chief minister between 17 May 2001 and 29 August 2004. On 30 August 2004, Antony left for Delhi to undertake organisational responsibilities in the Congress party, paving the way for Oommen Chandy to be chief minister. Chandy continued to be in power till 12 May 2006. In the twelfth assembly election held in 2006, LDF won with 98 seats and V. S. Achuthanandan took office as chief minister on 18 May. He completed his term on 14 May 2011 and in the next election UDF secured a majority. Oommen Chandy was made chief minister and he ruled between 18 May 2011 and 20 May 2016. On 25 May 2016, the LDF returned to power with Pinarayi Vijayan as chief minister. In this way, Kerala has been under the rule of two groups of parties, alternating between the UDF and the LDF.

Development of the State

Local economic development necessitates specialised and focused territorial administration. When the state of Kerala was formed, it had only five districts—Thiruvananthapuram, Kollam, Kottayam, Thrissur and Malabar. It was clear that Malabar would not be feasible as a single district. Within two months, Malabar district was split into three districts—Kozhikode, Palakkad and Kannur. Similarly, the industrial growth of Alleppey presupposed its making into an independent district. Both Kollam and Kottayam were sufficiently large and economically enterprising. On 17 August 1957, Alleppey was separated from Kottayam and Kollam districts. Ernakulam, already a port town, was growing very fast as an urban centre. On 1 April 1958, Ernakulam was carved out as a separate district.

On 16 June 1969, Malappuram, a backward region, was made an independent district for focused development. It was created by taking parts of Kozhikode and Palakkad. Likewise, Idukki district was formed on 26 January 1972 with a special focus on development by separating parts of Kottayam and Ernakulam district.

It was with the same objective that the district of Wayanad was carved out of Kozhikode and Kannur on 1 November 1980. Pathanamthiṭṭa district came into existence with parts of the Alappuzha, Kollam and Idukki Districts in 1980. On 24 May 1984, Kasargod was separated from Kannur and constituted as a district, the last, in Kerala.

Architects of Modern Kerala

Modern Kerala was the outcome of several movements and contributions of many people of various sectors. We have discussed them in the earlier chapters. The contribution of Christian missionaries to the techno-economic and educational fields; socio-religious reforms by several sages like Vaikunda Swami, Aiyya Swami, Chattampi Swami, Sree Narayana Guru and Kumara Gurudeva; social revolutionaries like Ayyankali, Sahodaran Ayyappan, Pandit Karuppan, Kumaran Asan and others; and cultural leaders like V. T. Bhattathirippad are extremely important. Political leaders of the states of Tiruvitāmkur and Kochi, integrated Tiruvitāmkur–Kochi state and Malabar played decisive roles as well.

In the making of the modern Kerala state, the contributions made by two political personages, EMS and C. Achutha Menon, deserve special mention as the chief architects of modern Kerala. EMS was one of the founders of Congress Socialist Party, a faction of the Indian National Congress, and was elected as its All-India Joint Secretary from 1934 to 1940. He was also elected to the Madras Legislative Assembly in 1939. EMS was the first Chief Minister of Kerala State and the first non-Congress Chief Minister in the Indian republic. His first ministry pioneered radical reforms in land relations and in the field of education, which inaugurated the real making of modern Kerala. The process continued during his second ministry. Jeeval Sahitya Prasthanam, subsequently renamed Purogamana Sahitya Prasthanam (Progressive Association for Arts and Letters), a joint move initiated by EMS, Kesari, Balakrishna Pillai, Joseph Mundassery, M. P. Paul and K. Damodaran had significant impact in the process of modernisation of art, literature and culture. Kesari was the main visionary of the Progressive Movement in literature. Mundassery led the movement in the field of literary criticism. Mundassery, as the minister of education in the first ministry under EMS, was to bring about major reforms in the field of education, earning him the title 'the architect of modern school education in Kerala.' It was this ministry that enacted the Education Bill of 1958, a path-breaking legislation in the history of education in Kerala. It introduced a uniform system of education throughout the state, with a department well defined and a service well-organised. It stipulated service conditions of teachers, fixed their qualifications and extended direct payment of salary to them, including those in private colleges. Grants-in-aid scheme was introduced for private schools. As a measure to control mismanagement and corruption in private schools, the Bill contained precise definitions and stipulations. Government salary to teachers and aid to schools by way of maintenance grant was ensured. The Bill nationalised the textbook system as well. Later, in the political economy of the state, the decentralisation of power and resources under the People's Plan conceived by EMS marked the culmination of his sculpting of modern Kerala. A predominantly people-centred and empowerment-oriented development programme, the People's Plan of Kerala acquired a distinct place in the national decentralidation initiative for its principles of sustainability and local-level resource maximisation.

Achutha Menon started his political career by joining the Congress and subsequently becoming a member in the Kochi Praja Mandalam. In 1941, he joined the Communist Party of India and was actively involved in the labour movement. He continued to work in the Communist Party and was put in jail and subsequently remained underground during 1948–51. Menon was elected to the Tiruvitāmkur–Kochi State Legislature in 1952. He was the first finance minister of Kerala in the EMS Ministry of 1957. He was elected to the Kerala Legislative Assembly in 1960 as well. Later, Menon became a member of the Rajya Sabha during 1968–69.

He was the Chief Minister of Kerala for two terms (1 November 1969–1 August 1970; 4 October 1970–25 March 1977). Thus far, Menon holds the distinction of being the only Chief Minister who has come to power for two terms consecutively.

Menon's second ministry continued in power for about seven years, implementing radical reforms pending execution, such as the Land Reform Act and Agricultural Labour Law. It was his ministry which took private forests in possession by paying no compensation to their owners. Similarly, in 1972, his ministry introduced the famous 'One-lakh Housing Scheme,' the first remarkable move in the country to provide homes for homeless agricultural workers. Menon's contribution to the industrialisation of Kerala is quite significant as well. He was the lead in starting major developmental projects in the state. Establishments like Kerala State Electronics Development Corporation Limited (KELTRON) in 1972 and National Transportation Planning and Research Centre (NATPAC) in 1976 are some examples.

Menon is known as the architect of Kerala's higher education. All the major research institutions of Kerala were founded with his personal initiative. The Centre for Development Studies, Institute of Dravidian Linguistics and Sri Chithra Tirunal Institute of Medical Sciences and Technology are examples of such research institutions. Formulating a science policy for the state, Menon established a few Centres of Excellence in Scientific Research in the state, such as Kerala Agricultural University (KAU) in 1971, Kerala Forest Research Institute (KFRI) in 1975, Sree Chitra Thirunal Institute for Medical Sciences and Technology (SCTIMST) in 1976, National Centre for Earth Science Studies (CESS) in 1978, Centre for Water Resource Development (CWRDM) in 1978 and Regional Cancer Centre (RCC) in 1981.

Kerala Model of Development

The Kerala model was originally a set of recommendations about certain chosen issues regarding the development of Kerala. It was proposed in a UN study by a team headed by K. N. Raj during the 1970s. It is meant as a model of equitable growth which emphasised land reforms, poverty reduction, educational access and child welfare. The Kerala Model is the name now given to the means and measures that enabled the state government to achieve high literacy, wide social access to healthcare, low infant mortality, improved life expectancy and remarkable social development. The state attained a very high rate of literacy, a life expectancy almost equal to that of developed countries, the lowest ever infant mortality rate in the world and one of the world's best-controlled population growth. Kerala achieved all of this as a result of the state's affirmative action about development consisting of basic education, healthcare, land reform and social security by way of employment and pension as top priorities. Kerala's achievements are the culmination of systematic development in various interrelated fields, such as economy, society, intellectual thought and political consciousness. On top of all, it is a state that is economically, socially and politically quite different even from West Bengal which bears comparison in certain attributes.

The economists discovered that in spite of low income, the state had a politically active, highly literate and healthy population. What surprised economists was the incompatibility between the advanced development indices of the state and the state's per poor capita income, which was quite below the national average. How could a state with extremely high unemployment rate and huge budget deficits attain top indices of progress that is common only in developed countries? Kerala had also successfully addressed gender gap and access disparity in higher education.

In this regard, Bill McKibben, an eminent anthropologist and environmentalist famous as a protagonist of sustainable development, notes the following in his *The Age of Missing Information* (2006):

> Kerala, a state in India, is a bizarre anomaly among development nations, a place that offers real hope for the future of the

> Third World. Though not much larger than Maryland, Kerala has a population as big as California's and per capita annual income of less than $300. But its infant mortality rate is very low, its literacy rate among the highest on earth, and its birthrate below America's and falling faster. Kerala's residents live as long as Americans or Europeans. Though mostly a land of paddy-covered plains, statistically Kerala stands out as the Mount Everest of social development; there is truly no place like it.

Economic migration to countries in the Persian Gulf became a significant phenomenon from the 1970s onwards and the remittance by non-resident Keralites became a good source of income for the State. As a very poor state, Kerala experienced a boon in the Gulf boom because the Left government required economic growth to sustain its social development programmes. Sustenance of high literacy, low infant mortality rate, administered population growth, wider healthcare service and enhanced life expectancy demanded a stable finance. The continued efforts of successive governments had to ensure economic growth for usual development as well. This involved high levels of political participation and activism among ordinary people, along with substantial numbers of dedicated leaders at all levels.

Modern Culture

The people of Kerala had experienced the modern culture with the arrival of the Europeans. Soon, they understood it as the colonial modern. Western values, passions and worldviews had influenced them to different degrees, depending upon the level of education and exposure. People of each caste and community had begun to understand themselves and others in this lens of modernity. It was a process of invention of one's own culture. Accordingly, all of them discovered their traditions self-consciously, but without knowing that they were becoming modern through the process. An ensemble of new self-perceptions of castes, communities and religions constituted the modern in people's everyday culture. In short, the colonial and the modern converged in their traditional life, facilitating a new visibility of the tradition as modern.

We have discussed earlier how new social perspectives, but rooted in the old, emerged urging for reforms of beliefs, rituals, rites and institutions ordained by religions. There is manifestation of modernity in the form of tradition in all such reforms. In the process of the communication of reformist ideas, Malayalam language was enriched. Subsequently, the literature and art of Kerala embodied the passions and values of idealism and romanticism. The popularity of the printing press and the wider use of paper in the nineteenth century played a major role in the onset of modern culture. The Malayalam script was used in print for the first time in Amsterdam for the publication of *Hortus Malabaricus*. Rev. Benjamin Bailey, an Anglican missionary at Kottayam, was the first to establish a printing press in Kerala in 1821. He printed the first Malayalam book in 1824. It was printed at the C.M.S Press from 1848 onwards. With the publication of the first Malayalam newspaper called *Jnjananikshepam* by Bailey, the printed script became the most influential object of public sensibility. Bailey's print letter types of the Malayalam script was in use for a long time until standardisation of the script based on the recommendations of the Sooranad Committee in 1967. Printing had a decisive impact on the growth of literature in the twentieth century.

During the reign of Swathi Tirunal, a government press was opened at Thiruvananthapuram in 1836. Later, in 1865, a lithographic press in the private sector added to the printing facility. Nevertheless, most printed works of Malayalam were carried out in the London Missionary Society press established at Nagercoil in 1820 or in the Basel Mission Press established at Mangalore in 1842. In Cochin, Rev. Fr Chavara Kuriakos had established the St. Joseph's Press in 1844. Dr Hermann Gundert started his lithographic press, the first press of Malabar, in the Illikkunnu Bungalow at Thalasseri in 1845. It was through this press that the earliest newspapers like *Rajyasamacharam* and *Paschimodayam* were published in 1847.

In the field of literature, new genres like the novel and the short story became popular. The old type of musical drama based on the Tamil theatre gave way to the theatre of social plays. They were instrumental in bringing tremendous changes in the society, polity and culture of Kerala. Following the celebrated trio in Malayalam poetry—Kumaran Asan, Vallathol Narayana Menon and Ulloor S. Parameswara Aiyer—there appeared a group of nine poets who brought in a new era of rich and splendid poetry: Sankara Kurup (1901–1978), P. Kunhiraman Nair (1905–1978), Edasseri Govindan Nair (1906–1974), Balamani Amma (1909–2004), Vailoppally Sreedhara Menon (1911–1985), N. V. Krishna Warrier (1916–1989), Olappamanna Subrahmanian Namputiri (1923–2000), Akkitam Achutan Namputiri (1926–) and N. N. Kakkad (1927–1987).

In the field of art, Raja Ravi Varma (1848–1906) stands distinct for his paintings that combined Western techniques of execution and traditional Indian aesthetics. His paintings are realistic in their conception, design and sensibility, but highly representational. The reality that he captures in his paintings is engendered by passions of modernity. Similarly, his aesthetics is traditional but invented by him through notions of modernity and under the Victorian normative pressure. His paintings exemplify how tradition becomes an invention through representation enabled by the techniques of modernity.

Some of the poems of N. V. Krishna Warrier are based on non-literary themes. His work *Missionary* deals with the colonial strategies of constructing intellectual bondage under the colonial subjugation by Western authorities in the eighteenth and nineteenth centuries. It has to be noted that the intellectual apparatus in this poetic experiment exhibits a thorough understanding of modernity and its multifarious programmes. Here, NV observes the fact that ancient Indian thought and wisdom are superior to the Western sciences, which is wisdom designed mainly for the endless exploitation of nature and is characterised by inherently limited resources. His *Nannangaatikal* is based on the Megalithic monuments widely scattered in South

India in general and in Kerala and Tamil Nadu in particular. The poet develops the subject with insights and information from the disciplines of history and anthropology. Similarly, Edasseri Govindan Nair presents a critique of the paradigm of the nation-state in modern historiography in one of his poems called 'Kutiyirakkal' in *Kaṛutha Cheṭṭichikaḷ*. He notes that the boundaries of countries in maps are meaningless and that 'Wherever the mud pots of the poor are/Thrown out in this world,/And that is their country'.

P. Kunhiraman Nair, another great poet, asks in one of his poems, 'what kind of education is this, which suffocates the natural genius unto death'. Similarly, Vailoppilli, another prominent member of this group, has several poems on various aspects of modern Kerala. He praises the developmental projects such as construction of dams and channelising water to the paddy fields in one of his poems entitled 'Jalasechanam' (Irrigation). At the same time, he is slightly afraid to note the all-pervading influence of machines in the life and culture of the people. In one of his poems he predicted with an atom of fear: 'Tomorrow the machine will sow the seeds,/the machine will harvest the crop today,/we see that this has come true in our life.'

Novels and dramas in Malayalam were instrumental in bringing about basic changes in economic and social life in Kerala. Thakazhi, Ponkunnam Varkki and others wrote about the plight of the downtrodden sections of the erstwhile Thiruvithamkur. K. T. Muhammed's dramas played a decisive role in introducing revolutionary changes in the māppiḷa muslim families in Kerala. Above all, it is a widely acclaimed fact that the socio-political dramas of Thoppil Bhasi and the drama troupe of Kerala People's Arts Club (KPAC) were major transforming influences. The dramas and the troupe played a decisive role in spreading the ideas of the Leftist movement in Kerala.

In art, literature and culture the term modern refers to a trend. However, it is not mere trend explicit in terms of the style of expression, the nature of content and so on. Instead it refers to the context of knowledge culture. It is the nature of knowledge in terms of its reliability, authority and authenticity that the term 'modern' indicates. Isaac Newton, the author of *Mathematica Principia*, presented knowledge with mathematical precision. This knowledge became the model of knowledge that had to be emulated by everyone in the eighteenth century—the Age of Enlightenment. Newton provided the foundation of the knowledge for future. The scientific temper that originated from his mechanics though was recognised only during the nineteenth century. The modern is built intellectually on the foundation of scientific knowledge distinct for certainty, finality and universality. Its origins out of the industrial capitalist economy are another fundamental link not adequately understood. Students of history have to understand that art and literature have no history in themselves but only in their relations with the socio-economic processes.

Similarly critics in art and literature discuss the meaning of the postmodern almost entirely as a matter of stylistic trend. As in the case of the modern, postmodern also has to be understood against its approach to and perception of knowledge. Contrary to the foundational knowledge of modernity, the epistemic base of the postmodern is the post-Newtonian micro-mechanics of uncertainty and complexity. There is no precedence of the universal grand theory over the particular. This upsets the modernist convention of making knowledge teleological, unitary and logo-centric. It decentres and limits knowledge as particular and context bound. Students of history should also know the fundamental link between the late capitalist economy and the postmodern knowledge of uncertainty.

XIII

Stages of Social Development

This chapter sums up the region's past as socio-economic and juridico-political aggregates for a conceptual consideration to see how they relate to systems and structures well known to historiography. It is a discussion of changes by way of formations and transformations of systems. Marx's theory of history conceives the socio-economic and politico-cultural aggregate as mode of production that binds together economy, technology, polity, jurisprudence, ethics, religion and culture. Establishing economic correlations to social power relations, institutions of control, structures of domination and cultural practices, the theory explains the causality of the formation-transformation continuum by attributing it to the contradictory dynamic of the process. Discovering modes of production and their sequential order in world history, Marx describes their principles individually and integrates them through a general theory of formation and transformation. Primitive communism, slavery, feudalism, capitalism and socialism/communism are the names that Marx gives to the modes of production in history. Historians have been debating over the identification and labelling of socio-economic systems in different geographical and cultural regions. This chapter seeks to familiarise students of history with such debates in historiography and methodological aspects of identification of modes of production relevant to the understanding of Kerala's past.

In earlier chapters we have briefly discussed the tentative history of the Kerala region from the earliest to the relatively recent times in the chronological order by focusing on important events and their processes. It is the region's archaeology of the

Stone Age with which we started this narrative. Despite the considerably long span of time since the Stone Age, the knowledge available about the period is abysmally limited. However, when it comes to the question of conceptualisation, it is the material process of appropriation of nature for subsistence that needs to be focused. Life in the Stone Age was based on the primitive means of subsistence namely hunting and gathering. An unstructured and inseparable combine of economy, power relations and culture, it precludes discussion of their aggregate in the perspective of mode of production. According to Marx's evolutionary scheme, the primitive mode phases out into the slave mode, but it is the agro-pastoral without slavery which evolved from the primitive in the history of Kerala. Nevertheless, one can conceptualise it as agro-pastoral social formation.

Theoretically, social formation and mode of production are more or less one and the same. Perhaps the only difference between the two is that the concept of social formation takes into account all co-existing economies under the dominant one in a given time, while the concept of mode of production focuses only on the dominant economy. Agro-pastoral social formation was co-existence of uneven forms of subsistence, varied power relations and diverse cultures, but under the dominance of a redistributive pastoral economy through its predatory polity and heroic ideology. One social formation dissolves itself into another as a result of intensification of basic contradictions within the dominant economy. The identification of basic contradictions as prime movers that brought about the transformation of agro-pastoral social formation is, therefore, central to conceptualisation. It is possible to presume that, over a few centuries, practices like redistribution had generated differentiation, and the dominance of agro-pastoral economy declined due to its inherent incapability of growth under kin-based relations of production. As an economy based on kin labour, it had no potential to move on to new forces of production. It was virtually impossible for the agro-pastoral social formation to sustain itself any longer with its low labour productivity and inability to reproduce the economy efficiently. Institutions like plunder raids and redistribution would not be sustainable beyond a certain period. Both kin labour and raids were unable to provide favourable conditions of growth for wet-rice agriculture, the potential source of economic surplus. In short, social formation was anticipating an inescapable production crisis. Under the pressure of these contradictions a series of transitions happened around the mid-first millennium CE—the transitions from kin labour to non-kin labour, from millet to paddy, from clan and kin ties to hereditary occupation groups and caste, from chiefdom to monarchy, and from heterodox religious ideology to brāhmaṇism. These transitions became complete during the period from the eighth to ninth centuries CE.

Actually, transformations of the aforesaid type should lead to the making of a hierarchical system of agrarian relations with landlords at the top, tenants at the middle and poor peasants and tillers at the base. Such a social formation is called feudalism, according to the theory of mode of production. What emerged in Kerala was a social hierarchy with landlords at the apex and in the descending order the lease-holders (kārālar), artisans/craftsmen (kuṭiyāḷar) and the slave-like primary producers (aṭiyāḷar). In addition, there were many who had small strips of land as hereditary holdings (*kāṇi*), which were also tilled by the primary producers. One cannot equate the system with feudalism, although certain features like widespread tenements in land, subject peasantry, entrenched system of land dues and various obligatory services are common to both. A significant component that developed in India and, particularly in Kerala, was the institution of jāti. Being an agrarian economy based on hereditary occupation groups and hierarchical productive relations, the jāti system could accommodate all of them into a corresponding social order of its own. EMS called the system 'jāti, janmi, nāṭuvāḻi sampradāyam' (a system of the caste, the landlord and the local ruler). In feudalism, the primary producers, called serfs, enjoyed possession of small strips of land, while in the janmi system, the primary producers were landless. Such differences are natural because feudalism was a regional system that had no uniformity even within Europe.

As elsewhere in India, the jāti system became an institution integral to the stratified agrarian society. It acted as fetters that tied fast entire groups of people to the system of hereditary occupations (kulatoḻil) and obligatory services, institutionalising their servitude permanently. Nevertheless, in popular parlance, the janmi system is equated with feudalism.

The janmi system expanded itself and continued for three to four centuries without any fundamental changes, in spite of monetisation of exchanges, extensive overseas trade and formation of trading community settlements of religious identities, as exemplified by Jews, Syrian Christians and Islamic Arabs. Such new settlements were largely replicas of the dominant agrarian structure, functions, relations and obligations. It became well-entrenched in the wake of the breakdown of the Perumāḷ rule and the rise of principalities. How it finally dissolved itself into a new social formation has to be conceptualised by examining the development of contradictions at the fundamental level. Theoretically, it should encounter a serious production crisis and go dysfunctional due to intense contradictions at the level of technology, economy and productive relations. However, history shows that the janmi system was hegemonic when the European overseas trading companies arrived at the seaboards of Malabar. European companies superimposed themselves over the janmis, not only forcibly shared the agrarian surplus but also introduced changes in productive technology. This intensified contradictions and aggravated tension in the relations of appropriation. The Mysore raids added to exploitative relations and control among people. During the period of overseas trade operations by the European companies, a new economic system that emerged in the Mediterranean and Western Europe penetrated into Kerala.

In the Mediterranean and Western Europe, a new economy began to emerge out of the decadent feudal system during the fourteenth–fifteenth centuries. Mercantile circuit of goods became wide-ranging, markets proliferated and the use of money became extensive. Money enabled tenants to pay the feudal rent in cash. A new class of country gentry, distinguished from lords and involved in enterprises of commodity production, was coming up in the marketing centres. They were increasingly in need of human labour. Independent labour collectives began to emerge through peasant movements against lords who were oppressive. Several peasants got freed from the clutches of lords. In England, the Black Death took the lives of many labourers and caused their scarcity. It constrained several lords to hire the labourers from those who had enough. All this increased the number of unencumbered labourers available in the market towns. Wage labour gradually got institutionalised. It marked the rise of a new mode of production centred on manufacturing that thrived on wage labour. As the enterprise turning money into capital, it is called capitalism.

As a mode of production destined to be catering to the consumption beyond the local through mass production, capitalism indispensably required technological development. As a result, its instinctive urge was to open up markets in and secure raw materials from wherever possible and by whatever means. Crossing the geographical limits of Western Europe was indispensable for the economy. It began to expand far and wide through various institutional structures, particularly monopolistic overseas trade. During the fifteenth and sixteenth centuries its monopolistic trade network spread to the Ottoman and Russian empires. Soon it reached the Mughal and Vijayanagara empires. Finally, through trade, it colonised a large part of the world. Using the seaboards of Kerala, India was colonised too. The colonial economy became a world system by penetrating itself into all the empires of the time and Western Europe emerged as its nerve centre.

It was this colonial phase of capitalist economy that impacted the janmi system in Kerala. Theoretically, a mode of production is *sui generis* and not a transplant. Nevertheless, being a universal mode of production, capitalism reaches everywhere through forceful penetration. Penetrated by the colonial economy, the janmi system precluded the possibilities of generating contradictions of its own and prime movers within. Therefore, there is no scope for a conceptual appraisal of the development within the jāti, janmi, nāṭuvāḻi system. Instead, the peculiar historical situation of Kerala demands conceptualisation of the contradictory relations that emerged consequent to the colonial penetration of capitalism into the jāti, janmi, nāṭuvāḻi system.

In the wake of the arrival of the European companies, Kerala was dominated by agrarian economy based on the jāti, janmi, nāṭuvāḻi system of land relations, reinforced by the jāti system of social organisation. All arts, crafts and other labours were hereditary, as ordained by the jāti system. Attached to land, workers were virtually immobile. A janmi had *de facto* control over all the settlers in his land. This situation presupposes no economic enterprises demanding labour freed from the janmi and the jāti system. When foreign trading organisations like maṇigrāmam and ancuvaṇṇam were allowed to found their settlements during the early medieval period, they were granted service men along with land. This practice had to continue when the monopolistic trading companies were given permission to build their warehouses and factories. All the captains of the East India companies of the Portuguese, the French, the Dutch and the English in their initial stage of securing land space for establishing their warehouses and factories had encountered the absence of masons and workers as a major problem. Therefore, all of them had to approach the local rulers to grant them the required artisans and craftsmen.

During the colonial period, there was a steady increase in the demand for free labourers (i.e., labourers not at the disposal of janmis and nāṭuvāḻis), because the European companies were eager to hire them. We have discussed in Chapter Ten how this demand pressure intensified in the nineteenth century and provided an added context for working class movements to free themselves from the bondage under the janmis and nāṭuvāḻis. All the anti-caste and related movements for the right to wear upper-cloth or for the freedom to use public paths or for entry to the temple, etc. have to be seen against this economic context of labour demand that was growing in the wake of the European colonisation by trading companies. It cannot be seen as altogether accidental that all these happened to be movements for freeing the body of the lower-caste people who constituted the primary labour force. Indeed, there were new ideas and perspectives gaining currency, especially new worldviews based on new religions of transforming influence. We do not underestimate their role in developing a new sensibility among the common people. Nevertheless, the fundamental pressure at work was that of labour demand.

It is quite reasonable to infer that the demand for labour on the one side and the bondage of labour in the agrarian system on the other was a catalyst with an emancipatory urge among some of the subjected labourers, particularly those who had come under the influence of new religious worldviews. In Chapter Eleven, we have shown the British colonial system having superimposed itself on the jāti-janmi-nāṭuvāḻi system causing over-exploitation and unbearable bondage leading peasants to revolt. These movements also led to the rise of a class of unencumbered workers who had escaped from the clutches of the jāti, janmi, nāṭuvāḻi system. Naturally, one of the major changes under the colonial economy was the beginnings of the disintegration of the jāti, janmi, nāṭuvāḻi system and the rise of unencumbered labour force, the fundamental necessity of the rise of capitalism.

German missionaries who accompanied the monopolistic colonial trading companies were responsible for the introduction of Western technology to the field of commodity production in Kerala. We have already discussed how the Basel Mission took the lead in bringing about technological transformation in the manufacture of tiles and textiles of Kerala. Kozhikode emerged as the main centre of tile industry and Kannur as the major centre for textile industry in the nineteenth century under the initiative of the German missionaries. East India Companies introduced the factory mode of production in the sector of coir manufacture and marketed the products all over the world. This marked the beginnings of the capitalist mode of production in Kerala. The company of James Darragh and Henry Smail is perhaps the best example. The British colonial enterprises made the industrial mode of production in its full-fledged form by purchasing several companies from the other owners and improving them with new technology during the period of World War I. Powerlooms of the period exemplified a typical capitalist industry of contemporary England.

To conclude, the history of Kerala represents the formation and transformation of social formations starting from the primitive to the capitalist through the development of basic contradictions in the economy and social relations leading to dissent and protest. There are several features unique to the history of the Kerala region, to be highlighted when a conceptual generalisation is attempted. Hence, it is important to retain the terms in the source material for naming the social formation. Certain terms like feudalism, despite their claim of universal application, are found unsuitable in the history of different regions. Nevertheless, it is important to view the history of any region against convincingly-defined social formations of broad universals. This is not to suggest a reductionist approach, but to underline the methodological significance of conceptualising history as socio-economic and politico-cultural aggregates, identifiable into systems and structures. A student of history has to realise the primacy of methodological pre-occupation in understanding history, a form of knowledge invariably tentative. What turns up essential in historical knowledge is empirical basis, holistic perspective and the logic of interpretation.

Bibliography

Ayyar, L. K. Anantakrishna. 1926. *Anthropology of the Syrian Christians*. Ernakulam: Cochin State Government Press.

Baldaeus, Philip. 1996. *A Description of East India Coasts of Malabar and Coromandel and also of the Isle of Ceylon*. Reprint of the 1703 edition, translated from High Dutch in 1672. New Delhi and Madras: Asian Educational Services.

Thapar, Romila. 2013. *The Past Before Us: Historical Traditions in Early North India*. Cambridge: Harvard University Press.

Bernard, K. 1980. *Flashes of Kerala History*. Cochin: Victory Press.

Béteille, André. 1965. *Caste, Class and Power*. Berkeley: University of California Press.

Bhaskaran Unni, P. 1994. *Kollathinte Charitram*. Kollam: Public Library and Research Centre.

Bowring, B. Lewin. 1899. *Haidar Ali and Tipu Sultan*. Oxford: Clarendon Press.

Bristow, Robert. 1959. *Cochin Saga: A History of Foreign Government and Business Adventures in Kerala, South India, by Arabs, Romans, Venetians, Dutch, and British, Together with the Personal Narrative of the Last Adventure and an Epilogue*. Second edition. London: Cassell.

Brown, L. W. 1956. *The Indian Christians of St. Thomas*. Cambridge: Cambridge University Press.

Bruce, Henry. 1901. *Letters from Malabar and on the Way*. London: George Routledge and Sons.

Buchanan, Francis. 1870. *A Journey from Madras through the Countries of Mysore, Canara and Malabar*, Vol. II. Madras: Higginbothams.

Champakalakshmi, Kesavan Veluthat and Venu, eds. 2008. *State in Pre-modern South India*. Thrissur: Current Books.

Day, Francis. 1863. *The Land of the Perumals, or Cochin, Its Past and Present*. Madras: Gantz Brothers.

Ganesh, K. N. 1915. *Keralattinte Innalekal*. Fourth edition. Trivandrum: Kerala Bhasha Institute.

———, ed. 2013. *Exercises in Modern Kerala History: Historical Study*. Second edition. Kottayam: Sahitya Pravarthaka Co-operative Society Ltd.

Godelier, Maurice. 1977. *Perspectives in Marxist Anthropology*. Cambridge: Cambridge University Press.

Gopalan, A. K. 1959. *Kerala, Past and Present*. London: Lawrence and Wishart.

Gopinatha Rao, T. A., ed. 1988. *Travancore Archaeological Series*, 3 Vols. Trivandrum: The Government Press.

Gurukkal, Rajan and Raghava Varier. 2005. *Cultural History of Kerala*, Vol. I. Trivandrum: Government of Kerala.

Gurukkal, Rajan. 1990. *The Kerala Temple: Agrarian Relations in Early Medieval Kerala*. Edapal: Vallathol Vidyapīṭham.

———. 2009. *Social Formations of Early South India*. New Delhi: Oxford University Press.

———. 2015. *Rethinking Classical Indo-Roman Trade*. New Delhi: Oxford University Press.

Haridas, V. V. 2015. *Zamorins and the Political Culture of Medieval Kerala*. Hyderabad: Orient BlackSwan.

Iyer, L. K. Anantha Krishna. 1981. *Tribes and Castes of Cochin*, Vols II and III. New Delhi: Cosmo.

Iyer, S. Krishna. 1984. *Travancore-Dutch Relations 1729–1941*. Trivandrum: University of Kerala.

Kareem, C. K. 1973. *Kerala under Haidar Ali and Tipu Sultan*. Cochin: Kerala History Association.

Kailasapathy, K. 1968. *Tamil Heroic Poetry*. London: Clarendon Press.

Kawashima, Koji. 1998. *Missionaries and a Hindu State Travancore 1858–1936*. New Delhi: Oxford University Press.

Kerala District Gazetteers. Ernakulam and Trivandrum: Kerala Gazetteers, 1965.

Kerala State Gazetteer, Vol. I. Trivandrum: Kerala Gazetteers, 1986.

Kerala State Gazetteer, Vol. III. Trivandrum: Kerala Gazetteers, 1989.

Koshy, M. O. 1989. *The Dutch Power in Kerala 1729–1758*. New Delhi: Mittal Publications.

Krishna Ayyar, K. V. 1938. *Zamorins of Calicut: From the Earliest Times to AD 1806*. Calicut: Norman Printing Bureau.

———. 1966. *Short History of Kerala*. Ernakulam: Pai & Co.

Krishna Ayyar, K. V. and Mary Samuel David. 1979. *Making of History*. Trivandrum: Charithram Publications.

Kunju, A. P. Ibrahim. 1975. *Mysore-Kerala Relations in the Eighteenth Century*. Trivandrum: Kerala Historical Society.

———. 1975. *Studies in Medieval Kerala History*. Trivandrum: Kerala Historical Society.

———. 1976. *Rise of Travancore: A Study of the Life and Times of Martanda Varma*. Trivandrum: Kerala Historical Society.

Kurup, K. K. N. 1975. *Ali Rajas of Cannanor*. Trivandrum: College Book House.

———. 1981. *A Study in the Agrarian Relations of Malabar*. Calicut: Sandhya Publications.

———. 1988. *Modern Kerala: Studies in Social and Agrarian Relation*. Delhi: Mittal Publications.

Malekandathil, Pius. 2010. *Maritime Trade: Trade, Religion and Polity in the Indian Ocean*. New Delhi: Primus Books.

———. 2012. *The Mughals, the Portuguese and the Indian Ocean: Changing Imageries of Maritime India*. New Delhi: Primus Books.

———. 2016. *The Indian Ocean in the Making of Early Modern India*. New Delhi: Manohar.

Mateer, Samuel. 1871. *The Land of Charity*. London: John Snow.

———. 1883. *Native Life in Travancore*. London: W.H. Allen.

Mathew, K. M. 1988. *History of the Portuguese Navigation in India, 1497–1600*. Delhi: Mittal Publications.

Mathew, K. S. 1983. *Portuguese Trade with India in the Sixteenth Century*. New Delhi: Manohar.

Mayer, Adrian C. 1952. *Land and Society in Malabar*. Bombay: Oxford University Press.

McKibben, Bill. 2006. *The Age of Missing Information*. New York: Random House.

Menon, A. Sreedhara. ed. 1964. *District Gazetteers*. Quilon and Trivandrum: Kerala Gazetteers.

———. ed. 1965. *District Gazetteers*. Trivandrum: Government Press.

Menon, C. Achyutha, 1911. *Cochin State Manual*. Ernakulam: Cochin State Government Press.

Menon, P. Shungoonny. 1878. *History of Travancore from the Earliest Times*. Madras: Higginbothams.

———. 1983. *History of Travancore*. Trivandrum: Kerala Gazetteers.

Mohan, P. Sanal. 2015. *Modernity of Slavery: Struggles against Caste Inequality in Colonial Kerala*. New Delhi: Oxford University Press.

Nair, Adoor Ramachandran. 1986. *Kerala State Gazetteer*, Vol. II (Pt. 1). Trivandrum: Kerala Gazetteers.

———. 1986. *Slavery in Kerala*. Delhi: Mittal.

Narayanan, M. G. S. 2013. *Perumals of Kerala*. Thrissur: Current Books.

Padmanabha Menon, K. P. and T. K. Krishna Menon, eds. 1924. *History of Kerala*, Vols I, III and IV. New Delhi: Asian Educational Services.

Panikkar, K. N. 1989. *Against the Lord and State: Religion and Peasant Uprisings in Malabar, 1938–1921*. New Delhi: Oxford University Press.

Pillai, P. N. Elamkulam Kunjan. 1970. *Studies in Kerala History*. Kottayam: National Book Stall.

Polanyi, Karl. 2001. *The Great Transformation: The Political and Economic Origins of Our Time*. Boston: Beacon Press.

Poonen, T. I. 1948. *Survey of the Rise of the Dutch Power in Malabar (1603–78)*. Trivandrum: University of Travancore.

———. 1978. *Dutch Hegemony in Malabar and its Collapse (AD 1663–1795)*. Trivandrum: University of Kerala.

Raghava Varier, M. R. 1997. *Madhyakala Keralam: Swarupaneethiyuṭe Caritrapṭhangaḷ.* Kottayam: SPCS.

———. 2004. *Sthānārohaṇam, Caṭangukaḷ.* Edapal: Vallathol Vidyapeeṭham.

———. 2012. *Jainamatam Keralathil.* Kottayam: SPCS.

———. 2012. *Keraleeyatha: Carithramānangaḷ.* Kottayam: Sahithya Pravarthaka Co-operative Society (SPCS).

Raghava Varier, M. R. 2012. *Kolezhuthu and Malayalam Manuscripts in the Biliotheque Nationale de France.* Thiruvananthapuram: KCHR.

Raghava Varier, M. R. and Kesavan Veluthat. 2013. *Tharisappaḷḷippaṭṭayam.* Kottayam: SPCS.

Ramanath Aiyar, S. 1904. *The Royal House of Travancore.* With a Brief Memoir of H. H. The Maharaja. Trivandrum: Malabar Mail Press.

———. 1907. *The Problem of Charity in Travancore.* Trivandrum: Malabar Mail Press.

Terray, Emmanuel. 1972. *Marxism and Primitive Societies, translated by Mary Klopper.* New York and London: Monthly Review Press.

Vaidyanadhan, Ramachandran. 1997. *Communication History of the Dutch in India.* Madras: Artline Printers.

Veluthat, Kesavan. 1993/2012. *The Political Structure of Early Medieval South India.* Second edition. Hyderabad: Orient BlackSwan.

———. 2014. *Brahmin Settlements of Kerala.* Thrissur: Current Books.

Appendices

Genealogy of the Cēra Perumāḷs

This genealogy is prepared on the basis of what M. G. S. Narayanan has given in his *Perumāḷs of Kerala*. We have incorporated the indications available in the *praśasti* of Rājaśekhara found at the Kuṛumāttūr Vishnu temple inscription (Pukkōṭṭuchōla, Areekode, Malappuram district), the only *vamśāvali praśasti* (genealogy) available in Kerala, which significantly updates the order of succession under the Perumāḷ rule.

Sthāṇu Ravi (844–871 CE)

|

Rāma Rājaśekhara (871–883 CE)

|

Kōta Ravi Vijayarāga (883–913 CE)

|

Kōta Kēraḷa Kēsari (913–943 CE)

|

Indu Kōta (943–962 CE)

|

Bhāskara Ravi Manukulāditya (962–1021 CE)

|

Ravikōta Rājasimha (1021–c. 1036 CE)

|

Rājarāja, Ravirāma Rāya, Ādityan Kōta Raṇāditya (c. 1036–89 CE)

|

Rāma Kulaśēkhara (1089–1122 CE)

Inscriptions of the Perumāḷ Period (c. 800 CE–1122 CE)

Place	*King*	*Date*	*Purport*	*Historical importance*
Vāḻappaḷḷi, Tiruvārruvāi, Kottayam district	Rajaśēkhara	12th regnal year; 9th century CE	Endowment, temple	Political history, dynastic history
Bishop's palace, Kottayam	Sthāṇuravi	5th regnal year; 849 CE	Grants, privileges for foreign merchants like ancuvaṇṇam, maṇigrāmam	Urban development, other economic aspects and state formation
Kūṭalmāṇikyam temple, Irinjālakuda	Sthāṇuravi	11th regnal year	Temple committee resolution	Temple personnel management
Tiruvārruvāi	Sthāṇuravi	17th regnal year	Temple committee resolution	Political and social history

(*Contd*)

(*Contd*)

Place	*King*	*Date*	*Purport*	*Historical importance*
Tillaisthanam, Tancāvūr district Tamil Nadu.	Sthāṇuravi with Rājakēsari Varman,	Undated	Royal grant; granting military honours	Political processes, Political history
Tirunadikara, temple	Kulaśēkhara Dēva and his son-in-law Vijayarāga Dēva	9th century CE	Temple affairs	Relation of the Perumāḷ with the Cōḻas
Kurumāttūr	Rāma Rājasēkhara	871 CE	Regarding the repair of a tank; connects Rama Rājasēkhara with the Iṣkwāku line of kings	The only *praśasti* of a Cēra Perumāḷ found in Kerala thus far
Vāḻappaḷḷi, Tiruvārruvāi, Kottayam district	Rājaśēkhara	12th regnal year; 883 CE	Temple committee resolution	Economic growth; expansion of cultivation
Chōkūr, Puthūr village, Kozhikode district	Kōtaravi	15th regnal year; 898 CE	Arrangements for various donation	Economic aspects
Neṭumpuramtali, Thrissur district	Kōtaravi	17th regnal year; 900 CE	Temple committee resolution	Land grant to temple

(*Contd*)

(*Contd*)

Place	*King*	*Date*	*Purport*	*Historical importance*
Aviṭṭattūr, Thrissur district	Kōtaravi	20th regnal year; 903 CE	Temple committee resolution	Designations like *sabhaiyar*, *potuval*, *variyar*, etc.
Ṭṛiprangōde, Malappuram district	Kōtaravi	27th regnal year; 910 CE	Temple committee resolution	Economic history
Poṛanghāṭṭiri, Malappuram district	Kōtaravi	27th regnal year; 910 CE	Temple committee resolution	Economic history
Indianūr, Malappuram district	Kōtaravi	27th regnal year; 910 CE	Land grand to temple.	Economic history
Tripūṇittuṛa, Ernakulam district	Kōtaravi	913 CE	Temple committee resolution	Economic history
Thiruvoṛṛiyūr, Tamil Nadu	Kōtaravi	913 CE	Mentions Kerala Rāja Vijayarāga Cēramānār or Vijayarāgadēvar. Land grant to village by Iravi Nīli.	Relation between Cēra Perumāḷs and the Cōḻas; important for political history

(*Contd*)

(*Contd*)

Place	*King*	*Date*	*Purport*	*Historical importance*
Trikkākkara	Kerala Kesari	913 CE	Land grant	Economic History
Mānipuram, Kozhikode district	Indu Kōta	3rd regnal year; 943 CE	Temple committee resolution	Socio-economic history
Putukkōde, Kozhikode district	Indēśwaran Kōta	3rd regnal year; 946 CE	Temple committee resolution	Political and social history
Thiruvanvandūr, Aleppey district	Indu Kōta	5th regnal year (?); 948 CE	Temple committee resolution	Socio-economic history
Tirumūḻikkaḷam, Eranakulam district	Indu Kōta	5th regnal year; 948 CE	Temple committee resolution	Socio-economic history
Trikkākkara	Indēśwaran Kōta	10th regnal year; 953 CE	Gift of lamb to temple.	Socio-economic history
Trikkākkara	Indu Kōta		Temple committee resolution	Mentions Governor of Kālkkaraināṭu
Trikkākkara	Indu Kōta	17th regnal year	Temple committee resolution	Socio-economic history

(*Contd*)

(*Contd*)

Place	*King*	*Date*	*Purport*	*Historical importance*
Neṭumpuṛamtaḷi	Indēśwaram Kōta	17th regnal year	Temple committee resolution	Socio-economic history
Trikkākkara, Ernakulam district	Bhāskara Ravi	6th regnal year (2+4)	Temple committee resolution	Socio-economic history
Pantalāyanikollam, Kozhikode district	Bhāskara Ravi	11th regnal year	Consecration of the temple	Political and economic history
Trikkākkara, Eranakulam district	Bhāskara Ravi	13th regnal year (2+11)	Temple resolution	Socio-economic history
Trikadithānam, Aleppey district	Bhāskara Ravi	year 14 (2+12),	Royal order Koyilatikārikaḷ appoints Go-vardhana Mārttānṭa, Governor of Vēṇāṭu as Governor of Nanṛuḻaināṭu also	Informs about the over-lordship of the Perumāḷ
Trikadithānam, Aleppey district	Bhāskara Ravi		Temple committee resolution	Socio-political history

(*Contd*)

(*Contd*)

Place	*King*	*Date*	*Purport*	*Historical importance*
Perunna, Kottayam district	Bhāskara Ravi		Temple committee resolution	
Jewish Synagogue, Ernakulam	Bhāskara Ravi	38th regnal year; 1000 CE	Grants and privileges to Iravi Kōrttān, a jewish merchant.	Royal charter, economic aspects
Trikkākkara, Ernakulam district	Bhāskara Ravi	42nd regnal year; 1004 CE	temple committee resolution	Socio-economic history
Tirunelli, Wayanad district	Bhāskara Ravi		Temple committee resolution	
Tirumūḻikkaḷam, Eranakulam district	Bhāskara Ravi	48th regnal year; 1010 CE	Temple committee resolution	
Trikadithānam, Aleppey district	Bhāskara Ravi	48th regnal year; 1010 CE	Temple committee resolution. Refers to the *kūṟu* lines of Kuṛumpoṛaiyūr	
Pullūr Koṭavalam, Kasargod district	Bhāskara Ravi	58th regnal year; 1020 CE	Revenue information	Income to the Perumāḷ's treasury

(*Contd*)

(Contd)

Place	*King*	*Date*	*Purport*	*Historical importance*
Eramam, Kannur district	Bhāskara Ravi	58th regnal year; 1020 CE	Temple committee resolution	Political history
Trikadithānam, Aleppey district	Bhāskara Ravi	58th regnal year; 1020 CE	Temple committee resolution	Political history
Trikadithānam, Aleppey district	Bhāskara Ravi	58th regnal year; 1020 CE	Temple committee resolution	Political history
Trikadithānam, Aleppey district	Bhāskara Ravi	13th regnal year (6+7)	Temple committee resolution	Political history
Neṭumpuṛamtaḷi, Thrissur district	Bhāskara Ravi	18th regnal year 2+16	Temple committee resolution	Political history
Trikkākkara	Bhāskara Ravi	21st regnal year (2+19)	Temple committee resolution	Political history
Trikkākkara	Bhāskara Ravi	31st regnal year	Temple committee resolution	Political history
Tirunelli, Wayanad Dist.	Bhāskara Ravi	43rd regnal year; (2+35+6)	Temple committee resolution	Political history

(Contd)

(*Contd*)

Place	*King*	*Date*	*Purport*	*Historical importance*
Trikadithānam, Aleppey district	Bhāskara Ravi	48th regnal year	Temple Committee resolution	Political history
Trikadithānam, Aleppey district	Bhāskara Ravi	26th regnal year; 988 CE	Temple Committee resolution	Political history
Perunna, Kottayam district	Bhāskara Ravi	33rd regnal yearl; 995 CE	Temple committee resolution	Political history
Tiruvangād, Kannur district	Bhāskara Ravi	35th regnal year	Nil	Lost
Tirumirrakkōde, Malappuram district	Ravi Kōta	8th regnal year	Temple committee resolution	Politico-cultural history
Panniyankara, Kozhikode district	Ravi Kōta		Temple committee resolution	Political history
Thālekāt, Wayanad district	Rājasimha Perumānaṭikaḷ	3rd regnal year	Village assembly resolution; growth of a bazaar is mentioned	Economic aspects of the region

(*Contd*)

(*Contd*)

Place	*King*	*Date*	*Purport*	*Historical importance*
Maṇṇākōyil Ambāsamudram, Tamil Nadu	Rājasimha	Nil	Temple Committee resolution	Socio-political history
Maṇṇākōyil Ambāsamudram, Tamil Nadu	Cēramānār Rājasimha		Temple committee resolution	Socio-political history
Maṇṇākōyil Ambāsamudram, Tamil Nadu	Cēramānār Rājasimha	Nil	Temple committee resolution	Socio-political history
Tiruvancikkuḷam Thrissūr district	Rājasimha	1036 CE	Temple committee resolution	Socio-economic history
Trichambaram, Kannūr district	Rājarāja Cōḻa	4th regnal year 1040 CE	Temple committee resolution	Socio-economic history
Tiruvannūr, Kozhikdode district	Rājarāja Cōḻa	8th regnal year; 1044 CE	Temple committee resolution	Socio-economic history
Indiyanūr, Malappuram district	Rājarāja Cōḻa	Nil	Temple committee resolution	Socio-economic history

(*Contd*)

(*Contd*)

Place	*King*	*Date*	*Purport*	*Historical importance*
Trikkaṭittānam, Aleppey district.	Ravi Ràma	2nd regnal year; 1050 CE	Mentions punishment for theft.	Crime and punishment
Paṛampantaḷi, Malappuram district	Ādittan Kōt	Nil	Temple committee resolution	Crime and punishment
Nallūr, near Feroke, Kozhikode district	Ādittan Kōt	7th regnal year; 1089 CE	Temple committee resolution	Crime and punishment
Tiruvālūr, Ernakulam district	Kulaśēkhara Perumāḷ	3rd regnal year	Temple committee resolution	Crime and punishment
Perunna, Kottayam district.	Kulaśēkhara Perumāḷ	10th regnal year; 1099 CE	Royal order; mentions *nālutaḷi*	Political history
Neṭumpuṛamtaḷi, Thrissūr district.	Rāma	10th regnal year	Temple committee resolution	Political history
Neṭumpuṛamtaḷi, Thrissūr district	Rāma	11th regnal year	Temple committee resolution	Political history
Kollam, Kollam district	Rāma Kulaśēkhara	13th regnal year	Royal order	Political history

(*Contd*)

(*Contd*)

Place	*King*	*Date*	*Purport*	*Historical importance*
Kollam, Kollam district	Rāma Kulaśēkhara	Nil	King sitting in council; nālutali āyiram; Mānavikrama alias Pūnturaikkōn, Governor of Ēranātu and others	Important record for political history of Kerala; mentions some the *nātuvālis*
Pantalāyinikollam, Kozhikode district	Kulaśēkhara	Nil	Royal order	Political history
Tiruvālancuḻi, Tancāvūr district, Tamil Nadu	Mentions Cēramānār Rāmavarma	Nil	Temple committee resolution	Political history
Irinjālakkuta, Trissūr district	Not available	Undated	Temple committee resolution	Political history
Talakkulattūr, Kozhikode district	Tiruvaṭi	Undated	Temple committee resolution	Political history
Tiruvalla, Kottayam district	Not available	Undated	A set of copper plates containing rich materials for studying socio-economic aspects	A document in the set mentions Bhāskara Ravi as heir apparent.

Chronological Outline of the History of Kerala

Years before present	*Historical/time period*	*Notes (Events, processes and sources)*
38000–30000 BP	Old Stone Age (Upper Palaeolithic Age)	Stone tools of Kanhirappuzha and Shendurney (Thenmala)
30000–25000 BP	Middle Stone Age (Mesolithic Age)	Rock-art sites in the Marayur forest Human habitation in the high ranges (c. 25000 years BP)
25000–7000 BP	Late Stone Age (Microlithic Age)	Rock-art sites at Eaṭakal and Tovari
7000–3000 BP	Late Stone Age (Neolithic Age) c. 5000 BCE c. 3000 BCE	Rock art at Tovari depicts terraced field of cultivation Beginning of agriculture; human habitation in the red soil hillocks (c. 5000 years BP)
3000–2500 BP	Iron Age (Megalithic Age) c. 1000 BCE–c. 500 BCE	Archaeological remains of burial systems, viz., dolmens, cists, rock-cut chambers, stone circles, cairns and urns
		Evidence of maritime contacts during the pre-Roman Egyptian phase (Torpedo Jars and Turquoise Glazed Wares)

(Contd)

(*Contd*)

Years before present	*Historical/time period*	*Notes (Events, processes and sources)*
2500–2300 BP	c. 500 BCE–c. 300 BCE	Tamiḻakam; landscape ecosystem peoples
		Metal-smelting, weaving, glass-making, stone-cutting, pottery and other crafts
2300–1700 BP	Tamil heroic Age c. 300 BCE–c. 300 CE	Potsherd of the Indian Rouletted Ware at Paṭṭaṇam with the Brāhmi label 'amaṇa' indicating the presence of inland merchants from northern India
		Puṟanānūṟu, *Patiṟṟuppattu*, *Periplus of the Erythraean Sea*; Pliny's *The Natural History*; Ptolemy's *Geography*
		Tamiḻakam; vēntar (Cēras, Cōḻas and Pāṇḍyas) and vēḷir chieftains; kiḻār; *tinai*-based subsistence economies; redistributive agro-pastoral social formation; kin-based relations of production; predatory political control
1700–1300 BP	Great Landscape Ecosystem Transformation c. 300 CE–c. 700 CE	Roman and punch-marked coins at north Kottayam, Eyyal, Valluvalli, Panangad, Kanhirapally and Paṭṭaṇam, vouching for transactional relations between Graeco-Roman mariners and inland merchants on the Kerala coast
		The illustrated Christian topography *Cosmas Indicopleustes*

(*Contd*)

(*Contd*)

Years before present	*Historical/time period*	*Notes (Events, processes and sources)*
		Kaḷabhra interregnum (?); dissolution of earlier social formation; institutionalisation of hereditary occupation groups as castes; the making of paddy fields out of waterlogged and water-saturated lowlands
1300–800 BP	c. 700 CE–c. 1124 CE	Stone and copper plate inscriptions indicating a wide variety of economic, social, political and cultural affairs
		Cilappatikāram; *Periyapurāṇam*; Keralōlpatti tradition; Muhammad al-Idrisi
		Transformation of individual brāhmaṇa households into corporate village settlements; hierarchical relations based on differentiated land rights; shift to paddy as the dominant crop; agrarian economy of marginal surplus; state formation; reign of the Perumāḷs of Mahodayapuram; Āḷvār/Nayanar bhakti movement; establishment of kavu shrines, brāhmaṇical temples, Jain basadis, mosques, synagogues and churches; theatre personnel attached to temples; marumakkattāyam
		Commencement of Kollam Era, 825 CE
800–500 BP	c. 1124 CE–c. 1400 CE	Rise of principalities (*swarūpams*)—a class-structured society, dominated by landlords who become an oligarchic body; Sāmūtiri (Zamorin); beginnings of the circulation of coins and use of money
		Maṇipravāḷam literature (*sandesakavyas*)—*Śukasandēśam*, *Uṇṇunīlisandeśam*; Marco Polo; Ibn Battuta; *Payyannurpāṭṭu*, oral tradition; Kollur Maṭham

(*Contd*)

(*Contd*)

Years before present	*Historical/time period*	*Notes (Events, processes and sources)*
		plates; Divakara's *Amogharāghava*; Cirāman's *Rāmacaritam*; Mādhava's *Veṇuāroham*; Paramēśvaran
500–400 BP	c. 1400 CE–c. 1500 CE	Duarte Barbosa; *Vaṭakkan Pāṭṭukaḷ*; *Thorrampāṭṭukaḷ*; Niraṇam poets; *tullal* poetry; Nīlakanṭha Somayājī's *Tantrasamgraha*, *Sidhāntadaṛpaṇa* and *Āryabhaṭīyabhāṣya*
		Rise of higher mathematics and astronomy; arrival of Vasco da Gama
400–200 BP	c. 1500 CE–c. 1700 CE	Arrival and establishment of European traders; their travelogues; records of the East India Companies
		Establishment of palaces by local rulers; royal government records of Travancore and the Zamorin's court (Kozhikkotan granthavari); records of local chiefly families (Kūṭāḷi records); defeat of the Kunhali Marakkars by the Portugese; agrarian revolt in Germany and the arrival of Germans in Kerala; arrival of the Dutch in Malabar; arrival of the English in Malabar; arrival of the French in Malabar; Kerala Varma Pazhassi Raja and the Pazhassi episodes; establishment of English hegemony
		Shaik Zainuddin's *Tuhfat-ul-Mujāhiddīn* (1583); Tuncattu Rāmānujan Eḻuttacchan; Jyeṣṭadeva's *Yuktibhāṣā*; Shaik Zainuddin's *Tuhfat Ul Mujjahiddin*; *Patappattu*, oral tradition of the māppiḷas; *Hortus Malabaricus*

(*Contd*)

(*Contd*)

Years before present	*Historical/time period*	*Notes (Events, processes and sources)*
	1721 CE	Attingal Revolt
	1741 CE	Battle at Colachel
	1766 CE–1767 CE	Mysorean invasion under Hyder Ali
	1789 CE–1790 CE	Mysorean invasion under Tipu Sultan; beginning of centralised administration in Kerala, effective revenue collection machinery
200–100 BP	c. 1800 CE–c. 1920 CE	Pazhassi Kerala Varma's death (1805); Kundara Proclamation of Vleu Thampi Dalawa (1809); Pāṭṭa Viḷambaram (1865); construction of the first major bridge (hanging) at Punalur (1878); Malayali Memorial (1891); īḻava memorial (1896); Kāyal Sammēḷanam (1913); Khilafat Movement (1919); socio-religious reform movements—cānnār agitation (1813–59), mūkkutti agitation, kallumāla and irumpuvaḷa agitation (1915), community movements and establishment of Sree Narayana Dharma Paripalana Sangham (SNDP); local rulers of Tiruvitāmkur and Cochin introduce tenancy 'reforms', such as ensuring fixity of tenure, fairness in rent and freedom to transfer; Velu Thampi and upper-class rivalry against the growing dominance of the British, and Kundara Proclamation; Paliath Achan; kurichya revolt (1812)
		Opening of coffee plantations in Wayanad and tea plantations in Munnar by the British; modernisation of coir production technology;

(*Contd*)

(*Contd*)

Years before present	*Historical/time period*	*Notes (Events, processes and sources)*
		technological transformation in the traditional handloom industry initiated by Basel mission and emergence of Kannur as the main centre of textile production; modernisation of roads; establishment of first printing press at Kottayam; William Logan's *The Malabar Mannual* (1886); Edgar Thurston's *Castes and Tribes of Southern India* (1909); Francis Buchanan; Sree Narayana Guru's *Atmopadesa Satakam*
100–50 BP	1921 CE	Agrarian movements; Khilafat movement; Malabar māppila rebellion, Muhammad Abdurahaman; Kerala Provincial Congress Committee (KPCC)
	1921 CE–1946 CE	Peasant revolts; formation of Kerala Provincial Congress Committee (1921); Vaikom Satyagraha (1924–25), E. V. Ramasami Naikar (Periyar); Narayana Guru; Independence movement, second phase of Civil Disobedience Movement; Nivarttana (Abstention) Movement (1932); Kumaran Asan; formation of the Congress Socialist Party (CSP) (1934); All-India Kisan Sabha and All-Malabar Karshaka Sangham; formation of the Communist Party unit of Kerala (1939); Kayyur Revolt (1941)
100–50 BP	c. 1946–1956 CE	Aikya Kerala Prasthanam (1948) and the making of modern Kerala; Punnapra-Vayalar Revolt (1946); declaration of independence by Tiruvitāmkur and eventual accession of Tiruvitāmkur to the Indian Union; merger of Kochi and Tiruvitāmkur;
	1957 CE	First Communist ministry elected; Agrarian Relations Bill and Land Reforms Act aimed at ending janmi system

Index